PRAISE FOR *A SHORT*
(NEARLY) EVERYTHING PARANORMAL

'Simonsen describes his book as "A travelogue from the twilight zone," but he is far too modest. *A Short History of (Nearly) Everything Paranormal* is a sprawling work, meticulously researched, in which the author deftly, and with engaging wit, pulls together the various strands of 'psi"— telepathy, clairvoyance, precognition, telekinesis, and healing—and presents them for our consideration ... If you are not convinced, well then, he hopes that you will be at least entertained. I was.'

Teresa Carpenter, Pulitzer Prize winner, author of the New York Times *number-one bestseller* Without a Doubt.

'As an encyclopedic introduction to the psychic side of the fascinating but puzzling domain known as the *paranormal*, there is no better choice than *A Short History of (Nearly) Everything Paranormal*.'

Dean Radin PhD, Chief Scientist at the Institute of Noetic Sciences (IONS), California. Author of the award-winning The Conscious Universe *(HarperOne, 1997),* Entangled Minds *(Simon & Schuster, 2006) and the 2014 Silver Nautilus Book Award winner,* Supernormal: Science, Yoga, and the Evidence for Extraordinary Psychic Abilities *(Random House, 2013).*

'This is an outstanding book and it deserves all the attention it can get. Not only is *A Short History of (Nearly) Everything Paranormal* a book for all seasons, it is a book for all reasons!'

'[A] superb survey of the paranormal ... *A Short History of (Nearly) Everything Paranormal* [is] a veritable cornucopia of odd facts and fascinating information stitched into a much-needed survey of a vitally important subject. ... Although serious in content, it is written in a light, often humorous, style which is a delight to read. As someone who has myself made a lifelong study of the paranormal, I cannot recommend it highly enough.'

'Terje Simonsen is a remarkably balanced and insanely well-read guide into a literally impossible subject. He employs the elegant metaphor of a Mental Internet remembering and connecting everyone to explore an astonishing array of psi phenomena...'

'...a very readable, informative, and entertaining book. It is also one of the most comprehensible books on psi I've run across that's aimed toward the general audience. It would be a great book for anyone with a general curiosity in the subject. However, I think it's valuable for scholars too. Overall, a very impressive and valuable book.'

'…a very enjoyable read, an engaging introduction to parapsychology for the general public. It creatively combines historical, anthropological, biological, and physical perspectives on psi in a way that I have never seen before in an introductory book concerning our research area.'

Assessments from committee members in The Parapsychological Association, granting A Short History of (Nearly) Everything Paranormal *the esteemed PA Book Award for 2019.*

'Terje Simonsen in *A Short History of (Nearly) Everything Paranormal* has put together an engaging and informed overview of this evolution (in consciousness) that is worth your attention.'

Stephan A. Schwartz PhD, Fellow, William James Center for Consciousness Studies, Sofia University, Palo Alto, California. Author of The 8 Laws of Change.

'Terje Simonsen's sense of humor and fair coverage of a vast and complex area provides a good introduction to a topic that is often tainted by shallow thinking and uninformed bias despite considerable scientific evidence for its reality and its intrinsic fascination to most people.'

Etzel Cardeña PhD, Thorsen Professor of Psychology, Lund University, Sweden. Editor-in-Chief of the Journal of Parapsychology *and co-editor of* Parapsychology: A Handbook for the 21st Century.

'This book evidences ... a superb use of English, admittedly in a journalistic manner but also highly captivating, jovial and easy-to-read style. This is not easy given the topic is highly controversial and many of the more scientific findings demand expertise in specialist areas. To successfully write about this area also demands an optimal combination of skepticism and open-mindedness.'

Adrian Parker PhD, clinical psychologist. Parker is professor at Gothenburg University, Sweden, where he is currently carrying out research into lucid dream states and exceptional experiences among twins and teaches an international course on 'Consciousness Studies and Psychical Research.'

'If you wanted to study parapsychology in one single book, I think this one might just be the best one available today. I highly recommend it!'

Jeffrey Mishlove PhD, clinical psychologist, host for the TV series Thinking Allowed.

'It is some time since I last read a book on the paranormal, and I cannot imagine a better refresher course than *A Short History of (Nearly) Everything Paranormal* ... [it is] written in a lively and often witty manner, and evinces an eloquent use of English ... Simonsen casts his net both wide and deep, drawing on the history of paranormal research as well as on recent findings ... Altogether a most informative and thought-provoking work.'

Christopher McIntosh PhD, (prev.) Centre for the Study of Esotericism Exeter University, author of Beyond the North Wind: The Fall and Rise of the Mystic North *and a series of other books on occultism and related subjects.*

'Terje Simonsen's personal style inevitably involves his readers in the exciting material of the non-material, in a manner that makes the book read like a thriller ... Far from being just for the theoretically inclined, it can serve as a door-opener to your own inner, still untapped potential. An international classic on a topic that affects us all to our core!'

Annkathrin Puhle PhD, author of Shakespeare's Ghosts Live: From Shakespeare's Ghosts to Psychical Research.

'...the language is simple, fluid and elegant ... Simonsen provides us with a work that covers almost all the aspects and phenomena of parapsychology, all exposed in a simple and rational way, without attitudes that are too compliant or too a priori negativistic.'

Bruno Severi, Dr. Scient, professor em. in biology, University of Bologna

'... from the first page the reading was smooth and compelling. The author, a Norwegian writer, a historian of ideas, is a passionate connoisseur of the esoteric traditions; asking himself questions, keeping the interest and the dialogue with the reader alive. He certainly does not lack a sense of humor and some of his comments are really amusing.'

Anja Riceputi, Professor in Archaeology, University of Bologna

'Well-researched and comprehensive, *A Short History of (Nearly) Everything Paranormal* is a must-read for anyone interested in psi or the paranormal. Highly recommended.'

Bruce Olav Solheim PhD, author, Fulbright professor, distinguished professor of history, Citrus College, California

'The best book on the paranormal I have ever read … It covers the entire field leaving no stone unturned. It is extremely thorough and informative as well as written in an engaging style which makes the book difficult to put down … My prediction (or perhaps precognition) is that this book will become a primary standard bearer in the increasing acceptance of the psi field within the present century…'

Dr Jerry Hirschfield, bestselling author of Your Soul Is Calling: Healing Our Ego Addiction.

'I've been reading about parapsychology for nearly 50 years. I've read several histories of the discipline, and have never before gotten such an in-depth feel for it … His idea of the "mental internet" is an excellent analogy for contemporary folks … whether your interest is in a great read, a highly informative history of parapsychology, or a deeply challenging philosophic adventure, I highly recommend Terje Simonsen's book.'

Don Salmon PhD, author of Yoga Psychology and the Transformation of Consciousness: Seeing Through the Eyes of Infinity.

'I enthusiastically recommend A Short History of (Nearly) Everything Paranormal as a wonderful gift for the person "who has everything," since most certainly they will not already have this book, which just might positively transform their world.'

Cynthia Sue Larson, bestselling author, life coach.

'[…] provides the survey of psi evidence, history, and research that is never provided in our conventional educations, and which should be considered absolutely essential for our consideration and more complete understanding of the world in which we find ourselves.'

David Warner Mathisen, author, Star Myths of the World *series.*

'a unique book ... engaging scholarly and journalistic content providing new, surprising and intriguing information not previously, or very rarely, appearing in other books on the history of the paranormal ... It takes a unique personality to lead us through such territory with wit, irony and other creative and accepted distortions of rationality ... you come away as confident of the reality of the paranormal as you care to be...'

Henry Reed, PhD, author of The Intuitive Heart: How to Trust Your Intuition for Guidance and Healing.

'Terje Simonsen offers the model of the Mental Internet as a way to think about psychic phenomena and the "secret powers" that human beings inexplicably sometimes seem capable of. I find this idea appealing and explanatory of so many fringe and paranormal experiences people have...'

Toby Johnson, author of Finding Your Own True Myth: What I Learned from Joseph Campbell.

'Terje Simonsen provides his audience with diverse yet authentic stories on psi phenomena which are both engaging and entertaining. His passion for historic and multi-cultural research studies shine through his work in every chapter of the book ... I highly recommend this book to anyone who is interested in understanding the history of the human mind/consciousness and its relation to matter (reality).'

Aida Askry, PhD, author of Book of Present.

'I really enjoyed reading this book and would recommend it to anyone who would like to better understand the scientific evidence proving the existence of psychic powers. Unlike most books on this subject the author maintains an unbiased, sometimes critical perspective on the data presented and his writing style is easy-going, often humorous...'

> Steven Richheimer PhD, author of The Nonlocal Universe: Why Science Validates the Spiritual Worldview.

'What Dr Simonsen has done is provide one of the best-detailed paranormal reference books currently available.'

> Norman W. Wilson PhD, author of Shamanism: What It's All About.

'...thorough and entertaining ... I've always found these phenomena endlessly fascinating and this book covers them all!'

> Stacy Horn, internet pioneer, journalist, author of Unbelievable: Investigations into Ghosts, Poltergeists, Telepathy, and Other Unseen Phenomena.

'...a comprehensive guided tour through the dense forest of the paranormal, a feat which he accomplishes with deft, open-minded ease. The paranormal has always challenged conventional thinking and often makes for dry reading. By contrast, this book must be one of the most readable, entertaining, and perhaps thorough guides to this complex and at times exotic terrain ever written. It is a pleasure to read and may well be destined to become a classic in the field.'

> Barry Cottrell, author of The Way Beyond the Shaman: Birthing a New Earth Consciousness.

'This is an enchanting book—brimming with knowledge about the esoteric and the paranormal, presented in a joyous way that entertains, as well as educates, the reader.'

Anne Kalvig PhD, Professor of Religious Studies, University of Stavanger, author of The Rise of Contemporary Spiritualism.

'a sympathetic, charming and personal book ... easy to read ... a fine introduction to the misty landscapes of parapsychology.'

Tom Egeland, fiction author and critic, published in 25 countries.

'The author overviews an impressively broad scope of the research that has been conducted about and within the paranormal field.'

Vinjar Fønnebø MD, PhD, director of the National Research Centre in Complementary and Alternative Medicine at the University of Tromsø.

'...a great, exciting and well-written book.'

Jan-Erik Ebbestad Hansen PhD, Professor of the History of Ideas, University of Oslo, author and editor of a number of books on mysticism and related subjects.

A SHORT HISTORY

OF *(NEARLY)* EVERYTHING

PARANORMAL

A SHORT HISTORY

OF *(NEARLY)* EVERYTHING

PARANORMAL

OUR SECRET POWERS – TELEPATHY,
CLAIRVOYANCE & PRECOGNITION

TERJE G. SIMONSEN

WATKINS
Sharing Wisdom Since 1893

This edition first published in the UK and USA in 2020 by
Watkins, an imprint of Watkins Media Limited
Unit 11, Shepperton House
89-93 Shepperton Road
London
N1 3DF

enquiries@watkinspublishing.com

Design and typography copyright © Watkins Media
Limited 2020

1 3 5 7 9 10 8 6 4 2

Printed and bound in the UK by TJ International Ltd.

A CIP record for this book is available from the British
Library

ISBN: 978-1-78678-357-8

www.watkinspublishing.com

To Tore, my father, Siri, my mother,
and Ole Peter, my brother

ABOUT THE AUTHOR

Terje G. Simonsen is a Norwegian Historian of Ideas and non-fiction author, specializing in the esoteric and occult. He is educated at the University of Oslo, where he also has taught introductory courses on philosophical and literary works. His dissertation on the anthroposophical journal *Janus* received much acclaim and was released as a book in 2001. In the prestigious series *The Cultural Library* and *The World's Holy Scriptures,* Simonsen has published essays on *I* and *Thou*, the mystically inspired main work by the dialogue philosopher Martin Buber, and *The First Book of Enoch*, an esoteric text from antiquity. Simonsen has received several grants, and is a full member of ESSWE, the European Society for the Study of Western Esotericism.

In addition, Simonsen is educated in gestalt therapy and psychosynthesis, and his varied career has also included stints in psychiatry, kindergarten, museums, security, catering etc. Today he works as a freelance writer. Simonsen is also a café aficionado, salsa dancer, amateur pianist and chess player.

Since childhood Simonsen has been fascinated by 'magical' phenomena as telepathy, clairvoyance, precognition, and healing—an interest based on some peculiar experiences of his own as well as strange stories told by friends and family. Later, this fascination led to extensive forays into esoteric and occult traditions, where such phenomena are not seen as chimera but as part of an expanded consciousness, and also into the science about such phenomena, i.e. parapsychology. The result is the present book, an entertaining, colorful and multifaceted good read, endorsed by several of the world's foremost experts in the field as well as a number of other authors and critics.

TABLE OF CONTENTS

INTRODUCTION

A Travelogue from the Twilight Zone

A Great Man's Dream

One April evening in 1865, President Abraham Lincoln was sitting in the Red Room of the White House, along with a few of his closest friends. One of them was W.H. Lamon who had previously been Lincoln's partner in a law firm and now worked as his bodyguard. In Lamon's auto-biographical notes, we read that Lincoln told the following story that evening:

> *About 10 days ago, I retired very late. I had been up waiting for important dispatches from the front. I could not have been long in bed when I fell into a slumber, for I was weary. I soon began to dream. There seemed to be a death-like stillness about me. Then I heard subdued sobs, as if a number of people were weeping. I thought I left my bed and wandered downstairs. There the silence was broken by the same pitiful sobbing, but the mourners were invisible. I went from room to room; no living person was in sight, but the same mournful sounds of distress met*

me as I passed along. I saw light in all the rooms; every object was familiar to me; but where were all the people who were grieving as if their hearts would break? I was puzzled and alarmed. What could be the meaning of all this? Determined to find the cause of a state of things so mysterious and so shocking, I kept on until I arrived at the East Room, which I entered. There I met with a sickening surprise. Before me was a catafalque, on which rested a corpse wrapped in funeral vestments. Around it were stationed soldiers who were acting as guards; and there was a throng of people, gazing mournfully upon the corpse, whose face was covered, others weeping pitifully. 'Who is dead in the White House?' I demanded of one of the soldiers, 'The President,' was his answer; 'he was killed by an assassin.' Then came a loud burst of grief from the crowd, which woke me from my dream. I slept no more that night; and although it was only a dream, I have been strangely annoyed by it ever since.

Lincoln's unrest was hardly surprising, as this dream definitely has 'something' about it that almost inevitably gives one goose bumps. And for us, a grim extra dimension is added by the fact that Lincoln related this story on April 11—three days before he went to the theater, where he was shot by an assassin and died from his injuries the following day. But how, then, are we to interpret this dream? Powerful people are frequently targets of attacks, and there had been an attempt to assassinate Lincoln a few years earlier. So maybe it was just his fear of such an eventuality that was expressed in the dream, and by pure coincidence the dream occurred shortly before the murder? Or maybe Lincoln's old and intimate friend had a desire to build myths around the president, and therefore compromised with the truth in his retelling? Or maybe it actually was the case, in line with how Lamon presents it, that Lincoln had a precognitive dream, i.e. that during sleep he got a glimpse of the future?

Now, this we can never know for sure. However, what is certain is that Lincoln, who was a very intuitive man, often consulted his dreams. Among other things, he believed that on several occasions his dreams had given him information regarding the outcome of key battles in the ongoing Civil War. And Lincoln is by no means the only person who has claimed to have had such experiences: many cultures, for example, Indian, Chinese, Greek, Roman, Jewish, Muslim, Viking, Indigenous Africans, Americans and Australians, are replete with accounts of precognition in dreams—tales which, of course, may be nonsense. But there are reputable scientists who think that some of these stories could be about *real* experiences of precognition i.e. paranormal foresight.

And there are also scholars who have argued that dreams allow for telepathic communication! In 1922, Sigmund Freud, the founder of psychoanalysis, wrote that it is 'an indisputable fact that sleep creates favorable conditions for telepathy.' During sleep, we are more relaxed than when awake, and our mental filters are on a little vacation. We are therefore more open, more receptive. Could it be that this lowered threshold enables us to receive information that we usually filter out? For more than a decade during the 1960s and 1970s, the possible relationship between dreams and telepathy was researched in the Dream Research Laboratory at the Maimonides Medical Center in New York. The leaders of these experiments were Professors Stanley Krippner, psychologist and parapsychologist, and Montague Ullman, psychiatrist and psychoanalyst, and they, in fact, came a long way toward reaching the same conclusions as Freud! Such ideas are obviously outside of the mainstream, but since reputable scientists are prepared to devote their energies to researching them they cannot simply be dismissed as delusional.

The Paranormal

Experiences of telepathy, precognition and related phenomena seem a poor fit with the typical modern, rational Western worldview. But statistics show not the least regard for this, and impertinently insist that more than half of us will have experiences of this kind during our lifetime—experiences of something beside the normal, namely something paranormal (*para* = beside). So statistics would suggest that paranormal experiences are, in fact, quite normal!

These phenomena could be said to belong to the *twilight zone*, the borderland of consciousness—a sphere that we may have a vague notion about, but that most of us are not really familiar with. Seventeen years ago the American Psychological Association launched a mapping project in the exciting book, *Varieties of Anomalous Experience* (E. Cardeña, S.J. Lynn and S. Krippner, eds.). Here a number of psychologists write about quirky themes such as lucid dreams, out-of-body experiences, telepathy, precognition, healing and other strange experiences that are not in harmony with our usual perception of reality. However, it becomes evident from the case studies in the book that such experiences do not have to be confusing or intimidating, but in fact can also be deeply meaningful. For example, many people experience a new and more serene relationship with both life and death after so-called near-death experiences, where one typically has a feeling of leaving the body, being enclosed by a great light, meeting deceased family members, angels or other spiritual beings, and the like.

The authors of *Varieties of Anomalous Experience* emphasize the *experience*, and especially the aspects connected with *personal meaning*, and largely refrain from telling us how these phenomena are to be *objectively* understood. Psychologists and psychiatrists will typically explain (or explain away) such experiences, resorting to pathological descriptions: hallucination, psychosis, dissociation, trauma, etc. But, interestingly enough, two of the three editors of *Varieties of Anomalous Experience* (Krippner and Cardeña) have said elsewhere that they think at least some of these strange phenomena are likely to be objectively real—i.e. that beyond people's *feelings* of having telepathic contact there may also occur *genuine telepathy* (a direct transfer of thoughts, feelings and sensations from one person to another).

A similar stance has been taken by a number of talented physicists, including Nobel Prize winners, who have argued that these kinds of phenomena, rightly understood, need not be contrary to the Laws of Nature. For example, Cambridge Professor Brian Josephson, who won the Nobel Prize in Physics in 1973, claims that both telepathy and psychokinesis (direct impact on the physical world by the power of mind) are 'objectively occurring phenomena' (not just hallucinations, etc.).

Throughout the book we will therefore consider the possibility that paranormal phenomena, or at least some of them, may be objectively real. This is not something I set out to *prove*; rather it is something I hope to *probe*. The reader is thus not asked to 'believe' in anything but simply to keep an open mind. I'll tell some quite unusual stories I feel deserve to be told, and the reader will (of course) draw his/her own conclusions as to how to interpret them. Personally, I don't think all the stories related in the book are best explained as being just chimeras. But if the reader disagrees with me that's fine—I hope he/she will still be entertained!

Psi

Unlike UFOs, aliens, ghosts and the like, some paranormal phenomena seem to be a direct result of the human will and abilities, e.g. clairvoyance and healing. There are even professionals—psychics, healers—who make their living from their claimed abilities in this field. This type of paranormal phenomena is often called 'psi,' after the first letter of the Greek word *psyche*. The term 'psi' was introduced by psychologist Robert Thouless in the *British Journal of Psychology* in 1942. He introduced the word, coined by his collaborator Bertold Wiesner, to be able to discuss these phenomena in a neutral manner, without reference to religion or belief. For some readers the word 'psi' might perhaps sound a little strange, but it is well established in parapsychological literature, and the term is—just as Robert Thouless intended—quite neutral, and therefore very handy.

The main forms of psi, often referred to as the 'Big Five,' are:

1. *Telepathy*: direct transference of thoughts and/or feelings

2. *Clairvoyance*: psychic sight, remote viewing, mental television

3. *Precognition*: paranormal foreknowledge, premonition

4. *Telekinesis*: direct mental influence on physical objects

5. *Healing*: direct mental interactions with living systems

The first three phenomena are about transmitting information, and are often called ESP (Extra Sensory Perception). Traditionally they are seen as an expression of 'the sixth sense,' and constitute the main focus of this book. The last two phenomena are about transfer of energy, and are often called PK (Psychokinesis), and we will most certainly say a thing or two about them, also.

The majority of the considerations in this book are based on strange incidents reported by scientists of one kind or another—archaeologists, anthropologists, psychologists, physicists and philosophers. Such people are more often than not very resourceful with well-developed skills in observation as well as in thinking. It therefore seems reasonable to take their reports seriously, even when—or *especially* when—they dare to speak against the consensus and vouch for the paranormal. It is not unusual to think that those scientists who report having experienced paranormal phenomena are misinterpreting their experiences at best or are fraudulent at worst. I suggest we take 'the road less traveled' and regard 'the defendants innocent until proven guilty' and seriously listen to their stories. They were there—we were not.

We shall also pay a visit to the parapsychologist's laboratory, where such strange phenomena are being researched with rigorous scientific methods. However, the present book is by no means a textbook in parapsychology. Rather it is a peacock's tail of paranormal perspectives, presenting many a quaint and curious idea of forgotten lore, as well as trailblazing projects from present-day research. This is mixed with a cornucopia of entertaining stories collected during forays (both my own and those of others) into the unknown regions of the mind.

The book can thus be seen as a travelogue from the *twilight zone*, the exotic borderland of consciousness. Some of the researchers who have dealt with this field have made suggestions as to how such events can be scientifically understood. An explanatory model that everyone can agree upon has not yet crystallized, but one idea persists: that *consciousness* is something completely different and far more extensive than we usually imagine it to be. By routine thinking

inside the box, we tend to take for granted that consciousness merely exists inside our own head, and that 'the brain
is alone with the brain,' to quote the Norwegian pop band
deLillos. But perhaps the brain is not that alone after all?
For it has been suggested from several quarters that our own
consciousness may be understood as being a part of a greater
Consciousness, a Mind at Large.

'The Mental Internet'

Based on this idea, we launch a quite simple model, called
the 'Mental Internet.' The basic metaphor here is that somewhat in the way our computers are linked together via the
internet, the 'consciousnesses' of all humans, and perhaps
all living beings, are linked together via some sort of Mental Internet. Consciousness, like the internet, is—on some
level—something that we are all doing together; it is net-
working. And telepathy is the communication that drives
this network. I am of course aware that such a model is a
gross simplification. But as the great statistician George
E.P. Box once put it: 'Essentially, all models are wrong, but
some are useful!'

Early psychic researchers found wireless telegraph and radio to be helpful metaphors when trying to grasp how telepathy could be possible, as these technologies demonstrated
that information could be transmitted instantly across vast
distances. If a crude apparatus could perform such a miraculous feat then our highly advanced minds might also be able
to accomplish such operations in ways yet to be discovered.
Today, however, the internet will probably make for an even
better analogy. There are two reasons for this: The internet is
intrinsically a web, thus collective, connective and more reciprocal than the radio. (A friend of mine related that when

he was a small boy, he found it utterly frustrating that the man in the radio was *speaking* all the time and never showed the faintest interest in *listening!*) And also, the internet is not only a medium for the *transmission* of information but also for *storing*.

Some people seem to be quite allergic to such models, saying: 'We know how radio and the internet works, but telepathy—if real—must surely be a totally different matter, thus these models are useless.' With this I don't agree; on the contrary, I feel such simple models may help to stretch the imagination, making it a little more flexible, perhaps opening us up to new possibilities. So once more in the wise words of George E.P. Box: 'Essentially, all models are wrong, but some are useful!'

I therefore invite the reader to engage in a little thought experiment throughout the book: namely that an Internet Model of consciousness may have some relevance. Galileo once invited the Inquisition to look through his telescope in order to see what he himself had seen. But, as we know, the inquisitors were not very keen on having their horizons expanded and instead muttered murkily of 'the work of the Devil.' However, I take it for granted that the reader has a radically more open attitude than those darkened souls, and I am therefore confident that my invitation will be well received.

Chapter 7 is entirely dedicated to skepticism related to the paranormal, which will help raise awareness about some common mind traps. And instead of either drowning in a swamp of naive acceptance, or crouching in the trenches of dogmatic skepticism, we will with poise and deliberation walk down the golden road of sober openness! In this respect it is interesting to note that not all skeptics are dismissive of the paranormal per se. For example, Sam Harris, the philosopher, neuroscientist and high-profile skeptic, author of *The End of Faith*, has stated:

> *My position on the paranormal is this: Although many frauds have been perpetrated in the history of parapsychology, I believe that this field of study has been unfairly stigmatized. If some experimental psychologists want to spend their days studying telepathy, or the effects of prayer, I will be interested to know what they find out. And if it is true that toddlers occasionally start speaking in ancient languages (as Ian Stevenson alleged), I would like to know about it.*

But even so, Harris does not think this field to be so interesting as to deserve much time and attention. Here I part ways with him, because I find it intriguing to think that our everyday perception of Space and Time may, in some respects, be merely a mental frame, a habit. And therefore it might be possible to think outside the box in a more radical way. The proposed thought experiment about a Mental Internet allows for this, and telepathy can then be considered as the 'emails' sent and the 'downloads' made via this mental network. Many phenomena that otherwise would appear inexplicable will in light of this model fall quite nicely into place. More (much more) about this later!

Based on the model of the Mental Internet—the thought experiment that I hope the reader will sign up for while reading this book—a psychic is simply a person who has an active relation to this network. Basically, that's it! But of course, competence will vary greatly, much like musical ability: most people can learn to play for their own pleasure, but not all are gifted enough to be musicians. And very few will be a Mozart, a John Coltrane or a Jimi Hendrix.

In addition to literature, the bibliography contains many links to valuable articles and reports that can be downloaded

from the internet (i.e. the *physical* internet!). These will enrich and deepen your reading experience along the way.

Then it only remains for me to say: Welcome, dear reader,
to the following journey in the Borderland of Consciousness—a fairytale kingdom which more often lies bathed in
moonlight than in sunshine, where telepathy is the prevailing language, where Space doesn't limit our view, and where
the Past, the Present and the Future are one!

Chapter 1
OPENING THE VAULTS OF TIME— ARCHAEOLOGY AND PARAPSYCHOLOGY

There are More Things in Heaven and Earth...

On-screen archaeologist and Intelligence agent Sophia Hapgood, who for a period was the girlfriend of Indiana Jones, was probably not the most warmhearted person around, as Jones on one occasion complained to his mentor, Dr Marcus Brody: 'You know, Marcus, the coldest year of my life was the one I spent in Iceland with Sophia.' However, Hapgood possessed other qualities that within both Intelligence and archaeology could presumably be at least as important: she was strong-willed and she was psychic. But, archaeology based on clairvoyance—does such a thing ever occur apart from in the movies? Well, it must be admitted this can hardly be said to be the preferred method in archaeology. But something extraordinary took place in 2012 that might make at least *some* archaeologists consider broadening their methodological scope an inch or two. After being lost since 1485, the remains of King Richard III—'A horse! A horse! My kingdom for a horse!'—were sensationally discovered after the Scottish screenwriter and amateur historian Philippa Langley did a nice little piece of clairvoyant archaeology, so it seems!

Langley had long been an enthusiast and defender of Richard III, the last Plantagenet king, believing his reputation had been willfully and unfairly tainted by Tudor propaganda. Archaeologists had given her a fairly good idea of the possible location; that of the former Greyfriars Church in Leicester, in which Richard's body could have been placed some time after his death. The church was demolished by Henry VIII and today the remains lie sealed under asphalt and buildings. But no one knew anything for certain, not about the abbey and definitely not about King Richard. One common opinion held was that his remains had been thrown in the River Soar. Langley has been interviewed many times about the case, and has given the following account of the historical site:

> I walked around that car park and I just knew there was nothing there. It was 'dead.' As I walked away, I saw another, private car park over to the right. I know how mad this sounds, but I snuck under the barrier and, on a very particular spot, I had the strongest sensation that I was walking on Richard's grave.
>
> It was a hot summer and I had goose bumps so badly and I was freezing cold. I walked past a particular spot and absolutely knew I was walking on his grave. I am a rational human being but the feeling I got was the same feeling I have had before when a truth is given to me.

On the basis of this clairvoyantly conceived idea, Langley organized an excavation, and—lo and behold!—about three feet (one meter) under the ground at the spot she had pointed out, a skeleton was found. It was DNA tested against the living descendants of Richard III's sister, Anne of York, and found to be a 99.999 percent match!

Regrettably we are not able to close the story in the full fairytale fashion, by announcing that Philippa, after having found her much sought-after king, married him and lived happily ever after. But even if we cannot herald love and a wedding and showers of white roses, there was a happy ending for Philippa—she was awarded an MBE by the Queen for 'services to the exhumation and identification of Richard III.' And as regards King Richard, he was reburied on March 26, 2015 with due pomp and circumstance in Leicester Cathedral following a week of commemorative events.

So, then, did the discovery of Richard III come about by an amateur archaeologist having more than her fair share of 'beginner's luck'—a one-in-a-million fortuitous shot, based on pure accident? Even if the chances are small, it *is* possible to win the Lottery. That question will of course be for each of us to ponder. But Langley herself, as we heard, clearly thinks of the incident as something other than sheer luck; she felt that her hunch, accompanied by strong bodily sensations, provided her with real information: 'The feeling I got was the same feeling I have had before when a truth is given to me.' (Speaking of truth, the old word 'soothsayer,' now used to mean a person who predicts the future, literally means 'truthsayer.' Perhaps hard to believe, but still…). Even if we shall never know whether Langley's intriguing combination of synchronized feeling and finding was based on clairvoyance or just on sheer luck, what is certain is that her case is not unique. There are, in fact, several instances where (professional) archaeologists have claimed to make significant discoveries based on information obtained via clairvoyance. Let's have a look at some classic cases.

Mysticism in Mexico

Clarence Weiant (1897–1986) is recognized as one of the people instrumental in rewriting the history of ancient Mexico. This came about in the following manner: Weiant, a multifaceted man who had begun his career as a chiropractor but later opted for anthropology, was working on his doctoral thesis when, just before World War II, he was invited to participate in what was to become an epochal excavation at the ancient cultural field of Tres Zapotes, Veracruz in eastern Mexico. The excavation was conducted under the auspices of the distinguished National Geographic Society and the Smithsonian Institution.

The environment was challenging: there were snakes, tarantulas and a variety of other nasties such as we've all seen in movies, and in some places the crew were forced to wind their way through waist-deep mud. It was arduous work, the anticipated findings did not materialize and frustration built up. In a most interesting lecture presented to the American Anthropological Association in December 1959 (http://bit.ly/125gC8A), Weiant recounts what then happened:

After we had spent some days in fruitless digging in the immediate vicinity of the Cabeza Colosal—a giant stone head, six feet high [2m], 18 feet [5.5m] in diameter and weighing 10 tons [9,000kg]—and had used a plough to tear up the small plaza situated between the giant head and the nearest mound, I was approached by Emilio Tegoma, one of our workmen, reputed to be the oldest man in Tres Zapotes. He assured me that he possessed the power to see things at a distance and things hidden. If we would listen to him, he would lead us to a place where we would find what we were looking for. He led us to what is referred to in our reports as the zone of the burials. Within twenty minutes after ground was broken here, the first beautiful and unbroken figurine of a Maya priest came out of the ground.

This became the first of a series of highly significant finds, including 15 statues and a number of stone tablets with descriptions containing time references as far back as the year 31 BCE—the oldest references yet found on the American continent. Frustration was turned into success, and Weiant was given the rare honor of having his dissertation published as a special Smithsonian bulletin. Together with follow-up excavations conducted by others, Weiant's findings led to radical changes by scientists in their understanding of the history of the area. Hereafter it was no longer assumed that the Mayans or the Aztecs constituted the original culture of Mesoamerica—the broad cultural field covering 'the middle' of the two Americas—but rather that it was the obscure Olmecs (c. 1500 BCE–400 BCE) that had formed the 'mother civilization' of the area. In other words, the whole Mesoamerican cultural history was revised!

Not an insignificant result from the clairvoyant visions of an elderly Indigenous worker…if clairvoyance really was involved? Maybe Emilio Tegoma just had a lucky day at work? Or maybe he simply conveyed knowledge that was common among locals? Of this we cannot be certain. But Weiant, for his part, was inclined to see the information provided by Tegoma as stemming from clairvoyance rather than from plain luck or from the 'social stock of knowledge.' This was due to several experiences of the kind, including the following:

Later, on a Sunday afternoon, when it had occurred to me that this might be a good man to consult for information on the history and ethnology of Tres Zapotes, although I did not know how or where I might find him

on an off day, he suddenly appeared at the camp, told me
that he knew I wished to ask him some questions, and he
gave evidence that he knew in advance what the ques-
tions would be.

Weiant lists a string of cases, involving different researchers, where paranormal abilities, according to his perspective, could have been involved. He remarks that even if separate episodes cannot be considered scientific evidence, he nevertheless—based on his own experience and that of others—would recommend that 'every anthropologist (in the US archaeology is usually regarded as a subdivision of anthropology), whether believer or unbeliever, should acquaint himself with the techniques of parapsychological research and make use of these, as well as any other means at his disposal [...].' And Weiant concludes his lecture on a visionary note: 'Only a few times in the history of civilization, it seems to me, has an intellectual challenge of this magnitude presented itself. How can a science which purports to be the Science of Man ignore it?'

A Modern Merlin in the Kingdom of Arthur

Some years earlier a gifted English architect and archaeologist had reached a similar conclusion, namely Frederick Bligh Bond (1864–1945. And since we are now in parenthesis, let me parenthetically add that Bond's grandfather was the nephew of Captain William Bligh of *Mutiny on the Bounty* fame.). Bond frequented societies involved with the

occult in one way or another—the Freemasons, the Theosophical Society, the Society for Psychical Research, the
Rosicrucian Society of England and the Ghost Club—and
in due course he also worked as an editor for a couple of journals of occult lore. 'Occult' may perhaps sound somewhat
sinister in the ears of some modern readers, but its original
meaning is not connected to black magic or any other evil;
the word is derived from the Latin *occultus*, meaning 'secret'
or 'hidden', and is a neutral term for phenomena that are
obscure to us. For example, Isaac Newton, who first formulated the law of gravitation, describes gravity as having
'occult' qualities, as it cannot be seen and it exerts its power
at a distance and in a secret way.

Bond first had a successful practice as an architect in
Bristol, designing official buildings including public halls,
hospitals, university buildings and schools. Later he became recognized as an expert on the restoration of medieval churches, but today he is primarily remembered for
his pioneering archaeological work in Glastonbury Abbey
in southwest England. The first abbey was founded in the
700s, and Glastonbury was, for a period, the largest and
richest abbey in the land. After the last abbot, Richard
Whiting, was executed in 1539, a casualty of Henry VIII's
proclivity for violence, the abbey was dissolved and started
to deteriorate, and during the following centuries it fell into
complete ruin. Furthermore, the abbey's proud history almost disappeared into oblivion.

The area is mythical to its core: Some believe that Cad-
bury Castle, a fortress from the fifth century on a nearby
hill, might perhaps be the legendary Camelot—the castle of
King Arthur and the Knights of the Round Table. Nobody
knows if there was indeed a historical King Arthur, but in
anno Domini 1191, the monks of Glastonbury reportedly
found an oak coffin, containing the skeletal remains of a

human couple and a lead crucifix with an inscription that spawned protracted speculation as to whether the tomb could have belonged to King Arthur and his Queen Guinevere. If this were the case, then Glastonbury, which in the early Middle Ages was surrounded by wetland areas, might have been the mystical *Avalon*—the island to which Arthur, according to legend, was brought after being mortally wounded. However, the common (and sadly more prosaic) perception is that the tomb was fabricated in order to entice more pilgrims to finance the rebuilding in 1184 following a fire. Be it Avalon or not, Glastonbury Abbey is for many reasons—Celtic, Christian, political-historical, literary, and occult—an important monument, and is visited annually by more than 100,000 people.

What Goes Around Comes Around

With such a mystical haze hanging over the area it was perhaps only to be expected that 'the invisible hand of destiny' would entrust the assignment to excavate the ruins to a person with a deep commitment to the occult, perhaps even a little *too* deep. For in 1921—in spite of his success with the excavations that he had been working on since 1908—Frederick Bligh Bond was fired by his employer, the Church of England, since it had become clear that he had applied spiritualistic methods to accomplish his discoveries! As early as 1907 Bond and his intuitive assistant, the former navy captain John Allan Bartlett, had received communications from spirits—or 'spirits' if you'd rather—via so-called *automatic writing*. This is a technique used by spiritualists—and also by some psychologists and artists—that involves allowing the hand to write without conscious control, so as to leave the spirits (or eventually the subconscious mind) in command. Bond would ask his questions of the spirits, and Bartlett would then let his hand be 'taken over' to become a tool for writing—and sometimes also drawing—their answers: 'Stand ye and be as waxe in our hands,' the spirits urged them (a little creepy, I would say!).

The messages claimed to originate from a group of persons/spirits who called themselves 'The Watchers'—important among them being the penultimate abbot of Glastonbury, Richard Beere (deceased 1524), and an otherwise unknown monk, Brother Johannes Bryant. Messages were partly delivered in Latin (of varying quality), partly in medieval English and partly in relatively modern English. In general, the spirits seemed to respond based on their personal interests and perspectives—don't we all, really—be that of an abbot, a mason or a monk.

Abbot Beere was a highly cultivated man. We know he corresponded with Erasmus of Rotterdam, the learned humanist, and he commissioned a number of exquisite buildings in Glastonbury. In 1503, Henry VII sent Beere as an ambassador to Rome to congratulate the new pope, Pius III, on his election. After returning from Italy, Beere took the initiative to build what was likely a spectacular chapel, in the new, ornamental Italian style, and dedicated to Our Lady of Loretto. (Legend has it that the house in which the Virgin Mary lived was carried by angels to the Italian town of Loreto, which has been a pilgrimage destination for centuries.) This chapel eventually became an increasingly significant theme in the later conversations between Bond and the spirits.

The spirits gave Bond instructions as to where to find the remains of multiple buildings, among them several chapels, most famously perhaps the chapel dedicated to St Edgar. The excavations conducted in 1908 and 1909 had already proved the spirits' words to be more than just nonsense, as

Bond actually found the sought-after ruins. He went on to uncover statues, tombs and carvings, secret tunnels, water-courses and drainage systems. And according to his detailed analysis in *The Gate of Remembrance* (1918), where he showed his true colors and for the first time disclosed his unconventional approach, the excavations so far had confirmed much, even most, of what the spirits had related. For example, concerning the chapel dedicated to St Edgar, the spirits had explained that *azure* glass was used in the windows. This—according to Bond, who was an expert in the field—was not to be readily expected. The more common stained glass in a 16th-century chapel in England would be toned in white and gold, and the blues often tended toward steely grey. But interestingly enough, when the Edgar Chapel was excavated, Bond found a large amount of crushed, azure glass...

The Loretto Chapel

After some years apart, Bond and Bartlett were reunited during WWI and agreed to continue with the channeling. The first séance in the new series was held on December 4, 1916. Bond had thought the spirits would perhaps comment upon the war, whereas Bartlett had hoped for some enlightening hints concerning sacred geometry, a keen interest of his. But the spirits obstinately proceeded in their own manner, and chose to deliver new and quite detailed information pertaining to Glastonbury, in particular the beautifully decorated chapel dedicated to Our Lady of Loretto. That such a chapel really had existed was mentioned in scattered historical sources, but the evidence was partly anecdotal, and the location, let alone the specifics, of the chapel remained a mystery.

In the above-mentioned and later séances—the interrogation was interrupted because of the war—the spirits informed Bond where the Loretto Chapel could be found, its dimensions and how it was built. Here are a few tidbits.

> *Obliviscor. So long we have slept near Capella Loretta under the bank full thirty paces from the Navis. Ye did not go farre enow beyond the (bank) they cast up there. It was full five feet in, and buried in the place where he [Abbot Beere] didd drawe the Chapitre Howse [...].*
>
> *The syde of it was distant from ye navis thirty-one feet and a half, and from ye aisle of ye transept he was fulle tenn feet with a covered way unto, and four steppes up unto ye aisle aforesaid. Yt...was ybuilded by Bere [Abbot Beere] most faire and wonderfull in ye newe style brought from Ytaly when he didd goe there upon ambassadrie.*

These are just a couple of examples from the large catalogue of revelations. The spirits further provided many descriptions, with accompanying sketches, of the chapel's decorations—descriptions indicating that the style of embellishment was unknown at that time and place. No wonder, because as we have just heard, it was made in 'ye newe style brought from Ytaly.'

The next phase in the excavation began some months after the end of WWI. Bond initially had trouble finding the chapel, and hence had to consult the spirits again. But they repeated the same instructions, and by taking a closer look and digging deeper, he eventually found the remains of a chapel, which would seem to closely resemble the information provided by the spirits—concerning location, size, etc. The building, which therefore appeared to be the chapel of Our Lady of Loretto, was dilapidated to an unusual extent, even for a ruin, and Bond did not have time to explore the site before he was fired. In the fourth edition of *The Gate of*

Remembrance he supplies further instructions from the spirits—instructions that have yet to be implemented. It would be highly interesting, then, to see what could be in store for the person inclined to execute the spirits' 'last will and testament'!

An Open Mind—the Brain Still in Place

It seems that Bond did quite a good job at Glastonbury. Dr Ralegh Radford, the archaeologist excavating the site in 1962, attested that Bond's methodology was 'as advanced as any at the time.' So his openness to the occult seems not to have been in conflict with a rational approach. But since it is widely believed that Bond made his momentous discovery in accordance with an ostensibly 'irrational' way of collecting information, we have to ask: what kind of phenomenon are we really looking at here? Could it be, as many spiritualists would likely consider, that persons from 'the other side'—souls of deceased people, disembodied spirits—provided Bond and Bartlett with the information? Or could it rather be, in line with the model we suggest in this book, that the information was downloaded via telepathy from our collective Consciousness, the Mental Internet? Bond himself apparently was open to both these perspectives but, underscoring his rational approach, he puts more weight on the latter. He says he is inclined to think the information came from a

> *cosmic Memory, conscious or unconscious, active or latent [...] embracing not only all individual experience and revivifying forgotten pages of life, but also [...] involving yet wider fields, transcending the ordinary limits of time, space, and personality.*

But if one is skeptical of spiritualism, of our model and of Bond—perhaps the explanation simply could be that we are dealing here with an unusually talented archaeologist, who, with the help of his sensitive assistants, was able to eloquently 'read' the patterns of the site? (Medieval churches and their premises are often built according to standardized structures.) Such 'reading' could perhaps have been made possible through a combination of in-depth historical studies and 'subliminal perceptions'—that the brain perceives far more of a landscape than one is consciously aware. Perhaps this is how they were able to obtain all this strangely accurate information? And that thereafter they, for some reason, mystified the process by involving spirits? Nobody knows. But what we in fact *do* know is that it was Bond, and not some conventional, hidebound archaeologist, who detected these long lost buildings.

The news that the Church of England was actually involved with an archaeological 'secret service' under the leadership of Commander Bond—*Bligh* Bond—was, as stated, not well received when it first came to light in 1918 with the release of *The Gate of Remembrance*. When the actions of secret services are brought to light, and thus are secret no more, those involved will often be compromised, and archaeology is no exception. The church felt compromised by being associated with Bond's spiritualistic practices, and probably even more so since they actually seemed to work. In addition there was other bickering. Bond (being, after all, related to *HMS Bounty*'s notoriously headstrong Captain Bligh) was certainly not the world's most diplomatic person, and his superiors for their part appear to have been quite smug and inflexible, exhibiting 'the insolence of office.' On top of this, Bond's estranged wife ran an unusually toxic smear campaign—berating him in the press, in court and on social occasions—accusing him of a highly uncommon form of child abuse, namely that of exploiting their daughter as a spiritual medium! (The daughter sided with her father, proclaiming he had never done such a thing.)

So alas! after a prolonged controversy, Joseph Armitage Robinson, Dean of Wells, known for his critical research on the myths surrounding the place, sacked Frederick Bligh Bond, the man who had applied his occult resources—be they spirits, be they subliminal perceptions, be they mystifications—as a magic wand to lift the curse of oblivion, and thus conjured forth the mighty Glastonbury Abbey from the twilight of history.

Psychic Pathfinders on Indian Lands

Professor John Norman Emerson (1917–1978) did a most formidable job pertaining to the cultural history of the Huron-Iroquois First Nations people of Ontario, Canada. Emerson led no fewer than 50 excavations, he started several institutions in archaeology as well as an archaeological journal, and for a period he was also president of the Canadian Archaeological Association. Emerson differed, however, from his colleagues in that he did not limit himself to merely 'interpreting stones and bones,' as he dubbed it, but eventually chose to make use of 'intuitive archaeology'—i.e. he would sometimes seek assistance from clairvoyants. And he also recommended that archaeology, as a discipline, should be open to information collected in this very unorthodox way.

What brought him to take his profession down this unusual road was his acquaintance with George McMullen (1920–2008). Emerson first met McMullen in a private setting, and was initially curious as well as skeptical of McMullen's alleged psychic abilities. It all began as an innocent party game, where McMullen would get to hold some ancient artifacts and then try to come up with their particulars—location where found, age, use, etc. And astonishingly enough, according to Emerson, McMullen repeatedly provided both significant and hereto unknown information, although he neither had any qualifications nor any prior experience in archaeology. One thing led to another, and when the 'party games' were expanded with a similar success to include field tests at various excavation sites, Emerson became increasingly convinced that McMullen's strange ability was genuine. And also that it was not just some kind of psychological oddity, devoid of any meaning and significance, but—as Weiant and Bond had earlier concluded—that archaeology *as a science* could benefit from 'psychic' persons such as McMullen.

McMullen had since childhood experienced a strong capability for the type of clairvoyance called psychometry, i.e. the ability to paranormally 'read' objects. He explains:

As a young child I could pick up an object and by just holding it I'd know who made the object, where the object came from and who had owned the object. I'd also know about the owners of the object; where and how they had lived, whether they were still alive or had died and the manner of their death.

This sounds preposterous, but psychometry is actually an ability that has been reported many times. McMullen had also on occasion the experience of communicating with different 'contacts,' i.e. beings of a spiritual nature, which would supply him with information. These contacts sound as if they could be akin to the spirits (or 'spirits') which, as we heard above, delivered messages to Bartlett and Bond—birds of a different feather, perhaps, but still birds... And in light of our suggested Internet model, the information contained in the 'downloads' could therefore conceivably stem from the bulk of information stored in the collective Consciousness, the Mental Internet, the Mental Cloud.

McMullen had never seen any point in such abilities, but now, through his collaboration with Emerson, a scientist of high esteem, he finally felt his powers could be applied in a valuable way. McMullen subsequently cooperated with other archaeologists, however they were usually afraid that their colleagues might find out, and therefore typically asked him to visit the excavation sites when their teammates were on holiday, and also to keep quiet about the whole affair afterwards! For a scientist to meet with a psychic is likely to be a *liaison dangereuse*, which might easily develop into a brutal career killer. If one is perceived to be unscientific or unserious it could swiftly become *adios* to collegial respect, promotions, scholarships and support. Emerson, however, enjoyed such a degree of recognition beforehand that he could afford to disregard his colleagues' well-intentioned warnings—and they are said to have been manifold!—that he stay away from such stuff and nonsense.

Let us briefly hear how McMullen assisted with an excavation east of Toronto in 1973. The young archaeologist C.S. Reid, a student of Emerson, had been unable to find the palisade—the long fence encircling the settlement—that is of utmost importance when mapping a village. After two seasons of fruitless exploration, entailing filtering through tons of earth, a widespread confusion ruled, tracks led in different directions, and no one really knew what to do. Such was the situation on May 19 when George McMullen, following

Emerson's suggestion, took the matter in his own hands. He strode around the site, gesticulating and explaining what he could 'see,' and hot on his heels was Reid, putting white marker sticks in the earth. Within minutes McMullen 'saw' that large parts of the palisade had been covered by a huge heap of gravel, and said that by digging on the eastern side of this pile, remnants of the palisade would be found. He also marked its direction and added that it had not fully encircled the village. None of this was according to expectations, and hence McMullen's information was received with skepticism. Emerson says: 'It was completely wrong. They would not have placed a palisade there…'

However, it soon became clear that McMullen had been spot on: the palisade was found in accordance with his instructions, and followed the precise direction he had predicted. It also turned out that it formed a partial, not a full, enclosure of the village. McMullen had moreover said that at the end of the palisade there would be some kind of 'cattle gate'—Reid dug, and sure enough, the gate was there!

McMullen spent a few days on the site in this first round, and apart from the palisade he marked the possible positions of two larger buildings. These were both found—the first of them less than 18 inches (half a meter) away from the place he had pointed out! At a later visit McMullen gave further successful indications. The only thing he seemingly got wrong was some burial places that he had marked, but which were unable to be detected by the team (though some claim these graves have since been found).

Anyway, what McMullen did was nothing short of impressive. If you are in Rome, it may be said with some justification that you just have to break ground and you will make archaeological finds. But in our case the sought-after structures had, as we heard, escaped the archaeologists' keen eye for two seasons when McMullen appeared on the scene and saved the day. According to Emerson, the area was without character, flat, covered with grass, straw, shrubbery, a group of poplars and a large pile of gravel that had been dumped there in the 1950s—'there was not much to see, I can tell you.' So it cannot reasonably be said that McMullen's findings were obvious. Emerson used McMullen on many other sites as well, and estimates loosely that his success rate was about 80 percent. Whereas Stephan A. Schwartz, who we will become acquainted with very soon, estimates McMullen had a score of about 70 percent. Still fairly impressive, I would say!

Emerson sums up his thoughts on 'intuitive archaeology' in the following words:

> *Although I do not claim that my studies have achieved the status of being scientific, neither can they be ignored or dismissed as nonsense, imagination or hallucinations. The key to the matter appears to lie in the concept of intuition. I found for my purpose a workable definition of intuition is that individuals exist who have 'an immediate knowledge or knowing of events without the obvious use of learning or reason.' Intuitive or psychic individuals can tell about past events and circumstances by a poorly understood process of immediate knowing. […] I propose to use an innovative approach to this understanding by combining the disciplines of archaeology, science and psychic studies.*

In truth, a most remarkable proposal from a highly respected researcher who is sometimes referred to as the 'father' of Canadian scientific archaeology!

In addition to his own clairvoyantly informed fieldwork, Emerson walked the talk by engaging in the milieu that formed the SAC, the Society for the Anthropology of Consciousness (www.sacaaa.org)—a subdivision within the

American Anthropological Association. Here all kinds of off-beat themes such as trance, altered states of consciousness and psi are dealt with simultaneously in an open-minded and scientific way. Psi, then, are the paranormal phenomena that seem to be directly related to our own consciousness, will and abilities—telepathy, clairvoyance, precognition, healing, etc.—as opposed to the phenomena apparently caused by 'external agents' (UFOs, ghosts, crop circles, etc.). In the bibliography there is a link to an article on 'intuitive archaeology' where Emerson shows how this quite special method could eventually be put into practice. And in McMullen's book *One White Crow* can be found some entertaining and easy-to-understand lectures Emerson held on the topic.

Indiana Schwartz and the Lost Treasures of Alexandria

After his cooperation with Emerson, McMullen also engaged in other archaeological endeavors—most importantly the so-called *Alexandria Project*, led by Stephan A. Schwartz. Schwartz is certainly a colorful character in the world of archaeology, undoubtedly gifted but considered by many conventional archaeologists to be eccentric, even a bit kooky, and could perhaps be described as a kind of paranormal Indiana Jones. Schwartz has hosted spectacular expeditions and discovered shipwrecks and ruins, he cooperated with the American military in the so-called Stargate project which we will look at in chapter 2, and he has also written a couple of paranormal 'good-reads,' *The Secret Vaults of Time* and *The Alexandria Project*, which are both classics within the intriguing fringe field of intuitive archaeology.

The Alexandria Project deals with an exploration undertaken by Schwartz and his Mobius team in the huge harbor area of Alexandria, Egypt, starting back in 1978. 'Mobius' is a reference to the 'Mobius strip'—a surface with only one side (take a strip of paper, twist it half a turn and glue the ends together and you'll have it). As I was a bit uncertain as to why Schwartz had given his team such a strange name I sent him an email and asked. He wrote back that the Mobius strip, with its twisted, seamless continuity, symbolized to him 'that the local and nonlocal were one if you only understood the twist.' Hence the Mobius team consisted both of 'normal crew'—divers and engineers—working 'on location' as well as 'paranormal crew'—psychics, paragnosts—working 'nonlocally' (using clairvoyance). In addition, the team was given important external assistance from an eminent Polish archaeologist who helped to collate and interpret the resulting findings.

The team's technological expertise was represented by electrical engineer Harold Edgerton, a professor at MIT (Massachusetts Institute of Technology). He had developed sophisticated photography and sonar systems and had earlier cooperated with the charismatic French diver, inventor, filmmaker, environmentalist and author Jacques Cousteau. The paranormal component was taken care of by no fewer than 11 psychics. Most essential were the aforementioned George McMullen, and Hella Hammid, who was a kind of real-life Sophia Hapgood. Hammid was a photographer who had worked for several years as a so-called 'remote viewer' on the Stargate project (see chapter 2). A remote viewer is a professional clairvoyant, who uses extrasensory perception (ESP) to sense with the mind rather than with the physical senses. In the Stargate project, the

American military and the CIA sought to use clairvoyance in military contexts, for example to locate military installations in foreign countries. One would think such experience to be an excellent qualification when on a mission to discover ancient ruins!

And indeed, in the giant Eastern Port area the Mobius team soon found many highly interesting and important architectural remains. The ensuing information is attested to by Professor Mieczyslaw Rodziewicz, a specialist in the Graeco-Roman antiquities of Egypt and then leader of the Egyptian-Polish Archaeological Mission in Alexandria. The team discovered ruins of what was probably the *Timonium*, a small 'vacation palace' to which Marc Antony withdrew after having been defeated by Octavian, the future Emperor Augustus. The team also found remains of an Isis temple, a major breakwater, and of what was most likely the palace of Cleopatra (yes, *the* Cleopatra!). Also discovered were a small stone sphinx, a cluster of bead-like stones, a large crown from a statue and various other objects. And last, but certainly not least, some distance outside the harbor they found huge blocks of chiseled stone that in all likelihood belonged to the impressive and almost mythical lighthouse on Pharos Island (not *The Faroes!*) This tower was considered to be one of the Seven Wonders of the Ancient World, and according to one estimate it was about 400ft (134m) high.

A large part of the work underwater has been filmed, and hence these quite spectacular finds are well documented. Apart from his book, much information can be found on Schwartz's website: www.stephanaschwartz.com

Schwartz sounds surprisingly modest considering all that they found—I, for one, would undoubtedly have been euphoric if I had discovered something like the palace of Cleopatra! But it had long been known that much of old Alexandria lay submerged in the harbor area and hence that

ruins of the above-mentioned edifices were probably to be
found there. Schwartz therefore chooses to primarily underscore *the effectiveness* provided by the combination of technology and clairvoyance:

> *Other diving teams could also have found what we
> found, but not as quickly or as easily. It would have
> been extremely difficult to do several of these findings if
> we only had sonar to guide us. To apply search patterns
> would have taken many weeks. But using historical
> sources and the psychics we were able to make a reason-
> ably good first estimate of what one might see on the sea-
> bed already within a few days.*

However, it turned out to be impossible for the divers to
investigate the area as thoroughly as they'd hoped since the
water was extremely muddy—according to Schwartz it was
'like swimming in minestrone soup.' (In the aftermath of the
expedition, the above-mentioned professor Harold Edgerton and Schwartz co-authored a paper which was presented
at the Annual Meeting of the Society for Underwater Archaeology, January 11, 1980.) A more in-depth exploration,
both figuratively and literally, became the lot of successors
with bigger budgets and more available resources. This happened in the 1990s under the auspices of a French-Egyp-
tian cooperation led by renowned Egyptologist Jean-Yves
Empereur in partnership with Franck Goddio, marine archaeologist of much acclaim. Goddio's work was covered by
the Discovery Channel—which regrettably had not existed
when Schwartz's team were in and around the Alexandrine
waters (or minestrones). Today, scuba trips to the area are
arranged, so that not only scientists (and psychics) but also
tourists can get to see these exciting ruins.

Well, then—was Schwartz's paranormal thrust into this
area to be considered archaeologically valuable? Or was it

just some sort of reckless adventure, of which the history of archaeology is all too rich? Heinrich Schliemann's infamous use of dynamite to 'excavate' Troy, which he had newly discovered, comes to mind. (Speaking of Schliemann: Schwartz in an interview has recounted that Schliemann was led to searching for Troy at this specific site based on a series of dreams...) But let's get back to the archaeological value of Schwartz's foray: The assessment of Professor Mieczyslaw Rodziewicz, the above-mentioned archaeological expert, was as follows: 'As an archaeologist with twenty years' experience working in Alexandria, I would say the discoveries are of the highest importance [...],' and even more forcefully: 'I, as an archaeologist, would classify it higher than the discovery even of the tomb of Alexander the Great.' That is *some* endorsement to get from an expert within Alexandrine archaeology! It seems, then, that Indiana Schwartz because of—or perhaps some would say in spite of—his unconventional methods managed to do some pretty valuable archaeological science.

So, once again we have seen that important archaeological discoveries were made with the help of information obtained via clairvoyance. Such, at least, is the perception of the maverick archaeologist who made these discoveries (though I have an almost clairvoyant hunch that some slightly more conservative souls might disagree...).

Hunger for Mysteries in Christiania

As I suppose it might entertain some readers—perhaps for more than one reason—I will conclude the chapter by recounting my own little venture into intuitive archaeology or, perhaps more correctly, intuitive historical research. A few years ago I decided to dig up some facts regarding my great-great-grandfather, Olaus Johnsen, who lived in Christiania in the mid to late 1800s. ('Christiania' is the old name for Oslo, the capital of Norway.) When I set out on this modest historical journey, I knew next to nothing about him, not even his name, just that he had a son (my great-grandfather) who was an architect. Clearly, I could use a little qualified help, and hence I summoned the experienced archive researcher, Terje Gudbrandson, the former chairman of the Norwegian Genealogical Society. I also had the idea of simultaneously doing a little paranormal research, just for fun. I therefore contacted a lady (she has said she prefers to remain anonymous) who on some previous occasions had impressed me with her seemingly strong psychic abilities. I told her about the project and asked what we were going to find. She then right away, without asking any questions, said that I would discover that my great-great-grandfather was far more influential than I had until now thought. And further, that he had done much to help the poor.

When the archives were opened a few days later, Gudbrandson could tell me that the documents showed Olaus Johnsen had gone through a most remarkable social elevation: starting out very poor (his grandfather was listed as 'beggar'), then finding his way into manufacturing, and ending up as a very wealthy real estate developer. Among other things he built many of the tenements at Meyer-Lökken (a district close to the center), and he both dealt and socialized with the movers and shakers in Christiania. For example, the nobleman Herman Wedel Jarlsberg leased half of the second floor of Olaus' private apartment at 2, St Olav's Place. In those days, St Olav's Place was a powerhouse, and number 2 was the central and most fashionable building. The walls were decorated with stucco ornaments, and in the middle of the 'star square' (so called because five roads meet in a node) was a water fountain with a beautiful statue of Cupid.

That Olaus proved to be such a big shot came as a great surprise to me. I therefore have to admit that the psychic certainly was on to something when she said that Olaus would turn out to have been far more influential than anticipated.

But what about the second point she mentioned, concerning helping the poor? A few days later Gudbrandson called me again. This time he had found Olaus' last will and testament, and reading it had brought tears to his eyes. For the will, dictated by Olaus on his deathbed, instructed that large sums be used to create an endowment for health care for artisans and workers (who were often so poor that they could not afford any proper treatment). According to the statutes the sick could get financed sojourns to Sandefjord Bad, a balneological (medical bath) facility. This was Norway's premier spa resort with an excellent medical standard for the times. And to keep spirits high, the acclaimed composer-conductor Johan Svendsen and his orchestra gave concerts for the patients, who quite often were members of the *glitterati*—the well-to-do, fashionable and glamorous. An endowment portion appears to have been equivalent to approximately £15,000/$19,500 in today's money. And if not fully recovered after one stay—Olaus dictates, contemplating how he himself had got help for his rheumatism at Sandefjord Bad on several occasions—it was possible to arrange for another one! Such bountifulness bestowed on a sick artisan or worker must surely have been something quite out of the ordinary.

Then again, were the predictions of this exceptional lady just arbitrary guesses snatched out of midair? Sure, she did not provide any detailed information, that's true. But I must admit I find it intriguing that she was able to give a fitting thumbnail sketch of the—quite unexpected—results before the 'excavation.' At least it seems this way to the (perhaps a little too fascinated?) author. But if this actually should be the case—that it was not just lucky guesswork on her part— perhaps it is not so strange after all. Because according to the thought experiment suggested in the introduction, i.e. the Internet model of consciousness (and I hope I still have the reader with me on that one!), all the necessary information would conceivably be available on—and could thus be downloaded from—the Mental Internet.

Now, I did not discover any Mayan statuettes, nor any chapel dedicated to Our Lady of Loretto, nor a palace having belonged to Cleopatra. And most of my great-great-grand-father's fortune has long been gone because of market crashes, gambling and inflation. But I am still pleased to have discovered new parts of our family history, and some interesting buildings at Meyer-Lökken. This is particularly the case with Olaus' own residence at 2, St Olav's Place. In the world-famous novel *Hunger* by author and Nobel laureate Knut Hamsun (by many seen as the originator of literary modernism: James Joyce, Franz Kafka, Virginia Woolf, etc.) the main character, who most likely is Hamsun himself, is trailing two ladies—one of them being Ylajali, the woman of his feverish dreams—until they arrive at St Olav's Place:

*Outside No. 2, a large four-storied house, they turned
again before going in. I leant against a lamppost near
the fountain and listened for their footsteps on the stairs.
They died away on the second floor. I advanced from the
lamppost and looked up at the house. Then something odd
happened. The curtains above were stirred, and a second after a window opened, a head popped out, and two
singular-looking eyes dwelt on me. 'Ylajali!' I muttered,
half-aloud, and I felt I grew red.*

Who, then, was this mysterious Ylajali in reality? Could it
have been Ida, the painter-sister of Herman Wedel Jarlsberg
(Olaus' aristocratic tenant), who often visited her brother at
2, St Olav's Place? This is the opinion of a number of *literati*,
as Hamsun is known to have had a soft spot for ladies of
the Arts. Or is it more likely that the real Ylajali was Olaus'
then 22-year-old daughter, Nathalie? The protagonist in
Hunger is delirious and hence could have twisted 'Nathalie'
into the quite similar sounding but more exotic-romantic
'Ylajali.' We know that both ladies in question had at times
their abode on the second floor—the very floor where Ylajali appeared... Given our focus on mystical matters, and
also because the novel Hamsun wrote after *Hunger* is called
Mysteries, it would perhaps be suitable to have a small team
of intuitive or clairvoyant historians solve this piquant little
historical literary riddle? I don't know about the international learned literary community, but I am quite sure that
at least Weiant, Bond, Emerson and Schwartz would all
have cheered and approved!

Chapter 2

MILITARY MYSTICISM—A CLAIRVOYANT VIEW OF THE COLD WAR

Paranormal Paranoia— or Perhaps Not

2009 saw the release of the movie *The Men Who Stare at Goats* featuring, among others, acting heavyweights George Clooney and Kevin Spacey. The film is based on the US military involvement with the paranormal, which included experiments where soldiers tried to kill goats by staring at them! These are weird cases and one is inclined to think of the whole thing as just one of those conspiracy theories for which the American people—with their historical roots in persecuted religious minorities—have always had an affinity: where God is eager to implement his plans, Satan is likely to conspire against it! Thus the findings from a 2013 Public Policy Polling showed that about 20 percent of Republicans and 5 percent of Democrats thought their very own President Obama to be the 'anti-Christ'—the false Messiah mentioned in the New Testament. While a corresponding perception of former prime minister Theresa May—as the 'Mother of Harlots and Abominations of the Earth' (Revelation

17:5)—is rare among Britons regardless of party. Regrettably we haven't here the opportunity to delve into this exciting theme, which is treated in, for example, *American Exceptionalism* by Dorothea L. Madsen among other works.

So—given their strange nature, the incidents in *The Men Who Stare at Goats* could easily be thought of as being no more than conspiracy fantasies and the 'fake news' of yesterday. But as stated at the beginning of the movie: 'More of this is truer than you would believe!' And that is probably correct.

The Weird Ways of War

The film traces the goat-staring and other military paranormal usage back to the 1970s, when the pervasive paranoia of the Cold War created a mental climate conducive to the entrance of psi phenomena into the political arena. The reason the *paranormal* so easily bonds with *paranoia* is the emphasis on hidden connections—connections lying *parallel* to those that are obvious (*para* = beside). And given an atmosphere of fear, wherein one feels subjected to continuous surveillance, the susceptibility to lurid theories is likely to be high. In addition, the era was infused with the hippie movement and their spiritual approaches to most aspects of life. This also had an impact on a group of people who aren't normally associated with any kind of hippie philosophy whatsoever, namely the Intelligence service. One noteworthy case is Major General Albert Stubblebine, head of the United States Army Intelligence and Security Command. Stubblebine demanded that his personnel practice bending metal using the power of thought. And on various occasions he himself tried to walk through walls! No joke, it really *is* true—on YouTube you can find videos where Stubblebine confesses his disappointment at not having succeeded.

So, both the paranoia and the particular spirituality of the era, the *Zeitgeist*, served to promote a strong increase in the interest in all things paranormal. In addition there were specific reasons why both military and civilian Intelligence were attracted to the potential of such phenomena. It had become clear that the Russians had been conducting exhaustive experiments of this nature for some time. This was confirmed by both Intelligence information and also via more public sources. The International Parapsychology Congress held in 1968 in Moscow made public films with the *paragnost* (i.e. a person who claims to have paranormal abilities) Nina Kulagina, where she demonstrated telekinesis by moving various physical objects, apparently with just her mental powers (clips of these films are easily found on YouTube). Kulagina was examined by many Soviet scientists including two Nobel laureates, and most of them seem to have concluded that her power was the real deal.

Well, it's one thing to move inanimate objects around, but on March 10, 1970, Kulagina was reported to have taken full control of the heart of a frog: she first increased the frog's heart rate—and then stopped it completely! A skeptical psychiatrist, who thought the reports of this event to be plain bogus, challenged Kulagina to take control over *his* heart. A military doctor, who had researched Kulagina for some years, set up an experiment where the heart rates of both Kulagina and the psychiatrist were monitored by ECG. Kulagina increased her heart rate gradually, whereas the heart rate of the psychiatrist speeded up so dramatically that—because of health concerns—the experiment was stopped after just a couple of minutes! These seemingly impressive events may of course have been based on a combination of complicity and cheating with instruments. But what if these effects were real? And what if a person with Kulagina's abilities became bored with just controlling the hearts of frogs and volunteers, and instead directed her attention to the heart of the American President?

In 1972 the English parapsychologist Benson Herbert was allowed to do some experiments with Kulagina. The following happened the first time she demonstrated her powers on him: '[...] she held my arm and produced an intolerable sensation of heat, which I could not endure for more than two minutes.' At a later meeting he had decided to steel himself, and from that occasion he recounts the following:

> *As far as I was concerned, it felt like acute physical pain, and I had to clench my teeth and beat my forehead with my free hand in order to continue with the experiment. It soon became clear beyond doubt that the sensation was pure heat, and electrical in nature. Apart from the heat, restricted roughly to the area beneath her hand, I felt no other symptom. I cannot be sure how long I held out, but guess it was between four and five minutes, after which time I involuntarily collapsed on a nearby couch, and Kulagina released me of her own accord.*

Following these experiences, Herbert no longer doubted the authenticity of the heart-stopping experiment: 'It is now not difficult for me to believe that she can stop a frog's heart. I think it possible that if Kulagina had maintained her grip on my arm for half an hour or so, I would have followed the way of the frog.'

Such reports were obviously likely to fire the imagination of an already paranoid US Intelligence service. In addition, there were rumors of Russian experiments with so-called 'psychotronic weapons.' These devices were said to utilize the type of energy generated by telekinesis. And if they were to be installed in a satellite, for instance, they could—at least in theory—affect the physical and mental health of people in large areas. The previous KGB general Oleg Kalugin has since confirmed that there *were,* in fact, attempts to develop such weapons. He has also—perhaps to make himself a little more interesting?—indicated that one actually managed to achieve some results. For instance, Kalugin suggested that Boris Yeltsin's heart attack in 1991, following the coup that initiated the end of the Soviet Union, was triggered by psychotronic weapons used against him by the regime. Well, regardless of whether this is true or not, there is obviously something valid in the modern saying: 'Just because you are paranoid doesn't mean they *aren't* after you!'

Clairvoyance—Spy Camera of the Future?

However, the most extensive military projects involving paranormal capacities did not focus on completely curious stuff such as staring at goats, controlling frogs' hearts, etc. This is possibly because such psychokinetic abilities are hard to develop and even harder to control—even according to those who are completely convinced of the possibility of cultivating such powers. But with respect to the ESP trio, telepathy, clairvoyance and precognition, the situation is very different. Quite a few of the researchers, officers and agents involved have reported developing ESP with notable success. But of course, in spite of their competence and integrity, these people cannot be regarded as neutral observers.

The main objective for the military was to develop what was termed 'remote viewing.' This is basically the same as *clairvoyance*, i.e. the experience of 'seeing' through inner vision, places which are unreachable by physical sight. The 'viewer' may also receive additional impressions and information in the form of sounds, strange ambiance, odors, etc. When cultivating remote viewing, clairvoyance is exercised in a highly structured manner, with fixed procedures and exhaustive protocols. The cultivation of such an ability is obviously potentially very useful, for instance, with regards to the location of enemy installments, transport and maneuvers.

The fact that the US military started to experiment with this ability was also motivated by the following: They realized that the Russians, through unknown means, had accessed sensitive military secrets. And around the same period, they acquired information that the KGB had used tens of millions of rubles to fund the training of clairvoyant spies. So doing the math, and adding a little—as the climate of the period definitely encouraged—some of the hawks were left with a nagging suspicion that it was thanks to clairvoyant spies that the Russians had accessed these secrets. They therefore concluded: 'If the Eastern bloc has such people on its rosters, we definitely should acquire some too!' The irony was that the Russians had possibly started *their* research based upon similar assumptions about what the Americans had achieved in the paranormal field...

Project Stargate

The Stargate Opens

These were diverse projects which, in different ways and under the auspices of various personnel, involved military-oriented clairvoyant activities, such as Sun Streak, Grill Flame, and Center Lane. These projects are often subsumed under the umbrella term 'Project Stargate,' which is the label I will use for the sake of simplicity.

The first military program for remote viewing was developed by Captain Fred Holmes Atwater in 1977, and for years to come Atwater also organized the training of clairvoyant spy candidates. He describes this work in his autobiography *Captain of My Ship, Master of My Soul*, and there he also reports on some of his own paranormal experiences, which in the first place had caused him to become seriously interested in this special topic. Atwater mentions how odd it was to read discussions in the newspapers on the feasibility of remote viewing while he—according to his perception—saw it demonstrated in the laboratory every day! From his perspective the question was therefore not about the *existence* of such abilities, but rather whether they could be developed, and how reliable they eventually would become. It goes without saying that when many lives and material wealth are in the balance, as is often the case in military operations, decisions need to be based on meticulous and precise information. This aspect—the stability and reliability of the information—was also (no big surprise) decisive in the final fate of the paranormal military programs.

The physicists Russell Targ and Harold Puthoff at Stanford Research Institute, a renowned institution linked to Stanford

University, developed much of the program's scientific foundation, theories and training methods. Targ and Puthoff were pioneers in the field of laser technology, and had undertaken assignments for NASA and the CIA among others. Their psychic research had begun during the early 1970s. And partly based on the goodwill of the famous and infamous rocket engineer, Wernher von Braun—the main brain behind both Adolf Hitler's V2 rockets and the American Apollo project—the project had received partial funding from NASA. Von Braun, James C. Fletcher (the administrator of NASA) and others were standing on a pier, chatting informally during a conference, when Targ suggested that his and Puthof's psychic project should receive financial support. Von Braun then turned to Fletcher and said: 'Oh, give him the money, Jim. We all know that this stuff is real. My grandmother always knew when the trains would crash or when someone was about to die.' Targ and Puthoff became known to the public in the wake of their experiments with Uri Geller—the Israeli magician, illusionist, medium or whatever we might call him (he refers to himself as a 'mystifier')—who rose to international stardom based on his paranormal (or perhaps 'paranormal') demonstrations on TV, where he seemingly excelled both in telepathy and the telekinetic 'bending of spoons.'

As Targ and Puthoff were developing the techniques for remote viewing they were assisted by the artist Ingo Swann (1933–2013), who some would consider to be an exceptionally talented psychic. In addition Targ and Puthoff got help to look into the theoretical aspects from some talented, playful and imaginative 'hippie physicists' from the so-called Fundamental Fysiks Group at Berkeley. We will become acquainted with this exciting pack of scientists in chapter 6.

In their book *Mind-Reach: Scientists Look at Psychic Abilities* (1977) Targ and Puthoff explain the basic methods used to cultivate remote viewing abilities in the test subjects. The main features of the technique are quite simple: While the test subject—the remote viewer—is stationed in the laboratory, a member of the research team jumps in the car and drives to another location where there is a 'target.' This target has characteristics that are easily recognizable. It can, for instance, be a building with a special shape, a unique natural form or anything with a distinct visual identity. When the experiment starts, the remote viewer tries to 'see'—by visualizing, acquiring images, feeling, associating, sensing, etc.—what the target looks like. The viewer then sketches the most characteristic traits of the target, say, an oval pool, a triangular tower, a meandering river, a cliff shaped like a half moon, etc. The viewer also gives an accompanying verbal description of what she/he sees, feels, senses, etc.

Targ and Puthoff maintain that the majority of around 100 test subjects actually managed to develop certain remote viewing abilities within the space of a few months. However, very few acquired consistency in their results.

The Stanford Research Institute remote viewing exploration became integrated in the military Stargate program during 1977–1978. It was subsequently classified with restrictions that lasted until 1995. After the research became directed toward military usage, the remote viewers would typically be recruited from among soldiers—often personnel who repeatedly had managed to survive under 'impossible' conditions. The assumption was that these individuals might have a well-developed sixth sense that had helped them to pull through against all odds.

Due to a limited number of suitable candidates and qualified trainers, only a small number went through the training to become remote viewers/clairvoyant spies. Through the years Stargate seems to have had about 20–25 remote viewers employed—successively, not all at once—and some 40 inner-circle personnel.

The Taurus Experiment—
Clairvoyance from the Deep

In 1977, a field-oriented slant was given to some experiments conducted by Stephan Schwartz (the psychic archaeologist we got to know in chapter 1) on board the mini-submarine *Taurus*. The boat, which was brand new, was at the Institute for Marine and Coastal Studies, University of Southern California, for her sea trials. The Institute graciously financed the sub, the surface support ship and all the people involved in the operation for three days to help Schwartz carry out the Deep Quest study. During the experiment, the submarine with the viewer on board was submerged hundreds of miles out in the Pacific, at depths varying between 80–170 meters (260–560 feet) according to the reports. The idea was, among other things, to check if distance, the water shield, and electromagnetic isolation would impact the viewer's abilities. Because of space considerations I'll restrict myself to describing only select episodes from the experiment (protocol is found in the bibliography).

A pair of experimenters, a 'target demarcation team,' would visit a site (that the viewer had no prior information about), and the viewer would then attempt to 'see,' describe and sketch it. The first site visited was a giant oak on a hilltop in the Portola Valley in California. The viewer, Hella Hammid—located in the submerged submarine out in the Pacific—closed her eyes for a moment, then said in a rush: 'A very tall, looming object. A very, very, huge tall tree and a lot of space behind them. There almost feels like there is a cliff or drop-off behind them.' Not a bad description, considering that she was located deep in the ocean, hundreds of miles away! The other site visited was a shopping mall in Mountain View, California. The viewer, now Ingo Swann, described it—correctly—as follows: 'flat stone flooring, walls, small pool, reddish stone walk, large doors, walking around, an enclosed space,' and made a sketch descriptive of the site. Barring collusion between the researchers and the viewer, such accurate representation is difficult to explain. And don't take my word for it!—the reports, including photos from the sites and the viewer's sketch, are found in the bibliography, giving you the opportunity to make up your own mind.

Related experiments tested the ability to 'see' pictures (rather than sites). A viewer would be asked to describe a picture located several kilometers away (these experiments were land-based). The report describes the first three trials as follows: The first target picture chosen by the experimenters was a photograph of the Cheops pyramid in Egypt. The subject person (the remote viewer) depicted a square building in a dry place. He felt that his arms and hands were being bandaged, and his head and face also. He thought of the word 'mummy.' The second picture was a painting of a gorilla looking out of a window. The subject reported seeing a disfigured black man with his face cut in half by something (the window frame). The third picture showed fishing boats on a Mexican lake. The main elements of the subject's descriptions were 'seafood' and 'the ocean.'

These are of course not *perfect* descriptions of the pictures. Nevertheless, the degree of accuracy seems much too great to be dismissed as 'purely coincidental.' As with the first case, I see here only two possibilities: 1) complicity or 2) authentic clairvoyance. The second alternative is of course very convenient for our model of a Mental Internet!

An everyday version of such an experiment could be staged in the following way: You travel to, say, Paris, and settle in front of the Eiffel Tower with a laptop hosting a webcam. You then start to chat with a friend who is downtown (or in a submarine, if you happen to know a crew member). This person will probably be able to quickly describe your environment relatively well: 'Braid-like metal structure in the background, seems to be tall, even monumental, arches beneath, an urban environment, people going to and fro.' And voilà!—you have remote viewing à la internet. I am the first to admit that it may sound simplistic to depict an apparently mystical ability in such a trivial way. Nevertheless, if our consciousness actually has a collective dimension— that we are all connected on some level—the example may be a good approximation of the way this ability functions.

Remote viewing, given that the phenomenon is real, is an application of *clairvoyance*. But as there were people present by the targets, perhaps the aforementioned episodes could just as well be seen as an application of *telepathy*—that staff members had accidentally acted as 'transmitters.' This is an interesting question that I think would be impossible to answer. It is quite often hard to differentiate between *clairvoyance* (where information is downloaded from the Mental Internet without a specific 'sender') and *telepathy* (where the information stems from a specific person). When using *clairvoyance* in a military connection one attempts to directly 'see' landscapes, buildings, things or activities of strategic importance. While using *telepathy* in a similar context, one would rather attempt to 'read' the thoughts and plans of, for instance, an important enemy general. Such use of telepathy has almost certainly been attempted, but within Stargate the focus was on the development and use of clairvoyance.

Shaken and Stirred, and the Need for Martinis

Well, then, how did the remote viewers perform? Puthoff maintains that the results were sometimes so staggering that they were scared to report them—they feared they wouldn't be believed! Such cases were called 'eight martinis'—an Intelligence expression for events so shocking that one has to wash down eight martinis to regain one's composure. An early 'eight martini' occurred when a policeman, Pat Price, and the artist Ingo Swann, two of the most trusted remote viewers in the early days, were independently given a set of latitude and longitude coordinates. Both men gave quite similar descriptions of the location (in West Virginia). The descriptions were not perfect, but still surprisingly good. But what led to an acute need for the eight martinis was Price's depiction of a top secret, underground military installation at the location! Moreover, Price gave a telling characterization of the activities in this installation; among others the use of code names with references to pool—cue ball, cue stick, etc. According to Puthoff, who at the time was not aware of the installation, all of this was confirmed in retrospect. I assume that the martini cocktails mixed by Targ and Puthoff that evening became more than normally shaken, as they themselves clearly must have been both shaken *and* stirred!

Pat Price was also impressive in one of the most famous police cases from the period—in fact, one of the most famous police cases of all time. On February 5, 1974, Stanford Research Institute was asked to assist the police with the Hearst case. Patricia Hearst, granddaughter of the media mogul Randolph Hearst, had disappeared the day before and the police hadn't a clue about the circumstances or her whereabouts. Amazingly, Price could tell them that the disappearance was a kidnapping, but one that primarily had been politically—not financially—motivated. And from a large police catalogue of mug shots, Price identified as suspects three people from the Symbionese Liberation Army (SLA)—an extreme, leftwing urban guerrilla group, which staged robberies and used violent means. Later it transpired that it *was*, in fact, this particular group that had kidnapped Hearst, and also had managed to brainwash her into taking part in a bank robbery. A photo showing Hearst holding a machine gun during the robbery has become one of the iconic images of the 1970s. Price also managed to locate the car of the kidnappers. And although the information he provided did not become decisive in the release of Hearst, the *accuracy* of the information remains mind-boggling—assuming, of course, that the story is correctly recounted.

Some critics, among them the well-known skeptic Martin Gardner, have pointed to the fact that several of the remote viewers were connected to the Church of Scientology. This is no surprise because back then the Church of Scientology was one of the few organizations that had training programs designed to activate paranormal abilities; if you're interested in learning kung fu, it makes sense to join a kung fu club! Nevertheless, Gardner maintained that this link could have created an 'unholy alliance,' and thus influenced *which* results were included in the reports and *how* they were reported. This is surely a legitimate point of view. But as the public evaluation of Stargate did not arouse any suspicion that the results had been manipulated in any way, such insinuations have to be put on Gardner's tab.

Puthoff resigned as project manager in 1985. The particle physicist Edwin C. May subsequently became the most prominent administrative and scientific leader within Stargate. My friend, the film maker Terje Toftenes, interviewed May in October 2017—the link is found in the literature list. During May's tenure success was reported in a number of cases, among others an incident regarding a spy suspect arrested in South Africa. A remote viewer 'saw' that the suspect had used a radio transmitter hidden in a pocket calculator to smuggle information. When confronted with this paranormally acquired information, the spy confessed and chose to cooperate. Other cases, under much more dramatic circumstances, took place during the Gulf War (1991). Here Stargate's remote viewers reportedly assisted in locating both SCUD missiles and hidden laboratories designed for research in biological and chemical warfare. Tunnels and underground military installations are also said to have been detected with their help. These accounts are based upon sources with connections to the project; hence they might have had a vested interest in promoting the enterprise.

But we have also had external confirmation of Stargate successes, one even stemming from the very highest levels. According to *Reuters*, President Jimmy Carter confirmed in a speech to students at Emory College, Atlanta on September 20, 1995, that during his term as President (1977–81) a 'special plane' (probably a Russian spy plane) that had crashed in the Congo was found with the help of remote viewing. Carter recounted that detailed searches with spy satellites had failed to find any traces of the wreck. Then, without Carter's knowledge, the CIA had proceeded to put a remote viewer on the job. Carter reported that, 'She gave some latitude and longitude figures. We focused our satellite cameras on that point and the plane was there.' Unless Carter was fundamentally misled by CIA Director Stansfield Turner (they were classmates at the US Naval Academy in Annapolis, and Turner was sworn in to the CIA position by Carter, but one never can be fully sure with these Intelligence people!), it certainly looks as though Stargate can record a very satisfactory result in this case.

The Stargate Closes

Regardless of such positive reports, Stargate was closed in 1995 after having completed no less than 504 separate spying missions. The CIA, which eventually had taken over the coordination of activities, requested that the American Institutes for Research perform an evaluation. They employed two external consultants with no link to Stargate, who then evaluated a (very small) selection of the experiments. One of these consultants was Jessica Utts, a statistics professor with several published textbooks in her field. She contended that the viewers had significant scores 34 percent of the time, which was far beyond what one could expect if one had used good, old-fashioned guessing. Utts declared:

> *The statistical results of the studies examined are far beyond what is expected by chance. Arguments that these results could be due to methodological flaws in the experiments are soundly refuted. Effects of similar magnitude to those found in government-sponsored research at SRI and SAIC have been replicated at a number of laboratories across the world. Such consistency cannot be readily explained by claims of flaws or fraud.*

Utts goes on to say, 'Using the standards applied to any other area of science, it is concluded that psychic functioning has been well established.' So, backed by a substantial amount of other research within the field, Utts quite categorically concluded that Stargate's results could not be attributed to chance or faults in the experimental procedures. And on this basis she recommended that Stargate should continue.

The other external consultant was Ray Hyman—a psychology professor and magician, and also a notorious debunker of the paranormal; it would be tempting to describe Hyman as a 'celebrity skeptic.' Hyman starts his report by commenting that Stargate represents a marked step forward with commendable improvements as regards scientific methods. And he agrees with Utts that the positive statistics are difficult to explain.

We agree that the effect sizes reported in the SAIC experiments are too large and consistent to be dismissed as statistical flukes [...] I tend to agree with Professor Utts that real effects are occurring in these experiments. Something other than chance departures from the null hypothesis has occurred in these experiments.

Still Hyman maintains that the 'something' that occurred does not need to be successful remote viewing. He hints that the effects (i.e. the positive statistics) could perhaps be attributed to undiscovered faults in the methodology.

Although I cannot point to any obvious flaws in the experiments, the experimental program is too recent and insufficiently evaluated to be sure that flaws and biases have been eliminated.

As we can see, Hyman was not convinced by the results. But interestingly he *does* explicitly say that he has not been able to find any faults or mistakes. At the end of his report he provides suggestions for future research. Among others, he suggests evaluations should be left to fully independent judges—i.e. experts without any prior knowledge of either the targets or the viewers involved.

The committee which evaluated the fate of Stargate was—take note!—not interested in remote viewing per se, but focused on the eventual military value of such an ability. The reports from Utts and Hyman were an essential part of the decision-making process. And with one of these experts not convinced that remote viewing was a reality at all, the committee, after a short deliberation, concluded that Stargate didn't have adequate military usefulness to merit further support. Among the reasons stated was the following:

> *The information provided by remote viewing is vague and ambiguous, making it difficult, if not impossible, for the technique to yield information of sufficient quality and accuracy of information for actionable intelligence. Thus, we conclude that continued use of remote viewing in intelligence gathering operations is not warranted.*

The committee recommended that Stargate be phased out—a recommendation quickly followed up by the CIA. And so it happened that the Stargate was closed, barred and bolted!

Some informed sources have claimed that the closure was partially motivated by stigma: many top military officials found it embarrassing to be involved with an oddball project that so far had only a *possible* value. Several of them wanted to *use* Stargate, but very few wanted to be associated with it. The fear of being regarded as ridiculous was great, and obviously not without reason. Stargate had become one of the many hot potatoes of the Cold War, and as the well-known viewer Joe McMoneagle put it: 'Anybody associated with it could kiss their career goodbye.'

Some Thoughts in Retrospect

Stargate was a long and relatively comprehensive project. It is estimated that the various component programs, which sometimes ran simultaneously and also partially replaced each other, were active for roughly 20 years with a total budget of approximately 20–25 million dollars. Even if the budget was quite modest—adjusted for price index increases it equals about 40 million dollars in 2020—the accrued documentation was quite formidable. Among the American public institutions and bureaux which at one point were involved in Stargate we find the CIA, FBI, Defense Intelligence Agency, National Security Council, National Security Agency, Secret Service, US Special Forces Command, Drug Enforcement Agency, Navy, Army, Air Force, and the US Customs. In other words, a most powerful motley crew you wouldn't want to have as enemies! Russell Targ once humorously commented that this was the *really* paranormal thing about Stargate; that this strange program was treated with positive interest by the authorities over such a long period! But all things must pass, and as previously stated, the magic faded in 1995 and Stargate was closed.

A substantial amount of the internal documents has been declassified. Since 2004, anyone interested has been able—funnily enough—to order this material directly from the CIA. In January 2017, the CIA released even more documents which can now be downloaded freely from their own website. By studying the roughly 100,000 declassified pages you can reach your own opinion on Stargate. Note that when visiting and using the CIA website you may be registered by those states spying on the USA—perhaps not a very pleasant thought... So let me give a mention to the informative website of Daz Smith, an English viewer who had part of his training within Stargate: http://www.remoteviewed. com/index.htm. Here one can download a selection of the Stargate documents released by the CIA. Smith has told me that there are parts of the Stargate material that still remain unpublished, and that in the published documents sections have been blacked out and removed...

Most of us would probably want a slightly easier approach than having to trawl through piles of documents, and to that end I have the pleasure of announcing that we are fortunate, as various insiders have written about Stargate. *Reading the*

Enemy's Mind: Inside Star Gate, America's Psychic Espionage Program by retired army major Paul Smith gives an excellent overview. Major Smith was associated with the project during the period 1983–1990 and was a remote viewing instructor of the utmost importance. Also Russell Targ, the physicist who for so many years was one of the 'backroom boys,' has published a string of books germane to the theme. And from the outsiders we have journalist Jim Schnabel's classic *Remote Viewers: The Secret History of America's Psychic Spies.*

As a little service to those readers who want to proceed in making their own attempts at remote viewing, I have included a link to a brief 'Do-it-yourself' instruction written by the aforementioned Major Paul Smith. There is also a link to the original training manual used within Stargate, which neatly sums up the basic methods, and which also explains some of the theoretical foundations. When reading it I was suddenly struck with the thought that the movie *The Matrix*, considered one of the greatest science fiction films ever, may conceivably have been inspired by this training manual; this includes the film's title, as one of the central concepts in the manual is—'matrix'!

As far as I have ascertained, virtually all the people previously involved in Stargate claim that remote viewing is an undeniable reality—this includes the physicists, the officers and the agents (though these people are, of course, not unbiased observers). At the same time, all of them have admitted that there were problems involved in basing military decisions on this highly arbitrary ability. Nevertheless, several of the more high-profile agents have managed to develop careers based on purported clairvoyant proficiency acquired through their training within Stargate. Some of them have been employed as advisors by companies searching for oil and other natural resources. And some have used their alleged paranormal powers to assist police and other organizations searching for missing persons. The artist Ingo Swann, one of the creators of the methods used in Stargate, has stated that it is a heavy burden to work with such cases; this is because it often entails 'seeing' abuse, murders, rotting corpses, etc. Swann has reported being successful in only three of 25 attempts. (He was apparently not satisfied with this.) Whereas Joe McMoneagle, who—given his professional military background—is probably a much more robust viewer, claims to have given a fairly accurate location of the missing person in 10 of the 26 cases he has been involved in as of 2012. If this is correct, hats off to him!

McMoneagle was also the first of the military remote viewers and had a marked James Bond flair to his ID code— namely 001. He currently has the highest public profile of the former Stargate viewers, and in addition to his books and lectures he has participated in television programs. On such occasions he has demonstrated his special abilities close to 100 times. To appear on live TV demonstrating remote viewing is brave; however, not everyone has been overwhelmingly impressed—the well-known skeptic Brian Dunning said that what impressed him most was the editing of the television recordings!

Let me also mention that McMoneagle has become something of a star in Japan after having appeared a number of times on Japanese television. He has assisted the Japanese police in solving cold cases, and he has also been involved in psychic archaeology with the aim of finding the historical truth about Himiko, the famed shamaness-queen of Yamatai-koku, an ancient Japanese kingdom.

There are several videos of McMoneagle available, so it is possible to see an experienced viewer in action—and perhaps thereby also to form an opinion of his abilities?

Glimpses from Behind the Iron Curtain

Stargate was developed as a response to real as well as imagined paranormal research conducted in the Eastern bloc—in particular, of course, the Russian activities. At the same time the former Czechoslovakia and Bulgaria were also carrying out parapsychological research of high quality, but the Russians were the most eager, and had reportedly between 20 and 50 (estimates vary quite a bit) institutes working on partially military-oriented paranormal research. Mention of this will perhaps bring to some readers' minds, particularly if they are chess players, the legendary 1972 World Chess Championship match between Bobby Fischer and Boris Spassky that took place in Reykjavik, Iceland. Accusations of every imaginable form of manipulation and trickery were swirling all over the place—and no wonder. The Russian chess team had help from a parapsychologist, and Reykjavik suddenly had a surprise visit from Fischer's brother-in-law—none other than Russell Targ of Stargate! This apparently innocent match was in fact significant propaganda as it was seen as a fight between the Eastern bloc and Western systems. Thus both sides most probably applied paranormal as well as normal means in their attempts to secure the victory/take home the prize.

We are aware of such curiosities, but the true extent of military-oriented paranormal activities within the Eastern bloc during the Cold War is still relatively unknown. Testimonies from eyewitnesses presumed credible do exist; Oleg Kalugin's description of psychotronic weapons has been mentioned, and Larissa Vilenskaya, an engineer and parapsychologist who emigrated to the US in 1981, has reported that talented mediums were recruited to use telepathy, in the more literal sense, to 'psyche out' the leaders of other countries when they appeared on television! Another program was focused on internal politics: according to the biochemist and parapsychologist Milan Ryzl, with whom we shall soon become acquainted, the aim was to use telepathic hypnosis to 're-educate' (= brainwash) antisocial elements, i.e. opposition and criminals (groups which then were often surprisingly analogous...).

Through the years popular books have been published on this topic, such as *Remote Viewing: History and Science of Psychic Warfare and Spying* by Tim Rifat (1999). An older easily accessible work is *Psychic Warfare: Threat or Illusion* by Martin Ebon (1983). Both books contain interesting information but do not discriminate well enough between the facts and paranoia. An even earlier account was *Psychic Discoveries Behind the Iron Curtain* (1970) by journalists Sheila Ostrander and Lynn Schroeder. This is probably the most popular classic that contains the most extensive information on Cold War paranormal activities within the Eastern bloc. Ostrander and Schroeder have a flair for the fantastic, and there is a sensationalist slant to their book. Still, *Psychic Discoveries Behind the Iron Curtain* provides valuable information as the authors were 'on location.' In 1968 they visited the International Parapsychology Congress in Moscow and afterwards they traveled in other Eastern Europe countries, interviewing psi researchers.

The sensationalist slant in popular works is quite understandable and to some extent also forgivable; one wants to increase the 'wow factor' so as to sell as many books as possible. More troublesome is when the same weakness also pertains to the primary sources, as different firsthand reports from the Eastern bloc appear to be conflicting: some sources say the paranormal programs were enormous, whereas other sources downplay their importance. An example of the first

kind of source is former KGB General Boris Ratnikov, who
was responsible for various psychic operations. In an interview with the *Russian Gazette* in 2006 Ratnikov said:

> *You can't even conceive what sort of war of minds was
> unfolding in this field in the first half* [sic!] *of the twen-
> tieth century. I'd hardly be exaggerating if I say that
> sometimes real 'astral'* [an occult term denoting 'psychic']
> *battles were waged. And all of this was classified and
> camouflaged, probably no less than the nuclear project.*

Ratnikov further explains that the main practical purpose
for the Russian research was to be able to exercise distant
influence/control of the human psyche.

> *Around 50 institutes in our country studied the possi-
> bilities of acting on the psyche remotely. Expenditures
> for these goals were counted in the hundreds of millions
> of rubles. And although the investments justified them-
> selves, the results we got were not developed.*

Ratnikov also gives a couple of concrete examples of their
activities:

> *Back at the beginning of the 1990s, we 'worked' with
> Robert Strauss, the new US ambassador in Russia.
> Having read his thoughts, we came to the conclusion that
> within the embassy there was a device for psychotronic
> influence on Muscovites, but it was deactivated. We also
> received other information from his subconscious.* [...]
> *A couple of weeks before the start of the bombardment
> of Yugoslavia by American aviation, we held a séance
> to connect with the subconscious of Secretary of State
> Madeline Albright.* [...] *First of all, within Madame
> Albright's thoughts we discovered a pathological hatred*

for Slavs. She was also incensed that Russia possessed the largest reserves of minerals in the world. In her opinion, in the future not just one country should dispose of Russian reserves, but all humanity under the supervision, of course, of the United States.

Well, well, well—I must say… Ratnikov has, in fact, impressive military credentials and unless he has severe mental problems, or a personal interest in lying—giving us 'alternative facts,' as it is called in the Trump era—I would say that the typical Cold War paranoia becomes more than partly justified by such depictions! The Russians were apparently both heavily investing in, and also practically applying, this most curious form of weaponry.

But Ratnikov's statements seem to be countered/modified by that of other high-ranking officers. 2015 saw the release of a book called *ESP Wars East & West: An Account of the Military Use of Psychic Espionage as Narrated by the Key Russian and American Players* (Edwin C. May, Victor Rubel and Loyd Auerbach). As of today this is probably the best book on the market pertaining to the theme (but I am aware that parts of its representations are considered tendentious by some and are being challenged). Here, former KGB Major General Nikolai Sham seems to be painting a more modest picture of the Russian paranormal activities. Sham is quoted as saying that: 'There was nothing comparable to the U.S. Star Gate program.'

Even if their names might seem to suggest otherwise—Ratnikov, Sham—both are men of merit and high standing, so who to trust? Neither being a telepath nor a prophet myself, I can still hear a little voice telling me that the FSB (the descendants of the mighty KGB) will not release a single page from their archives even if I bribe them with the best vodka and the best caviar and in addition ask politely. And since my own remote viewing abilities are not that well developed I can't rely on them either to peep into the subterranean bunkers in Moscow or gaze over the vast steppe of Siberia. Therefore I recently (January 2017) contacted three different Russia experts—a former professor in Russian History at the University of Oslo, and two fulltime researchers at NUPI, Norsk Utenrikspolitisk Institutt (the Norwegian Institute of Foreign Policy)—but none of them knew of reliable sources related to this peculiar aspect of the Russian secret services. Then I tried to contact Andrei Soldatov, who is running Agentura.ru, a website frequently used as a source on Russian affairs by international media, but Mr Soldatov did not respond. Apparently we still have some way to go before being able to get a valid picture of the 'para'-military activities of the Eastern bloc, comparable to what we have of Stargate following the CIA release of documents.

So for now, I think we'll have to content ourselves with having a brief look at the more civilian part of the activities. I purposely write 'more civilian' since during the Cold War civilian research in many fields was also, to a large extent, regarded as part of the East–West conflict.

The Red Square—Not Square At All

It is clear that the scientists in Eastern Europe were researching all the phenomena that were being studied in the West: telepathy, clairvoyance, precognition, telekinesis, healing, etc. And furthermore, that this was by and large done within the framework of the so-called 'diamat,' *dialectical materialism*, which was the obligatory philosophy in communist regimes. Therefore the phenomena were not viewed in light of some kind of spiritual New Age or 'hippie philosophy,' even though researchers like Professor Giorgi Lozanov had visited India to study yogis. Accordingly with this 'hard' and purely materialistic approach, Eastern bloc researchers would often explain psi phenomena as being caused by low-frequency electromagnetic waves, or eventually by forms of energy so far undetected by classical science.

In Eastern Europe, psi research typically involved the use of hypnosis and also various forms of electrical equipment. Among these was the well-known 'Kirlian photography'—a photographic imaging of the bioelectric field (the 'aura') surrounding all living beings. Another project focused on developing 'psychotronic dynamos' with the purpose of generating and concentrating the type of energy supposedly involved in telekinesis (the 'spoon-bending' type of energy). This energy was to be used for healing, but was also thought to have the potential for far darker deeds… When reading about all this, one senses a strange ambience: a mixture of Gothic, Red Square, and science fiction—as if Frankenstein, Stalin and Arthur C. Clarke were to lock hands and perform a circle dance. (And by the way, Stalin himself was fascinated by the paranormal, and had witnessed persuasive demonstrations by the famed medium Wolf Messing.) One also senses a *dead end*—that history has taken another route forever.

Two Wise Men from the East: Milan Ryzl and Giorgi Lozanov

Two prominent researchers among the greats of Eastern European parapsychology who have directly influenced the West are the recently deceased professors Milan Ryzl (1928–2011) and Giorgi Lozanov (1926–2012). These men also had an explicit humanistic and spiritual agenda, which far exceeded the confines of both the laboratory and the era.

From Czechoslovakia With Love—Milan Ryzl

Toward the end of the 1960s, the Czech biochemist and parapsychologist Milan Ryzl chose a one-way ticket to the West, after many years of the Communist regime taking a rather sinister interest in his research. Ryzl had focused on hypnosis as a means of developing ESP in his volunteers, and through the years he systematically hypnotized several hundred people for this purpose. He has estimated that approximately 10 percent of the volunteers developed reasonable abilities for telepathy, clairvoyance and precognition. The official interest in Ryzl's research is said to have increased greatly following reports that his students had won the national Lottery several weeks running! Ryzl contended that the Lottery was an excellent training ground for precognition, and had developed a unique symbol system that the students used to more easily identify the winning combinations.

But the authorities wanted Ryzl to not limit his multifaceted expertise to Lottery stakes; rather they asked him to use it in good old-fashioned spying on Western colleagues, combined with paranormal surveillance as later employed by Stargate. But the invitation he received was what in *Godfather* terminology is called 'an offer you can't refuse.' As Ryzl had too much integrity to accept any kind of sleazy spying assignment, he soon experienced being followed by agents and having his manuscripts stolen. This was not an expression of personal paranoia: during the early 1970s, the award-winning American psychologist Stanley Krippner went on a study trip to Eastern Europe, and he confirmed that there was—in keeping with the spirit of the times—extensive monitoring of parapsychologists. In his book *Human Possibilities: Mind Exploration in the USSR and Eastern Europe*, Krippner reports that films showing experiments with telekinesis had to be smuggled across the border with utmost care. And Edward Naumov, one of the most well-known Russian parapsychologists, was in fact sent to a labor camp because of his 'incorrect' association with Western researchers.

After some time Ryzl found the situation unbearable, and in 1967 he managed an escape worthy of an agent, including a border crossing at night and shifting between diverse escape cars. Many might view the following as a textbook example of a self-fulfilling prophecy, but Ryzl actually claims that a psychic friend had prophesied his dramatic escape—including both the escape route and specific details—no less than 15 years in advance!

Ryzl ended up in the US, where for many years he generously shared his parapsychological capabilities with universities. He also wrote some 20 books on the topic and published over 100 scientific articles. Many of his works are mainly theoretical, but Ryzl was also a practical man who wanted to touch people's lives—his book *How to Develop ESP in Yourself and Others* (1973) is an example of this.

Ryzl contended that parapsychology should not limit itself to providing explanations for so-called anomalies, phenomena that appear to be in contradiction to the laws of nature (*a* = not, *nomos* = law). He thought that parapsychology should have a much bolder and broader objective. Ryzl believed that modern humanity experiences an unfortunate and unnecessary divide between science and religion—'religion' understood not as dogma, but as contact with the deeper, spiritual dimensions. By conveying the psi phenomena and their mysterious world and by helping to integrate them into the story of our lives, parapsychology, according to Ryzl, could assist in bridging this unhealthy divide, and could thus positively affect Western culture at large. We could come to see ourselves as heroes and heroines on a quest, not just as purposeless puppets without any higher meaning in life than to consume, pay our taxes and then die.

To apply parapsychology as a therapy for Western culture is no small ambition, and might sound too optimistic. Regardless, Ryzl's *diagnosis* probably makes good sense. Diverse thinkers, for instance Mikhail Bhaktin, C.G. Jung, Gaston Bachelard and Michel Foucault, have maintained that the modern Western trend to *rationalize* is often characterized by abuse and oppression, exacting a high price. The parts of our character that do not fit the rational, the well-ordered, the productive, tend to be powerfully denigrated—even dismissed. The aforementioned thinkers, and also a number of others, have pointed out that our earlier history provided more space for the irrational, for the so-called crazy, the unproductive, and also for the realm of trances and ecstasy. And they all seem to be in agreement that humanity has lost something substantial through the modern fear of such 'anarchistic' experiences.

Might it be that with our rationality, our 'square' lives and tendency to stick to 'the way things have always been done,' we reduce access to the *Transcendent*, the *Realm of the Gods*, i.e. the spheres going beyond our daily trivialities: Love, Art, Music, Holiness, Ecstasy, Meetings, Mystery, Meaning—in short, all those experiences which lift us up, and confirm us to be more than just biological robots? Might the hesitant attitude toward psi and the paranormal in modern Western culture also be part of this unnecessary and unhealthy limitation?

In his book *Ancient Oracles*, Ryzl goes back to the Mediterranean cultures of antiquity and portrays the central role of oracles and mysticism; humankind then had a completely different sensitivity toward the sixth sense, to the 'Voice of the Gods.' Through his experiments with ESP and hypnosis, with his books and articles, Ryzl not only wants to map an unknown part of reality, he also wants to act as a bridge builder across the gap between religion and empirical science, and to teach us to interpret the symbolism of the spirit, to reopen the road to the transcendent—to the Kingdom of the Gods. In truth, this *is* an ambitious project! But, then, nothing ventured...

'The Limitlessness of Mind'—Giorgi Lozanov

The Bulgarian psychiatrist Giorgi Lozanov is best known in the West as the founder of *Suggestopedia*. This is a teaching method that many, including a UNESCO panel, have held to be conducive to fast language training (so-called 'super learning'), but of which others have been critical. The method uses games, drama, music and different art forms, including yoga techniques, to activate the slumbering resources within our consciousness. But Lozanov was not only a pedagogue, he was also one of the most respected parapsychologists in Eastern Europe, and furthermore an expert on hypnosis and altered states of consciousness. For many years Lozanov led a government-funded laboratory in Sofia, which became known as the Institute for Suggestology and Parapsychology. Here he had available the most advanced mind-mapping equipment of the day, and the institute employed no fewer than 30 highly qualified professionals— doctors, psychologists, engineers, physicists, etc. Lozanov believed that an interdisciplinary approach was necessary to properly understand the psi phenomena. There has been speculation as to whether Bulgarian Intelligence was also linked to the institute, and given the macro-political situation at the time it is more likely than not that this was the case.

In his laboratory, Lozanov researched diverse types of extraordinary and anomalous phenomena, as for instance savantism (extreme abilities in areas such as calculation and memory) and twin telepathy. Lozanov claimed to have discovered that if a wave pattern is artificially induced in the brain of one twin, the same pattern has a tendency to spontaneously manifest itself in the brain of the other twin—even if that person is in a different location! This is in line with the results of the telepathy experiment of Professor Adrian Parker, which is presented in chapter 6, and the experiments with distant mind-influencing described in chapter 8. In particular, Lozanov took a strong interest in precognition— he dedicated over 20 years' work to mapping every aspect of this quite mysterious phenomenon. Lozanov became so renowned for his ability in this field that the Russian Communist elite, spearheaded by no less than Secretary General Leonid Brezhnev, trooped into his laboratory and asked for (= demanded) predictions regarding their political careers!

Baba Vanga—Lozanov's Primary Medium

Lozanov used a large number of volunteers as experimental subjects as he was of the same opinion as Ryzl, that paranormal capacities—'our secret powers'—are part of our collective heritage as a species, and to some degree are shared by everybody. In addition, he examined 65 professional psychics. His primary subject was Vangelia Gushterova (1911–1996), usually referred to as Baba (grandmother) Vanga, a medium of great repute, who during her lifetime received tens of thousands of visitors from many countries. Around 1960, a government committee that tested her was so impressed that their report declared: 'We have to do more research on this phenomenon, we have no choice.' Lozanov was given the task, and Baba Vanga was given a state salary (possibly identified in the salary structure as 'tenured psychic').

Baba Vanga also practiced healing, based on a combination of medical clairvoyance and herbs. Over the years, she became established as a Bulgarian national icon, and even though she did not profess any religion, a kind of spiritualist church was built in her honor after she died.

As a young and unknown doctor, Lozanov had become curious about Baba Vanga and, together with a university friend, paid her a visit one day. When his friend came into her presence, Baba Vanga told him straight away—without any prior introduction whatsoever—his name, where he was born, and gave a description of the apartment in which he lived. She proceeded to name his mother and described an illness she had, and afterwards she told him when his father had died, including the cause of death. She then observed: 'You have been married for seven years, but you have no children.' But this, she said, would change in the coming year. And, according to Lozanov, so it came to be that within a year the couple had their first child!

Following this impressive introduction, Lozanov himself was next in line. Baba Vanga started by addressing him by his first name (this happened many years before he became famous), and then she said: 'You are a doctor, and heal people with the help of hypnosis. You have come here to test me,' something Lozanov confirmed. All of this sounds like the ingredients of a magazine story of the best/worst kind, but was in fact reported by one of the most renowned psychiatrists in Eastern Europe!

Lozanov estimates that there were several hundred people present (Baba Vanga's house functioned as a place of pilgrimage) and further relates that he and his friend had deliberately avoided all conversation while waiting in line to enter—to prevent the possibility of hidden assistants picking up information. This was long before the existence of the internet, and Baba Vanga was at the time completely blind. So—from a normal perspective, it seems incomprehensible how she managed to acquire such detailed and specific information about two completely unknown men. However, if we assume the existence of a *Mental Internet* from which information can be downloaded, then...

And Baba Vanga has, in fact, explained that when she spoke with a person, she often could see a stream of pictures in her inner vision, containing all sorts of information about this particular person, almost as if she were viewing a movie. But she often had no control as to *what*—past, future or specific topics—this movie would show her.

Vanga would sometimes receive exact times for specific events. Lozanov has mentioned an incident involving an unsavory person—a guy who behaved rudely and visited her just for the hell of it. She told him: 'You will be the victim of a serious accident on November 11 this year. You will be seriously injured but will survive.' And, according to Lozanov, this is exactly what happened: On that very day of November 11 the man became involved in a traffic accident! Of course, one may wonder if perhaps he, by some sort of autosuggestion, unconsciously steered himself right into this crash, and thereby created a classic self-fulfilling prophecy.

But Baba Vanga also gave many predictions regarding circumstances over which the subjects involved had little or no control. Just before World War II, she moved to Petrich, the village in which she would live for the rest of her life. A few years after, Boris Gurov, one of the neighbors, asked her about the fate of his brother Nikola, who had mysteriously disappeared 20 years previously. No one had heard from him since. Vanga told Boris that Nikola was still alive, and that she could 'see' him clearly. He now lived in the Soviet Union, where he was a scientist, but at the moment he was a German prisoner of war. She went on to say that he would come back to Petrich that same spring, and that he would then be wearing a grey uniform and carrying two suitcases. Here it sounds as if she is describing something seen in a movie, just as she had explained. And sure enough, two months later, following an absence of no less than 20 years without any contact or sign of life, Nikola, the lost brother, came back to the village in that very manner!

Lozanov related that through the years he probably had several hundred conversations with Baba Vanga. And since their connection lasted for two decades, he had the opportunity to check many of her predictions (which, in contrast to what is sometimes claimed, focused on personal matters rather than world events). Lozanov says that even if some of the stories regarding her gifts are exaggerated—she had some bad days on the job in which her abilities barely functioned—he is of the opinion that she was correct in nearly 80 percent of her predictions! And again, the source of this startling number is the respected psychiatrist, Lozanov.

Meeting with a Master

In 2008 Lozanov visited Norway in connection with his teaching activities, and I had the privilege of meeting him for lunch at the Bristol Hotel in Oslo. I had long felt an urge to discuss these topics with a person who had really dug deeply into the matter. Among other things, I wanted to discuss the following: Is it really possible to predict future events accurately, sometimes many years in advance? And if such paranormal predictions do take place, how can one explain them? And of course I also wanted to ask him about Baba Vanga. Lozanov responded pleasantly and openly, but he seemed tired (he was then over 80 years old). And he also seemed to be a marked man (he explained the reason for this during our conversation, see below).

Lozanov was a respected scientist within the Eastern bloc countries and for a long time all was well and good: he enjoyed government support, free rein, etc. He even had his own weekly TV show. However, when he started receiving international attention and recognition during the early 1980s, things gradually became problematic. Lozanov told me that he had been held under house arrest by the authorities for nearly 10 years! He was only allowed to move between his home and the clinic in which he worked. This was combined with a ban on all contact with Westerners, even by phone. And the authorities went on to confiscate nearly all his research material—a devastating blow for a serious scientist. As a consequence Lozanov has published very little of his parapsychological research. As he exclaimed: 'I cannot publish without documentation—I am a scientist!'

During lunch Lozanov confirmed the main outline of the stories of the exceptional abilities of Baba Vanga, including her accurate predictions. As we have heard, these predictions could impart both exact dates and precise circumstances (cause, location, etc.) surrounding specific events in the lives of individuals—a pregnancy, an accident, a homecoming from a war, etc. When I asked him how this could be possible, he simply answered: 'The limitlessness of Mind!' He enthusiastically elaborated on this, and stated that this assumption was the foundation for his research both within the paranormal and pedagogy. And further he believed that learning and developing both normal and paranormal abilities primarily had to do with the steady opening up to more of this limitlessness.

Hence, I got the clear impression that Lozanov did not reduce Consciousness to just an *epiphenomenon*, a secondary phenomenon, a mirror expression of the chemical activities within the brain. Rather, he seemed to regard the brain as an extremely well equipped office in which Consciousness works. I am therefore convinced that Lozanov's idea of consciousness is fairly close to the one presented in this book: that Consciousness is not limited to the brain, but that it also has non-local and non-temporal dimensions, as we shall explore elsewhere, especially in chapters 6 and 8. Based on this perspective, which is shared by many other parapsychologists, we can all be considered dormant savants, magicians—not stage magicians but the Merlin type—and Baba Vangas.

A Chapter Closes— or Maybe Not?

Following these deliberations regarding the lives and thoughts of Milan Ryzl and Giorgi Lozanov, the chapter on military mysticism is drawing to an end in this book, as it has already done in real life, where both Stargate and the corresponding activities in the Eastern bloc countries can be considered closed chapters. Can we ever be completely certain about this, though? From time to time there are rumors that Stargate is still secretly in operation! Some contend that the rapid phase-out in 1995 was a 'managed bankruptcy,' a pro forma arrangement, in which the CIA sought to salvage some of its secrets from the public domain. There are indications that the CIA stopped activities within Stargate and transferred employees to other projects three months *before* the report recommending closure was presented. If this is correct, it may not be farfetched to think that the CIA had prepared an official closure of Stargate—for who knows what reasons—far in advance. In which case the report was just a prop, a 'good reason' for closure made after the fact.

Well, regardless of what opinion one could have on this, I would imagine that the story of Stargate has shown, possibly to the surprise of many readers, that paranormal phenomena have played a relatively large political role, not only in the days of the ancient Greek oracles and Roman augurs, but also in our modern 'rational' times. And if one has an inclination for conspiracy theories, one can, of course, spend quite some time pondering what might be the content of the roughly 20,000–30,000 pages of Stargate documents that have *not* been released.

Chapter 3

ANTHROPOLOGICAL ASTONISHMENTS AND PECULIAR PERSPECTIVES

Man also possesses a power by which he may see his friends and the circumstances by which they are surrounded, although such persons may be a thousand miles away from him at that time.

~ Paracelsus

On Safari in Outer and Inner Landscapes—Considerations Upon Embarking

On the following safari we will learn about specific incidents that have occurred when people from our Western culture, out on diverse research missions, have met with Indigenous people. Apart from the entertainment value such tales of the strange and the bizarre may provide, the point is to show that from Greenland to Australia, from antiquity to modern times—in spite of all the cultural differences and the worlds and times apart—there appear some surprisingly similar reports about individuals who have the ability to see/perceive sites utterly far beyond the reach of physical sight. In fact, it was just this capability that Stargate sought to cultivate! Here is surely a treasure trove full of stories; even a little too full according to the flawed judgment of a friend of mine—a former friend, that is (just kidding!)—who I think got overwhelmed by some kind of paranormal 'culture shock.' Yes, it's an encompassing journey, like the spiral dance of Life itself, full of twists and turns, but there is order in chaos for all these cases are closely linked together by their common theme. They thus constitute a lustrous necklace of paranormal Biwa pearls thread on a string of clairvoyance!

We will generously disregard the 'order of discourse'—the often arbitrary and unnatural distinctions made between social anthropology, cultural anthropology, ethnography, ethnology, etc. Different countries have their own academic subdivisions, so if our envoys may reasonably be described as 'anthropologists' in the broad sense of the word, they are very welcome in this chapter. Our foremost intent is not to engage in snazzy theories and the splitting of hairs, but rather to embark on a good old-fashioned treasure hunt in the anthropological archives! Those with an interest in more theoretical elaborations could, for example, check out *Being Changed by Cross-Cultural Encounters: The Anthropology of Extraordinary Experience*, Young and Goulet (eds.), and *The Ashgate Research Companion to Paranormal Cultures*, Jenzen and Munt (eds.).

For practical reasons I shall by and large use the 'etic' perspective, an outsider perspective, which means I will apply Western categories about what is normal and paranormal, natural and supernatural, physical and spiritual, etc. These ideas may of course differ quite a bit from the 'emic' perspective, i.e. the notions held by the Indigenous people and their shamans. And talking of which, a *shaman* (the word originally comes from Siberia) is, as many readers will already know, a trance medium—a person who through his/ her expertise in altered states of consciousness is able to liaise between the physical and the spiritual world, and thereby may bring about healing, and perform psychic counseling and other spiritual tasks. Shamanism is often regarded as the earliest form of religious practice, going back to at least 30,000 BCE.

Anecdotes and the 'Emperor's Wrath'

Trigger warning! Most of the ensuing stories don't fit well with the prevalent 'map of reality'; they may thus prompt slight confusion, 'cognitive dissonance' and eventually activate defense mechanisms. Perhaps it may seem naive to present them in such a candid way as I do. But since most of the stories originate from esteemed scholars—not from raconteurs and spinners of yarns—they deserve better than to be dismissed as 'anecdotes.' The word 'anecdote' will in scholarly circles often be uttered with a slightly derogatory tinge, and used more or less as synonymous with 'unreliable' i.e. non-verifiable evidence. Originally, though, it was a neutral term, simply meaning 'unpublished' (Greek: *an-ek-dotos* = un-out-given). And, as we know, there may be many reasons for a book not to get published—some good, some more questionable.

A classic example of the latter is *The Secret History* by the Roman historian Procopius (c. 500–c. 554 CE), which was not published for fear of the wrath of the Emperor Justinian, and which during the Middle Ages was referred to as 'Anecdota.' Procopius' fears were most likely well founded, as the Emperor is portrayed as corrupt and tyrannical, while his consort, Empress Theodora, is exposed as celebrating her carnal desires *in extremis*, wallowing in a variety of sexual pleasures and to such an extent so as to make Casanova a model student in Sunday school. The work thus remained anecdotal—unpublished, that is to say—until 1623, partly because of these descriptions (the readers are in particular cautioned against his chapter 9…).

The stories that we shall deal with are less rabid than those of Procopius, and since they actually are published, they are no longer anecdotes in the literal sense. And what is really wondrous is that when anecdotes become published they often are indistinguishable, or almost so, from anthropological data collected by interview… Fear of the 'emperor's wrath'—thumbs down from colleagues, loss of promotion and financial funding, ridicule and ostracism—made, in fact, many researchers hesitate to publish their paranormal stories. And according to people familiar with the field, there are still those who hesitate, muzzling themselves lest the 'emperor's wrath' be incurred…

Enigmatic Episodes—Different Districts, Common Kernel

Charles Darwin

Charles Darwin (1809–1882), biologist, naturalist, geologist and father of our modern ideas about evolution, was also an anthropologist. 'Lhis is evident both from the book *The Descent of Man, and Selection in Relation to Sex* (1871) and from the rich and engaged cultural considerations about Indigenous people and colonists found in his travel diaries. Darwin recounts an episode that is of extra interest to us.

Jemmy Button (named so because he had once been traded for a mother-of-pearl button!) was a member of the Yamana people from Tierra del Fuego at the tip of South America. After a year's stay in England, Jemmy was on board the HMS *Beagle*, sailing back to his homeland. One night, while asleep in his hammock, he had a dream in which he was approached by a man who whispered to him that his father had died. The next day Jemmy related this rather somber dream to a couple of friends, Bennett and Bynoe. One of them just laughed the whole thing off. Jemmy, however, took the dream's 'announcement' deadly (so to speak) serious—and it would indeed prove to be correct. Captain FitzRoy writes in his journal: 'He [Jemmy] fully believed that such was the case, and maintained his opinion up to the time of finding that his father had died,' word of which reached them on their arrival in Tierra del Fuego. Captain FitzRoy comments further: 'Poor Jemmy looked very grave and mysterious at the news, but showed no other symptom of sorrow. He reminded Bennett of the dream [...].' Darwin writes in his diary: 'Jemmy heard that his father was dead; but as he had had a "dream in his head" to that effect, he seemed to expect it & not much care about it.'

They did not learn much about the particulars concerning the sad incident, as discussing such matters was considered taboo among Jemmy's people. So although the dream's message indeed proved to be correct, we shall never know if it was delivered at the exact same time as the death of his father. Darwin apparently took the co-occurrence of the dream/death to be purely coincidental, but Jemmy was, as we have heard, of a completely different opinion. And *if* Jemmy was right, the incident could be described in 'etic' terminology—meaning outsider terminology—as *dream-telepathy*, a subject we shall explore in some depth in chapter 8. (Jemmy himself would, of course, have expressed it differently.)

Peter Freuchen

Danish explorer, anthropologist and author Peter Freuchen (1886–1957) had an unusually close relationship with both nature and Inuit (Eskimo) culture, and was also as tough as they come: he once killed a wolf with his bare hands! In Greenland Freuchen collaborated with Knud Rasmussen (1879–1933), whose maternal grandmother was Inuit, and whose scientific expeditions facilitated Greenland's incorporation into the Danish 'commonwealth' in 1933. In his memoirs Freuchen relates that when Rasmussen traveled eastward on his second major survey in 1916–18, he himself remained in the camp on the West coast. One evening during a celebration, Inaluk, an elderly woman, suddenly got up and left the room. A few minutes later they heard singing outside, and when they went out to see what was going on they saw Inaluk standing in the moonlight, swaying in a state of trance. She was heard singing: 'Those who went to the East side have returned. Those who went to the East side have returned.' When Inaluk came out of the trance, Freuchen asked her if all was well with Rasmussen's expedition. Inaluk answered that two people were dead, but that Rasmussen himself was among the survivors.

Freuchen kept an unintended vigil because of this upsetting scene. Then suddenly, in the middle of the night, a ravaged Rasmussen appeared in the doorway! After greetings and salutations Freuchen asked if everyone had survived, whereupon Rasmussen responded that two were dead: their good friend, Hendrik Olsen, was lost and had probably been eaten by wolves, and their ailing botanist, Thorild Wulff, had, at his own request, been left to a certain fate in the icy wilderness. Drama at the highest level! For us the challenge is, thank goodness, far more trivial, namely to understand how on earth (or on ice) Inaluk could have gained this information? Rasmussen's expedition had been away for more than a year, and no one knew if, let alone *when*, they would eventually return. And of course, all specific information about their condition was completely unknown. If Freuchen's representation is correct, then maybe psi could be the answer? That Inaluk intuitively sensed that something was going on, and then, going into the trance, she opened up to a 'download' with specific information from the psychic cloud, the Mental Internet?

Sven Hedin

The Swedish explorer Sven Hedin (1865–1952) was an internationally known and admired scientist, and was even knighted for his scientific achievements. This was especially due to his contributions in geography and cartography, but also in archaeology and anthropology. Hedin led several expeditions to the interior of Asia, and early in the 20th century he charted large parts of Tibet. He recounts an occasion where he had rented the services of a caravan guide from an isolated nomadic tribe to help him through a *terra incognita*, a completely unknown territory. Unfortunately, the guide perished shortly after, and the expedition had to turn around. On their way back to the nomads they met the brother of the deceased, and before they had time to inform him he said he knew of the sad news. He also provided a detailed account of the death and the place where it had occurred. But how come, Hedin wanted to know, did he have all this knowledge? The man answered he had seen it all with his mind's eye! So—if the nomad was not mad and Hedin's account is to be trusted, this seems to be a classic case of clairvoyance, that is, in 'etic' terms; the man himself had of course used his own, 'emic,' words. Anyway, I guess Stargate would have hired this guy on the spot!

Henri Trilles

The French missionary and anthropologist Henri Trilles (1866–1949), author of among other books *Les Pygmées de la forêt équatoriale* (*Pygmies in the Equatorial Rainforest*), was doing much of his work in Gabon, then a French colony. He relates that an Indigenous man was able to present him with a precise description of his home in Paris. This occurred many decades before the mobile phone entered the world stage. But perhaps this wise person had the opportunity to tap information from a person close to Trilles, say a friend, a co-worker or an assistant? Not impossible... But, the man also announced that Trilles' father had recently died (which was unknown to Trilles himself at the time) and described the illness from which he had suffered. A few weeks later Trilles was able to confirm this information through more normal channels. So—was it just pure coincidence, a lucky/unlucky guess? Or could it perhaps have been a striking example of clairvoyance? One begins to wonder...

Adolphus Peter Elkin

A.P. Elkin (1891–1979) was a renowned—and controversial—expert on Australian Aboriginal culture, and for a period was president of the Australian Anthropological Association. In his book *Aboriginal Men of High Degree: Initiation and Sorcery in the World's Oldest Tradition*, Elkin describes the so-called *karadji*, a type of traditional Australian shaman. Among the skills ascribed to the karadji is healing (and murder!) by the means of psychic powers. Furthermore they are said to be able to move at paranormal speed and to master what in etic (outsider) terminology would be called clairvoyance and telepathy. Another interesting feat of theirs is the ability to create 'magical illusions' in the minds of other people through telepathy.

The ability to project images in mysterious ways is also known in a number of places, e.g. Siberia and Norway, where it is sometimes called 'synkverving,' meaning 'sight-twisting.' The well-known psychic Marcello Haugen (1878–1967) from Lillehammer is known to have been a dab hand (or mind) at this. For example, when young he warded off an attack by a bunch of bigger boys by projecting the image of his father standing right by him. The mob reportedly split and ran off as though having seen a ghost! (Perhaps not so far from the truth...) And when working as a stoker he, just for fun (albeit insensitively), projected into the mind of the train driver the image of a man standing in the middle of the railway track, reportedly causing the driver to panic and hit the brakes. Whether Marcello was just a natural virtuoso in NLP (Neuro-Linguistic Programming), somewhat like the great entertainer and stage magician Derren Brown (check out Brown's videos on YouTube), or if the projected images really were created by telepathy is not for me to decide.

But let's now return to Australia and Professor Elkin: On his 'walkabouts,' visiting villages in the wilderness, he realized that people knew beforehand of both his (unannounced) coming and also the purpose of his visit. Moreover, Elkin learned that people in some enigmatic way seemed to be updated about noteworthy events—deaths, births, successful hunting, etc.—pertaining to family members living far away. Elkin is not dogmatic but he suggests that all this could be due to telepathic communication. He has also suggested that maybe the Aboriginals' tranquil lifestyle was what enabled them to pick up 'vibes'—subtle ESP signals—that more fast-paced city dwellers and suburbanites typically wouldn't perceive.

Stories from *Sami Ednan*— the Land of the Sami

The Nordic Indigenous people, the *Sami* (formerly referred to as Lapps or Laplanders), living in the northern parts of Finland, Sweden and Norway, have long been regarded as being really savvy in such matters. In 1555, Olaus Magnus, the Swedish bishop, ethnographer and cartographer, described in his *Historia de Gentibus Septentrionalibus* (*History of the Nordic Peoples*) how the Sami have special abilities that enabled them to gather information about kith and kin residing far away.

The mystical/spiritual aspects of traditional Sami life and culture were eventually suppressed and this silencing was justified by both Christianity ('paganism!') and rationality ('superstition!'). This didn't mean, though, that the spiritual traditions were forgotten, but they went underground and were practiced in secret. However, the times they are a-changin', and especially during the past 20 years the old traditions have seen new recognition. Ole Gunnar Ballo, former MP and head of the Institute of Forensic Medicine, has for many years practiced as a physician in northern Norway. And in 2009 he publicly stated that the old Sami tradition of *blodstemming*—stopping of bleeding by psychic means—actually works! (Without trying to *explain* the phenomenon as due to say placebo, telepathy, healing, and so on.) And Helga Pedersen, deputy head of the Labor Party, has stated that among her people (Pedersen has Sami background) it is customary to consult individuals with this kind of expertise. Today, the ancient spiritual traditions are sometimes combined with New Age philosophy, and syntheses of this sort—often referred to as 'neo-shamanism'—are thriving.

Let's now consider an interesting little cultural historical piece by the Norwegian priest and historian Peder Claussøn Friis (1545–1614). In *The Finns'* [i.e. Sami] *Beliefs and Religion*, released posthumously in 1632, he says that the Sami at will can 'fly off and find out what's going on elsewhere.' The Sami then lies down and 'gives his spirit away, and is as if he was dead, and is black and blue in the face, and such he lies in an hour or an hour and a half, because the place that he is off to visit, is far away, and when he wakes up again, he can say what is happening and what certain people do and have at hand in the place which he was asked to visit.' Within Sami tradition it is assumed that a person has a 'body soul' and a 'free soul,' and it is this 'free soul' that one can send off to wherever one wants. Within Western esoteric tradition a similar phenomenon is very well known, and is called 'astral projection' (where consciousness is separated from the body).

Friis continues with a delightful description of a real-life demonstration that took place in Bergen in the house of Johan Delling, a *Hanseat*, meaning a merchant of German ancestry. A Sami visitor was asked to use his special abilities to 'fly' off to Germany there to suss out Delling's family members and what they were up to. The Sami went into a trance in a quite dramatic way. At the start he 'was sitting, raging, just as if he were drunk, and then he suddenly jumped up, ran around a few times, and fell down, and was lying in front of them, just as if he had been dead, and when he at last woke up again, he told them what the members of his family [i.e. Delling's family in Germany] were up to and doing, and it was immediately recorded in the guestbook, and was later found to be true, what he had said thereof.'

Certainly not a bad performance by the Sami!—regardless of how it could be explained. Friis goes on to relate other stories that obviously must be based on plain superstition and/or misunderstandings. But the feat performed in the home of Johan Delling, which, as said earlier, would be called 'astral projection' in Western occultism, is reported from spiritual traditions over virtually the entire world. The phenomenon implies that consciousness may in some way be separated from the body, and—as is occasionally experienced by 'astral travelers'—is able to whiz off and see and collect information from other places.

In more modern language the similar phenomenon is often referred to as an 'out-of-body experience'; it is found to occur spontaneously under various conditions—occasionally when a person goes into cardiac arrest or is under anesthesia. After regaining consciousness some patients will describe how they—as if witnessing the scene from above—could see themselves lying on the operating table observing the surgical procedures, the medical team, their comings and goings, the movements of instruments, etc. Under the auspices of the British intensive care specialist, Dr Sam Parnia, there has, for some years, been a medical project called AWARE—with a number of hospitals in the UK, US and Austria participating—that aims at charting the transition between life and death. And one of the many things they wanted to find out was whether the 'out-of-body' phenomenon is just something that the brain is 'making up,' or if a displacement of consciousness really occurs. So far it seems that in most cases 'out-of-the-body' is not synonymous with 'out-of-the-ordinary'—the experience of seeing oneself from outside (which most of us will have experienced during dreaming) does not necessarily indicate that the 'soul' has left the body. But there are, so it seems, a few exceptions. We'll comment a little more on this exciting project in chapter 6.

But now let's return to the Sami to make a proper farewell! This we'll do with a captivating tale found in the writings of Ernst Arbmann, Professor in Religious Studies at the University of Stockholm. Since the original version is rather long I will use an abridged version given by his successor in office, Professor Louise Bäckman, who herself has Sami background.

A Lapp, Lördal by name, offered to prove his 'magic art' to the Archbishop of Uppsala who was visiting his home in Lapland. Lördal burnt some herbaceous plants, inhaled the smoke and seemed to 'pass away.' After an hour he woke up and told the Archbishop that his wife was working in the kitchen, and he gave a detailed and exact description of the room. As evidence of his 'visit' to

Uppsala, he said that he had hidden the wife's wedding ring in the coal box. The Archbishop's wife confirmed his 'visit' in a letter later on and the ring was found in the coal box, as the man had said.

So—was this just a cleverly staged bluff? Maybe Lördal knew someone in the bishop's household—someone who had told him details about the kitchen, and in addition had agreed to stealing and hiding the ring? And then he could orchestrate his theatricals—the burning of herbs, inhaling, fainting, all just to prank the bishop. Or could the reported effects, inexplicable as they seem to be, really result from 'magical arts'—abilities that in 'etic' terms from parapsychology would be called clairvoyance and telekinesis? Or could there even be a third option: that Lördal had 'seen' the ring in the coal box via clairvoyance (a quite frequently reported ability, as we know from Stargate). And then he used the opportunity to boast of having placed it there himself by telekinesis (a rarely reported ability)? It will of course be up to the reader to eventually form his/her own opinion about this.

Three Anthropological P(s)ioneers

Clarence W. Weiant

Some anthropological researchers have tried to convince the scientific community to include psi in its horizon of understanding. One of these 'p(s)ioneers' was the anthropologist and archaeologist Clarence W. Weiant (1897–1986), whom we got to know in chapter 1, in connection with his exciting discoveries in Mexico. In his previously mentioned lecture about anthropology and parapsychology delivered to the American Anthropological Association, Weiant recalls a momentous experience he had with a medium in Puerto Rico:

> *With two friends I sat one night on the porch of a woman medium and listened with astonishment, as this lady described in detail my home at Peekskill, NY, including references to the location of trees and shrubbery, the colors of blossoms, the arrangement of furniture and pictures, an enumeration of the members of my family and their approximate ages, and even the correct diagnosis of an ailment from which my mother-in-law was then suffering. She referred also to intimate details of my personal life. The circumstances were such that only clairvoyance could account for her knowledge.*

And as we have already heard in chapter 1, Weiant felt these strange abilities were not only astonishing and amusing, but that they could also have far-reaching consequences for *science*: 'If it should turn out that the believers [in psi] are right, there will certainly be exciting implications for anthropology.'

Margaret Mead

Present at Weiant's lecture was Margaret Mead (1901–1978), the acclaimed and very versatile anthropologist, known for her cross-cultural studies of gender roles. This, in turn, contributed to her becoming one of the important figures in the sexual revolution in the 1960s and 1970s. Mead was considered an authority, and Weiant was acutely nervous to have her in the room! But there was no need for nerves. After Weiant had finished, Mead made a remark to the attendees supporting the general outline of Weiant's vision. She related that she herself had done some parapsychological research together with the renowned psychologist Gardner Murphy (who we will return to in chapter 8). She also put forward the view that anthropologists would likely benefit from mingling with psychics to get an increased understanding of their brand of mental powers.

Elsewhere Mead has stated that she thinks both to 'believe in' and 'not believe in' psi to be derailments, because in both cases one disposes of an investigating and scientific attitude. Belief and disbelief belong in church! Mead became a driving force for scientific studies on the paranormal. She was a board member of the American Society for Psychical Research (ASPR), and in 1969 she helped the Parapsychological Association become a member of the American Association for the Advancement of Science.

John Reed Swanton

Another prominent anthropologist who a few years earlier had tried to open academia's eyes to psi was John Reed Swanton (1873–1958). Swanton was a preeminent expert regarding the culture of North America's Indigenous peoples. For a period he was president of the American Anthropological Association, and he had also been editor-in-chief of *The American Anthropologist*, the association's foremost journal. Swanton was influenced by the philosophy of the mystic Emmanuel Swedenborg (see chapter 6), and this had contributed to his keen interest in and deep respect for native spirituality, that is rooted in, but not confined to, shamanism. His high regard for the spirituality of 'the other' was also cultivated by studying under the great Franz Boas, who taught the intrinsic value of cultural variation, and that cultures should always be met on their own terms ('cultural relativism') and not measured by alien (Western) standards of progression. Among the groups Swanton studied were Haida, Chinook, Dakota, Sioux, Tlingit, Creek, Chickasaw, and Choctaw. In addition he collected information about other, lesser-known groups such as the Biloxi and the Ofo.

After his long, distinguished and honorable career as an orthodox anthropologist, Swanton, to the astonishment of many of his colleagues, suddenly declared his belief in psi! This took place in 1948 in the form of a 'confessional' of 96 pages, called *Superstition—but whose?* His step had usually been light and his touch soft, but now Swanton revealed his polemical side, and he fiercely confronted the scientific community's lack of willingness to take the paranormal into account. He distributed his pamphlet to a number of his colleagues, and in 1953 he also published an article called *A*

Letter to Anthropologists, where he gives a short version of his stance, designed for a wider audience.

With respect to paranormal phenomena Swanton says: 'The evidence is, in fact, abundant. It is merely being smothered by a widely spread will to disbelieve [...].' He urged that science should not function as just another set of dogmas that the 'believers' must accept so as not to be 'condemned,' as he phrases it. Hence Swanton thought all truly scientifically minded anthropologists ought to familiarize themselves with parapsychology.

> *A significant revolution which concerns us all is taking place quietly but surely in a related branch of science [i.e. parapsychology]. It is not being met in an honest, truly scientific manner. Adhesion to current orthodoxy is always more profitable than dissent but the future belongs to dissenters. Prejudice and cowardice in the presence of status quo are the twin enemies of progress at all times and especially of the 'dispassionate method' in which science consists.*

Thus spoke John Reed Swanton! The loud and clear voice of this towering figure in American anthropology could not be misunderstood. But not much response came from his colleagues. Out of respect for his brilliant career his initiative was not opposed, but because of convention and tribal ritualism ('how things are done among us') it was not approved. Rather—to paraphrase St Matthew—his colleagues 'made light of it, and went their ways, one to his farm, another to his merchandise.' Though in private Swanton received some declarations of earnest interest. And so it came to pass that Swanton's initiative was mostly bypassed in silence. The anthropological community didn't react so very differently from the three wise monkeys: 'Hear no paranormal, see no paranormal, speak no paranormal!'

Zombie Time!—Joseph K. and the Coffin

But lo! soon there was to appear an anthropologist whose paranormal ideas would gain at least *some* traction within anthropology, namely Joseph K. Long (1937–1999). As some readers may recall, the famous, unnerving novel *The Trial* by Franz Kafka opens with the following sentence: 'Someone must have been telling lies about Josef K., for one fine morning he was arrested, though he had done nothing wrong.' If we should dare to rephrase Kafka with respect to *our* man it might read: 'Some scholarly tradition must have been telling lies about the paranormal, for one beautiful day Joseph K. was captured by surprise, though he had done nothing wrong.' What took hold of Long's thought process was the following: In 1970 Long was in Jamaica, comparing conventional physicians with local healers to obtain material for his doctoral thesis in medical anthropology. In the town of Mandeville the market square was buzzing with life (Long himself was situated some distance away) when 'The Coffin' suddenly came rolling into the arena. We'll let Joseph K. tell the story:

It was the height of market day and both shops and street vendors had a lively trade going when the thing appeared. It was a three-wheeled open coffin apparently steering itself into the midst of the crowd. There were three live vultures perched at one end and a dead arm hung limply over the side. As if that weren't enough, a hollow voice issued from the coffin's interior repeatedly inquiring the location of one Jim Brown. Hundreds of people saw it—and heard the voice.

Long arrived at the scene shortly thereafter and immediately interviewed a number of those present:

> *It was incredible. There were literally hundreds of people in that square and they all saw it, and heard the same words. More than that—and infinitely more important—they had all instantly reacted with behavior that showed they saw it. Within minutes the shops were empty, even of storekeepers. Everyone ran out to see the coffin and then just milled around, the way people do when they have seen something that has had a powerful effect on them.*

Aside from minor differences in the spectators' viewpoints, everyone told Long the same story. They also interrupted the story at the same point: 'Apparently, it just drove itself down the street and around the corner. Nobody followed. You can understand why.' At first Long thought that since people had had some time to chat before he interviewed them, it could maybe be one of those cases 'in which one or two people have the hallucination and then the emotion of the moment somehow carries the others along.' But he changed his mind when he learned that everyone had reacted spontaneously and left the stores *before* having talked together. It became clear to Long that 'they truly believed it had actually happened—self-steering coffin, vultures, hollow voice and all.'

But how was it possible that a non-existing 'something' could so strongly affect hundreds of people? Long had to admit, 'I didn't have a clue as to how to handle the matter. There was nothing in my anthropological training to prepare me for that coffin, and, had I seen it myself, I should doubtlessly have had myself committed.' He therefore didn't speak to his colleagues about what had happened that day: 'What was there to say?' But he never forgot it, and the event inevitably drew his gaze toward new horizons: 'To this day, I can't explain it except to say there must have been some kind of unique mass telepathic hallucination. That's pretty weak, I realize, but how else to explain that several hundred people are in agreement about an event that cannot occur?'

We cannot rule out that Long's idea of a 'collective telepathic hallucination' may be correct; seemingly such phenomena have manifested themselves in different places in the world. The most spectacular case on European soil would be perhaps the so-called 'Miracle of the Sun' that occurred on October 13, 1917 outside the Portuguese village of Fatima. Here, between 30,000 and 100,000 people (estimates vary) purportedly experienced the sun change colors in a most dramatic fashion while zigzagging across the sky. Many of those present described it as the sun 'dancing.' There are stacks of testimonies on record; a university professor in the natural sciences who witnessed the spectacle recounts the following:

> *This was not the sparkling of a heavenly body, for it spun round on itself in a mad whirl, when suddenly a clamor was heard from all the people. The sun, whirling, seemed to loosen itself from the firmament and advance threateningly upon the earth as if to crush us with its huge fiery weight. The sensation during those moments was terrible.*

Such celestial drama does not seem to be readily explicable by visual problems or the like. Initially, before the visions of the sun began, there had been sightings of the Virgin Mary, 'a woman more luminous than the sun.' This element of religious symbolism seems to indicate that what we have here is something other than just a normal meteorological phenomenon. So unless we apply a religious explanation, taking the incident to be a divine miracle, perhaps it could be seen as a most dazzling—in every sense of the word—example of just such a 'collective telepathic hallucination' as Long talked about.

Concerning the likelihood of collective hallucinations, Long had a paranormal peer in C.G. Jung, the psychoanalyst, who thought that these might occur when there is great turbulence in 'the collective unconscious.' This, Jung believes, will typically happen during traumatic events touching large numbers of people, e.g. natural disasters and war. So—perhaps it was no coincidence, then, that the Miracle of the Sun occurred in 1917, at the apex of World War I?

Well, anyway, after a long-lasting mulling over of 'The Coffin,' Joseph K. Long reached a conclusion congruent with that of Weiant, Mead and Swanton, namely that anthropologists ought to upgrade their understanding of parapsychology and altered states of consciousness. Long feared that without such understanding there may easily be 'cognitive dissonance' when anthropologists experience something out of the normal—something *para-normal*. The discomfort of having one's mental world slightly tilted out of orbit may lead to denial and the underreporting of 'disturbing' incidents. Long was himself no stranger to this problem:

> *Going over my field notes convinced me that I had witnessed a number of examples of psi phenomena, but instead of recognizing them for what they really were, I rejected that explanation because it did not fit into the model of scientific anthropology I had been taught.*

In his book *Extrasensory Ecology: Parapsychology and Anthropology* (1977) Long discusses the problem of 'cognitive dissonance' and other issues pertaining to this scientific no-man's land. The book also lists examples of experiences of psi reported by anthropologists. Long estimates that as of

1977 there were about a hundred reliable reports on record! Along with Stephan Schwartz and John Norman Emerson, both of whom we became acquainted with in chapter 1, Joseph K. became involved in a lengthy and complex process (hmm, that sounded strangely familiar…) which in the end crystallized into the Society for the Anthropology of Consciousness (SAC). Long and Schwartz were the initiators and Emerson joined in to lend SAC professional gravitas. In 1989 Schwartz, then president, successfully set up SAC to become a division within the American Anthropological Association.

Anthropology, Trance, Psi, Reason, and Stuff— Historical Perspectives

Around the middle of the 18th century the French philosopher Jean-Jacques Rousseau launched his soon-to-become influential notions of 'the noble savage,' which led to an extensive romanticizing of Indigenous people. These native peoples were said to possess all the virtues that we in the West lack: compassionate ethics, spontaneity, wisdom, a shame-free sex life, etc. And if upon closer inspection they did *not* prove to have all these virtues, it was more than once claimed that this was because their original culture had somehow been corrupted by Westerners. In reality, things are—as they usually are—far more complex and nuanced. For example, human sacrifice flourished among the Maya, Inca and Aztecs long before any violent Spaniard had set his conquering foot in South America. But *without* romanticizing it can be said that Indigenous cultures are generally far more open to altered states of consciousness and psi than our own society. Many groups have highly developed practices for shifting the gears of consciousness: drumming, meditation, ritual suggestion, dancing, singing, storytelling, psychedelics, etc. There will often be a Master of Ceremonies—a shaman, a noaidi, an angakok, a karadji— who is an expert in such techniques, and in the capacity of being a 'traveler between worlds' is familiar with the different mental landscapes, their dangers and opportunities, and therefore will be able to act as a guide. While our own priests and psychologists, people who according to their profession perhaps ought to be familiar with the depths of the soul, are seldom highly qualified in such matters.

The Western shutting down of these spheres is probably not, as some seem to think, due to our philosophical/rational heritage from the ancient Greeks. Large parts of the population, including the philosophers—Pythagoras, Socrates, Plato and others—were not die-hard rationalists, but eagerly took part in the mystery religions. The Eleusinian mysteries in particular were popular, and some ethnobotanists believe that the *kykeon*, the holy brew drunk by the initiates, contained consciousness-expanding substances that—when imbibed during vigils in subterranean chambers and labyrinths—would easily arouse visions. And when celebrating the Dionysian mysteries, the point was certainly not to become 'rational'—quite the opposite: the rituals were aimed at inducing altered states of consciousness, and by going into a trance instead of coming to one's senses, one would sometimes open up to the sixth sense. An ancient text says that the initiates *threw their head back with glassy eyes, dancing to the beat of the drum, causing the blood to rush. In this ecstatic and enthusiastic state they indulged themselves, danced wildly and shouted Euoi! And at this moment of intense rapture they were united with God. They were filled with His Spirit and obtained divine powers.*

We're obviously here talking about *psychic* powers rather than physical.

The ancient Greeks were in general quite open to what in 'etic' language would be called psi. The Delphic oracle is very well known. (And speaking of which, the Pythia, the High Priestess of the Temple of Apollo at Delphi, did not just present her visitors with banal 'oracle answers,' as the modern, persistent myth would have us believe; many of her rulings were clear as crystal.) In addition we have reports of dozens of *mantis*, meaning 'seers.' Several of these are just fictional characters, but we also know of very real people of this type (psychics/clairvoyants) who were consulted by kings and coachmen, queens and courtesans. The 'seers' took part in people's everyday affairs: business, marriage, moving, disputes between neighbors, etc. And Greek armies never fought a campaign without a competent seer in their ranks! Hence, within ancient Greek society skilled seers tended to have high status, high salaries, and often belonged to the societal elite. This, however, certainly did not mean that it was always hats (or hoplite helmets) off to the seers, for already in the *Iliad* and the *Odyssey*, they are, on occasion, denounced as too ambiguous, too unreliable or too gloomy.

Even when the Greeks gradually moved 'from mythos to logos' (from myth to philosophy), Plato still found a place for the seers in his 'ideal state.' And both Democritus (who coined the term 'atom') and Aristotle took certain forms of what we would call psi for granted, and tried to give philosophical explanations for the phenomena. Later, the *Stoics* held that the human soul contained an element that could be stimulated to develop precognition. Thus, together with the rationality they rightfully are so famous for, the ancient Greeks allowed plenty of space for phenomena we would call paranormal!

When the Romans eventually established dominance in the Mediterranean area, the mental space seems to have become somewhat narrower, expressed by shutting down some significant holy sites used for initiation into the Greek mysteries. However, this was by no means a regulation: as long as one worshiped the emperor's genius and paid one's taxes, the pragmatic Romans would often allow for participation in the mystery cults *ad libitum*. And as the alert reader of *Asterix* will have noticed, the Romans definitely took prophecy and foresight into account. They practiced, among other things, 'reading' the patterns in the liver of sacrificial animals and the patterns in the flights of birds. From a parapsychological point of view there will of course be no information in the patterns themselves—any possible information lies in the images that the seer projects into them. The same is also true for other divinatory means, such as cards, crystal balls, tea leaves, coffee grounds, yarrow stalks, charred bones, black mirrors, etc. They are canvases onto which our mental images—which perhaps contain elements of clairvoyance and precognition—may be projected. One might imagine that with tools as, say, tea leaves, yarrow stalks etc. the patterns formed could perhaps to some extent be influenced by psychokinesis. But when using crystal balls or black mirrors, it is obvious—since there are no patterns in the balls or mirrors—that all information (and misinformation…) stems from our own projected images.

Modern Europe has, as opposed to earlier times, quite rigid restrictions in relation to ecstasy, trance and psi—phenomena that are not identical but which often go together (we will delve more into the co-occurrence of these phenomena in chapter 6).

An important reason for this, perhaps even more important than Enlightenment philosophy and natural science, is the emergence of urban lifestyle; loud noise, hurried pace, rational organization, regulated working hours and all the other blessings of Protestant ethics that led to diverse 'unproductive' phenomena being declared *non grata*. It is therefore hardly a coincidence that it is within groups on the fringes of society, such as the Romani people, that we find the most vibrant cultures for utilizing paranormal abilities. As the saying goes: *Use it or lose it!*

When a 'reasonable' person from a 'sensible' Western culture has to deal with African time, Balinese spirits or other 'irrationalities,' it may sometimes trigger a 'culture shock' to use the classic anthropological term. This is also true in the face of the Indigenous accounts of psi phenomena. Many early anthropologists who, stated or implied, adhered to the notion of white supremacy 'solved' this problem by interpreting stories about the paranormal as remnants and rudiments from an earlier stage of development—end of story! Later, genuine interest was shown in the symbolic aspects of these stories; an account of telepathy could for example be interpreted as 'a close, reciprocal connection,' or the like. But that the touching story—of, say, a woman suddenly feeling her child to be in need, rushing home just in time to save it from a wild animal, a fire or another danger—might also be about *real* telepathy; the direct transfer of information across distance, was more rarely considered. This could have challenged the fundamental assumptions of the Western worldview to an uncomfortable degree. Suddenly, before you know it, we would no longer be defining *their* reality, but they would be starting to define *ours*. Clearly, one should be careful not to allow for *that* much understanding!

Bronislaw Malinowski (1884–1942) is often considered the father of modern social anthropology. He advocated 'participant observation' as a norm for the discipline i.e. one ought to actively seek a duality—to be both inside and outside a culture, so as to achieve an understanding that neither mere participants (Indigenous people) nor mere observers (detached anthropologists) would be capable of. Malinowski had already promoted such ideas in the interwar period, but we had to reach the 1960s before anthropologists began to take part more systematically in rituals that included altered states of consciousness, induced by drumming, dancing, meditation, vigils, isolation, and entheogenic plants. Thus they came closer to a firsthand understanding of vital elements in the actual culture. Suddenly it became very clear that, for example, the shaman's drum was much more than just a 'culturally coded symbol of wisdom' or something of that ilk. Such somewhat 'geeky' interpretations were frequent with 'structuralist' anthropologists who perceived a culture to be a 'text,' and thus tried to 'read' the culture's beliefs, actions and objects in light of the latest (Western) literary theories.

Shamanistic 'drum travel' caused many an anthropologist to experience altered states of consciousness, and some also had psi experiences, such as astral projection, telepathy, clairvoyance, precognition and spirit manifestations—experiences that *can*, but probably don't *have to* be attributed to hallucinations. Some of these 'experienced' anthropologists have become involved in the Society for the Anthropology of Consciousness, where our friend 'Coffin Long' was a prominent figure. While other researchers in this field—often called 'transpersonal anthropology'—have chosen a more biological approach. One of them is Professor Charles Laughlin (b.1938), a Canadian anthropologist who has studied both African and Canadian ethnic groups with emphasis on rituals. He has also lived in Asia and for years meditated in the Tibetan Buddhist tradition. Laughlin combines field experiences with spiritual experiences and a bunch of different sciences to describe the interaction between brain, culture and consciousness. Regarding psi he notes that there is 'evidence within quantum physics, parapsychology and ethnology from alternative states of consciousness—evidence that suggests that human consciousness is able to exert effects on distance and communicate using telepathy.' Laughlin proposes that this may happen because the brain is a 'quantum computer' that can convert energy into information and information into energy (not easy, this one...). Although Laughlin believes that psi is real, he doesn't believe consciousness to exist independently of the brain. Hence his view differs from, for example, *Irreducible Mind*, a model that will be presented in chapter 6.

An Anthropologist Goes Native—Michael Harner

It sometimes happens that an anthropologist becomes so engrossed in the culture of his/her study that it gets close to possession. This phenomenon is humorously referred to as 'going native.' The humor is, however, a tad sarcastic rather than friendly; to do such a thing is a no-no, and is seen as heralding goodbye to proper science, for 'to go native is to go naive.' And the poor anthropologist who has gone native will more often than not incur the ridicule of superiors, and encounter a loss of respect and grants, and sometimes even employment. However, there are honorable exceptions, who by virtue of their expertise continue to be taken seriously even after going native. One of these is Michael Harner (b.1929), who has taught at renowned universities, including Berkeley, Columbia and Yale. But Harner is also a practicing shaman! In particular, he is committed to spiritual healing, reportedly with far better results than those achieved by placebo.

During his studies in the early 1960s, Harner visited various tribes of Indigenous people living by the Amazon River and was there introduced to trance-inducing drumming as well as the consciousness-expanding brew *ayahuasca*. And as Harner succinctly says: 'It worked!' In addition to creating visions, ayahuasca reportedly sometimes facilitates telepathic contact with plants, animals, kinsmen and ancestral spirits. Because of such spectacular effects, one of the crucial components in this two-component concoction was, back in the day, given the highly descriptive name *telepathine!*

Harner emphasizes, however, that one does not need psychoactive plants to experience altered states of consciousness; many shamanic traditions use only drumming or other auditory stimuli. He explains that the way this works on the technical level is by changing the brainwave pattern: shamanic drumming will typically have a base pulse in the theta range, i.e. about 4–7 beats per second. The frequency following response (FFR)—the response that makes us want to dance when listening to awesome music—causes the brain to adjust its pulsing to the drumming. Thereby it will start to produce more theta waves. Intense activity in the theta range is often associated with dreaming and creative processes and—based on research on shamans and long-term meditators—facilitates trance and perhaps even healing and other paranormal phenomena, so it seems. Harner was once connected to an apparatus designed to read brainwave patterns. After just a few minutes of drumming his brainwaves had markedly changed and he was 'deeply into theta.'

Learning to change the brainwave pattern is an essential part of the technical repertoire in shamanism, but according to Harner there are many more insights to be learned from the shaman's world—insights that could be of importance for Westerners. Harner emphasizes that although there are many versions of shamanism, there is also a surprising degree of similarity all over the world, a more or less transcultural essence, a 'core shamanism.'

Belonging to this core is a profound understanding of the connectedness of human beings to the Whole, and the recognition that Nature can't be bossed around according to human discretion and whim. This holistic consciousness is eminently expressed in the Oscar-nominated Sami movie *Pathfinder* (1987). In one scene, Raste, the *noaidi* (the Sami shaman), instructs the young protagonist, the pathfinder Aigin, on 'the big picture' and the connectedness of all things. Aigin, however, doesn't really get it, and says he cannot see it. Raste then—with a dramatic gesture—places his hand tightly over Aigin's face and for a few seconds prevents him from breathing. This very simple but profound 'direct pointing', worthy of a Zen master, gives Aigin an intense psychophysical experience of his continuous relationship with and dependence on Nature.

Spirits—an Unknown Species

In addition to the respect for Nature's elements and beings, belonging to the 'shamanic core' also means having the utmost regard for a species that most Westerners rarely take into consideration, namely the *spirits*. Harner relates that through his shamanistic practice he eventually had experiences that forced him to reconsider his own worldview. His point of departure, which is shared by many—I would think most—anthropologists, was that 'everything is culture.' So, if during a trance you should meet with a spirit, this would usually be interpreted as your culturally coded beliefs structuring your experience. The spirit experience is seen as 'subjectively valid' (whatever that might mean), but I daresay there is only a small minority of anthropologists who would seriously consider the possibility that an *objectively* existing spirit had dropped by!

Fredrik Barth (1928–2016) was the doyen of Norwegian social anthropology who held professorships at both Boston and Harvard Universities. Barth belonged to the same generation as Harner, and decades before the mobile phone made its entry, he ran field studies among the Swat Pathan— an ethnic group in East Pakistan. On one of his trips he met with people from a particular clan, known to have a very close connection to their deceased ancestors (their 'spirits'). They would provide remarkably detailed descriptions of what was going on in the village where Barth had his base camp, even if it was several days' journey away. How they got all this information Barth said he simply could not understand. And then he added, tongue-in-cheek: 'Well, I *hope* that I do not understand it!'

Harner was less hesitant than Barth to take the power of spirits into account and, as we just heard, he eventually became convinced that such intelligences, entities, or whatever one chooses to call them, are objectively real. Harner claims to be in contact with these nonphysical beings on a regular basis, e.g. when he is engaged in healing. He is certain that many encounters of this kind are not just 'cultural' or arbitrary products of the chemistry in the brain. Of course, different cultures create different versions of the Spirit World. And obviously brain chemistry is involved in the trance-experiences as in all experiences. But according to Harner, there is an objective spiritual reality behind the different mythologies and vast individual experiences. In the book *Cave and Cosmos* he writes:

Shamans differ from those who believe in spirits, because they know from firsthand experience that spirits exist. They see the spirits, touch them, hear them, smell them, and converse with them. [...] You know your family, friends, and acquaintances exist because you talk and otherwise interact with them daily. Similarly, shamans know spirits exist because they interact with them daily [...].

Unlike Harner, most anthropologists do not recognize spirits, angels and the like as independent beings. Rather they would, in keeping with traditional academic psychology, exhort the spirits to be content with an existence as 'sub-personalities'—parts of ourselves that under certain circumstances, e.g. in trance, can appear to have their own individuality. Sub-personalities are similar to the characters appearing in dreams. If I should happen to be dreaming of, say, a wise old man and a gorilla, a possible interpretation (for dreams are highly ambiguous) could be that they represent respectively my own wisdom and my own strength. But one would rarely conceive of this sage and gorilla enjoying an independent existence, and next morning to be strolling down some ghost town lane to get a coffee after a long night's work!

Within *transpersonal psychology*—which we will discuss in chapter 4—one is often quite open to paranormal phenomena. Here sometimes spirits, angels and similar beings are seen as psychological 'tools' established by our psyche to manage our paranormal abilities. Such powers, to the extent they may be real, could obviously be problematic when it comes to taking responsibility. It is easier if one can say, 'No, *I'm* not psychic—it is my late grandfather's spirit who knows all these weird things!' Or, 'No, *I'm* not clairvoyant—it's my guardian angel that performs the feat of viewing far-off places!' etc. Things become a bit safer that way (and in addition one cannot be held accountable for possible mistakes...). And through rituals, trance, prayer and other techniques, one can conjure these characters— the grandfather's spirit, the guardian angel, etc.—when one needs to activate their (= one's own) secret powers of precognition, clairvoyance, and so on.

Harner eventually left the university system, not because he was unwelcome for, as already mentioned, he has taught at various prestigious educational institutions. However, he preferred to pursue his shamanic interests in a more practical way; shamanism is not primarily a theoretical thing. So to 'beat the drum' for shamanism in the most literal sense possible Harner now gives courses in drum traveling, healing and other shamanistic skills. He has also formed the Foundation for Shamanic Studies, an organization working for the preservation of traditional shamanistic traditions still to be found around the world. For those who would like to pursue this further, let me mention that interviews and lectures with Harner are available on YouTube.

More About Spirits—Edith Turner, Eileen Garrett

One of those who traveled with Harner on his 'drum journeys' was Edith Turner, colleague and spouse of the distinguished Scottish anthropologist Victor Turner. She was originally a conventional anthropologist, but she did eventually experience things that her university education had not prepared her for... In 1985 in Zambia, she was quite taken aback when a shaman during a healing ritual bent down while singing and drumming to extract a malicious spirit:

Suddenly Meru [the patient] raised her arm, stretched it in liberation, and I saw with my own eyes a giant thing emerging out of the flesh of her back. It was a large grey blob about six inches across, opaque and something between solid and smoke: I was amazed, delighted. I still laugh with glee at the realization of having seen it [...].

Apparently the patient became fit as a fiddle after this ritual. Turner deliberates:

Then I knew the Africans were right. There is spirit stuff. There is spirit affliction; it is not a matter of metaphor and symbol, or even psychology. And I began to see how anthropologists have perpetuated an endless series of put-downs about the many spirit events in which they participated—'participated' in a kindly pretense. They might have obtained valuable material, but they have been operating with the wrong paradigm, that of the positivists' denial.

Interesting perspectives, indeed! However, it is well known that shamans often apply techniques to stage the perception of the illness leaving the sick, thereby activating a healing placebo effect. And initially Turner had been served a beverage:

a cup was handed to me and I drank the liquid, which tasted pleasantly of fresh leaves. Immediately my head fired up and swam. The drink contained no alcohol, but I felt the same recognizably loosening effect as before. Nevertheless I went on writing my field notes with no change in legibility.

The potion apparently didn't induce any twist in her perception of reality, but even so, could Turner in the midst of

tumult and drumming, her head 'fired up,' have been duped
by shamanistic sleight-of-hand? Well, this we shall never
know. But regardless of what might have caused her observation, she maintains she has seen on a number of occasions
that trances, in addition to affecting the mood of the participants, also produce phenomena of the psi type:

> *I have taken note of the effects of trance and discovered*
> *for myself the three now obvious regularities: frequent,*
> *non-empirical cures; clairvoyance, which includes find-*
> *ing lost people or objects, divination, prediction, or forms*
> *of wisdom speaking; and satisfaction or joy—these three*
> *effects repeating, almost like a covenant.*

No big surprise, then, that over the years Turner's professional interests took a markedly spiritual course. Among
other thing she went on to conduct studies of healing
and spirit manifestations with the Alaskan Native people
(Inupiat), and she also portrayed her field experiences in
several books.

Now, have Harner, Turner and countless likeminded researchers among spirit-familiar shamans gone completely
astray on the vast plains of our inner worlds? Or *are* there
really such beings as spirits? Maybe we ought to lend an ear
to 'the skeptical medium,' as she called herself, Eileen Garrett (1893–1970). She was one of the most significant paragnosts (person with alleged paranormal abilities) in the 20th
century. Garrett was in contact with spirits as often and as
easily as with the pigeons in the park, and she was once asked
if they really were independent beings (as the spirits themselves stubbornly claimed during her séances), or whether
they were part of her own subconscious (as her Jungian analyst suggested). She quipped: 'On Monday, Wednesday
and Friday I think that they are actually what they claim to
be... on Tuesday, Thursday and Saturday, I think they are

multiple personality split-offs I have invented to make my work easier... on Sunday I try not to think about the problem.'

Apparently a wise and humorous lady, this Eileen Garrett! So in her spirit—a most apt metaphor when talking about Garrett—perhaps we should avoid drawing any categorical conclusions about Harner's, Turner's, Garrett's, our ancestors' and other people's spirits—if they should be seen as independent beings, or if alternatively they should be understood as parts of our own subconscious? Or if perhaps these two approaches can be combined, in a somewhat similar way that one can see a human being both as an independent individual and also as an expression of our common human genetics. Both conceptions are equally valid, but from different perspectives. As always, it will be up to the reader to draw his/her conclusions.

Modern Myths from Mexico: Carlos Castenada— Shaman or Sham-man

When speaking of anthropology and the paranormal we cannot avoid mentioning the famous and infamous social anthropologist Carlos Castaneda (1925–1998). Castaneda, who was a doctoral student, and for a period also gave courses at UCLA, created a sensation in the 1960s and 1970s with his books about Don Juan Matus, a Mexican shaman from the Yaqui people. Castaneda tells of a vast amount of paranormal experiences such as telepathy, synchronicities, spontaneous movements through space, magical transformations, etc.—often in connection with altered states of consciousness. In his first two books such states are described as being induced by peyote cactus and Mexican 'magic mushrooms,' plants containing respectively *mescaline* and *psilocybin*, two powerful hallucinogenic substances. In the following books, however, when Carlos has 'awakened' from his limited frame of mind, and has come to realize that there is another reality behind the visible, Don Juan teaches him a sophisticated system of mental techniques, based on self-observation, meditation and physical exercises.

University professors lined up to bow in the dust to Castaneda, wowed by the young, brilliant anthropologist who took 'participant observation' to new heights, and thus obtained radically new insights into Yaqui culture. But as the Romans said: *Arx tarpeia Capitoli proxima*—the Tarpeian Rock (from which criminals were thrown to their death) is close to the Capitol—and Castaneda soon fell from academic favor. For even though his books about the things he and Don Juan experienced together are both entertaining and contain a lot of interesting psychology, it eventually became clear that Castaneda primarily had literary and philosophical ambitions, and that his accounts were not based on field studies with the Yaqui to any large degree, if at all...

Daskalos—the Cypriot Sage

In his book *The Magus of Strovolos: The Extraordinary World of a Spiritual Healer*, Kyriacos Markides, professor of sociology at the University of Maine, describes a wealth of episodes that could have been taken straight out of the Bible: healings, mind reading, nature miracles, astral projection, psychokinesis and more! The person who is said to have been responsible for all these events was the mystic Stylianos Atteshlis (1912–1995). In Cyprus, where Atteshlis was a celebrity and had many admirers as well as many detractors, he was known as *Daskalos* (= teacher) because he ran seminars in spiritual development. His daughter has informed me that Daskalos had no fewer than two doctorates, one in theology and one in philosophy, as well as five masters' degrees!—all from the University of St Andrews in Scotland. Some of Daskalos' teaching videos are available on YouTube.

Professor Markides, who grew up in Cyprus, wanted to use 'participant observation'—the central method in social anthropology—when meeting with Daskalos. He would not give up the role of observer, but at the same time he would be involved in Daskalos' highly personal variant of Christian Gnosis, with strong elements from Asian traditions. The book portrays a series of meetings between the two, where Daskalos' complex philosophy emerges through their dialogues. And in addition, as initially mentioned, we are witnessing a plethora of what we usually would call miracles. Daskalos didn't think, however, that there was anything miraculous about these events. He spoke of them very casually, as 'phenomena,' and perceived them to be expressions of natural, but little known, forces: 'If we knew how nature works, we would not call them miracles.' Let's have a look at such a 'phenomenon.' Markides recounts the experience of an Italian journalist:

In front of several witnesses, Stylianos Atteshlis healed a three-year-old English boy of polio. I stared with curiosity at the English woman holding her child. Only when

*she placed the boy in Stylianos Atteshlis' arms did I notice
that [the boy's] left leg was covered with a heavy plastic
brace. It was atrophied and clearly shorter than the other
leg... Stylianos Atteshlis sat on a chair with the child in
his arms and began to speak to him with a very sweet
tone in his voice. As he was doing that, he began to gen-
tly stroke the sickly leg. He pulled it a few times as if to
make it longer... Ten, twenty minutes must have passed;
I don't remember. I had my eyes glued sometimes on the
child and sometimes on Stylianos Atteshlis. Suddenly, the
child made a pained grimace. At that point he raised the
boy up, gave him a light slap on his buttocks, and said,
'Now, run, my boy.' And the child began running around
the room. Was it a miracle! Was it suggestion! One can
make whatever conclusions one wishes. I just describe
what I saw.*

We obviously cannot decide what happened here, but will
have to restrict ourselves to passing on the tale as one example of those stories that circulates *en masse* about this
modern mystic. Daskalos' obituary in *The Cyprus Weekly*,
September 1–7, 1995 stated:

*There are many authenticated stories of the apparently
miraculous cures that he achieved. One does not have to
read Markides' books to learn of them: Cyprus is full of
people who, often as a last resort, had visited Atteshlis in
the hope of being treated for ailments that conventional
medicine was unable to help.*

*There is no shortage of convinced and grateful patients,
although equally one can find many people for whom the
initial apparent cure turned out to be short lived.*

*Whether one 'believes' in Stylianos Atteshlis or not,
it cannot be denied that he was a unique thinker and
teacher with a 'magical' personality. His death will leave*

a far greater gap than most people in Cyprus could possibly realize.

Bushmen—Pioneers in Web-Based Education

When we're speaking of 'collective consciousness,' we usually refer to what is agreed on within a group. Europeans, for instance, would mostly agree, say, that human rights form a valuable part of their tradition, that Beethoven was a great composer, that Americans for the most part are their good friends on the world scene (even though they elected Donald Trump...). Such perceptions, shared by many, are sometimes said to belong to the 'collective consciousness,' but there is of course nothing paranormal about this. However, some anthropologists report that certain Indigenous people know a qualitatively different form of collective consciousness—one that is founded on telepathy!

Professor Bradford Keeney (b. 1951) at the University of Louisiana is a renowned theoretician in cybernetics (systems theory) and psychology and has published about 30 books, including classics on group dynamics and counseling. But Keeney has also worked as an anthropologist with among others the San people of the Kalahari and the Ju/'hoan people in Namibia and Botswana. These are ethnic groups who are often referred to as 'Bushmen.' (The term has been debated, but most of the Bushmen themselves are apparently fine with it.) It is said that Keeney is the only Westerner to be initiated in their ancient spiritual tradition to the level of becoming a shaman, a *n/om-kxosi* (as to the pronunciation, I'm afraid I cannot help...). He portrays the Bushmen as having a far more direct, complex and nuanced kind of collective consciousness than a collective appreciation of fish and chips or a shared football roar.

> [*In the strongest of such experiences*] *one's consciousness will seem to slide or slip into another domain of being where one merges with the knowing of previous ancestors. In this domain of collective consciousness, sometimes called a 'classroom' by the Bushmen, you receive knowledge. It is visionary and is directly absorbed—like being downloaded. Here songs, dances, information about plants, beadwork, and all kinds of matters are passed on. This is why the Bushmen have no written or oral custodians. They enter into domains of collective consciousness and get downloaded through a heartfelt absorptive experience.*

Keeney says that Bushmen do not depend on the usual types of transmission of knowledge, because their culture from days of old has used online teaching! These are indeed strong statements, but Keeney cannot easily be dismissed; in addition to being a highly respected psychologist, he has also headed the *N/om-Kxaosi Ethnographic Project*—a long-standing collaboration between the Texas Medical Center and the University of Witwatersrand (South Africa), to which both Megan Biesele and David William Lewis, two of the world's foremost experts on Bushman culture, are affiliated.

Since there is no widely accepted explanatory model for telepathic communication of knowledge, researchers have often ignored the Bushmen's stories of this kind, or have reinterpreted them as symbols of 'a sense of closeness to the ancestors' or the like. We shall not attempt to prove that the Bushmen's telepathic experiences are objectively valid—we simply open up to the possibility that they *may* be so. I also note with pleasure that Keeney's descriptions seem to fit surprisingly well with our own model. The Mental Internet really seems to be the epitome of a World Wide Web!

Some researchers have suggested that groups among Indigenous Australians have, or at least used to have, 'classroom experiences' when entering into 'dreamtime'—the timeless sphere which we briefly mentioned earlier in this chapter. Bushman and Australian Aboriginal cultures are immensely old; in 2012 a set of Bushman tools was discovered dating back to 44,000 BCE! Perhaps this collective sphere, this 'classroom,' this 'dreamtime', may be the very basis of our human consciousness? And in that case, perhaps telepathy is our original means of communication? As we will see in the next chapter, Sigmund Freud thought that this is probably the case. He believed, however, that ordinary language is preferable. But we may not need to choose, for if there actually is a capability, a 'language,' which in a subtle way allows for direct communication between people, this could perhaps help strengthen the feeling that we, on a basic level, all are connected, and that we are part of something bigger. These insights form an intrinsic part of many primordial cultures, and we Westerners probably could benefit from becoming a little more aware of them as well.

Back from the Expedition—Epilogue

So—during this foray into some exotic paranormal forests we have seen that qualified anthropologists have had their eyebrows raised and their jaws dropped in encounters with primeval cultures more open than our own to the enigmatic world of psi phenomena. And even if the tales conveyed are not as luscious as Procopius' stories (especially his chapter 9, against which the reader has already been warned!), we have seen that it is by no means risk-free to 'come out of the closet' waving reports of phenomena that don't fit well with a standard Western worldview. But truth should always take precedence over docile acceptance of tradition. Otherwise we will live in a perhaps pleasant, but still somewhat twisted version of reality, namely the 'erality' as modernist poet Jan Erik Vold humorously expressed it:

-erality

you say, erality
is much eralier
than reality, don't
you think? Yes, it's probably
so, I answer, but
reality
is more real,
still. You say: Of what help
is that
up against erality
being as eraly as it is!

There are unquestionably many *eralities*—personal, religious and neo-religious—that we may lull ourselves into if we, for the sake of comfort, close our eyes to the realities. (And these days the political erality of Trump's White House obviously tries to dethrone our known political reality.) Moreover, it seems there even may be some *professional* eralities around: diverse traditions, as for instance conventional psychology, medicine and biology, have made for themselves a quite transparent world, where a tacit assumption is that paranormal phenomena do not occur. Now, such a neat universe will undoubtedly represent many researchers' beloved *erality*, but—does it also represent *reality*?

The long string of surprisingly similar stories from the different corners of the world rendered in this chapter suggests that there still might be vast unchartered terrains out there (and in there!), and that our everyday notion about human abilities and Space might be limited. This chapter has presented some perspectives provided by a number of nonconformist members of the anthropologist tribe, and the list could easily have been made longer. And now it will of course be up to the reader to find the answers that are valid for him or her!

Chapter 4

FROM THE HISTORY OF PSYCHOLOGY: IGNITING IDEAS AND PARANORMAL PONDERINGS

William James Throws Down the Gauntlet in America

William James (1842–1910) started out as a physician, taught medicine/physiology at Harvard, but eventually opted for philosophy and psychology and is considered both a founding father of the branch of philosophy which is called 'pragmatism,' as well as one of the most important psychologists in history. Among James' many contributions is his influential textbook *Principles of Psychology*, where he describes our consciousness as being a continuous flux; thus the well-known concept 'stream of consciousness' stems from James.

James, who was the brother of novelist Henry James and diarist Alice James, had grown up in an intellectually stimulating home, where his father had introduced him to much philosophy, in particular the ideas of the Swedish scientist and mystic Emmanuel Swedenborg (who we will have a closer look at in chapter 6). These teachings gave James' view on human beings a spiritualistic slant—the soul/consciousness is seen as something different from/more than the brain—a belief which proved to be lasting (even though he later, in keeping with his pragmatic philosophy, also included complementary perspectives).

Hence James did not limit his interests and activities to mainstream psychology but took a keen interest in the paranormal as well and eventually went on to become president of the ASPR, the American Society of Psychical Research. James' study of the prominent medium Leonora Piper (1857–1950) led him to conclude that her trance states expanded her knowledge to a degree and in a way completely impossible to explain on the basis of existing science. James thus felt that scientists denying such phenomena were hindering the progression of science, a process that depends on being willing to let the outworn and outdated go.

> As a matter of fact, the trances I speak of have broken down for my own mind the limits of the admitted order of nature. Science, so far as science denies such exceptional occurrences, lies prostrate in the dust for me; and the most urgent intellectual need which I feel at present is that science be built up again in a form in which such things may have a positive place. Science, like life, feeds on its own decay. New facts burst old rules; then newly divined conceptions bind old and new together into a reconciling law.

One of history's greatest psychologists had thus thrown down the gauntlet claiming that that there are objectively real paranormal phenomena which merit—nay, demand—

our attention, and which must be accounted for and integrated in our understanding of reality! Some decades later, in 1927, R.B. Rhine would pick up James' gauntlet, and start doing trailblazing scientific parapsychological research at Duke University. However, the buzz of the day in American psychology at the beginning of the 20th century was 'behaviorism'—stressing the measurement and conditioning of behavior—and within this school of psychology the elusive psychic phenomena were seen as irrelevant.

Psychoanalytical Perspectives I—Sigmund Freud, the Secret Mud Bath

In Europe, however, psychoanalysis—which attaches much more importance to subjective experience and our inner world than does behaviorism—was about to gain traction. This made it possible to consider 'the depth of the soul'—complex emotions, thoughts, the unconscious, such stuff that behaviorism considers unimportant—as relevant in scholarly circles. Serious discussion, though, about the paranormal was all but easy, for in European universities, as in American colleges, fear of the 'emperor's wrath'—the fear of being punished by ostracism, loss of respect, funds and employment as explained at the beginning of the former chapter—was looming...

The most preeminent psychoanalyst by far is Sigmund Freud (1856–1939), and as most readers will probably already know, Freud was also the originator of psychoanalysis. But what is less well known is that Freud also took a keen interest in the occult. The textbooks in psychology will often cite Freud's famous call to stave off 'the black tide of mud of occultism.' But one sentence quoted alone and out of context does by no means give us the true picture. For Freud was an honorary member of both the Society for Psychical Research (SPR) in England and its American counterpart the ASPR. And even if he may have begun as a skeptic he eventually became completely convinced of the reality of telepathy and wrote various pieces in the affirmative about it.

Freud believed he might have experienced telepathic contact with his fiancée, later wife, Martha, early in their relationship. He also did some experiments on telepathy together with her and their daughter, Anna, who became a renowned child psychologist. His belief in the reality of telepathy became firmly established in 1910 when Freud and Sándor Ferenczi, a Hungarian student and colleague, had an extensive correspondence on the subject. And on August 20, Freud wrote with enthusiasm that some exciting observations of Ferenczi's 'finally eradicates the doubt about the existence of telepathy.'

In public, however, Freud chose to keep silent. And the reason is, as we mentioned initially, fear of the 'emperor's wrath'! Psychoanalysis already had a whole slew of enemies, partly due to the fact that Freud and most of his colleagues were of Jewish descent. Anti-Semitism was rife in Vienna, and Freud had repeatedly been denied professional promotion and had felt the need to deny that his work was a 'Jewish science.' Another ground for friction was that psychoanalysis, through its pursuit of meaning in dreams and the irrational, was regarded by many to be unscientific 'mysticism,' and furthermore, a mysticism with a most contaminated content. Freud had argued that the child—the Victorian innocent, the pure and semi-divine child—houses sexual feelings toward the parent of the opposite sex, combined with a jealousy-based hatred of the parent of the same sex (the Oedipus complex). The late-Victorians and the Edwardians were not amused... And as if this was not enough, Freud had asserted that God, the Heavenly guarantor of morality and values, is nothing more than the image of a gruff or, at best, loving father projected onto the sky by infantile people. Should psychoanalysis on top of all this now also be seen as a mouthpiece for occultism? Freud thought no! And he therefore cautions Ferenczi: 'Let us be completely silent about this.'

However, both Ferenczi and C.G. Jung—the Swiss analyst whom Freud considered to be his most important pupil, his 'crown prince,' and whom we will get to later in the chapter—had become really gung ho about exploring these exotic borderline areas of consciousness. But, in a letter of May 11, 1911 Freud seemed resigned to Ferenczi and Jung going it alone, 'I see that I cannot hold you back. [...] These are dangerous expeditions, and I'm not able to go with you.' It was Jung, a natural born mystic, who eventually became the most ardent explorer of the paranormal primeval forests.

But as the years went by, Freud, in spite of his initial reservations, joined in for some minor excursions. In 1922 he published an article called 'Dreams and Telepathy,' where he says that it is 'an undeniable fact that sleep creates favorable conditions for telepathy.' (We will elaborate on this theme in chapter 8, where we shall become familiar with some mind-boggling experiments in dream telepathy.)

Around the same time Freud also composed a somewhat longer lecture on the subject, probably with the intention of delivering it at a conference. But the 'Committee,' the inner circle of his associates, seemingly talked him out of it. The lecture, entitled 'Psychoanalysis and Telepathy,' was released posthumously. Here he argues that 'There is little doubt that if attention is directed to occult phenomena the outcome will very soon be that the occurrence of a number of them will be confirmed; and it will probably be a very long time before an acceptable theory covering these new facts can be arrived at.' These seem to be wise considerations.

Psychoanalysis and Occultism— Brothers-in-Arms?

Freud believed that in principle it should be possible to envision a fruitful interaction between psychoanalysts and occultists (Freud use the term 'occultist' more or less as synonymous with 'spiritualist'); both groups are 'fringe dwellers' whose ideas about the depths of the human psyche are rejected by mainstream psychology. But such cooperation would hardly be a bed of roses. Most occultists, according to Freud, are too gullible and would probably right off the bat take paranormal phenomena to confirm their spiritualist worldview. But even if, say, telepathy should occur, this does not prove, of course, that there is a spirit world, with angels, etc. And although psychoanalysts are very open to finding meaning in dreams and the irrational, they are mostly diehard materialists—Freud thought that there was not even a theoretical possibility for a life after death!

Neither was Freud open to precognition or paranormal foresight—a phenomenon most occultists assume to be real. He discusses a couple of cases of *apparent* precognition, but concludes that it is telepathy that has been at work: that one person 'tuned into' the thoughts of another, and thus became able to perceive what was coming. If I get to know about Jack's plan to buy a fishing rod and Jill's plan to buy sneakers, there is certainly no precognition needed to predict that fishing rod and sneakers probably soon will be theirs. And whether I should learn of their plans via snooping in their shopping lists or via telepathy, in neither case is there a direct experience of the future, and therefore no true precognition.

In a quite candid lecture from the mid-1920s, published in 1933 under the title 'Dreams and Occultism,' Freud advocates the intriguing idea that telepathy, the direct transfer of thoughts and feelings, may in fact be the *Ursprache*, the original means of communication used by humanity before developing verbal languages!

> *One is led to the suspicion that this [telepathy] is the original, archaic method of communication between individuals and that in the course of phylogenetic evolution it has been replaced by the better method of giving information with the help of signals which are picked up by the sense organs [i.e. verbal language].*

Nevertheless, Freud believed that this ancient ability lies dormant; it is a discarded but not dismantled system of communication, and can therefore be reactivated e.g. by collective excitation: 'But the older method (telepathy) might have persisted in the background and still be able to put itself into effect under certain conditions—for instance, in passionately excited mobs.' The mass can then become almost like an swarm of angry bees or a flock of fleeing sheep, possessed and controlled by one, collective feeling, rushing off without any individual reflection, as is sometimes seen in political and religious rallies, war psychosis and even rock concerts and sporting events. If one accepts Freud's premise—that telepathy is our human protolanguage—it seems reasonable, then, to assume that such mass hysteria could possibly facilitate collective telepathic hallucinations such as those we have discussed in connection with anthropology, that is Long's coffin and the Miracle of the Sun.

There are, in fact, significant overlaps between psychoanalysis and anthropology, as both disciplines are hunting and gathering the meaning of symbols (psychoanalysis focuses on individuals while anthropology focuses on cultures) and both Freud and Jung have contributed to both fields. As opposed to Jung, who liked traveling to exotic places, Freud was more of a couch potato, sitting in his living room, puffing 20 of his beloved cigars a day (but as Freud reputedly said: Sometimes a cigar is just a cigar...). But even so, his thoughts, especially in the book *Totem and Taboo* (1913), which for a great part is based on anthropologists' experiences, became important to anthropology. Freud claims there are striking parallels between the rituals of Indigenous people and the neuroses of Westerners, and he thus subtitled his book: *Resemblances Between the Psychic Lives of Savages and Neurotics*. Henceforth, anthropologists visiting the 'savages' would often have a well-worn copy of *Totem and Taboo* readily available in their haversacks. Freud and his ideas on telepathy such as the *Ursprache*, our original method of communication, are clearly indebted to the anthropologists' depiction of phenomena occurring in tribal trance rituals.

But—fear of the 'emperor's wrath' caused Freud to keep quiet about his paranormal ideas for a prolonged period of time. This silence most likely contributed to an academic taboo that perhaps could be termed *psi-phobia*: the fear of touching anything paranormal. This neurotic fear has in turn caused, and still causes, many accounts of paranormal experiences to remain anecdotal, that is to say unpublished.

So—the man who had once publicly warned about occultism's 'black tide of mud' now privately enjoyed a veritable mud bath—soaking and steeping in the titillating occult phenomena. In a 1921 letter to Hereward Carrington, a psychic researcher and prolific author, Freud lays bare the depth of his fascination with the paranormal mud pit, confessing, 'If I had to live my life over again, I should devote myself to psychical research, rather than psychoanalysis.'

Psychoanalytical Perspectives II—Carl Gustav Jung, the Abdicated Crown Prince

The psychoanalyst who actually devoted large parts of both his professional and private life to the paranormal was C.G. Jung (1875–1961). In 'alternative' and New Age circles Jung has long been a grandee, and following the release of the movie *A Dangerous Method* (2011), his fan base has probably been extended to include other groups as well. This film primarily deals with relationships, conflicts and sexuality, but it also makes evident that Jung held paranormal phenomena to be very real.

Breaking Free from Freud

Jung had become Freud's premier student and was, in Freud's own words, the 'crown prince' of the psychoanalytic kingdom. But as happened on more than one occasion in Freud's empire, the heir rebelled. An important bone of contention was the role of sexuality vs. the spiritual: Jung thought, as opposed to Freud, that neuroses are not necessarily explained by repressed sexuality and/or the accompanying family conflicts. He instead felt that the quest for Wholeness—the religious question, the yearning for Meaning—constituted a force even more essential than libido, i.e. sexual desire, especially with mature people. Freud was, however, no great believer in open dialogue; his pupils more often resembled disciples, and when anyone had the audacity to oppose him, there would be trouble... Jung recounts several of their disagreements in his autobiography *Memories, Dreams, Reflections* (1962), and the most interesting from our paranormal perspective took place in Vienna in 1909. Freud had then, because of 'his materialistic prejudice,' dismissed as nonsensical some of Jung's questions concerning precognition and parapsychology.

> *While Freud was going on in this way, I had a curious sensation. It was as if my diaphragm were made of iron and was becoming red-hot—a glowing vault. And at that moment there was such a loud report in the bookcase, which stood right next to us, that we both started up in alarm, fearing the thing was going to topple over on us. I said to Freud: 'There is an example of a so-called catalytic exteriorisation phenomenon.'*
>
> *'Oh come,' he exclaimed. 'That is sheer bosh.'*
>
> *'It is not,' I replied. 'You are mistaken, Herr Professor. And to prove my point I now predict that there will be another loud report!' Sure enough, no sooner had I said the words than the same detonation went off in the bookcase.*

Jung, then, took this 'catalytic exteriorisation phenomenon' to be a physical manifestation of the emotional conflict between them. Freud also mulls over this episode in a later letter, and confesses that it made a strong impression on him, but without, in the end, agreeing with Jung's interpretation.

After his final break with Freud, Jung underwent a painful period during which he gradually freed himself emotionally and intellectually from the yoke of his mentor. This liberation was facilitated by the psychiatrist Theodore Flournoy, whom Jung once referred to as 'my highly respected and fatherly friend.' Flournoy was a versatile scientist, who also made in-depth studies of spiritual matters. Jung says that Flournoy helped him to see Freud's limitations, and also encouraged him in his research on religion and the paranormal.

The Collective Aspect of the Psyche

An important concept that Jung developed was 'the collective unconscious.' This, he assumes, is a 'mental reservoir' created by the experiences that humanity has accumulated throughout history. Jung once dreamed he entered a basement (a common symbol of the subconscious), and suddenly he discovered that under the floor of the basement there was an ancient cave ('the collective unconscious'). This dream was one of the sources that eventually sparked off the idea that the psyche might have a collective aspect—a notion which, Jung felt, threw light on many phenomena, e.g. the development of the human psyche during the course of history, some otherwise apparently inexplicable mental problems, religious revelations and various paranormal phenomena.

Another source for Jung's idea of 'the collective unconscious' was the observation that some people diagnosed with schizophrenia had visions closely resembling those depicted in ancient Gnostic and alchemical texts. These patients were people with little or no education, and Jung therefore thought it unlikely that they could have acquired their unusual imagery from 'quaint and curious volumes of forgotten lore' hardly known to anyone but a coterie of researchers. It then struck Jung that they might instead have obtained the information directly from the collective unconscious! In a memorable television interview for the BBC in 1959 (easily found on YouTube), Jung relates one such case, and the interviewer John Freeman asks: 'And this you felt proved that there was an unconscious which was something more than personal?' Jung answers with a warm and somewhat teasing smile: 'Oh well, that was not a proof to me, but it was a hint, and I took the hint.'

To throw some light on the idea of the collective unconscious from another angle, let me mention that the well-known English healer Matthew Manning relates in his first book, *The Link: The Extraordinary Gifts of a Teenage Psychic*, that during his automatic writing sessions he had suddenly started to jot down words and phrases in Arabic and Greek—languages he had never learned! Manning's publisher sent the Arabic messages to Professor Suheil Bushrui at the American University in Beirut, who informed him that they were written in Arabic script of different varieties and quality. Strange, indeed... But perhaps Manning could have picked up these letters and words unconsciously when reading books or watching TV? This seems to be a very reasonable idea, but could it also apply to those long sentences, with internal logic and correct syntax, which he sometimes produced? One message came in writing of such high quality that, according to Professor Bushrui, it seemed to have been written by a scholar skilled in calligraphy.

And what was *really* wondrous was that material 'came through' that contained information that was unavailable to the public. Over a period Manning 'received' a number of 'letters' pertaining to the internal affairs of the Orthodox Church—letters that seemed to have come from the hand of a deceased Greek bishop Nektarios (albeit these messages came in English). Some of the letters were addressed to the head of the Orthodox Church in London, Archbishop Athenagoras, and they were therefore passed on to their rightful recipient. After having read them Athenagoras stated: 'The case of Matthew Manning is beyond any form of logical investigation. I can say positively that the young man has been in no position to know of certain things which were contained in those "letters."'

So unless Manning and Archbishop Athenagoras here have joined forces to prank us—and Manning has no affiliation with any Christian church—this would seem to corroborate the Jungian idea that in addition to our individual psyche there exists a collective memory, where all our experiences, thoughts and feelings are stored. Or as we in this book describe it: that in addition to our computers, tablets, smart phones and our brains, there is a Mental Internet where our impressions and thoughts are uploaded, and where people with a 'good search engine,' i.e. those who are 'psychic,' can browse and download this information. Interestingly enough, Manning is not the only one who is said to have received messages in foreign languages in mysterious ways. The Cypriot mystic Daskalos, whom we got to know in the previous chapter, reportedly experienced multiple 'downloads' in ancient languages, conveyed by the spirit (or 'spirit') of a medieval monk.

But now back to Jung, who was becoming increasingly fascinated by this expanded perspective on the psyche. He therefore chose not just to let the 'the black tide of mud' run its own slow course, but rather he pried the floodgates wide open. And if we take Freud's metaphor even one step further it would probably be apt to say that Jung excelled in occult mud wrestling: Over a period of 30 to 40 years he participated regularly in spiritualist séances, and researched at least eight different mediums. In addition to his own extensive paranormal experiences, as well as those he read in Gnostic and alchemical texts, Jung also received significant inspiration from the works of the English philosopher, poet and spiritualist Frederick Myers, with whom we will become acquainted in chapter 6.

Jung—also for fear of the 'emperor's wrath' (we're getting used to this now...)—chose to keep silent about the paranormal aspects of his business. Hence outwardly Professor Jung remained a respected psychiatrist, a well-regarded guest at conferences and conventions. While inwardly, he was Basilides, an antique Gnostic teacher, who roamed around in the spiritual worlds, guided by Philemon, his guardian spirit, who revealed to him 'ineffable secrets.' Some of these revelations are described in Jung's book *Seven Sermons to the Dead* (1916), which he chose to publish pseudonymously because of its special (to put it mildly) content.

But there is a time for everything: In *Memories, Dreams, Reflections*, Jung finally and unequivocally showed the flag and acknowledged a wealth of mysterious events, significant visions, telepathy and precognition. For example, he recounts having 'seen' Europe lying bathed in blood a year before World War I broke out. Jung also writes about various psychokinetic phenomena—a tree being cleaved from crown to root, a manifestation which Jung attributed to his family's extensive spiritualistic activities; a bread knife exploding in the drawer; doors opening and closing by themselves (which Jung certainly did not believe was caused by a draft).

Equally quirky phenomena, which obviously are not easily verifiable, are known from many sources. Psychokinetic events are often reported in connection with *poltergeists*

(German for 'noisy ghost')—a phenomenon which became part of urban folklore after the 1982 horror movie by the same name. The roughly 90 well-witnessed cases in Lalm kindergarten in 2010—objects flying around, things apparently coming out of thin air—which we will discuss in chapter 5 seems to be an excellent example of poltergeists.

Also some of the actions traditionally ascribed to goblins, gnomes, kobolds, sprites, tomtes, etc. could quite reasonably be seen as the activities of poltergeists. But—take note!—in parapsychology, poltergeist activity is *not* seen as caused by goblins, gnomes or kindred creatures, but as spontaneous psychokinesis; that psychic powers in the human consciousness are manifesting physically. English geneticist and mathematician Dr George Owen, who was one of the world's foremost experts on poltergeists, believed that such phenomena tend to manifest themselves around people with emotional conflicts—the events are not manifestations of an angry ghost, but rather of the ghost of anger. The loud reports in the bookcase that Freud and Jung experienced appear to fall neatly into place within Owen's model. Both men experienced this to be a serious crisis in their relationship—a crisis with great emotional, symbolic and practical significance. Probably they both felt intensely something like: 'Unless that [expletive!] shuts up right now there's going to be an explosion!' And that was also pretty much what happened...

The Archetypes and Synchronicity—
Patterns, Coincidences,
Themes and Meaning

The collective unconscious is supposedly the habitat of essential patterns associated with particularly momentous human experiences and characteristics, such as birth, death, heroism, sexuality, aggression, wisdom, etc. Jung dubbed these patterns 'archetypes.' He developed his theories over a long period and his descriptions are not without ambiguities, but often he will portray the archetypes as 'force fields' of psychic energy. There have been attempts to modernize Jung, wanting to clean him of 'occult mud,' and thus some choose to interpret the archetypes more as 'dispositions' or the like. This author believes such rationalization to be a deviation, obscuring the *numinous* quality of the archetypes—their awe-inspiring presence and their possessing power—that was so often underscored by Jung.

Jung argued that ancient mythologies, with their plethora of Venuses and Marses, fertility goddesses and war gods, heroes and divine children, sages and witches, are galleries where archetypes are on display. Also modern mythologies, such as *Star Wars*, the Harry Potter books, *Lord of the Rings*, etc., are spheres where archetypes come to expression, e.g. characters such as Yoda, Voldemort and Gandalf are utterly archetypical—their presence can almost be felt, even if they are just fictional (or are they...?). It is the archetypes' *numinosity* (their awe-inspiring spiritual quality) that gives these myths their allure and thus can explain why they exert such an attraction and cast their spell on us.

Based on the idea that all humans participate in the same collective field, Jung also dedicated much work to the mythologies of Indigenous cultures. By social anthropologists he is often dismissed as being 'uniculturalist,' i.e. without an eye for cultural differences, but according to the standards of his own day by which in all fairness he ought to be judged, Jung was probably an anthropologist as good as any: he went on excursions to Latin America, Africa and India where he engaged in 'participant observation.' Many readers probably have heard 'The Rhythm of the Heat' by

Peter Gabriel; this hypnotizing track is based on a frightening trance experience that Jung had when participating in a drum ritual in Ethiopia.

Jung definitely had an interest in conventional parapsychology; he corresponded with, among others, the trailblazing parapsychologist Professor J.B. Rhine (discussed in chapter 8). But Jung's ultimate concern was not the peculiar phenomena in themselves, but rather the *meaning* they might create for the person experiencing them. Jung had observed that psi phenomena often manifested themselves when the archetypes, the psychic energy fields in the collective unconscious, are activated. This typically occurs in association with existential crises—when our quest for meaning completely fills us, and where we are driven beyond the limits of everyday life. People then tend to go 'deep' into themselves, into the subconscious, the 'basement' of the psyche. And, according to Jung, they sometimes go even deeper, into the sphere below the basement, to the collective unconscious. This may evoke and awaken the archetypes, which will often cause the occurrence of strange and meaningful coincidences, 'synchronicities,' as Jung called them. He mentions diverse examples from his therapeutic practice—let's have a look at a classic case.

Jung had a patient who was struggling with a compulsively rational approach to life. She was an intellectual control freak, who had completely shut off the emotional/irrational, fruitful/chaotic aspects in Life—the precise aspects that, according to Jung's understanding, could have helped to redeem her. To phrase it in the 'archetypical' language: She was much of an Athena, but very little of an Aphrodite. The therapy had stalled, and Jung did not know what to do. He yearned for something unexpected to occur, something that would cause her intellectual 'glass cage' to crack. And so it came to be.

One night the patient had a dream in which she was offered a valuable piece of jewelry, designed as a golden scarab—the sacred beetle that for the ancient Egyptians symbolized transformation and rebirth—that, symbolically speaking, is the very goal of Jungian therapy. As she recounts her dream to Jung, he suddenly hears a tapping on the window right behind him, and turning he sees a beetle 'knocking' on the glass. He opens the window and in flies a rose chafer, a golden beetle in the family *Scarabaeidae*, which is as close as you can get to an Egyptian scarab at more northern latitudes (check *Cetonia aurata*—it is quite beautiful!). Jung catches the beetle in the air and presents it to the patient with the words: 'Here is your scarab!' According to Jung this made a strong impression on her and helped her to open up to the irrational—exactly what was needed for her therapy to progress. Jung adds that he had never—neither before nor since—seen a rose chafer behave in such an intrusive way!

To describe this kind of event that, from his perspective, involved both the physical and the psychical, Jung introduced the term 'synchronicity—'same-timeness'; when coincidences are incidences coordinated. One definition of synchronicity is the 'acausal relationship between two or more psychical and physical phenomena.' The events in a synchronicity—in our example: the psychic (the woman's dream about a scarab) and the physical (the beetle incident)—are, according to Jung, coordinated from a level beyond them both, namely from the collective unconscious. The psychic energy stored there, he argues, can manifest itself both psychically and physically. This is quite abstract, but we could perhaps use a thunderstorm as an illustration. Both thunder and lightning are expressions of electrical discharges; one expression comes in the form of sound (thunderclap), the other in the form of light (thunderbolt).

But both are expressions of the exact same underlying level, namely the electrical discharges.

Jung formulated his idea of synchronicity based on inspiration from various physicists. He recalls that it was Albert Einstein, with his ideas about the relativity of space and time, who had first given him the idea that perhaps *causality*—the relationship between cause and effect—could be somewhat more relative than is usually thought. And by the way, in the early days when they were developing their respective philosophies, Jung and Einstein often synchronized their suppers by having dinner together!

In addition, Jung was influenced by the Danish physicist Niels Bohr, who assumes that reality is intrinsically paradoxical and therefore can best be described by models that both contradict and complement each other. In a similar way, Jung believed that his concept of synchronicity both contradicts and complements normal causality. Artists and creative people of different hues—those thinking a bit more 'out of the box' than most of us—quite often become fascinated by Jung's notion of synchronicity. For example, many readers will certainly be aware that Sting, the great pop singer, released an album entitled *Synchronicity*. This is kudos to Jung. Sting also went into Jungian psychotherapy.

Support from 'The Conscience of Science'

Perhaps quite a few of us feel that Jung, with his concept of synchronicity, stands in acute danger of finding patterns and meaning when there are none—a tendency often referred to as *pareidolia* or *apophenia* (this will be discussed in some depth in chapter 7), and thus that he deviates from a proper scientific approach. But, interestingly enough, Jung had strong and enduring support from one of the outstanding figures in modern physics, Wolfgang Pauli (1900–1958), who received the Nobel Prize in 1945. Even Albert Einstein was an admirer of Pauli's and is said to have thought of him as a kind of successor despite their significant theoretical disagreements.

Several preeminent physicists of the day sent their manuscripts to Pauli to have him propose improvements. But they did not do so without apprehension! Pauli did not beat about the bush; he was a merciless critic, too rigorous rather than too lenient. As he once said: 'It may be that I have rejected something that was correct, but I have never accepted anything that was wrong!' This severity had given Pauli the nickname 'the conscience of science.' On one occasion when a colleague presented Pauli with some calculations of inferior quality he received the devastating feedback: 'This isn't right. It isn't even wrong.' In other words: mere garbage.

Pauli believed, however, that Jung really was onto something with *his* theories. This was partly due to the fact that Pauli, as he saw it, had experienced many synchronicities in the form of psychokinesis. Typically Pauli would feel that 'something' built up inside of him, and a little later it would 'blast' a surrounding object. A chair, a vase, a motor, some electrical apparatus would suddenly break, crack, smash or snap. Laboratory equipment, which until then had functioned smoothly, repeatedly failed for unknown reasons when Pauli was around. This had occurred in several laboratories throughout Europe, and was jokingly referred to as 'the Pauli effect.' Some have tried to explain (away) the phenomenon, claiming that Pauli was abnormally clumsy, and that *this* was how the damage came about. Each is of course entitled to his/her opinion, but Pauli himself had quite another view; according to Pauli's biographer and assistant, physicist Charles Enz, Pauli seemingly took the strange events to be expressions of his inner imbalance, a psychic chaos, manifesting psychokinetically as outward havoc.

Pauli would readily joke about the whole thing, but he also seems to have been deeply disturbed by it. Also other physicists were concerned about 'the Pauli effect': Otto Stern, who received the Nobel Prize in physics in 1943, was a good friend of Pauli's. But even so, Stern forbade Pauli to visit his laboratory—for fear of his precious equipment being blasted by Pauli's paranormal force!

Jung and Pauli stayed in contact for more than 25 years until Pauli's death in 1958. They exchanged many letters, discussing diverse philosophical, scientific and paranormal issues. And in 1952 they co-published the book *The Interpretation of Nature and Psyche*, where synchronicity is the central theme. Both argue that the sharp distinction between Consciousness and Matter, which after the philosophy of René Descartes (1596–1650) became part of 'the European (Cartesian) worldview,' is primarily an expression of a limited perception of reality, and gives us a flawed concept of the world. Jung points to the alchemical concept of *unus mundus* (One World), which implies that there is a deeper order underlying everything, and hence the observer and the observed are two sides of the same coin, of the same underlying reality. This entanglement of mind and matter would, according to Jung, allow for the creation of synchronicities. And Pauli for his part concludes—very cautiously, after all he was 'the conscience of science'—along similar lines: 'It would be very satisfying if the physical and psychical could be considered to be complementary aspects of the same reality.'

In recent times others have spun further on Jung's and Pauli's ideas on synchronicity, weaving them into a broader cultural tapestry. One notable heir of theirs is the British physicist F. David Peat with his book *Synchronicity: The*

Bridge Between Matter and Mind (1987) and *Synchronicity: The Marriage of Matter and Psyche* (2014). Other interesting voices can be heard in a collection of essays from 2008, namely *Synchronicity: Multiple Perspectives on Meaningful Coincidence*, Lance Storm (ed.).

Transpersonal Psychology

The Opening Toward 'the More'

Sometimes it happens that a person goes for a walk in the woods, and then suddenly starts to feel an almost mystical oneness with nature—an experience I am certain quite a few readers will be able to relate to. This could serve as an example of a *transpersonal* experience, an experience where one transcends (exceeds, goes beyond) one's everyday perception of oneself. Transpersonal experiences may involve the paranormal but not necessarily; the essence in a transpersonal experience is to perceive oneself as part of something bigger. Such episodes may happen in nature, at concerts or religious services, being with a loved one, or being engrossed in an idea, solving a scientific problem, engaging in the struggle for freedom, etc. Some schools in psychology regard the transpersonal to be a fundamental aspect of being human, underscoring that deep inside us there will always be this longing for 'the More,' as William James once expressed it. And without taking this into account, a person will hardly be able to experience life as meaningful and fulfilling.

The danger if this existential longing goes astray is of course that the yearning for meaning, for 'the bigger cause,' may drag people into the murky morasses of blind nationalism, religious extremism, etc. Therefore a constructive 'myth' must be found. And if this myth is to be not just a delusion, a 'life-lie' as playwright Henrik Ibsen famously dubbed it, but rather a life-truth, the big questions must be dealt with. Within transpersonal psychology one does not shy away from this—quite the contrary: It is when a person becomes refocused from the limited (I-me-mine) to the transpersonal (us-we-our) that a transformation can happen—that the crack may become an opening for the light, that the wounded may become a healer. For example, Beethoven, Dostoevsky and Martin Luther King struggled with major personal problems (deafness, depression, addiction, gambling, suicidal thoughts, etc.) but dedication to their respective 'More' (Music, Insight, Ethics) made their *souls*—their innermost being and intention emerging from the collective Consciousness—come alive and thus they discovered treasures of value to us all. At least, this is one way to look at it. The great Argentinian writer Jorge Luis Borges has said that in our modern, secular day one ought perhaps not to use the word 'soul' but rather 'subconscious.' But he then added, tongue-in-cheek, 'I prefer to have a soul!'

An early example of transpersonal psychology is *psychosynthesis*, which was developed by the Italian psychiatrist and student of Freud, Roberto Assagioli, and which to a large extent is built on esoteric traditions. *Analytical psychology* that stems from C.G. Jung is also a classic strand within the transpersonal family. Nowadays transpersonal thought will often be associated with figures such as Charles Tart, Stan Grof, Christina Grof, Ken Wilber, Ervin Laszlo, and a whole slew of thinkers and therapists from spiritual and humanistic traditions, e.g. psychodrama and Gestalt therapy.

The most important 'hatchery' for transpersonal thought in the past 50 years has been Esalen in California, an impressively versatile therapy center, research center, conference center, think tank, art scene, etc. The exciting story about Esalen is eminently told by the comparative religious scholar Jeffrey Kripal in his erudite but readable and engaging book, *Esalen: America and the Religion of No Religion* (2007).

Stan Grof—Spirituality and Therapy

One of the many exciting transpersonal therapists with a strong connection to Esalen is the colorful Czech-American psychiatrist Stan Grof, who first became known to the public through his work with psychotherapy and LSD back in the 1960s. (LSD was then a legal drug of which one had high expectations.) Grof began his career as a materialist with conventional perspectives on consciousness, but his own and his patients' experiences gradually led him to radically change his views. An important part of this *Umwertung aller Werte*, the revaluation of all values, to use an expression from Nietzsche, was taking the collective aspects of consciousness into account. For the mature Grof, consciousness and spirituality are central concepts.

> *We are not just highly evolved animals with biological computers embedded inside our skulls; we are also fields of consciousness without limits, transcending time, space, matter, and linear causality. And also: I had to open myself to the fact that the spiritual dimension is a key factor in the human psyche and in the universal scheme of things. I feel strongly that becoming aware of this dimension of our lives and cultivating it is an essential and*

desirable part of our existence; it might even be a critical factor for our survival on this planet.

Grof is in several respects a controversial thinker, but he has also received a lot of recognition; in 2007 he was granted the VISION-97 award, created by the legendary Czech dissident, philosopher, writer and later president, Václav Havel. In his speech at the ceremony Havel said the following:

I have always, all my life, thought that once something has happened, it cannot un-happen, that the entire history of the cosmos, of our solar system, of the Earth, and of humanity, are by some means recorded. That existence itself has some kind of memory.

It is clear that Havel supports the idea of some sort of 'mental cloud' where all and every piece of information is stored. He further said:

And the body of work of Professor Grof has all of a sudden shown me that, here and there, something is able to return, by a special pathway, from this memory, back to our time and place, into our consciousness. To our great surprise, we all of a sudden experience, identify with, or for a moment see something that happened many years ago, in remote places, and what we absolutely could not have previously known by any ordinary means. However, it is often possible to verify that it actually had happened.

Havel ended his speech as follows:

This is by no means the only thing that professor Grof teaches and researches. Nevertheless, for me personally, this—let us say—almost metaphysical dimension of his teaching speaks to me and continues to captivate me. I keep thinking about it, fully convinced that I am not a madman, who just believes in a delusion.

I now feel an urge to bow deeply and say: 'Thank you, Václav, for strongly supporting an idea so important for this book!'

Becoming Born Again...with Care

As an extension of his transpersonal orientation Grof believes that our self-understanding ought to develop from *hylotropic*, meaning materialistic (*hyles* = matter, *tropic* = turning or changing) to *holotropic*, meaning holistic in an extended sense. One not only—not even primarily—needs to acquire new insights but must also open up to new experiences. Grof, as stated, started out using the powerful hallucinogenic LSD as a catalyst. Later, he and his wife, the late Christina Grof, developed breathing techniques, *holotropic breathwork*, to facilitate 'rebirthing'—the experience of being 'born again' and getting a new sense of identity, a process described in a variety of myths since time immemorial. Grof comes across as an unusually robust person, and his therapeutic approach, which may involve unleashing torrents of emotions, can undoubtedly—as many have testified—have great transformative effects. Yet, such stirring up of emotions may, it seems, be a little too rough, even counterproductive, for some. So—even if there will be no big bad astral wolf to eat you, the results could still become unpleasant if using holotropic breathing to huff and puff and blow the doors of perception wide open without a good 'set and setting' (contructive mindset, harmonious environment, good friends, a skilled therapist), to use the famous expression coined by psychiatrist Norman Zinberg.

Whispers on the Way

Grof argues that when we start opening up to 'the things in us that are greater than us', psi phenomena tend to occur: precognitive dreams, telepathic experiences, and maybe first and foremost *synchronicities*—the kind of thematic meaningful coincidences we discussed in chapter 4 in connection with C.G. Jung. In his book *When the Impossible Happens* Grof relates a synchronicity he heard from Joseph Campbell, the renowned mythologist whose works on 'the hero's journey'—a metaphor for the universal spiritual quest—was an important source of inspiration for George Lucas when he crafted the mythology for *Star Wars*. Campbell told Grof the following story.

Early in the 1980s Campbell was deeply engaged in an important project on the role of animals in shamanic imagination. In the myths of the Kalahari Bushmen, the praying mantis, the somewhat creepy 'predatory grasshopper,' plays an important part. Once, when Campbell was sitting in his apartment on the 14th floor of a highrise building in Greenwich Village, New York, intensely immersed in myths about the mantis—mind full, books open, pictures on the wall—he suddenly got an irresistible impulse to rise from his chair and open a window facing Sixth Avenue. This particular window was always closed. According to Campbell, in the 40 years he had been living in the apartment, he had opened it no more than two or three times. Campbell now felt he *had to* open this window and in doing so he immediately peered out to the right. And there—on the exterior wall—a huge mantis was ambling along! Campbell said he felt it looked at him with a 'meaningful' glance...

Finding a mantis on the outside of the 14th floor of a building in New York is not a quotidian event (they, in fact, can be found in some parks in the city but are poor fliers).

Campbell was intensely focused on mantis mythologies and simultaneously felt an irresistible impulse to open this specific window that had only been opened every other decade. Moreover, this impulse occurred at the very moment the mantis strolled past. The statistical probabilities of this happening all at once seem, mildly put, to be low. So perhaps this could be seen as an epitome of synchronicity, when coincidences become coordinated?—a cluster of psychical and physical events thematically related, initiated by Campbell's intense focus and nicely orchestrated by the subconscious.

Well, anyway, Grof concludes, justified or not, as follows: 'Only a hardcore materialist committed to his or her worldview with a quasi-religious fervor could believe that something like this might have happened by pure chance.'

More than just a droll story about Campbell, Grof obviously also means this to be a story about *us*. For if we say yes to the 'call' and join 'the hero's journey,' being urged on by 'what in us that is greater than us,' then, according to mythology, Jung, Campbell, Grof and others, these kinds of quirky coincidences (which the abovementioned thinkers believe are organized from deep within the psyche) will start to happen in *our* lives. We will in some sense become like the heroes and heroines in the fairytales who are helped and given hints along the way by talking animals and other magical beings, to eventually win the prince/princess, half the kingdom, or whatever symbol is used for the highest good. A pleasant thought that is!—and perhaps there may also be some truth to it?

In order to recognize and understand the eventual messages coming from 'the King's palace' (the higher self, the depth of the soul)—to not ignore them, nor to neurotically over- or misinterpret them—one must according to age-old recipes learn to pay attention to one's hunches, intuitions, dreams, feelings and forebodings. Or as a more modern expression goes: you have to listen to the vibes. From the transpersonal perspective such vibes, such intuitions, such whispers, may contain psi-based information beneficial to growth and evolution, personally and collectively. And perhaps this is, in fact, exactly where psi phenomena might prove to be more than just curiosities? That in this connection they, if we are fortunate, might show their real meaning, acting as communication with 'what in us that is greater than us'? Perhaps *this* could be the most important secret of our secret powers?

Chapter 5

SCENES FROM A MARRIAGE— HISTORICAL GLIMPSES FROM THE RELATIONSHIP BETWEEN OCCULTISM AND PARAPSYCHOLOGY

Introduction—the Paranormal Tango

The period between 1500 and 1700 saw what is often called the Scientific Revolution, meaning that a breakthrough in natural science—mainly within astronomy, chemistry and physics but also in mathematics—took place. In addition, the 'mechanistic worldview' was introduced. Within this worldview the universe—including living organisms and heavenly bodies, which traditionally had been thought to be of a different, even spiritual, nature—is regarded somewhat like gears in a great mechanism, a cosmic machine, working according to laws that could be detected with rational

methods. Thus the idea of *anima mundi*, the world soul—
that the physical world 'deep down' had a spiritual essence,
perhaps a personality even—was dispensed with; as the
French philosopher René Descartes (1596–1650) dryly
summed up the new worldview: 'There is no spirit in sticks
and stones.'

Within this new horizon of understanding astrology—
where Venus, Mars and the other planets in the ancient
world had been regarded as personalities, 'gods'—developed
into modern astronomy. And alchemy—where mercury,
gold, silver and other elements were thought to possess
spiritual qualities—developed into modern chemistry. The
newborn sciences were based on the development of a whole
slew of new ideas and methods, but there was also clear
continuity—for example astronomy employed astrology's
detailed charts of stellar constellations, and chemistry utilized alchemy's equipment and vast knowledge of reactions
between elements. So in a certain sense the sciences became
heirs to their respective occult predecessors.

But—as is the case with so many of shady backgrounds,
modern science has proved to be sensitive to its ancestry, and
many scientists felt the need to disassociate themselves from
their parental 'black arts,' which they perceived to be backward and superstitious (e.g. astronomers deriding astrology's
horoscopes and chemists ridiculing alchemy's transmutation
of base metals into gold). The 'old-timers'— astrologers, al-
chemists—for their part would often scoff at their heirs'
contemptuous attitude, their hubris. The new scientists
seemed to think that they could just snap their fingers and
demand the Universe's innermost nature, its *quintessence,*
to reveal itself in observatories or laboratories, complying
with bureaucratic requirements and scientific protocols.
So during their first symbiotic centuries the natural sciences and the occult arts often had a somewhat strained

relationship—despite or *because of* their common interests—which in some sense resembled a *tango:* close and passionate but with an ever-present, underlying fight.

By the end of the 18th century, this tango—the love/hate dynamic between the occult and the scientific, the old and the new, the predecessors and the heirs—had manifested itself within early parapsychology. Those who had occultism as their *Weltanschauung*, their worldview, would typically be flattered by science's keen interest in the phenomena, but at the same time might feel that the scientists' approach of crude experiment and reason—rather than reverent invocation, meditation and ritual—was close to sacrilege. Rigorous scientists would maintain that no place, be it on Earth or in the Heavens, in the kingdom of man or the kingdom of spirits, ought to be protected from the scrutiny of human gaze and logic, and would regard the occultists' misgivings as silly leftovers from days of yore. In this chapter we shall become acquainted with a handful of the actors that have played their part—some as occultists, others as scientists—in this paranormal *tango jalousie* during the past 200 years. The first scenes take place under the heavy crystal chandeliers in the Parisian salons of the late 18th century.

French Opening Toward the Occult—Three Personalities in Paris

1. Magical Magnetism— Franz Anton Mesmer

Eighteenth-century Paris was the most open and dynamic European capital in its time and thus became the center for innumerable revolutionary and spiritual movements—two kinds of currents which, incidentally, often seem to flow in parallel. One of Paris' hottest names for a prolonged period of time was Franz Anton Mesmer (1734–1815). Mesmer was a German doctor who had built his practice on the notion of 'animal magnetism.' In Latin, 'anima' means soul, life, animal and living being. In the tractate *Propositions Concerning Animal Magnetism* (1779) Mesmer advances the existence of a kind of cosmic life force, a vital fluid, connecting 'the heavenly bodies, the earth, and animated bodies.' It seems fair to think of this proposed fluid as Mesmer's version of *ether*, an omnipresent, subtle substance, traditionally thought to be the 'stuff' that space is filled with. Mesmer believed this fluid to be essential to health, and just as the blood circulates in the body a circulation of this 'vital fluid' also exists. If one was to heal illness, one had to remove blocks and recreate the flow of this fluid. Mesmer attempted to attain this by utilizing powerful magnets and verbal suggestions, combined with the laying on of hands— hence transmitting animal magnetism from the therapist to the patient.

The French matrons, who constituted the majority of Mesmer's patients, were seated in groups of up to 20 in the *baquet*—a large, water-filled oak tub in which were installed magnetic iron rods which would magnetize the whole group at the same time. The treatments were often accompanied by pleasant fragrances and beautiful mood music; a miniature opera composed by no less than Wolfgang Amadeus Mozart had its premiere in Mesmer's garden, with the composer himself, then aged 12, in attendance. The treatment employed by Mesmer and his pupils could trigger substantial emotional and physical reactions in the patients—'crisis' was the term often used—and various forms of trance states would frequently occur.

And as for the effects? There were many reports of 'miraculous' healings, and also of diverse experiences of telepathy and clairvoyance. Such effects were thought to be a part of the *animal magnetism*. Somewhat like ordinary magnetism that has the effect of attracting metal objects, animal magnetism was thought to have the effect of attracting mental objects—thoughts, feelings and information. Mesmer says:

Magnetism can be compared to a sixth sense. The senses are neither defined nor described. They are rather felt. One cannot explain to a blind man what colors are. One would necessitate him to be able to 'feel,' them, that is, to see them. The same holds true for magnetism. It must be mainly transmitted through inward feeling. It is only feeling that can make the theory of it understandable.

In France a royal commission was appointed in 1784 to examine Mesmer's claims. Among the commissioners were the inventor and US ambassador to France Benjamin Franklin (the guy with the lightning rod) and the physician J-I Guillotin (the guy with the guillotine). The study was not primarily conducted to determine whether Mesmer's therapy had any effects—this was already proven beyond reasonable doubt by the many reported healings—but rather if Mesmer's claimed discovery of a magnetic, vital fluid was correct. The committee concluded that such was not the case, and stated that the healings, if not 'charlatanry,' could be ascribed to the 'imagination.'

This, then, must be said to be a modern conclusion, as it is now mostly assumed that what created mesmerism's diverse effects was suggestion, and only suggestion. As with so many therapeutic techniques, imagination/suggestion/placebo probably was a highly significant factor in Mesmer's treatments. But from the perspective of this book—that psi could, in fact, be real—we shouldn't ignore the possibility that Mesmer may have been an accomplished healer, or, in the terms of mesmerism, a man charged with *animal magnetism* (this *is* an amusing expression!). We should also be open to the possibility that the telepathic and clairvoyant experiences so often reported could have been real. Trance states, which often occurred with Mesmer's treatments, are known to be 'psi-conductive,' i.e. they facilitate the occurrence of psi phenomena. The reason is—as stated above—that such states, for both good and for bad, weaken the mental filters that organize our reality. In chapter 6, we'll take a closer look at this connection.

Mesmer's work aroused scientific interest in countries other than France. In 1812, King Frederick William III of Prussia appointed a commission to investigate the concept of 'healing magnetism,' and, in 1816, the use of this method was approved for medical purposes. In Berlin in 1817, Karl Christian Wolfart (1788–1832) was appointed professor of 'pathology, therapy, mesmerism and magnetism.' Some decades later, an English commission also got to work. In July 1870, following two years of investigation of 33 people who were each submitted to 50 sessions, the commission had not detected any of Mesmer's vital fluid, but confirmed the occurrence of striking and strange effects, and thus encouraged further research on the subject.

Mesmer's 'miracles' were eagerly discussed at the Parisian café tables, where absinthe's 'green fairy' exercised its alluring enchantments over the patrons' minds, and in the course of time Mesmer became a celebrity exerting influence over large parts of Europe. And even if Mesmer himself was not a particularly revolutionary person, his *concept of health*, emphasizing the creation of harmony via unrestrained flow, and that of healing occurring through crisis, became common stock in the rhetoric of many revolutionaries. To effect the healing of humanity, the unnatural rhythms, creating stagnation and disharmony in the body of society—such as the usurping of the poor by the rich—must be removed, and must be removed now!

Mesmer's impact continues to this very day. The strange phenomena that so often occurred during the treatment sessions conducted by him and his successors gave a far-reaching, perhaps decisive, impulse to the incipient scientific research on hypnosis, trance and psi that took place during the 19th century. Whatever one may think about his theories, he is still to be considered a significant pioneer in hypnosis. And the most widely disseminated, if hidden-in-plain-sight, cultural resonance of Mesmer's influence is our frequent use of a word that can mean *enchant, dazzle, spellbind* and *hypnotize*, namely—*mesmerize*.

2. Indian Intermezzo—Abbé Faria

In Alexandre Dumas' famous novel *The Count of Monte Cristo*, as many readers and/or moviegoers will surely remember, there features a mysterious monk who is said to be

mad; his name is Abbé Faria. In the Château d'If, a grue-
some penitentiary on a small island in the Mediterranean
where France used to deposit its 'enemies of the state,' Faria
assumes the role of mentor for the innocently imprisoned
Edmond Dantès, the future Count of Monte Cristo. Faria
inaugurates Edmond in the deep secrets—of philosophy,
physics and chemistry (and how to make poison...)—and
also reveals where the vast treasure of Cardinal Spada is
hidden, namely on the island of Monte Cristo off the coast
of Tuscany.

But what many probably do not know is that the character of Abbé Faria, as well as the plot of this exciting book,
is taken straight out of real life. José Custódio de Faria
(1756–1819) originally came from Goa in India; he was a
Catholic monk but also a revolutionary, and his involvement
in politics got him into trouble with the French authorities.
He served time as a political prisoner in the Bastille, and, at
least according to one biographer, he may also have spent a
period detained in the dreaded Château d'If.

Faria was an outstanding hypnotist—he was even consulted by Napoleon—and he had an unusually modern approach to hypnosis. Many of his contemporaries perceived
hypnosis to be a subdivision within the occult range of activities, and therefore either tended to write off its effects
altogether (superstitious humbug!) or to misinterpret them
(extraordinarily mysterious!). The same attitudes also applied to the occurrences of clairvoyance and telepathy that
were frequently reported. Faria, who had been a follower
of Mesmer, believed that these phenomena were definitely
real (he had experiences of the kind himself), but held that
mysterious powers or *animal magnetism* à la Mesmer were
not necessary to explain them. Rather, the key to the whole
thing was to be found within the consciousness of the hypnotized, 'the concentrated,' as was the term used by Faria.

Even though he no longer believed in animal magnetism, Faria was in every respect a magnetic personality, and he used his charismatic appearance—his intense eyes, his tall, dark and lean figure, and his mysterious oriental background (he was entitled 'Brahmin' on his visiting card)—for everything that it was worth. And with the contemporary fascination with the oriental and the world of *One Thousand and One Nights*—where powerful Parisian salon hostesses, the *salonnières*, would receive their guests in Eastern fashion, sitting cross-legged on a heap of cushions, sporting a turban and smoking a hookah—Faria's genuinely exotic image was an asset of no little value. The fascination with the Orient is also apparent in *The Count of Monte Cristo*, e.g. Haydée, the Count's beautiful slave-to-become-lover, is from Albania in the Ottoman (Turkish) Empire, and the use of exotic drugs is portrayed. In the wake of Napoleon's Egyptian campaign repatriated soldiers, having settled into oriental habits, stuffed their *narghiles* and *chibouks* and other Eastern smoking apparatus with more than just tobacco, and hashish would in the course of the following decades become fashionable in Paris. Dumas and his friends are known to have smoked *dawamesk*, a blend of hashish, cinnamon, cloves, nutmeg, pistachio, sugar, orange juice, butter and cantharides—some exotic tobacco, that is!

The Parisian 'proto-hippies' were, as goes with the trade, interested in everything exotic, in altered states of consciousness and in the occult. What, then, could be more chic than to be put into a hypnotic trance by a real Indian Brahmin! And Faria did not disappoint: daily he held sessions for approximately 60 people at a time. The gatherings were inundated with people, and during the course of his stay in Paris Faria seemingly hypnotized as many as 5,000 acolytes! Thus he followed suit with Mesmer, making altered states of consciousness, clairvoyance and related phenomena part of the buzz of the day. As we now know, altered states of consciousness—hypnotic trance, ecstasy, meditation, drug use, and other methods of breaking down the boundaries between subject and object—are 'psi-conductive.' The reason is that such states, for both good and for bad, weaken the mental filters that organize our reality.

With his countless therapeutic sessions and his books, Faria gave an impetus to the strong French tradition in hypnosis and suggestion, represented by outstanding figures such as J-M Charcot (pioneering neurologist and Sigmund Freud's teacher in hypnosis), C.R. Richet (Nobel laureate, physiologist and parapsychologist) and Émile Coué (the grand old man of autosuggestion). Faria is even considered by some historians to be *the* founder of medical hypnosis. Thus he can be considered prominent in the history of both parapsychology and the development of self-improvement techniques using autosuggestion to effect changes in one's body, mind and circumstances, such as autogenic training, positive thinking, creative visualization, NLP (Neuro-Linguistic Programming), etc.

3. In the Sibyl's Boudoir— Marie-Anne Lenormand

For 40 years, Paris was the home of Europe's most famous paranormal person, namely the hypnotist, clairvoyant, medium and fortune teller Marie-Anne Lenormand (1772–1843). Her list of clients was both long and wide and included some of the mighty leaders of the French Revolution, namely Robespierre, Saint-Just and Marat. And while all three were still riding high at the pinnacle of their power, she is said to have predicted a swift and brutal death for each of them, a prediction they allegedly received with laughter.

But, within a year—July 1793–July 1794—Marat had been stabbed to death in his bathtub, whereas Robespierre and Saint-Just had lost their heads on the guillotine!

So how did Mlle Lenormand know? Did she just happen to have a superb flair for the murky maneuvers in the labyrinths of power? Did any of her clients provide her with sensitive information? Or are we talking here about *real* precognition, paranormal foresight based on psi? No one knows. But what we do know for certain is that she was a woman of courage, as she dared to throw such grim predictions right in the face of these powerful persons, and later she even challenged Napoleon Bonaparte, the Emperor. Regarding her abilities, she was not in doubt. She saw herself in a direct line of descent from the divinely inspired seers and oracles described in the *Iliad* and the *Odyssey*, who in ancient times had been consulted by kings and commoners, warlords and philosophers. In some of her books—the good lady was both an author and a publisher—she consequently referred to herself as 'the Sibyl' (i.e. the Oracle).

According to Alexandre Dumas, both Napoleon and Joséphine, later his consort, had visited the Sibyl's boudoir in a fashionable apartment at 8 Rue de Tournon. In his book *The Whites and the Blues*, Dumas gives both a long and colorful depiction of these (separate) sessions, and in Dumas' rendition both Napoleon and Joséphine received clear messages about the spectacular fates that awaited them. As she grabs Joséphine's hand and falls to her knees, the Sibyl exclaims: 'Madame, I do not know your name, I do not know your rank, but I know your future. Madame, remember me when you are—empress.' While Napoleon a little later was told: 'You're going to be Alexander, you're going to be Caesar, you're going to be even more than that—you get to be Atlas who carries the world on your shoulders.' Dumas claims his account is reliable because it is based on information he received directly from the Sibyl's assistant. But this source can hardly be called neutral, so the words that were spoken in the boudoir will probably forever remain a well-kept secret. It is a fact, however, that Joséphine, who actually *did become* Empress, was convinced of Marie-Anne's precognitive abilities for the rest of her life. The two ladies became close friends, and Marie-Anne even published a biography of Joséphine.

And what, then, did Napoleon think about the Sibyl? In hindsight he should have had every reason to be pleased with the prediction (if Dumas' version is reliable). For although he may not have reached Alexander's or Caesar's (or Atlas') level, there was no other ruler in that era that even came close to having Napoleon's charisma, and who exerted such military and cultural influence. But still it seems he was not at all comfortable with the Sibyl's presence in the capital, and some time after he came to power, he tried to end all contact between the two friends, Marie-Anne and Joséphine. He later expelled the Sibyl from Paris on occasions—the reason was apparently that she had ventured to prophesy his downfall on the basis of his acquisition of a new female companion, namely Archduchess Maria Amalia of Austria, and also the defeat of his troops in Russia. This liaison, which primarily was initiated because Napoleon wanted an heir, made him abandon Joséphine (who for her part had already been unfaithful to him with a young cavalry officer).

Perhaps Napoleon himself has given us a key to understanding why he, *the boss of all bosses*, felt threatened—so it seems—by the Sibyl. During his final days, when a captive of the British on the island of St Helena, Napoleon made the following confession to his good friend, General Henri Gatien Bertrand, who records in his diaries, *Sketches from St Helena*, that:

She [Mlle Lenormand] drew a picture of this island on a wall panel in an apartment still to be found in Paris, in the Rue de Tournon. She described Longwood and Hudson Lowe for me [i.e. the villa where he was under house arrest, and the British governor of St Helena] ... I knew all this already when I was at the height of my power.

If General Bertrand's retelling is correct, Napoleon claims the Sibyl foretold this unimaginable state of affairs more than 10 years before it occurred! Certainly not bad—not bad at all... It is further known that Mlle Lenormand predicted 'a northern crown' to another of Napoleon's generals, whose name was Jean Bernadotte. And the very same Jean Bernadotte was later crowned King of Sweden and Norway under the name Carl Johan. A letter in which his wife, Queen Desideria, thanks Mlle Lenormand for her prediction is said to be in the ownership of a Swedish noble family.

What, then, was the background for the Sibyl's seemingly impressive accuracy in her predictions? Political flair? Luck? Counterfeit retelling? Or did she really possess an unusual ability of foresight, of premonitions—an ability to receive images and information from a future already laid out there, being present for those who really can 'see'? This idea that the future is, in some sense, already present is common stock within various occult traditions, and has, in fact, also been considered by serious philosophers and scientists. Such a view is today sometimes referred to as 'eternalism,' 'block time' and 'the B-theory of time'—a concept which was expounded in *The Unreality of Time* (1908) by the English philosopher John McTaggart. A significant comment on this view was made some years earlier by the esteemed physicist Oliver Lodge, who declared: 'The events may be in some sense in existence always, both past and future, and it may be we who are arriving at them, not they which are happening.' Special relativity, much in favor with present-day physicists, points to a theory of time similar to B-theory.

Well, be this as it may, one certainly does not have to be psychic to predict that a consensus regarding these matters will not be reached within a foreseeable future!

During her long career, Mlle Lenormand was visited by many a foreign dignitary, including the Duke of Wellington, Tsar Alexander I of Russia, Lady Elizabeth Shelley (mother of the poet) and the great Polish composer Frederic Chopin, as well as flocks of nobles, artists and celebrities from all over Europe. In addition, she was also approached by a good number of ordinary men and women. Mlle Lenormand was obviously a tourist attraction; in our day, many head to the Tuileries Garden when they visit Paris—in those days, a number of them might also have taken a trip to the Sibyl's boudoir. But people came not just for the purpose of entertainment. These were difficult times; first came the French Revolution in 1789, followed by the Reign of Terror; then came the years of the Napoleonic Wars, with their extensive devastation of land and people. And even in peaceful periods diverse diseases posed continual threats on a scale totally unknown to us: tuberculosis was a source of widespread suffering, especially among those living under poor sanitary conditions (it was the cause of about 25 percent of all deaths), while the more democratic flu regularly swept away both high and low, lay and learned. And from the colonies there continually came swarms of murky microbes; for example, the cholera outbreak in Paris in 1832 killed around 20,000 people.

Mlle Lenormand felt that her mission in this quite scary scenario was 'to comfort,' as she said. Because if she could 'see' that everything was going to go well with a brother fighting in the war, or a sister who was ill, this could of course be of great help to the family. She would also give her clients the choice: Would the questioner like to hear about *everything*, or just the good things that she saw? Let's have a look at an example of how the Sibyl comforted one of her celebrity guests.

Karl August Freiherr von Malchus (1770–1840) was an eminent person who held prominent posts; among other things, he was minister of finance in the German state of Württemberg, and he also authored a string of scholarly writings on economics. Moreover, he was a good friend of Ludwig van Beethoven. Von Malchus has extensively described his visit to the Sibyl, which took place in 1814. He decided to put her to the test, and therefore arrived on foot and in disguise, so as not to give her any clues regarding his identity, rank or position. In a small excerpt from their meeting we can read the following:

> For example, she said, 'You nourish great fear related to your family,' which I certainly did, because I knew my wife and my children had arrived safely at Elsen, but whether they had managed to get to Hildesheim, and if so, how it was with them there, I knew nothing about. 'But,' continued the sorceress, 'you can relax with respect to this, for within eight days you will receive a letter which will contain some things that will not be pleasant for you at all, but it will remove any concern with regard to your family.' And in fact, on the eighth day, I received a letter from my wife, where she informed me that she and the children were doing well. While the rest of the contents of the letter were not at all suited to please.

Again we must say: Well guessed by the Sibyl! For even if she knew the schedule for the mail coaches (which in those days could be delayed for many a reason), it was not easy to know when—if at all—a letter would arrive, and it would have been close to impossible to know what news the letter would eventually bring to von Malchus. This episode is but one of the stories he recounts. Again—how can this be so? Perhaps those who, like von Malchus, have written about their meetings with the Sibyl in their diaries or letters (and there are actually quite a few who have done so) were those who happened to visit her on a 'good day' when she managed a hit—based, perhaps, on a mixture of calculation, intuition and luck? Whereas the others—those who met her on a bad day—perhaps bypassed the matter in silence? Well, this we cannot know with certainty. But interestingly enough, we actually know a little about the experiences that some skeptics had in their encounters with her.

One of these skeptics was Narcisse-Honoré Cellier-Dufayel, a law professor who was also editor of a journal in which he had written warnings about charlatans. He went to the Sibyl with the intention of rebuking her for tricking money from the credulous and the poor. But, Professor Cellier-Dufayel became so impressed with all that she could tell him about himself, both about his past and his present, that he left totally confused. And within a year, so much of what she had prophesied about his future had happened that he gave in and was 'converted.' We know this because Cellier-Dufayel went on to become one of Mlle Lenormand's closest friends. He also wrote a biography of her, *The Truth about Mlle Le Normand: Memories, Intimate Revelations of the Mysteries of the Sybil and her Followers or Consultants.*

Let us end our visit in the Sibyl's boudoir with the partly irreverent, partly appreciative description from the pen of another skeptic, the English dandy R.H. Gronow. He records the event—which probably took place during his sojourn in Paris in 1815–1816—in his voluminous memoirs. Gronow was by profession a military man, he was one of England's best marksmen, and he fought in the Battle of Waterloo, where Napoleon—well, met his Waterloo! Whether or not Gronow's pen was mightier than his gun I cannot say, but it sure must have come pretty close—for just look at how he portrays our good lady:

It was impossible for imagination to conceive a more hideous being. She looked like a monstrous toad, bloated and venomous. She had one walleye, but the other was a piercer. She wore a fur cap upon her head, from beneath which she glared out upon her horrified visitors. The walls of the room were covered with huge bats, nailed by their wings to the ceiling, stuffed owls, cabalistic signs, skeletons—in short, everything that was likely to impress a weak or superstitious mind. This malignant-looking Hecate had spread out before her several packs of cards, with all kinds of strange figures and ciphers depicted on them.

Her first question, uttered in a deep voice, was whether you would have the grand or petit jeu, which was merely a matter of form. She then inquired your age, and what was the color and the animal you preferred. Then came, in an authoritative voice, the word 'Coupez,' repeated at intervals, till the requisite number of cards from the various packs were selected and placed in rows side by side. No further questions were asked, and no attempt was made to discover who or what you were, or to watch upon your countenance the effect of the revelations. She neither prophesied smooth things to you nor tried to excite your fears, but seemed really to believe in her own power. She informed me that I was un militaire, that I should be twice married and have several children, and foretold many other events that have also come to pass, though I did not at the time believe one word of the sibyl's prediction.

Mlle Lenormand was undoubtedly the most famous, but by no means the only, practitioner of the 'black arts' in the 'City of Lights.' The authorities tried to impose limitations, but the 'wild crop' of occultism—the ideas, the practices—flourished nonetheless in post-revolutionary France, and the peculiar, nocturnal aroma of these 'cultural belladonna-flowers' also seeped deep into the velvet curtains of the spectacular Parisian lounges. Francis W. Blagdon's *Paris As It Was and As It Is*, an English eyewitness account from 1803, says: 'At the present day, the ambulating magicians frequent the Old Boulevards, and there tell fortunes for three or four sous...' Quality-conscious customers, however, despised such low-grade charlatans and instead sought out the

> *fortune tellers of a superior class, who take from three to six francs, and more, when the opportunity offers... Formerly, none but courtesans here drew the cards [for fortune-telling]; now, almost every female, without exception, has recourse to them. Many a fine lady even conceives herself to be sufficiently mistress of the art to tell her own fortune; and some think they are so skilled in reading futurity in the cards, that they dare not venture to draw them for themselves, for fear of discovering some unwanted event.*

Since there were reports of a good number of astonishing 'magnetic' events—telepathy, clairvoyance, precognition, healing—skilled scientists became engaged in exploring the field. It would probably be fair to say this constitutes the starting point of modern parapsychology. These early efforts can hardly be said to have resulted in significant or lasting conclusions, probably because both the conceptual and the physical apparatus were undeveloped. But as a curiosity, let me mention that a commission of inquiry, appointed by the Academie nationale de médecine, in 1831 concluded that some people actually possess 'medical clairvoyance'—the ability to diagnose correctly based on clairvoyance. Whether the commission's successors in today's National Academy of Medicine would accede to this conclusion, I cannot say.

Hymns to the Night— Occultism and Science in German Romanticism

We are more closely connected with the invisible than with the visible.

~ Novalis

Bewitched by the Moon

Mesmer's activities gave impetus to the dawning research on the paranormal also in Germany, his homeland. Many observations regarding psi experiences from this period are embodied in the journal *Archiv für den Thierischen Magnetismus* (*Archive for Animal Magnetism*). The orientation in the direction of the paranormal fitted well with the dominant cultural movement of the day, namely Romanticism. One could perhaps say that while the philosophers of the French Enlightenment cherished reason, the bright day and the golden sunlight, the German Romantics instead hymned oceans of emotion, the dark night and the silvery moonlight.

As part of their reaction to what they saw as the rigid reason of Enlightenment, the German Romantics worshipped all that was mysterious, the enigmatic shadow side of our own psyches—dreams, sleepwalking, possession, irrationality, intuition, inspiration, imagination, and of course the paranormal phenomena.

In accord with this emotional and experiential approach to the world, Friedrich Schleiermacher, the main Protestant theologian of the Romantic era, declared that what constitutes one's relationship with God is neither citing a credo nor knowledge, nor morality, but rather it is *Feeling*. Romantic piety had a markedly pantheistic and mystical trait. God was less and less perceived as a heavenly Father, a strict Judge or a rational Watchmaker, and more and more as an eruptive Cosmic Force, surging forth, continuously creating the Universe and unfolding itself through the life of its creatures. 'The Spirit slumbers in the stone, dreams in the plant, awakens in the animal and gains consciousness in Man,' as Friedrich von Schelling, one of Romanticism's great philosophers, expressed it. Based on such an understanding, God and Nature can almost be seen as two sides of the same coin: 'Nature is visible Spirit, Spirit is invisible Nature,' as Schelling says. The German Romantics' emphasis on emotions, pantheism, nature, and also their fascination with the occult, makes it reasonable to regard them as the true forefathers and -mothers to modern 'alternative' movements such as the hippies and various aspects of the New Age.

Johann Wolfgang von Goethe— the Paranormal Poet

Magic rituals and astrological beliefs are important ingredients in *Faust*, the main work of Johann Wolfgang von

Goethe (1749–1832), Germany's greatest poet. Moreover, Goethe has related a number of personal experiences with the paranormal. In the famous conversations with his student/friend/secretary, Johan Peter Eckermann, Goethe revealed that he had experienced telepathy several times with his sweethearts (there were quite a few of them…). He also says: 'Between lovers the magnetic force [Goethe is here using the language of mesmerism] is particularly strong and works even over a very large distance.'

In the autobiographical work *Poetry and Truth*, Goethe describes an exciting vision in which he, as he later came to understand it, got a glimpse many years into the future. After a guilt-ridden split-up with his then-lover, Goethe rides off in full gallop through the deep forests along the border between Germany and France. Suddenly he has a vision where he sees his *Doppelgänger*, his double, riding toward him, wearing a special type of suit that Goethe himself had never worn. The color was 'pike-grey and with a little gold.' Eight years later, Goethe is riding down the same forest trail where his double had once appeared—and now it is *Goethe* who is wearing this very distinctive garment! Goethe recounts that this happened without any conscious planning, so it was not just a staging of a 'self-fulfilling prophecy.'

According to a report stemming from Dr August Klemm, Goethe also experienced an interesting and amusing episode in Weimar in 1813. After many hours of working together in a laboratory, Goethe and Klemm are having an evening saunter. Suddenly Goethe starts to behave strangely, gesturing and talking, as if someone is standing in front of him, although the street is completely empty. Klemm becomes worried, wondering if the great poet is in a daze. For listening to Goethe's words, he realizes that Goethe is experiencing the presence of his good friend, the renowned musicologist Friedrich Rochlitz (who according to their reports was supposed to be in Frankfurt). Goethe starts to laugh, and exclaims: 'Truly, it's him! My friend Friedrich!—here in Weimar!—But for God's sake man, what's the matter with you? In my dressing gown—with my slippers you're walking here, right in the middle of the street?'

After the vision had vanished, both Goethe and Klemm were a little uneasy, wondering if it could have been some sort of bad omen. But when they arrived at Goethe's home a little later, they had a pleasant surprise: There was Rochlitz, sitting on the couch—wearing Goethe's dressing gown and slippers! He had come on an unannounced visit, and being wet after a rainfall he had taken the liberty of borrowing some pieces of clothing from Goethe's closet. After a glass of wine Goethe told Rochlitz about the vision he'd had during his stroll with Klemm. Rochlitz then related that at that very same time he had dozed off on the couch, dreaming vividly about meeting Goethe, who in the dream had exclaimed: 'In my bathrobe and slippers in the street?'

A most charming tale! And, if the particulars are reliable, it could also be perceived as a stunning example of clairvoyance and/or telepathy; it would seem that the two men had a shared experience—participating in each other's worlds, even if physically separated. In chapter 8 we will find that there are things that may indicate that dreams create favorable conditions for this type of transfer of information.

Paranormal Philosophers

The great Romantic philosophers, such as Hegel, Fichte, Schelling and Schopenhauer, have all written about occult phenomena, usually in the affirmative, meaning that they saw these occurrences as objectively real and not as subjective chimera. Hegel, often regarded as the most influential philosopher of his day, says that there can be a magical tie 'between friends, especially female friends with delicate nerves (a tie which may go so far as to show "magnetic" phenomena), between husband and wife and between members of the same family.' Hegel also writes that under the influence of animal magnetism it may happen that the spirit 'frees itself from the constraints of time and space, and from all finite contexts.' Here he refers to what we would call telepathy and clairvoyance. Thus Hegel regards paranormal phenomena as real. He also considers them to be of great importance insofar as they show mechanistic philosophy (i.e. the philosophy of his competitors) to be flawed, being unable to account for such phenomena. But Hegel also thought occult phenomena to be regressive 'stuff' that typically would take place with those lacking mental balance—when the spirit/thinking becomes entwined with soul/emotions in an unsound way—and he therefore refers to such experiences as *Krankheit*, i.e. illness.

Arthur Schopenhauer, philosophy's grim pessimist, was convinced of the reality of telepathy, clairvoyance, precognition and magic. He thought all phenomena to be 'branches on the same trunk'—a view congruent with much modern parapsychology, where psi is often regarded as being basically *one* phenomenon (consciousness transcending Space, Time and Causality). Schopenhauer's personal library contained more than 100 books on paranormal topics, and he has also related his own experiences of this kind. One is a charming little telepathic episode from a dinner in Milan. His 'ravishing hostess' had asked him if, based on telepathy, he was able to determine on which three numbers she had placed her bet in the ongoing Lottery (it was possible to choose between a great many numbers). Schopenhauer says that, almost as if in a trance, he 'correctly provided the first and second, but provided the third one incorrectly because her enthusiasm confused me; then I came to myself, and began to reflect.' Schopenhauer took the incident as a sign he had a smattering of paranormal abilities.

He also relates an episode of what perhaps may have been a precognitive dream: One day Schopenhauer spilled ink in such a quantity that it flooded his desk and ran down onto the floor. He thereupon called on a housemaid to help him clean up. While doing the job, she told him that she had dreamed about this very situation—her helping him to wipe up ink from the floor—the previous night. Schopenhauer answered that he simply didn't believe her. But the girl insisted, and said she had also told one of the other maids of this dream. When this second girl entered the room shortly after, Schopenhauer questioned her right away—before the two girls had any chance to confer—and she confirmed that yes, sure enough, she had been informed about this ink-cleaning dream earlier that same day!

Schopenhauer recounts this little episode, which he swears to be true, in support of his idea that all things in this world happen by necessity, even trifles.

In Schopenhauer's *Essay on Spirit-Seeing and Related Issues* (1851) we get a sense of the great importance of the paranormal in the first half of the 19th century in *Deutschland der Dichter und Denker*—the Germany of poets and thinkers. Schopenhauer also makes the acerbic quip: 'Whoever nowadays doubts the reality of animal magnetism and the related clairvoyance ought not to be called unbelieving but rather uninformed.' Schopenhauer, who had an unusual talent for eloquence and wit, is often quoted as saying: 'All truth runs through three stages. First, it is ridiculed or distorted. Then it is combated. And finally, it is assumed to be self-evident.' It seems that he believed this to be the case also for 'magnetic' phenomena, but that the third stage had not yet quite occurred.

The Doctors Arrive

But the gentlemen (unfortunately there were very few women) poets and thinkers were not so much concerned with the practical as with the philosophical aspects of the occult: What do such experiences and phenomena tell us about human beings, about the relationship between people, and about Life and the World? The physicians, however, who now took to the task, had a more practical approach. One of the key figures in the field was Dr Justinus Kerner (1786–1862). He was also a poet, and combined scientific criticism with sensitivity in his approach to psi (as elsewhere, I will, for the sake of simplicity, use the term anachronistically). One of his major works is a 'medical biography' of the influencial clairvoyant mystic Friederike Hauffe. Kerner was a highly accomplished author, admired by many, including the great Danish philosopher and writer, Soren Kierkegaard.

Dr Carl Gustav Carus (1789–1869), a friend of Goethe's and one of the era's most versatile scholars, was, in addition to being a physician, also a psychologist, a philosopher and a painter. Carus had immersed himself in Mesmer's work, and had conducted his own research on visionary dreams, sleepwalking, clairvoyance and possession. The origin of these and related spiritual activities, Carus suggested, was located in a layer in the psyche he believed to exist below the threshold of consciousness, namely 'the unconscious.' Though he did not invent the term, Carus is, along with Schelling, the person who is usually credited with introducing this important concept in philosophy—a concept that about half a century later entered the vernacular thanks to Sigmund Freud, the father of psychoanalysis. Psychoanalysis and parapsychology have on several occasions promoted ideas closely resembling those of Carus, and which probably have been inspired by, if not taken from, him.

Die deutsche Gründlichkeit, the German thoroughness, began to fasten its grip around the paranormal from the 1870s onward with the launch of the journal *Psychische Studien* (*Psychic Studies*); for the ensuing 50 years this would be the main journal of parapsychology in Germany. A noteworthy episode in the intersection between occultism and parapsychology—'the paranormal tango'—from this period was the astrophysicist Dr Friedrich Zöllner's investigation of the famous and infamous American medium Henry Slade in 1877–78. Slade had been convicted of fraud in England (the judgment had a somewhat flimsy basis, though, and is said to have been primarily based on prejudice). Nevertheless, Slade had impressed both scientists and skeptics: The physicist and Nobel laureate Lord Rayleigh once brought along a magician to a demonstration of Slade's, but neither of them were able to understand how he produced his effects. Slade was later tested by Samuel Bellachini, Germany's most famous magician. After the test, Bellachini issued a signed statement where he declared that it was 'impossible' that Slade's effects could stem from tricks or sleight of hand, and that it would therefore be up to the physicists to provide an explanation.

Zöllner, who by the way was an expert in optical illusions, experienced some really strange incidents when he was together with Slade: knots on a string became untied in seemingly inexplicable ways, and messages were written on a blackboard, apparently by a telekinetically steered chalk/slate pencil. Hence he was becoming increasingly convinced that Slade was the real deal. However, Zöllner's positive representation of Slade gave rise, as one would expect, to vigorous debate in parts of the German scientific community, as many thought Slade to be solely an accomplished magician. Zöllner for his part tried to explain the abovementioned and related effects based on the notion that there are more dimensions than the three that for all practical purposes we usually take into account. This concept is sometimes dubbed 'hyperspace,' and the idea has been utilized both in geometry and philosophy, and also in science fiction where it will often be introduced to substantiate the possibility of traveling to distant galaxies.

Zöllner meant that what we experience to be paranormal phenomena could be thought of as 'shadows' thrown into our world from a higher dimension. Perhaps this could be illustrated with what happens when I stick my three-dimensional finger (having length, width and height) through the surface membrane of a puddle (the membrane has length and width, but almost no height). Even if the microorganisms living in the membrane should be extremely intelligent, they would—due to a (near) lack of three-dimensional perspective—be unable to perceive the finger in its entirety, and would most likely perceive my intrusion as a paranormal event.

Mysticism in Many Dimensions

Zöllner's approach to the paranormal is philosophically fascinating regardless of whether Henry Slade was just an accomplished deceiver or a true paragnost. And Zöllner was not the only one imagining a multidimensional universe. The year 1884 saw the release of the classic satirical novel *Flatland: A Romance of Many Dimensions*, written by cleric, grammarian and mathematics teacher, Edwin Abbott. The first part of the book could perhaps best be described as flat-out social satire of certain conditions in Victorian society, while the latter is a brilliant toying with the idea of multiple dimensions.

The protagonist is a Square who lives in Flatland, a world with only two dimensions. We join Square on his adventures, both in his own flat homeland and also in other 'lands', those with fewer dimensions, such as Lineland and Pointland, and those with more, such as Spaceland. In Pointland, the king is completely trapped in his own mind and doesn't really recognize visitors at all, while in Lineland, the king becomes murderously aggressive toward Square because of his utterly nonsensical talk about there being other countries outside Lineland!

Square meets with a Sphere coming from Spaceland, where there are three dimensions as there are in our own world. After initiating him in the mystical third dimension, Sphere exhorts Square to spread the 'Gospel of the Three Dimensions.' Square refuses, however, ignited by his newly acquired insight that each world is embedded within another, larger world, having one more dimension (dot within line, line within square, square within volume). He has thus become convinced that a three-dimensional world cannot possibly be the end of the story, and that there certainly must be 'countries' having even more dimensions!

In the preamble, Square says that he, who has become 'initiated into the mysteries of three dimensions having been previously conversant with only two,' publishes his writings hoping that the readers, living in 'the Celestial region' of three dimensions, will 'aspire yet higher and higher to the secrets of four, five or even six dimensions.' And toward the close of the book, Square says he is living in the hope that his memoirs 'may stir up a race of rebels who shall refuse to be confined to limited Dimensionality.' This surely sounds like an exciting intention!

The idea of multi dimensions can be demonstrated by imagining entering a theater right in the middle of a movie. You would neither know what is to come nor what has already been. While the director obviously has a completely different perspective—from his/her 'higher dimension' the film's whole action, past, present and future, is known. Perhaps our normal experience of the passage of time—revealing Life in sequences, second by second, day by day, much like a long-lasting film—is primarily due to the limitations of the equipment of our 'cinema,' our everyday frame of mind. While in a 'higher dimension,' both past and future can be seen as coexisting in an all-encompassing Presence—the dreams of Brahma, the mind of God—or the like.

This is an old philosophical idea, found in different portrayals, in Europe going back at least to Parmenides (late sixth or early fifth century BCE), whose thesis perhaps best can be summed up as 'It is'! (the totality of Being—past, present, future—IS, whereas change, becoming, and time are just illusions, a play of the senses.) Could it be possible, for example, through altered states of consciousness, to switch perspective and get an expanded view of this ever-present Presence? Perhaps such an expanded view is what we usually call precognition?

However, this would no doubt raise some quite complex philosophical questions as to what extent humans can be said to have free will. For, if the future already exists and can be known by precognition, what then about our ability to make choices? Without attempting to give a satisfactory answer—clearly here is material for shelves of books—let me just briefly air the very simple idea that a glimpse from 'the director's perspective' (if at all possible) might not need to constrain either our experience of the film or our free will.

Perhaps even just the opposite: that we could have the possibility to 'cut and paste,' to make freer and better choices based on the additional information provided by such a glimpse? Like an explorer using binoculars to detect resources and dangers lying ahead, thus becoming able to choose a better route. If so, a glimpse of the future could in fact increase our scope of opportunities, often referred to as 'freedom.' Such an opinion is held by the author and medical doctor Larry Dossey, and suggestions for using precognition in our daily lives can e.g. be found in his book *The Power of Premonitions: How Knowing the Future Can Shape Our Lives*. We'll get back to the exciting as well as frustrating conundrum of precognition in chapter 8 in connection with some laboratory experiments that—surprisingly enough—seem to indicate that at least some form of precognition *is* possible.

While writing this book I have been told a number of spectacular tales, as people trust me to not think they're crazy (they're mostly right), which almost merit a separate book. One story came from a man who had been my schoolmate for 12 years. Today he is a man with responsibility and position, and does not lean toward religion, New Age, and suchlike matters. One night he had been out drinking and became 'three sheets to the wind' (maybe even four…), as the old expression goes. As he was sleeping it off, he dreamt that a voice told him that a (specified and named) friend of his would win the Lottery. About two weeks later he got a call from this friend, and the conversation went something like this: 'Listen up!—I've got something to tell you!' Whereupon my schoolmate replied with a 'taken for granted' tone of voice: 'Yes, I know—you've won the Lottery.' And that was actually what had happened: the friend had won several million kroner! Considering the microscopic statistical probability of such a coincidence—the probability was so small it could even be compared to…well, to winning the

Lottery!—my schoolmate has started to wonder if there, in fact, might be something to the notion of parallel dimensions.

The idea of multiple dimensions is very old in esoteric philosophy. In Kabbalah, the Jewish mysticism, there are statements claiming there may be a thousand parallel dimensions! Paranormal events could then be understood as 'leaks' from a parallel or higher dimension—a bit like when someone is frying egg and bacon next door, and the smell seeps into our flat, or the music on the upper floor is heard through the ceiling. One of the most exciting theories in recent physics is the so-called M-theory, where the innermost building blocks of nature are thought to be membranes. Physicist Ed Witten, who has been crucial in developing this theory, has said that one can let the M stand for Magic, Mystery or Matrix, 'depending on your taste.' Witten, who is sometimes referred to as 'the Einstein of our times,' operates with the occult thought that the world has no fewer than 11 dimensions! And he does not mean these dimensions should only be perceived to be mathematical models, but that several of them may be folded into one another. Demanding stuff, this is! M-theory's multiple dimensions are now used by some as part of the explanation for the paranormal.

The Lights Are Lit by the Thames

Ah, it is the fault of our science that it wants to explain all; and if it explains not, then it says there is nothing to explain.

~ Abraham Van Helsing, vampire hunter, in *Dracula* by Bram Stoker

The late Victorian England saw the rapid emergence of various kinds of occult and esoteric groups. The reasons for this were, among other things, that Christianity had lost part of its power due to the influence of Enlightenment philosophy, and criticism from those engaged in science—biologists, physicists, social theorists, etc. People still asked their questions concerning the larger context and the meaning of Life, but the answers provided by the Churches did not seem as valid as they once were. For example, Darwinism had efficiently undermined (a literal interpretation of) the Bible's account of human origins. Hence, concerning the Meaning of Life there was a nascent philosophical vacuum—a vacuum that attracted alternative approaches to the Mystery. Hence, Europe's occult undercurrents resurged from their subcultural riverbeds: Hermeticists, Kabbalists, Rosicrusians and Freemasons were again to have their say and way. The different traditions also intermingled and entered into new relationships and combinations with one other.

One of the most interesting new occult lodges based on Western hidden traditions was *The Hermetic Order of the Golden Dawn*, started in the late 1880s by the Freemasons Robert William Woodman, William Wynn Westcott and

Samuel Liddell MacGregor Mathers. The Order eventually came to include many notable artists and writers: Gerald Kelly, Sax Rohmer, Algernon Blackwood and Arthur Machen among others. And in 1898, Sir Arthur Conan Doyle, the creator of Sherlock Holmes, also applied for membership. Soon after, however, he withdrew his application. This was because he had received, as he perceived it, an 'astral visitation' (i.e. a paranormal manifestation, an apparition) during which a person on the admissions committee examined him for membership! Conan Doyle experienced this incident both as strange and unpleasant, and even if it convinced him of the powers of the Golden Dawn, he was unnerved, and decided, 'their line of philosophy or development is beyond me.'

Bram Stoker, author of *Dracula*, had friends and associates within the high ranks of the Order, and he himself was said to have been a member. (One cannot quite keep track of these secret societies...). As some readers surely will remember, telepathy and clairvoyance play a role in Stoker's legendary work: Wilhelmina 'Mina' Murray, the female protagonist in *Dracula*, enters into a trance state, where she stays in telepathic contact with Count Dracula. And by exploiting this connection, her friends and the vampire hunter Abraham Van Helsing are able to track the movements of the bloodsucking Count. Later, the poet W.B. Yeats, who was awarded the 1923 Nobel Prize in literature, became Grandmaster (spiritual and ritual leader) of this fascinating Order.

Beyond the influence of Western occultism—which by the way includes the very word 'influence,' which originally referred to the astrological impact of the planets, the emanations 'floating' into the Earth through the ether—there were contributions from Eastern spirituality, primarily from Hinduism and Buddhism. The British had had close dealings with these mighty traditions in the colonies, first and foremost through the acquisition of the Empire's 'jewel in the crown,' namely India. Theosophy, the widespread esoteric system of Madame H.P. Blavatsky (who we'll get back to soon), poured mainly from these Eastern sources. And finally there arose various forms of more 'home-grown' spirituality; most importantly were probably the Spiritualist groups. Spiritualism can in part be regarded as a privatized, bourgeois form of religion: By means of séances one could acquire intimate contact with both the spirit world and deceased loved ones in the safety of one's own home—discreet and comfortable, without having one's nose exposed to the pungent odor of biblical brimstone.

Scholarly circles had often adopted some of the basic philosophical concepts of German Romanticism. And to a much higher degree than traditional Christianity, this Romantic pantheism was experienced as being compatible with both science and the occult. For example, it is striking that Darwin's theory of evolution, which infuriated so many traditional Christians, aroused far less opposition in those circles influenced by the *Weltanschauung* (worldview) of Hegel. Hegel had proclaimed that the world in itself was a developmental process, through which the *Weltgeist* (World Spirit, God) realizes itself, step by step, at ever-higher levels. So if humans should prove to originate from apes—well, where is the problem? It was of course intellectuals of this type, with a predominant interest in both philosophy and science, who first shone the Light of Reason on the occult landscapes.

The Society for Psychical Research—The Paranormal Detective Bureau

It is a capital mistake to theorize before one has data.
Insensibly one begins to twist facts to suit theories, instead
of theories to suit facts.

~ Sherlock Holmes, 'A Scandal in
Bohemia' by Arthur Conan Doyle

In was in 1881 that Sherlock Holmes fetched a good portion of strong shag tobacco from the Persian slipper on the mantelpiece in his apartment in 221B Baker Street. And while the smoke from his pipe rose in grey-blue spirals toward the ceiling, followed by meditative melodies from his Stradivarius violin, Holmes began to shed light on the criminal mysteries that are described in *A Study in Scarlet* (1887). A year later, in 1882, the Society for Psychical Research (SPR) was founded and began to explore its own brand of mysteries, a quest they engage in to this very day. One quite naturally associates Sherlock Holmes with the SPR, not only because of their shared desire to solve mysteries, but also because Holmes' creator, the physician Sir Arthur Conan Doyle, was, for many years, a member of this venerable association, whose purpose is to explore 'events and abilities commonly described as psychic or paranormal, by promoting and supporting important research in this field.'

It is tempting to see it as a symbol of the *Zeitgeist*, the spirit of the age, that this research started in the same period as the city of London (and likewise Paris) began to install electric street lighting on a large scale. The hidden nastiness, the prostitution and the violence, the concealed Victorian nightlife—often symbolized by the serial killer Jack-the-Ripper, though he came a little later—was still shrouded in a mantle of impenetrable smog. No—in the name of health, let there be light and air! In a similar way, the SPR intended to throw the light of science into the hidden, dark territories of the psyche and reveal their occult secrets.

The founders of the SPR were newspaper editor Edmund Rogers and physicist Sir William Barrett. Soon to become important were the prominent philosopher and economist Henry Sidgwick, and historian, philosopher and poet Frederick Myers (who we will return to in chapter 6, on Consciousness). The SPR soon included many of the foremost Victorian scientists, and when the various Nobel committees became established and began distributing their coveted awards, many of these found a home on the mantelpieces of members of the SPR. Thus the SPR was, like other concurrent private academies of science, a distinctly serious club, and many of the members during its first 50 years were political, scientific and cultural celebrities. We'll allow for a little name-dropping to emphasize this point.

In the member archives of the SPR are to be found William Gladstone (British Prime Minister—four times!), Arthur Balfour (philosopher, later Prime Minister), Sir William Crookes (physicist, chemist, pioneer in electricity and radiation), Sir Oliver Lodge (physicist, pioneer in electricity and radio technology), John William Strutt, Baron Rayleigh (physicist, pioneer in sound and radioactivity, Nobel laureate) Sir Joseph J. Thomson (physicist, discoverer of the electron, Nobel laureate). In addition, we find as members the authors Lewis Carroll and Robert Louis Stevenson and the poet Alfred, Lord Tennyson.

Let's drop some more names, now with a French flavor: Under the waving Tricolor we find such members as

Camille Flammarion (astronomer), Marie Curie (physicist and chemist, two times Nobel laureate), Charles Richet (physician, parapsychologist, Nobel laureate) and Henri Bergson (philosopher, Nobel laureate). The great psychiatrists Sigmund Freud and C.G. Jung also signed up with the English club. And finally, in the US, an offshoot of the SPR had around 250 members among the elite of contemporary American intellectuals, scientists, philosophers, doctors and psychologists from the best universities. All in all, the SPR was some society!

A precursor of, and operating in parallel with, the SPR was the Ghost Club, both of which are still in existence. This association was founded in 1862, and members included from the early days such luminaries as Charles Dickens, Sir William Crookes (pioneer of vacuum tubes), Sir Oliver Joseph Lodge (physicist and patent holder for radio) W.B. Yeats and Frederick Bligh Bond of Glastonbury fame. Over the years, several people were members of both the SPR and the Ghost Club, but the latter always had fewer members and operated more or less like a closed lodge until it became modernized and was 'opened up' in 1938 by the psychic researcher Harry Price. Another noteworthy society within the paranormal field was the British National Association of Spiritualists, which was founded in 1873, and which later appointed a scientific committee for the purpose of researching the paranormal. Some members of this association subsequently joined the SPR, which in turn laid down the template for most psychic research for the ensuing decades until J.B. Rhine, the American botanist, in the late 1920s launched his modern statistical methods. Offshoots of the SPR were then formed over large parts of the world. A good website where the SPR regularly publishes new articles can be found at: http://psi-encyclopedia.spr.ac.uk/

A Glimpse of Early Research on Psi

The SPR formed six committees with the purpose of conducting research on various aspects of the paranormal. Topics examined were: thought and emotion transfer (later baptized 'telepathy' by Frederick Myers), mesmerism, hypnotism, clairvoyance, contact with the dead, visions, levitation, and materializations (spirits or physical objects apparently appearing out of thin air). In 1886 the SPR published *Phantasms of the Living* (Gurney, Myers, Podmore)—a weighty tome that has become a milestone in the history of parapsychology. The work took as its starting point 702 reports of apparitions—sightings, visits, apparently by souls/spirits/ghosts of living persons known to the 'visited.' The reports were collected as responses to press appeals. In order to confirm their authenticity, the authors followed up with face-to-face interviews with the percipients who were living all over the country, and also often interviewing their family members and others who might provide supporting testimony. Many of the apparitions were related to 'crisis-telepathy.' The essence of this phenomenon is: When one person gets hit by crisis (injury, shock or death), another—related—person gets a strong sense of this specific crisis. The other person is usually a family member or a close friend, who at the time is far away, often in another city or even another country, and has no customary way of knowing about the crisis (this work was, as we know, released long before telephones existed). Let me illustrate the phenomenon 'crisis-telepathy' with the following example.

The famous polar explorer Roald Amundsen, the first person in the world to reach the South Pole, was convinced he could communicate telepathically with other people;

this he states in his diaries (1924–1925). And maybe he was right? The renowned author Tor Bomann-Larsen describes in his major Amundsen biography a quite thrilling episode involving Mrs Kiss Bennett, a Norwegian woman married to the English timber baron Charles Bennett, who had become Amundsen's flame. In June 1928, Amundsen was taking part in the rescue mission of the downed airship *Italia* that was carrying the Italian explorer Umberto Nobile, when his plane disappeared. Kiss Bennett in a mountain hotel in Norway experienced a telepathic 'visit' from Amundsen:

> *One morning when I just had put on my stockings, I distinctly heard his voice. 'Oh Kiss, now comes the terrible death struggle.' During the next three days I felt his presence in the room so close that I could have touched him. Then suddenly it was all over. I'm sure he died a slow death.*

We now know that Amundsen died on this very journey, probably after having crashed or made an emergency landing close to Bear Island. But Kiss, of course, had no knowledge of this when the 'visit' took place. I took the precaution to contact Bomann-Larsen regarding this unsettling incident. He told me that Amundsen had previously disappeared on a couple of occasions, later to reappear alive and well, and that the prevailing perception at the time of the 'visit' was that Amundsen most likely would return this time too. Bomann-Larsen also said that Kiss' portrayal is found in a diary entry of a relative, and was written down following a conversation with her. The information was, however, passed on in confidence, and Bomann-Larsen therefore has chosen not to disclose the source's identity.

The archives of the SPR are replete with similar reports of 'visits' from beloved ones in crisis. The visits have

manifested themselves in the form of visions, sounds and/
or distinct bodily feelings. The researchers in the SPR suggested a rational explanation: that these experiences should
be understood as telepathy (i.e. the workings of the human
mind) and not as hauntings by spirits or the like. *Phantasms
of the Living* is a huge work of over 1,300 pages: lots of
witnesses were interviewed and public documentation was
collected and signed statements recorded. The critical and
'disrespectful' way (as perceived by many) in which the SPR
researchers approached spiritual matters—for instance their
merciless debunking of the slate writing tricks of the medium William Eglinton, in 1886–87—exposed an incipient
schism within the organization, namely between *spiritualists* on the one side and *scientists* on the other. And within
the following few years many of the 'true believers,' among
them Stainton Moses, a former vice-president, had left the
SPR. So here we see some fiery steps in the aforementioned
'paranormal tango'—the passionate and conflicted relationship between occultism and parapsychology.

It was typical of the SPR to conduct their studies in the
grand style. When researching spontaneous hallucinations
in normal, healthy people (something which occurs from
time to time) and trying to identify whether these hallucinations contained telepathic, clairvoyant or precognitive
information, the SPR started out with a base material of no
fewer than 17,000 reports! From these it was estimated that
approximately 10 percent of the hallucinations contained elements of telepathy, clairvoyance and/or precognition.

The SPR also examined the quality of spiritual mediums,
and they became both famous and infamous for their 'debunking' of the revered Madame Blavatsky (1831–1891),
the charismatic founder of Theosophy. Theosophy is an extensive esoteric system which is based on a variety of both
Eastern and Western occult sources, and which has been

considerably important for many later esoteric religious groups and for the New Age movement as a whole. Madame Blavatsky acted as a medium who baffled her followers by conjuring the spirits of Koot Hoomi and Morya, two Tibetan spiritual masters. Occasionally, the masters would communicate through letters that apparently materialized right out of thin air. But—the scrutinizing eyes of Richard Hodgson, the researcher who was dispatched to India by the SPR to investigate the case, detected that there were thin, *paper thin*, cracks in the ceiling in the room where the letters from Koot Hoomi miraculously had materialized. And Madame's assurance that such cracks were common according to the building standards of the location at that period proved to be of no help whatsoever. This was because her housekeeper, Emma Coulomb, confessed to be an accomplice, and to have dropped the letters through the crack... After further investigation Hodgson wrote a 200-page report where he declared Blavatsky to be 'one of the most advanced, gifted and interesting impostors in history.' It was probably not easy for her to decide if she should feel flattered or ashamed by such a description!

For the sake of balance, let me add that not everybody agrees with the SPR's assessment of Blavatsky; some have claimed that Emma Coulomb's testimony was not at all trustworthy as she had earlier tried to blackmail Blavatsky. Furthermore, prominent cultural personalities, including Mahatma Gandhi and the present Dalai Lama, have maintained that both the teachings and the humanitarian efforts of the Theosophical Society are highly valuable, notwithstanding the moral flaws of its founder. The Dalai Lama has shown his support by visiting the headquarters of the Theosophical Society in various countries.

The SPR considered parapsychology to be a rigorous science that should follow the most stringent requirements for documentation. William James (1842–1910), one of the most influential psychologists in history, writes that should he be asked to name a scientific journal that has exemplary procedures in identifying facts and exposing flaws, he would refer to the SPR's journal, the *Proceedings of the Society for Psychical Research*. James explains this was because all the witnesses, as far as possible, were personally cross examined, the background facts were checked, and documentation was of the same objective quality as legal abstracts, so that anyone could form an independent picture on the strength of the evidence. Occultist and Nobel laureate in literature W.B. Yeats humorously said that the SPR's researchers were critical and scrutinizing to such a degree that had they been present when the World was created—to make sure that everything proceeded in an orderly fashion—they would have given God performance anxiety to such an extent that he would have been unable to complete the job!

Three Approaches to Psi— Laboratory, Nature, Spirituality

If we were to outline the ways which, from James' days and until our own time, we have related to psi in a serious way, we might talk about three main approaches: The first has its focus on experiments and is keen to engage in rigorous science on the paranormal. The second has a more natural practical approach to psi in relation to lived life. While the third approach emphasizes the spiritual aspect of psi, seeing paranormal phenomena as possible clues and connections to *the* big picture.

1. *Laboratory*: This approach claims that paranormal phenomena should be investigated in the same way as any other natural phenomena, thus the use of rigorous laboratory experiments is the best way to go. In the late 1920s, J.B. Rhine, the American botanist, launched rigorous statistical methods to evaluate telepathy, clairvoyance and precognition related to the drawing of cards. Nowadays, refined methods and advanced apparatus are utilized, as for instance MRI and fMRI (types of brain scans). Widespread are also experiments involving so-called *ganzfeld* (German, meaning 'total field'), where the test subjects' vision, hearing and other perceptions will be muted as far as possible. The idea is that subduing sensory 'noise' will make it easier to pick up the psi 'vibes,' such as inner images containing possible telepathic information. One avid 'laboratorian' is the engineer and psychologist Dean Radin, head of research at the Institute of Noetic Sciences. This is an important research center founded by Apollo 14 astronaut and MIT engineer Dr Edgar Mitchell (who, by the way, during his stay in space personally tested out the possibility of making telepathic contact with people on earth—reportedly with positive results!).

2. *Nature*: The second camp rather concurs with Jean-Jacques Rousseau and his classic call to 'return to Nature.' The psi-abilities (to the extent they are real) are developed as part of the natural evolution of humans. In prehistoric times the point of such abilities most probably was to survive: to avoid danger, to cry out for help, and to find partners. Therefore eventual psi-abilities will most likely be activated in demanding situations similar to those experienced by humans since prehistoric times. The epitome of such original psi is *crisis telepathy*, which quite often has been reported to occur in connection with shock, injury or death, as in the case with Roald Amundsen and Kiss Bennett mentioned earlier

in this chapter. The reason that the SPR felt that it was its responsibility to investigate this phenomenon was precisely the multiple accounts of it that were circulating. Crises are prototypical of a human *Urerfahrung*—an original experience—where telepathy possibly could have been of use to summon help from kinsmen. Thus a realistic study of the psi-abilities, the Nature camp argues, must take this into account. And for just this reason psi should not primarily be studied in sterile laboratories but in real life—in our contact with other human beings and with animals. Some anthropologists take this approach to psi, as does the English biologist and former Cambridge fellow Rupert Sheldrake.

3. *Spirituality*: And then we have the third faction, which emphasizes the spiritual aspect of psi. From spiritual traditions worldwide there are reported innumerable psi experiences taking place in connection with meditation, dance, prayer, trance, ecstasy, etc. Based on these accounts it seems psi typically tends to occur when people are searching intensely for Meaning, probing the depths of their soul. This aspect of psi was, as we saw in the previous chapter, underscored by C.G. Jung, and is also common in other branches of transpersonal psychology, i.e. the schools of psychology that emphasize our connectedness to the Whole. Among researchers with this orientation psi phenomena is often seen as a sign that 'what in us that is bigger than us' (the archetypes, our higher self, our spiritual guides, etc.) has been activated. Thus they will typically connect with spiritual traditions providing a framework for dealing with and utilizing such experiences, as shamanism, yoga, Sufism, Kabbalah, etc. Important figures within the transpersonal, psi-positive camp are psychiatrists C.G. Jung, Roberto Assagioli and Stanislav Grof, and psychologists Stanley Krippner, Charles Tart and William Braud.

There is not necessarily any implacable enmity between these three camps; some researchers can stroll peacefully between the three. The aforementioned Stanley Krippner was involved in laboratory experiments on dream telepathy for many years (we'll get back to this research in chapter 8). But Krippner has also done paranormal fieldwork (in Brazil), and moreover he is open to the spiritual aspect of psi (as a possible way to connect with 'the More,' with the bigger picture). However, even though there are no absolute divisions, this tripartite model nonetheless is of help to clarify different strains of thought.

The 'laboratorians' will not necessary hold studies by, say, anthropologists and ethnologists to be of immense value, as they are not fully replicable, nor are the results measurable in the positivistic sense (no grams, centimeters, ounces, inches, degrees, etc.). Of what help to science is it that people who are interviewed—the so-called 'qualitative method'—tell of being cured after visiting a healer, when there aren't any brain scans, either of the healer or of the patients, to find out what is going on physiologically? (Let me parenthetically add that even if the research is not unambiguous, some studies indicate that there likely will be increased theta activity, i.e. more brainwaves with 4–7 cycles per second.)

Further, the laboratorians tend not to be forthcoming as to how psychics, healers, soothsayers, gurus, etc. carry out their 'black arts.' For mantra chanting can easily drown out the quiet, sober voice of reason, and fogs of incense cover areas that ought to lie bathed in the clear, cool light of science.

Hardliners in the Nature camp highlight the utter irrelevance of sitting in a lab, guessing about drawing cards, throwing dice, color blinks on a screen, and the like. Building research on such petty games, they say, reveals a complete lack of sound judgment. Psi should be dealt with *existentially*, investigated as the tools in our primeval survival kit, as prehistoric alarm systems and mobile phones. And the Spiritualists are quick to point out these faculties lie at the very base of human consciousness and transcend the limitations of the ego, and might therefore serve as hotlines to the depth of the soul, to Being, Life, the Universe, Cosmos, the Great Spirit, God.

Both the latter approaches to psi—the Natural and the Spiritual—seem to concur very well with the large number of reports indicating that *intense engagement*—whether in war or in love, in crisis or in ecstasy—was a contributing factor for psi to manifest. For instance, the Scottish healer Bruce MacManaway claimed that his healing abilities became activated during World War II in connection with a grenade strike that badly injured one of his comrades. Whereas the opposite state of mind—boredom, that is— seems to be an impediment to psi function. Laboratory research on psi, consisting of endless repetitions for hours and days on end, could therefore perhaps be compared to—if I may be allowed—a sexologist doing erection research on test subjects immersed in a pool of ice-cold water. The frame conditions in the experiment effectively prevent the phenomena in question from arising (so to speak...).

This example is much more than a pure—or impure— wisecrack; the significance of the frame conditions seems to be reflected in the fact that different psi researchers get very different results. This fact is so palpable that the English psychologist and psi-researcher Dr Adrian Parker, professor of psychology at the University of Gothenburg, Sweden, has dubbed it 'The First Law of Parapsychology.' It turns out that scientists who are enthusiastic and have expectations that, say, telepathy or clairvoyance will occur tend to get more 'hits' than researchers with the opposite attitude. And take note: this does not *necessarily* have to do with over- or under-reporting, or differences in the honesty or competence of the researchers. Perhaps it would be apt to compare it with team sports: A coach with confidence in the team's possibilities, who creates enthusiasm, will as a rule get them to perform better and score more often than a skeptical coach. And given that they actually exist, psi-powers will most probably, like all other human faculties, be influenced by one's state of mind. It seems obvious that if the conductor of the experiments—'the coach'—has negative expectations this will hardly create a state of mind optimally 'psi-conductive.'

We will have a closer look at the three main approaches to psi—*Laboratory, Nature, Spirituality*—elsewhere. *Laboratory* has been awarded most of chapter 8, where we look at some exciting experiments supporting the psi hypothesis. *Nature* is discussed in chapter 9, and *Spirituality* is briefly discussed in chapter 4 in conjunction with C.G. Jung and transpersonal psychology, and will also be commented on again in depth in chapter 9.

Snapshots from Paranormal Norway

As the reader has probably already noticed this book is markedly oriented toward the international; haven't we already visited all continents at least once?—I think so, and more is yet to come! But as the author is Norwegian, I think it may enrich the palate if I give a little mention to 'stuff' from Norway. Due to space considerations I'll restrict myself to serve just a little paranormal finger food and some tidbits, but as we know, small canapés can sometimes be just as satisfying as a dinner!

Research and the Paranormal

My background is in the humanities, where research on the paranormal has focused not so much on the *phenomena* as on the *stories* about them, and where the patterns in storytelling, mythological motives, ideas about magic, etc. are eagerly analyzed. While all this may be well and good, the downside is that tales about psi are often reduced to exercises in literary theory—and suddenly one's own map has become much more important than the terrain! I don't concur with such an approach, and as the reader perhaps may have noticed my focus is solely on *what* is told about the paranormal and not on *how* it is told.

From the 1990s onwards Norwegian paranormal research has been mainly conducted within the framework of social science and the focus has often been on—forgive me, ye sociologists!—trivial stuff such as changes in society's belief systems and the like. Sociologists often try to determine the reasons for people believing in paranormal phenomena by asking 'diagnostic' questions, such as '*Why* do people believe in such things as healing, clairvoyance and spirits?' And the answers sociologists tend to find—that people believe in the paranormal because of, say, the estrangement of modern men and women, the privatization of religion, the yearning for resacralization (that the World again become holy), etc.—only serve to uphold the perception of paranormal phenomena as *symptoms* (of cultural and/or personal crisis).

Though not bluntly false, such a view on the paranormal is—in my perhaps not-so-humble opinion—as limiting as it is boring. I'll give the sociologists a clue for free: the reason why people believe in such things is that quite often they have experienced them...

So—paranormal research in Norway has focused on the stories and on society and there has been surprisingly little scholarly interest in the paranormal *per se*. Now, why is that? Well, the most likely reason seems to be the *stigma* that goes with superstition, or 'parapsychosis' as it was humorously dubbed by the playwright and critic Helge Krog. The prominent poet and translator André Bjerke is one of the few scholars who has publicly confessed to a keen interest in the paranormal and he once gave a witty description of the abovementioned stigma:

> *It is more dangerous for a professor to be caught red-handed doing research [on the paranormal] than it is for a Conservative politician to be found dead drunk in a brothel. What hitherto has dictated university science's sentiment towards parapsychology is an anxious sidelong glance towards colleagues: 'If it becomes known that I've seen a ghost, I'm done for at the faculty.'*

This is more than just a joke. I once spoke with a respected university professor, trying to convince her about going public with her *real* views on clairvoyance (which she is convinced is real). It was all but easy... The 'emperor's wrath' as described in chapter 3—i.e. thumbs down from colleagues, loss of prestige, position and pennies—ruthlessly rules the land! So even if Norway in some respects may be a country of otherness, most scholars are pretty much as scholars anywhere else, welcoming—for somewhat different reasons—neither polar bears nor paranormal phenomena into their offices!

Scholarly Mavericks

The Norwegian Society for Psychical Research, which today is called the Norwegian Parapsychological Society, was founded in 1917 and modeled on the SPR, the Society for Psychical Research, with which we have become acquainted earlier in this chapter. So last summer the Norwegian Parapsychological Society celebrated its 100 years jubilee—hooray! But as research on psi has had low status, ambitious scientists for their own good have mostly stayed far away from these muddy matters, and a proper research milieu was never established. Nonetheless, there have been a few skilled academics who—to the detriment rather than to the development of their careers—have engaged in parapsychology.

Harald K. Schjederup: Jack of Many Trades—Master of All!

The most prominent parapsychologist was perhaps the versatile philosopher, psychologist and psychoanalyst Harald K. Schjelderup (1895–1974). Schjelderup, who had also studied nuclear physics, was tenured as professor of philosophy at the University of Oslo in 1922 at the age of just 27. In 1928 his professorship was restructured and subsequently he became Norway's first professor in psychology. Schjelderup published numerous books and scientific articles and was also internationally recognized. The Norwegian Biographical Encyclopedia states that Schjelderup was 'above anyone else the one who built up psychology as a clinical discipline and university subject at the University of Oslo.' In his honor the premises of the Department of Psychology is named the Harald Schjelderup House.

Schjelderup, then, was definitely no fool; rather he was quite ingenious. But he had his occult side... In addition to his conventional respectable scholarly work Schjelderup for many years headed the Norwegian Parapsychological Society. His research within this field can be found summarized in an excellent book, *The Secret Man: Unconscious and Unknown Forces in the Life of the Soul*, where he theorizes about and relates multiple (seemingly) telepathic incidents from his clinical practice. The book has been reprinted several times and is established as *the* point of reference in Norwegian parapsychological literature. Links to the free download of this and the other Norwegian books mentioned below can be found in the bibliography.

Arvid Aas: The Psychic Psychologist

One of Schjelderup's most gifted students was Arvid Aas (1925–1969), who went on to become Norway's first professor in *clinical psychology* (which focuses on diagnosis/treatment). It was Aas' own psi-experiences that made him change his studies from medicine to psychology, as he repeatedly had dreams that were seemingly precognitive. For example, some weeks before his graduation in high school Aas had a dream that revealed to him the topic he would be tested on in his mathematics exams. On the basis of the dream Aas went to his teacher and asked whether he considered this specific theme to be a likely subject for the upcoming test, but the teacher replied in the negative. Nevertheless, the dream proved true, and Aas, who had listened to his dream rather than his teacher, was more than usually prepared—'paranormally well prepared' could perhaps be the *mot juste*—and thus got a good grade! Aas was the main editor of the Festschrift for Harald Schjelderup's 70th birthday, called *Research Journeys in the Depths of the Mind*. If he had not passed away quite early in his career, Aas would most likely have further developed the parapsychological lifework of Schjelderup.

Georg Hygen: Biologist of Mystical Habitats

The Norwegian scientist who, in addition to Schjelderup, was most systematically engaged in the paranormal was biologist Professor Georg Hygen (1908–1994). For several years he was president of the Norwegian Parapsychological Society. Hygen founded the society's journal *Parapsychological Notes*, and authored, edited and initiated a string of books within the field. He also wrote *Vardøger: Our National Paranormal Phenomenon*. Vardøger, which seemingly is more common in Norway than in most other countries, means that a person's approach is heard—say the sound of a car stopping outside, the opening of an entrance door, footsteps on the stairs—well before the arrival actually occurs. Hygen also wrote a popular book about telepathy, *Telepathy: Our Innate Cell Phone*.

Three Cases from the Field

The Snåsa Man

Norway has had from the Viking age a tradition of people who have 'warm hands' (healers) and the ability to 'see' (psychics). In rural areas this tradition is still alive, and several well-documented biographies have been written about people with such powers from our own times, e.g. Marcello Haugen, Lodvar Kaarstad, Anna Elisabeth Westerlund, Paul Hagerup, Ivar Flatmo, etc.

Today's most prominent healer and psychic is without comparison Joralf Gjerstad (b.1926), the so-called 'Snåsa Man,' named after the village where he lives. First and foremost Gjerstad is famous as a healer; he has received patients from several countries and during his long career has reportedly had more than 40,000 visitors! Gjerstad has also been consulted many times as a clairvoyant, assisting the Red Cross and the police in searching for lost persons. In 2008 Gjerstad rose to almost meteoric fame after his life was penned by the renowned biographer Ingar Sletten Kolloen, who has also written about Knut Hamsun. In the aftermath, Gjerstad toured the country for many months and thus became a household name in Norway. It is probably no exaggeration to say that at least once a week one of the big newspapers run a story about the 'Snåsa Man.'

Gjerstad has never taken any money for his services, believing that his claimed faculties are gifts from God and thus should be shared with others for free. He is generally very well liked, coming across as genuinely humble, free of the self-aggrandizement so typical of many 'gurus.' And having also been a local politician for the Labor Party, Gjerstad is often seen as the miracle man 'from the people and for the people.' He has even received the King's Medal of Merit in silver for his unselfish services. But of course, there has also been some controversy; the avid skeptic Ronnie Johanson has written a couple of books, claiming that the healings are due to the placebo effect, and that Gjerstad has accepted gifts as payment-in-disguise. Further, that Gjerstad is not to be trusted as he, according to Johanson, has told different—

contradictory—versions of episodes involving his alleged abilities in clairvoyance and precognition.

In 2016 the award-winning filmmaker Margreth Olin released a moving documentary about Gjerstad, where we follow him meeting and treating a series of patients, young and old. The film also has a section with follow-up interviews carried out a few months later. Some patients tell about initially feeling better, but without having experienced any long-term improvements. Whereas others claim that some of the positive effects are—at least so far—lasting. We shall look at some seemingly inexplicable events concerning the Snåsa Man in later chapters.

With respect to the international scene, let me mention that the Snåsa Man—who reportedly predicted the assassination of President John F. Kennedy a few days before it happened—has recently made the eerie prediction that the 45th President of the United States, Donald Trump, will suffer the same fate! In an interview with the local newspaper *Namdalsavisa* on January 17, 2017, the Snåsa Man says: 'They are going to get him. Trump will be shot.' He further says: 'Yes, I am disappointed with the Americans. They have made a scary choice.' With a little help from our multilingual friend Google Translate it should be possible for English speakers to read this—largely biographical, and non sensationalist—interview (link is found in the bibliography). According to scores of testimonials, the Snåsaman is a first rate healer, but is he also a reliable prophet? We'll see...

The Paranormal Lawyer (or Liar?)

One of the strangest books ever published in Norway—yet to be taken seriously—is *From an Unknown World* (1976) by the lawyer Thomas L. Aall, released by Cappelens Forlag, a respected publisher. The author, who belonged to an old, well-known and quite influential family that includes notable scholars, describes weighty personal paranormal experiences by the score: clairvoyance, telepathy, healings, telekinesis, poltergeists, ghosts, forebodings of death, etc. In the preface, the experienced and respected editor Waldemar Brögger says he doesn't know how such phenomena can be explained, but that he is confident that the author has experienced the events described. Aall had been an acquaintance of Brögger's for around 30 years, and in that context Brögger finds it 'completely and wildly implausible' that the recounted events should be just fabrications.

Aall was, as stated, a lawyer, obviously a somewhat 'macho' kind of guy, whose leisure activities were logging and boxing. He describes himself as 'not only a quick and agile boxer—I was also able to punch more than commonly hard.' Aall says modestly that he does not call himself 'a psychic' since the paranormal phenomena occurred spontaneously and were (to a large extent) beyond his control. And as he, by temperament, was more of a skeptic than a believer, he felt such experiences to be a disturbance rather than a blessing.

> With my orientation towards this planet and the delights of this world, my contempt for illusions in virtually all fields of life, my belief in the present and the tangible and nothing else—they [the paranormal phenomena] fit my intellect and my orientation much like a silk stocking which forcibly is pulled over a hedgehog; with an unpleasant lack of harmonic orientation as a result.

Hence Aall's story is intriguing, not only because of the enigmatic events depicted, but also on account of the author's relationship to them: analytical and reflective, not trading in any cheap sensationalism. His style of writing, charming and idiosyncratic as it is—a combination of quirky humor and deep seriousness—conveys a dense and arresting atmosphere, apparently much akin to the unknown world he is describing. Difficult to argue, of course, but one almost inevitably gets a feeling of *authenticity*, regardless as to how these events should be explained.

Aall casually depicts several humorous episodes, such as the chapter 'An Unusual Visit to the Doctor,' where he describes how his consciousness one night spontaneously moves off—a so-called 'astral projection'—to an unknown doctor's office. He is able to observe multiple specific details of the interior of the office, for example an orange lamp shaped as a cluster of grapes. But alas! Aall suddenly also gets to see his girlfriend being very thoroughly 'examined'—I shall refrain from further descriptions—by a young physician. Aall takes note of the physician's appearance, especially his peculiar hair, its cut and color. This weird phenomenon takes place about once a week for a couple of months before stopping altogether. Somewhat later Aall hears from the sister of his girlfriend that she (his girlfriend) during this period, in fact, had been dating a young doctor with looks very closely resembling Aall's observations! Not a very pleasant experience, obviously, but he kept his composure.

Aall's trepidation in connection with other experiences could, however, be considerable. While traveling abroad during World War II he suddenly experienced a projection of his consciousness. This time he found himself located in the gallery of the church in his hometown, hearing mighty baroque music from the organ—'vaults and walls vibrated under the fullness of chords in the bass.' Meanwhile, down in the aisle, six men are carrying a coffin. Aall notices with interest the pallbearers' asymmetrical attire: 'Five were in dark overcoats. The sixth had a light spring coat and a dark scarf around his neck.' So far the scene is peaceful.

Aall is poised and harmonious at heart: 'I found myself perfectly well.' But suddenly he hears *The Voice*: 'Thomas! It-is-your-mother! But-she-can-be-saved-if-you-go-home-now!' I daresay most of us would have become alarmed if experiencing something of this nature, as does Aall: 'Suddenly the situation had changed... I felt goosebumps spread, nerves contract, panic creeping into every pore and all the corners of my mind.'

Aall assumes that the projection of consciousness lasts for about half an hour. During this time he undergoes a crisis on several levels. His body is actually in a far-off country while he perceives himself to be located in the church of his hometown! In the aftermath more difficulties ensue. He is thrown into painful quandaries about what to do. Should he dismiss the whole experience as nonsense, or organize a trip home (not easily done during the war) to urge his mother, who to his knowledge was in the best of health, to undergo a medical examination? A long story cut short: Aall travels home and persuades his mother to visit the doctor. As the doctor finds nothing to worry about, just some trifling problem, her treatment is postponed some months. This proves to be fatal, as it was not a trifling problem—it was cancer... The scene at the grave seems so strangely familiar to Aall due to the pallbearers' asymmetrical attire: 'At the funeral, an icy winter day during the war, six men carried... Five were in dark overcoats. The sixth had a light trench coat with a blue scarf around his neck...'

I have given here only a short excerpt from this eerie story; I still get shivers when I read it in its entirety. His recounting seems authentic—this is something he has truly experienced (I shall refrain from alternative explanations of what could 'really' have happened). In hindsight Aall ruminates extensively on destiny vs. freedom: He believes he has 'seen' future events in a similar way on several occasions.

And also that things thus 'seen' would later occur regardless as to whether or not he tried to prevent them. If this should be the case—that it really is possible to 'see' the future—what then would be the consequences? Is it really possible to change the future if it is already 'written on heavenly tablets,' or in some parallel dimension? And what happens to free will and self-determination if we indulge in such fatalistic ways of thought?

Later in life, Aall became a Catholic—of a kind, as he still continued to doubt almost everything. Thus he chose the baptism name 'Thomas,' after the disciple famous for doubting Christ's bodily resurrection. Aall says wittily that as to which baptism name he should choose, there was *no* doubt...

Some time after his conversion word reached Aall that a certain Mr H. was terminally ill with cancer of the kidneys. This was a man who had once come to Aall's assistance when he had been severely injured by an axe (during logging, nothing criminal involved...). Mr H. was now hospitalized and, according to what Aall was told, had only a few hours left to live. Hearing this, Aall feels impelled to pray for—or perhaps we could also say 'send healing to'?—this terminally ill man (who, by the way, was not informed about Aall's initiative). And then, going deeply into prayer, Aall experienced an 'unknown Power who takes possession of one in a way I cannot explain or fully describe. It's like experiencing a partial inner division, infused with fear, that I am at the mercy of rather than being able to evoke.' Aall clearly enters a special state of altered consciousness through this mystical prayer. And what happens? Well, according to Aall, Mr H. survives and one month later is discharged from the hospital!

To get the whole story, Aall later contacts Mr H., who recounts the following:

It was like I had abandoned the body, and hovered for a while below the ceiling of the infirmary. I saw my body lying there, saw those standing around, saw it all. Next, it was as if I was led through the ceiling, out of the infirmary, over the roof of the hospital. I saw the city, the earth beneath me, saw everything clearly. And I moved with terrifying speed toward a very bright light, and it was a wonderful feeling; I felt so free, what shall I say, so detached from all ties heading toward this enormous light... But then, suddenly, it was like I felt a hand grabbing me in the neck and forcing me back to earth and into the body again...

Our man is not called Thomas for nothing, and the following dialogue takes place: Aall: 'Are you willing to answer me quite frankly one question?' Mr H.: 'Well, if I can.' Aall: 'Were you happy to return to your body and to this life here?' The man was obviously reluctant to answer, hence Aall emphasizes that he does not want politeness but the truth. Mr H. then responded: 'Well, when you put it that way, I shall have to tell it like it was, and that is, No. I would have preferred to be spared (the return) then.' He explained this is because he experienced 'such a wonderful freedom and I was so happy; yes, I can almost say that I was elated!'

Many people having had a near-death experience describe quite similar scenarios and emotions as Mr H. Spontaneous remissions of cancer also occur from time to time, but as Mr H. obviously had at least one-and-a-half feet in the grave, I think this case—if true—still must be considered quite exceptional. What I find unique in Aall's way of recounting the case is that he openly informs us that this man, so miraculously cured, had preferred to die! Many—I think it is fair to say *most*—healers/preachers/gurus, etc. in a similar situation would have been irresistibly tempted to use the incident for propaganda purposes: 'Prayer answered, healed on his deathbed, a miracle of biblical proportions, God is (or, I am) surely great!' While Aall, on the other hand, is neither blowing his own trumpet as some God-sent healer, nor is he currying favor with fellow Christians. He rather takes the sheen off the whole thing, leaving us with a puzzling feeling of ambiguity: 'A miracle... perhaps... but to what end, really?'

I feel this rigorous honesty to be a testimonial to Aall's integrity—that for him truth presides over illusions. And this of course also makes me more ready to consider his stories to be more than fantasy. It is a pity that Aall's extraordinary and exciting account has yet to be translated into English—I'll see what I can do about it!

Poltergeist—No Child's Game...

In press reports from 2010, Lalm kindergarten in Gudbrandsdalen (meaning Gudbrand's Valley) appeared to be a veritable haunted house. Between April 26 and June 15, all 15 employees witnessed diverse objects—cups, mugs, stones, jars, etc.—flying through the rooms! Sometimes these items seemed to appear out of thin air. In addition doors opened and closed by themselves, figures were drawn with crayons moved by no one's hand (no human's hand that is...), feathers used for decoration organized themselves into specific patterns, and so on. More than 90 seemingly inexplicable episodes occurred. And, interestingly enough, many of these events were observed by two or three adults simultaneously. In some cases there were even as many as 20 witnesses.

At first it was—of course—assumed that tricksters, young or grown-ups, were to blame. But since no one was ever caught and since the strange activities also eventually came to involve heavier objects and louder noises, both adults and children became increasingly perturbed. At last it was decided to take some action to end the turmoil. But how does one take action against something like this? Well, a priest was called in, and having him 'do his thing' provided, in fact, some alleviation. It proved short-lived, though, and the phenomena gradually returned. Then a clairvoyant was summoned, and after she did 'her thing' the relief—by cause or by coincidence—proved to be lasting. And subsequently Lalm kindergarten has only seen and heard the type of activities and noises that are *supposed* to occur in kindergartens.

However, all these strange phenomena had sparked off an interest in understanding what on earth had been going on! Therefore psychology professor Kjell Flekkøy was sent for. Flekkøy is a highly respected professional; he is a specialist in neuropsychology (the connection between brain and behavior) and is professor emeritus at the University of Oslo, and he has also been professor at Ullevaal hospital. Flekkøy has often prepared evaluations and reports for courtrooms and acted in other public and official capacities. In addition to his own expertise, Flekkøy requested assistance from a professor of physics at the University of Oslo.

Following inspections and interviews Flekkøy wrote a report where he outlined a cluster of possible explanations for the uncanny phenomena:

There are six alternative interpretations of these observations: (a) child's games, (b) lies, (c) psychosis, (d) delusion/ mass suggestion, (e) tricks and (stage) magic, (f) the incidents witnessed by many are physically real.

Flekkøy is of course well aware that these are exceptional circumstances he is evaluating, and in the introduction he says:

> In the following, I'll discuss the basis for confidence in the data, even if this thematically belongs in the discussion section. The reason is this: the phenomena portrayed are so unusual and little understood that the reader will be reluctant to take them seriously, as is the case with this report. Therefore it is necessary to evaluate the basis for confidence in the data as a first step.

One gets a clear picture of what Flekkøy means when reading the factual part of the report:

> Smaller objects suddenly appear without a sound 'like out of the air' at eye-height, eventually at ceiling height, hit the ground, always with a louder than usual sound, but with an otherwise normal character of sound. Where starting-points are located [it appears that] the movements have a very abrupt start with an 'explosive' character; the object whips away. Especially initially, the items concerned were mostly small and lightweight (a toy hammer, keys, blackboard magnets, etc.; see attached images); later also larger objects.

The flying objects are also said to have behaved in an unusual way:

> Breakable objects made of glass or ceramics do not smash into pieces as opposed to our usual experience with such items (cups, jars). When hitting the walls no marks are made despite what would be expected based on the item's weight, shape, speed and direction (e.g. a glue stick). On one specific occasion a jar of jam with a screw cap of metal

was crushed to very small fragments after hitting the
wall—but without leaving any mark on the wall.

These indeed peculiar events, according to the accounts of the kindergarten staff, would often be accompanied by unpleasant sensations—feelings of pressure in the head, sensations of cold, putrid odor, and sometimes also noises, such as bangs and crackles. In short: Here has been a poltergeist afoot! Within traditional occultism, activities of this kind will, as mentioned in chapter 3, often be blamed on spirits, goblins or the like. Whereas, in parapsychology they will be seen rather as a chaotic form of *psychokinesis*, a human ability, usually lying dormant. This assumption is partly based on the fact that poltergeist activities often seem to be linked to the presence of certain people; e.g. typically sensitive teens with dire inner conflicts. When such people are away say on holiday, or become more stable and harmonious, the poltergeist tends to disappear. (A cynical approach would be to say that this is due to the removal of the likelihood and/or the need to fake this sort of drama…)

An illustrative example would be the English healer Matthew Manning, briefly mentioned in chapter 3. Manning tells of telekinetic episodes with heavy furniture spontaneously sliding along the floor, cutlery flying out of drawers, stale bread appearing out of thin air, etc. Several cases of this type occurred at Manning's boarding school, and some are said to have been witnessed by more than 20 schoolboys. Manning relates that these events were quite stressful to him (no wonder…). But the problems were eventually resolved; the phenomena gradually ceased to appear, first when Manning took up automatic writing and painting, and later healing. Manning suggests that perhaps the same power that had been used to manifest as chaos now instead manifests itself harmoniously in the form of healing. For the past 30 years, Manning has enjoyed a reputation as one of the foremost healers in the world, with myriads of clients from a slew of countries. He has become an acquaintance of Prince Charles (it may not be an irrefutable proof of authenticity, but still...) and has lectured to members of the British Medical Association at their request.

Because of the alleged poltergeist episodes Manning was thoroughly investigated by researchers while young, in particular by George Owen (1919–2003). Owen was a mathematician and a geneticist with affiliations to the universities of Cambridge and Toronto, but in addition he was considered to be an expert on poltergeists. In the laboratory, he detected that Manning's brain exhibited a quite unique wave pattern, with sudden bursts and unusually strong activity in the theta range. As mentioned earlier, this is in the range of 4–7 oscillations per second, which is the same range that shamans will often stimulate with their drumming. Owen assumed that Manning's peculiar brain wave pattern was related to the poltergeist activity in some way.

Well, whatever explanation model one uses—spirits or psychokinesis—the experiences reported by both the personnel in Lalm kindergarten and by Manning are indeed something out of the ordinary! One is tempted, just as Flekkøy mentions in the introduction to his report, to dismiss the whole thing—which, in fact, many of the outsiders in Lalm initially did. But after a while, other people, not only the staff, started to experience the poltergeist... A parent, who initially was highly skeptical of the staff's account, claims to have seen a marker pen, two pebbles and a plastic lid manifesting seemingly out of nowhere! We'll give the word to this skeptic, as he is quoted in Professor Flekkøy's report:

Right after we [the skeptic and two others] had entered the eastern part of the kindergarten's living room, we heard a kind of snap from the ceiling. Then appeared a felt-tip pen of the sort we usually call a marker. It came at high speed from the ceiling and landed in a window facing south. The marker landed on the windowsill, and stopped as if had landed in glue. There it lay motionless. I picked it up and put it in my pocket...

Flekkøy comments: After about two minutes in this room, they once more heard the same sound from the ceiling, and a tiny light bulb right in front of them (the light bulb was of a type not used for regular illumination but rather for decoration). Together with the light bulb a pebble landed (of the size of a thumb nail). He picked up the items, and felt that the light bulb was warm, 'as if it just had been switched off!' In the same room, after a short while: The same sound, and now a plastic lid landed with a certain sliding motion along the floor. In the western section of the kindergarten:

In the same moment as we [the skeptic and the two others] entered this room, the sound came from the ceiling. Then there appeared a stone at head height that landed right before our feet. The stone had the size of the fist of a 3–4-year-old. The stone stopped right after it had landed. In the meantime another of the parents had arrived who also saw the event.

Some crazy stuff, this... Later that same evening, they heard once more the snapping sound from the ceiling, after which a toy log came down from above. Flekkøy comments dryly: 'Interestingly enough, the concerned parent had initially been markedly critical of the veracity of the accounts of the personnel—as had most of the other men. This was rapidly and lastingly changed after the self-observation.'

As stated, more than 90 different, very particular episodes were reported, and several of them were more complex and multifaceted—concurrent manifestations of strange movements, sounds, smells and sensations—than those given here as brief examples. After extensive deliberations back and forth, where the six options from the introduction were considered—(a) child's games, (b) lies, (c) psychosis, (d) delusion/mass suggestion, (e) tricks and (stage) magic, (f) the incidents witnessed by many are physically real—Flekkøy concludes mainly with the latter, namely that most of the reported episodes really (physically) happened: 'Overall, there is a basis for assessing the observations from Lalm and equally well documented observations as being physically real.' Flekkøy discusses possible explanations without coming down on the side of any specific one, and chooses—as is typical of sober scientists—to pass the ball on to future research. But indeed with a declared opening for new and exciting perspectives:

> *the implication being that the phenomena are merited a scientific elucidation of their nature. It is highly probable that such clarification will open doors leading to a more fundamental understanding of key aspects of our own nature as well as the nature surrounding us.*

Flekkøy's exposition is called 'Lalm kindergarten: Overview and assessment of ectopic incidents from April 26–June 15, 2010' and the link is found at the end of this book. The report is thorough in its descriptions and discussions, and is an exciting read—highly recommended! (It will demand a little extra effort, though, as Professor Flekkøy writes in *Nynorsk*, a special branch of Norwegian, not so easily read by translation programs.)

If Flekkøy's conclusion is correct, such 'magical' phenomena, defying ordinary human comprehension, occur not only in remote times, in distant realms or in fairy tales, nor only in the Baghdad of *One Thousand and One Nights* or at Hogwarts School of Witchcraft and Wizardry, but also in Lalm kindergarten deep in the Gudbrandsdalen. And it came to pass in those days where Barack Obama was the emperor of the USA and Jens Stoltenberg was the governor of Norway... Who would have believed—yes, who would ever have believed?

Chapter 6

CONSCIOUSNESS—THE ENIGMATIC KEY TO THE ENIGMAS

How it is that anything so remarkable as a state of consciousness comes about as a result of irritating nervous tissue, is just as unaccountable as the appearance of the djinn when Aladdin rubbed his lamp in the story.

~ Thomas Henry Huxley

The key to understanding paranormal phenomena is probably to understand a little more about what consciousness is and how it works. This is easier said than done, but we'll give it a try. However, the intention is by no means to reveal (God forbid such arrogance!) the Mystery of Consciousness. Rather we will modestly exercise a little 'mental chiropractic' by cracking and kneading some very common, very rigid perceptions. This is done by introducing ideas that violate what we could call 'the standard model' of consciousness. This model, commonly prevalent in psychology and biology, is based on the assumptions that consciousness can be fully explained by (i.e. reduced to) physical processes in the brain, and that it only operates locally (i.e. in the head of the individual)—a plateau of understanding from which it seems difficult to say anything useful about the paranormal at all.

Consciousness—the term is derived from the Latin *con* (with, together) and *scire* (to know)—is in one sense the most obvious and simplest phenomenon of all: At this very moment you are probably conscious of yourself without any difficulty whatsoever. But at the same time, consciousness is a most elusive entity, 'a ghost in the machine.' Although consciousness is the prerequisite for all our perceptions, it cannot perceive itself—much like the hand that can so easily grasp diverse objects, but is not able to grasp itself. Art, literature, psychology and neuroscience can tell us a great deal about what is going on within our consciousness. And as life goes by, experience will inevitably teach us all a thing or two or three about the multiple and complex activities going on in our inner world. But the phenomenon of consciousness—what it is in itself—is still a complete mystery.

The philosopher David Chalmers has spoken of 'the hard question' of consciousness. This is not a question about which chemical reactions in the brain are associated with consciousness. Neither is it a question about how the outside world is 'represented' in our consciousness, nor is it a question about how our beliefs and ideas are formed. And finally, 'the hard question' has nothing whatsoever to do with the many forms of cultural and political consciousness—Western consciousness, working-class consciousness, social consciousness and the like. So what, then, is 'the hard question'? Well, it can probably be formulated quite simply: Why does conscious experience occur at all? For perhaps we might just as well be living in a world of 'zombies' which by instinct perform all the actions of the average person but without consciousness, just as computers do myriads of ultra-complex calculations without having the slightest conscious experience of it. With respect to 'the hard question' we are, according to Chalmers, not even close to finding an answer. Yes, it seems as if many professionals hardly know where to start looking. The eminent British psychologist

Stuart Sutherland writes in the *Macmillan Dictionary of Psychology*:

> **Consciousness**—*The having of perceptions, thoughts, and feelings; awareness. The term is impossible to define except in terms that are unintelligible without a grasp of what consciousness means. [...] Consciousness is a fascinating but elusive phenomenon: it is impossible to specify what it is, what it does, or why it has evolved. Nothing worth reading has been written on it.*

So, neither philosophy nor psychology seems to be able to provide us with an overwhelming amount of help. Our itinerary will apparently lead us through a *terra incognita*, an unmapped landscape, swampy and covered in fog, where perhaps there even be dragons... But where marshes are shrouded in veils of haze, cloudberries are often many and juicy. And if there be dragons, the treasures they guard may well be vast. So let's just keep walking boldly ahead! I would be surprised if the fog didn't lift a little in the course of the chapter. And even if it is not within our scope to find an answer to 'the hard question', we may indeed come closer to a possible explanation for some of the highly enigmatic psi phenomena.

Consciousness—Urine of the Brain?

In biology and medicine—which are strongholds of 'the standard model'—it is sometimes claimed that consciousness is a greatly hyped and overrated entity; stated or implied, such a view is usually based on the idea that a human being is some sort of advanced, biological robot, whose actions are guided—or better still *controlled*—by a set of genetically programmed instincts and responses. Consciousness, therefore, is not free and objective, and hence cannot be trusted to give us true knowledge of ourselves and the world. Consciousness is by no means a solid anchor—nay, it could rather be described as an insignificant foam ball riding on top of the mighty waves of biology, while being swept hither and thither—like a ship without a rudder—by the indiscriminate winds of instincts and impulses. From this viewpoint consciousness is not regarded as having an independent existence, but is considered to be a mere *epiphenomenon*—a derivative phenomenon, a pure reflection of the brain's activities. Such a view is often called *physicalism*, the essence of which was poignantly expressed by the German 19th-century zoologist Karl Vogt in his apposite words: 'The brain produces thoughts like the kidneys produce urine.'

An upgraded version—perhaps we could call it BrainUrine 2.0—of this view argues that consciousness can be explained as a function of the right mix of chemical cocktails in the brain. If you blend in *un petit* amount of mirror neurons and stir 40 oscillations per second into the brain's electrical signals, *voila!*—consciousness will be served! According to this myth, the proper arrangement of an electro-physiochemical sort will not only constitute the necessary but also sufficient conditions to explain the occurrence of consciousness. New tales of this kind are continually released—the BrainUrine 3.0 upgrade, the 4.0 upgrade, etc.—and they all in one way or another claim that neuroscience, the discipline that combines medicine, biology, physics, chemistry and psychology, has solved the mystery of consciousness. But these myths

are probably just that—myths. Professor Richard Fracko-
wiack is an internationally renowned expert for his work on
brain imaging, and in 2004 he published, together with a
group of experts, a classic work of more than a thousand
pages, entitled *Human Brain Function*. Here he—apparently
a little abashedly—confesses:

> *We have no idea how consciousness emerges from the
> physical activity of the brain and we do not know
> whether consciousness can emerge from non-biological
> systems, such as computers [...] At this point the reader
> will expect to find a careful and precise definition of con-
> sciousness. You will be disappointed. Consciousness has
> not yet become a scientific term that can be defined in this
> way. Currently we all use the term consciousness in many
> different and often ambiguous ways.*

It seems clear, then, that neuroscience c. 2004 neither had
an answer to how consciousness arises, nor had any satisfactory explanation of what consciousness really is. Nevertheless, for decades it had been taken for granted within the
fields of biology, psychology and psychiatry that consciousness can be fully explained as a mere reflection of activities
within the brain. For, what could consciousness possibly be
except that?

Irreducible Mind

I regard consciousness as fundamental. I regard matter as derivative from consciousness. We cannot get behind consciousness.

~ Max Planck, physicist, Nobel laureate

In 2007, an alternative to 'the standard model' of consciousness was brought to the table with the release of *Irreducible Mind: Toward a Psychology for the 21st Century* (E. Kelly and E. Williams Kelly, eds.), which is a very comprehensive work. The book received favorable reviews in peer-reviewed journals, such as the *Journal of Mind and Behavior*, *Journal of Nervous and Mental Disease* and the *Journal of Consciousness Studies*, so there is probably good reason to take its viewpoints seriously. Funnily enough, this groundbreaking work was supported financially by the comedian John Cleese of Monty Python fame, who has also, as many readers are probably aware, on a number of occasions contributed—in his distinctive way—to books on psychology.

The authors of *Irreducible Mind* are professors and lecturers in psychology, psychiatry and neurobiology, and they believe—as the title more than indicates—that consciousness can *not* be reduced to a mere reflection of the brain's continuous activities. Consciousness should rather, they argue, be conceived as a sphere in itself, a collectively shared field of information, with which we all (and perhaps all other living beings) are connected.

The authors draw on historical sources, most importantly British philosopher and poet Frederic Myers (1843–1901) and American psychologist and philosopher William James (1842–1910), with whom we became acquainted in chapter 4. Both Myers and James were highly skilled academics—James is sometimes referred to as the single most influential person in the history of American psychology. But in spite of their 'scholarly squareness' they were telling strange stories—stories that, if they are to be trusted, strongly indicate that consciousness does not always stay neatly in place inside the brain... James, as already mentioned, did research on the famed medium Leonora Piper, and found that she was able to provide tons of information which, as James saw it, would have been virtually impossible for her to obtain via any usual channel.

It was fascinating experiences like these that led Myers and James to become actively engaged within SPR and ASPR, and they both served as president for their respective societies. Myers was also involved in the society's research on apparitions and crisis-telepathy, i.e. when one person experiences a crisis (shock, injury, death), the presence of this person and his/her suffering is purportedly perceived telepathically by a friend/relative. For example as in the chapter 5 story, where Kiss Bennett had a powerful experience of what she perceived to be the presence of the dying Roald Amundsen, contacting her by telepathy. It was, in fact, Myers who coined the very term 'telepathy' (*tele* = remote, *pathy* = sense, feeling, experience), and it was also he who introduced the concept of 'ESP' (Extra Sensory Perception).

The Brain as a Filter

Myers advanced the interesting idea—perhaps in part based on research done by Carl Gustav Carus (the German 19th-century physician and psychologist, Goethe's friend, mentioned in chapter 5)—that consciousness is not *created* by the brain; rather it is *reduced* by the brain. Consciousness is basically an immense field of information, and the brain can be understood as an ultra-sophisticated filter that condenses, sorts, modulates and organizes this field. And the reason that for most of us experiences of the paranormal are not everyday occurrences is simply that our brains filter out most of these episodes! Otherwise we would be overwhelmed with all kinds of strange stuff when trying (likely unsuccessfully!) to live normal daily lives. This is, in fact, a complaint frequently heard from psychics: that their lives suffer from 'too much information.'

However, in diverse altered states of consciousness the filtering can be suspended. Such states may occur e.g. during dreaming, meditation, trance, intoxication and near-death experiences. (The filtering can also be shut down by brain damage.) In line with our Internet model, such states could perhaps most aptly be described as conditions where our 'mental firewall' becomes partially disabled. And hence information from the Mental Internet—sometimes exciting stuff, but often just plain crap—is enabled to come through. A couple of American psychics told me that their abilities were 'awakened' after near-death experiences (drowning, car accident). When explained within our model, we would assume that the shock caused the 'firewall' to shut down, and accordingly the floodgates to the Mental Internet sprang open.

Such an increased flow of information happens, as already hinted at, for both better and worse: Many psychics tell about the strains and burdens that come with their visions. Norway's most high profiled psychic, Jordalf Gjerstad, the so-called 'Snåsa Man', has—as mentioned in chapter 5—been visited by literally tens of thousands of people during the past 40 years. He once told a journalist that it is a miracle he hasn't become *steintoillat* (completely mad), as he has the perception of 'seeing'—and thus to some extent also experiencing—his visitors' many fears, traumas and sufferings.

Unexplainable Phenomena

In *Irreducible Mind* Myers' and James' central thoughts are revised and updated in the light of current research in neurobiology and quantum theory, e.g. some quite complex thoughts are included from the physicist Henry Stapp regarding the possibility and even the necessity of free will. One conundrum he tries to solve is seemingly this: If consciousness is just a one-to-one reflection of processes in the brain, how can free will be possible? Aren't we, then, in the last resort, just biological robots fully determined by the brain's physiochemical reactions? Hence unless the undecidedness of the quantum processes is—in one way or another—taken to be an integral part of our consciousness, then no allowance for freedom has been made. I shall not deal with the subtleties of Stapp's model, on how we may make free choices, etc., as I believe the essence with respect to *our* theme—the collective aspect of consciousness—to be concurrent with Myers' and James' basic idea, namely that the brain is regarded as a *modulator* of consciousness rather than as a *creator*.

Savantism: The authors of *Irreducible Mind* argue that even if neurobiology has made tremendous steps forward in recent years, there is still a plethora of phenomena that is not accounted for—and probably never *can* be accounted for—within the prevailing theories. Such phenomena include the uncanny abilities of the so-called *savants* (meaning 'wise' in French), those who display, for instance, extreme skills in calculation, memory, music and other fields. Many readers will probably remember the movie *Rain Man*, with Dustin

Hoffman in the role of Raymond Babbitt, a mathematical savant. This character is partly based on the American Kim Peek (1951–2009), who could digest a book an hour, swallowing two pages at a time (left eye reading the left page, right eye reading the right!), and who afterwards would be able to reproduce about 98 percent of the content by heart. (This really could be named a 'peek-experience'!) Peek reportedly—and he was thoroughly examined—'scanned' more than 10,000 books in this peculiar way. We are obviously not dealing here with a normal memory function; it is much closer to the scanning, uploading and downloading done by computers.

And then we have Daniel Tammet (http://www.daniel-tammet.net) who, during a few weeks early in 2004, memorized pi (π, the unending number 3.141592...) to more than 22,000 places. And shortly after, on international Pi Day—which, of course, is celebrated on March 14 (3.14) — Tammet had his finest hour when reciting all these digits in public—without one single error! Tammet says he perceives the world of mathematics as a landscape where the numbers appear as forms and shapes with colors and other sensations, and also emotions, connected to them—a kind of neurological crosstalk. This mode of perception is called *synesthesia* ('sensing together' in Greek), and is, in fact, not unlike how some psychics experience *their* inner landscapes. A lady experienced within the field of psychic perception told me that all her senses work together as a whole, and that she will therefore often not be able to distinguish which of the senses is supplying her with the information. Incidentally, it may appear that a person has *both* these skills, both synesthesia and psychic perception. For example, reliable reports suggest that Mlle Lenormand and Marcello Haugen, both mentioned in chapter 5, had photographic, savant memory.

And anecdotes indicate that Kim Peek also had some telepathic abilities.

So, when Tammet wants to memorize thousands of digits, or do some crazy calculation stunt at about the same speed as a computer, he just mentally strolls around in this inner, synesthetical landscape and describes what he sees and feels—no big deal, really! Tammet, who has unusually good communicative skills for a savant (savants are often markedly introvert and not that verbal), has published several works of his own, and has also written a foreword to the savant book *Islands of Genius* by psychiatrist D.A. Treffert, who was used as a consultant by the team who made *Rain Man*.

According to the authors of *Irreducible Mind*, the incredible skills of Peek, Tammet and other savants are neither explained nor explainable by the prevalent theories of 'memory traces' in the brain or the like. But if one flips over the perspective and views the brain as a filter modulating and organizing the vast information in the Irreducible Mind (the collective Consciousness, the Mental Internet), well, then the skills of savants suddenly seem easier to explain. And if this is so, perhaps we are all dormant savants. One out of several examples indicating this could be the case is Orlando Serrell (http://www.orlandoserrell.com/about.htm). Orlando was a completely average child until, on August 17, 1979 at the age of 10, he was hit hard with a baseball on the left side of his head; this resulted in a brain injury that apparently caused parts of his filtering apparatus to cease to function. For subsequently he has been able to 'flash-calculate' the weekday of any date in the calendar, and he is also able to recall the weather conditions in his hometown on every single day since that fateful event back in 1979. This means being able to remember the weather on more than 9,000 separate days—utterly amazing, I must say!

Out-of-body experiences: Another phenomenon that seems difficult to explain within the framework of 'the standard model' of consciousness are the near-death cases where patients, after being resuscitated, are able to describe what happened while they were comatose. A classic case was related by heart surgeon Michael Sabom: A patient with cardiac arrest described how during the operation he had soared out of his body and calmly viewed the whole scenario from above. Then he lowered himself down over the operating table—where he could see himself lying! So far his experience could easily be dismissed as no more than a fantasy. But it turned out that he was able to provide a quite detailed account—not just a general description—of the procedures the surgeons had followed. He could also describe the movements of some of the surgical instruments at a time when he was demonstrably in a deep coma. So how could this be if consciousness is just a reflection of processes in the brain?

There are dozens of reports of similar incidents, which—if described in classical occult terms—could be called 'spontaneous astral projections.' My favorite example of this phenomenon is the experience related by the renowned Irish occultist and writer Herbie Brennan which can be found at: https://www.youtube.com/watch?v=O6zHbeMhuRA

Based on such findings, British near-death specialist Dr Sam Parnia in 2008 launched a project called AWARE (AWAreness during REsuscitation). It started out with 15 hospitals agreeing to map occurrences of this and related kinds. The project is described in Dr Parnia's book *The Lazarus Effect: The Science That is Rewriting the Boundaries Between Life and Death*. The results so far have not been quite as exciting as some of the researchers had expected (and probably also hoped for). There were only two apparently inexplicable cases, where the patients' consciousness seemingly was working and could observe the scene from the outside while the patient was in a coma. And due to ill-health only one of these patients could be interviewed strictly according to protocol. Thus the project documented only one case with 'a verifiable period of conscious awareness during which time cerebral function was not expected,' in the technical words of Parnia et al.

But perhaps even this somewhat meager result could corroborate an expanded view on consciousness? For as William James once said: 'If you wish to upset the law that all crows are black, you mustn't seek to show that no crows are; it is enough if you prove one single crow to be white.' Parnia's comments in the wake of the project have sounded affirmative with respect to this, whereas the comments by a number of skeptics have not (why am I not surprised?). Anyway, it should be noted that the project led by Parnia looked at cases in connection with cardiac arrest. There is also research (by Dr Pim van Lommel and others) with other criteria and which apparently confirms 'non-physical veridical perceptions.'

Other enigmas: There are still more phenomena which, according to the authors of *Irreducible Mind*, are difficult to explain within the horizon of 'the standard model.' We have for instance those thousands of people who have reported 'reincarnation memories'—i.e. a person presents (verifiable) memories, sometimes with detailed life histories, internal family affairs, secret episodes, etc., that appear to originate from a completely different life. Even the famed astrophysicist and high-profiled skeptic Carl Sagan was puzzled by this phenomenon, and thought that it merited serious investigation. But even if such memories should prove to be accurate, it does not mean that they are to be explained by reincarnation; from our perspective such memories could have been downloaded from the Mental Internet.

Other conundrums are those special people who have so-called *multiple personalities*, and where apparently totally distinct personalities live side by side within the same person. And last but not least of the enigmas—and of course of special interest to us!—we have the psychics and the various psi phenomena, such as telepathy, clairvoyance, precognition, healing and so on.

The authors of *Irreducible Mind* present their material over more than 800 closely written pages with a wealth of references. Thus the book constitutes a valuable documentation of psychological *anomalies* (*a* = not, *nomos* = law, rule), i.e. irregularities, events, occurrences which do not fit well with prevailing theories, or with the ruling *paradigm*, as it was famously termed by the historian of science, Thomas Kuhn. And—as Kuhn has described in his classic *The Structure of Scientific Revolutions*—since the anomalies are 'misfits,' they are mostly unwelcome and tend to be forgotten, bypassed or even outright embezzled by the scientific community. And to the degree that they are recognized at all, anomalies will typically be assigned to a lowly footnote, with the implied message: 'Does not fit with our cherished theory—are probably unimportant!'

The anomalies will therefore remain largely unexplained—to both the scientists' astonishment and (mainly) annoyance. But, as we have heard, the authors of *Irreducible Mind* believe that many anomalies within psychology can be explained with a 'change of paradigm' (Kuhn), if we start to view consciousness as a collective field of information. This field is the habitat of all the myriads of information that savants are able to remember; here is stored all the knowledge that psychics download; here are preserved the memories and experiences of the people who have lived before us; and here we all continually exchange 'telepathic emails' with friends and family. The brain is the device that enables us to connect to, upload, download and sort material from this sphere of information; however, the two—the brain and the Irreducible Mind—are most definitely not identical. Let's again apply our simple model: My computer is what enables me to connect to, download and sort all kinds of material from the internet. But the internet is obviously not identical to my computer!

Irreducible Mind currently represents one of the best scientifically substantiated alternatives to 'the standard model' regarding the nature of consciousness. But it is by no means the first work where ideas of this kind have been promoted. As we heard, *Irreducible Mind* is to some degree built on William James' and—in particular—Frederick Myers' thoughts. And as we pointed out in chapter 4, the great Swiss psychiatrist C.G. Jung also espoused the idea that the psyche has a collective dimension, 'the collective unconscious'—as he labeled it. Jung considered—at least in some of his works—this sphere to be almost a parallel universe. If we now expand our perspectives, both historically and philosophically, we find that various eminent thinkers of earlier times, such as Spinoza, Leibniz and Berkeley, go even further in emphasizing the preeminent position of consciousness. For not only do they conceive consciousness to be independent of matter, they—a bit simplified—even assume that the universe and all that it contains in the last resort are manifestations of a larger Consciousness (sometimes just referred to as 'God').

This view of the world, where everything is seen as filled with (and possibly created by) consciousness/spirit/psyche, is referred to as *panpsychism* (the prefix 'pan' meaning 'all'). Panpsychism was the prevalent philosophy in German Idealism, the Romantic movement we had a look at in chapter 5, where poets and thinkers such as Goethe, Novalis, Hegel, Fichte, Schelling and Schopenhauer were important figures. Now, if one assumes that consciousness permeates into the core of everything, then all humans, animals and plants, yes, in fact all that exists, *is already* intrinsically and intimately tangled together. Hence it hardly seems like a great stretch to take paranormal transference phenomena such as telepathy and clairvoyance into account. And—as we saw in chapter 5—the most influential thinkers within German idealism indeed considered psi phenomena to be objectively real and not just chimeras.

So, clearly the authors of *Irreducible Mind* are by no means alone in their highlighting of consciousness; rather they can be seen as representatives of a long and proud tradition of thinking.

Other Models

However, their model of consciousness is not necessarily the best alternative to 'the standard model.' There are also other models that allow for psi—I will briefly present some of these below.

The OrchOR: OrchOR is shorthand for Orchestrated Objective Reduction (a somewhat confusing name... I'll explain below). The main ideas in this model were launched in the late 1980s by the American anesthesiologist Stuart Hameroff and Roger Penrose—a mathematical physicist and colleague of Stephen Hawking. The model was then developed in Penrose's book *Shadows of the Mind: A Search for the Missing Science of Consciousness* (1994). Hameroff and Penrose believe that consciousness emanates in the brain as a result of 'bio-molecular computing'—complex quantum processes (please don't ask!) taking place in the *microtubules*, a plethora of tiny 'pipes' within the brain. Whereas quantum waves which, according to Hameroff and Penrose, can create consciousness when they 'collapse' (= get a specific structure), are ubiquitous. The Hameroff and Penrose model is therefore sometimes seen as a scientific 'light-version' of *panpsychism*, where consciousness is thought to be ubiquitous. Hameroff has in this connection stated: 'I disagree only slightly. I would say that what is omnipresent in the universe is proto-consciousness.'

Perhaps the rather abstract idea of an omnipresent 'proto-consciousness' that gives rise to consciousness could best be illustrated by how *electricity* emanates in batteries based on *electromagnetism* being present in every atom in the universe. Or with another image: Hameroff has said that proto-consciousness is to consciousness what noise is to music. Both noise and music consist of *sounds* (which therefore perhaps could be called 'proto-music'). But in noise the sounds are not organized, whereas in music the sounds are structured in a harmonious way—they are 'orchestrated.' This, then, is the reason why the word 'Orchestrated' is embedded in the model's name. Whereas 'Objective Reduction' refers to the quantum waves being 'reduced' by our brains, giving them 'objective' structure in the form of consciousness.

Hameroff has said he thinks their model allows for telepathy, based on the idea of *quantum non-locality*, an exciting concept that we will discuss later in this chapter. And Penrose has stated: 'I think there is strong evidence for precognition but I haven't done the maths yet to work out what else is allowed,' i.e. what other psi phenomena their model eventually opens up to.

The World as a Hologram: Yet another model that has ample space for psi stems from the great American physicist David Bohm (in his youth a colleague of Einstein) and the American neuropsychologist and neurophysicist Karl Pribram. This model is very complex, but is presented in an accessible way in the books of Michael Talbot—an author who had various paranormal experiences, including poltergeist and astral projection (out-of-body experiences), which gave him the urge to explore other, more inclusive models of consciousness. In Bohm's model consciousness and matter are not thought to be opposites (and one has to admit that they cooperate fairly well inside most human beings!) and both are seen as manifestations of an underlying 'holomovement.' Bohm believes that the world can be described as a *hologram*, a sort of three-dimensional image, where every little part contains information about the whole: 'The droplet reflects the universe' would probably be an apt expression for this idea. Hence our consciousness will in some sense be 'reflected' throughout the whole hologram, and is therefore not confined to the inside of our own heads.

If consciousness and matter really are as closely interconnected as Bohm suggests, the occurrence of psi phenomena such as telepathy and clairvoyance—which violates our common-sense idea about Space—would no longer seem strange. Bohm has explicitly stated that the common notion of consciousness suffers from not having included the revelations presented by modern physics. And he also participated several times in parapsychological experiments. After quite a few years on the margins, Bohm's interpretation of quantum physics has recently seen a partial renaissance because of an experiment conducted under the auspices of the physicist Aephraim M. Steinberg at the University of Toronto in 2016. The bibliography has a link to an article from the *New Scientist* describing this experiment. More recent experiments are being conducted at University College London.

Maybe Bohm's model could be even better suited than *Irreducible Mind* to explain clairvoyance? For, if a clairvoyant person is able to describe a specific building in a faraway country, one might imagine that this was possible because the natives of the country had 'uploaded' (i.e. by means of their thoughts, feelings and experiences) information about this building to the Mental Internet. Hence the information would be universally accessible, and could be 'downloaded' by the clairvoyant. But, if the clairvoyant could describe specific conditions on another planet, where there had never been a single human to 'upload' information—well, then it would be harder to see how such a feat could be possible. Nevertheless, it appears that Ingo Swann, one of the most important remote viewers in the Stargate project (chapter 2) managed to do just that. In a recorded session on the evening of April 27, 1973 Swann stated that he could 'see' there were planetary rings around Jupiter (much as with Saturn). This was a highly controversial claim at the time. But—in 1979 the *Voyager* probe confirmed that there *are* in fact such rings around Jupiter!

According to Bohm's model, our consciousness participates in the whole hologram (the whole world) at all times—'the droplet reflects the universe'—and it is therefore not separate from any place, even if the place is abandoned by both God and humans, and even if it is in another part of the universe. So could it perhaps be precisely such a Bohmian 'holographic ubiquity' of consciousness that enables clairvoyance to exist?

The Zero Point Field: And there are still more models (whew!—this will be the last one for now, I promise) such as the Hungarian systems philosopher Ervin Laszlo's exciting 'Integral Theory of Everything.' Laszlo's model is based on the idea of a *zero point field*. He often refers to this field with the old Sanskrit word *akasha,* which—among other things—denotes *ether*. In ancient Indian philosophy ether was considered to be the fundamental element (in Theosophy, 'the akasha chronicles' refers to a cosmic archive). Laszlo's zero point field purportedly contains every piece of information both thinkable and unthinkable—e.g. the totality of individual and collective memory, all the genetic codes in nature, all future possibilities, etc.—not just in our present universe, but in the *Metaverse*. In Laszlo's system the Metaverse comprises all past, present and future universes and all possible parallel dimensions. The *zero point field* could therefore be seen as an infinitely upgraded version of the Mental Internet!

To delve into the different models is demanding, and to determine which—if any—is correct is obviously even more difficult. Here is clearly material for a string of Nobel prizes for those with the vocation. These models are, as said at the beginning of the chapter, presented here mainly for 'chiropractic reasons'—to crack and knead some rigid perceptions by showing that there are, in fact, legitimate alternatives to the view of 'the standard model.' This model seems to rule out psi phenomena from the outset whereas the alternative models presented can quite comfortably include them. If we are not to believe that the millions of people who, according to statistics, have experienced such phenomena are naive, dishonest or flat-out crazy, perhaps we should seriously consider a new and more inclusive model of what consciousness is and how it works?

Eastern Perspectives

Eastern philosophies have in the main included the various types of psi phenomena. This is linked to the holistic approach prevalent in both Chinese and Indian thought. Many readers probably know of *Taoism* (*tao* is often translated as 'way,' 'mode,' 'law of life,' etc., referring to nature's intrinsic harmony). The key concepts here are *yin* and *yang*, which represent the eternal counterpoints that complement and interact with each other within life's great symphony: passivity/activity, contraction/expansion, night/day, death/life, etc. The symbol of Taoism, which is often depicted on jewelry of the 'hippie kind,' is two drop-shaped figures, one black and one white, inscribed in a circle. This expresses that opposites are closely interlinked with one other, and are involved in continuous exchanges. The person who co-operates with this flux—often referred to as *the supreme person*—through the attentive and meditative attitude called *Wu Wei* (effortless action, active non-action), will, according to tradition, elevate his/her consciousness and gain control over the *chi*, the life force, and hence will be able to perform healing, telekinesis and other 'miracles' (which are taken to be the natural activities of an expanded consciousness). The central text in Taoism, the *Tao Te Ching* from around 600 BCE, also describes the strong telepathic influence exerted by the person who is in harmony with *tao* and has an expanded consciousness: 'When the right person is sitting at the right place and is thinking the right thoughts, it can be felt more than a thousand miles away!'

Within the Indian tradition the holistic mindset is beautifully expressed by the metaphor of the *Net of Indra*, the God-King. Imagine an infinitely large golden fishing net with lots of parallel layers where each node in the yarn is a facet-cut jewel, and in its facets every jewel reflects the entire net with all the other jewels. This symbolizes how absolutely all things, objects and entities in the whole wide world—consciousness and nature, humans and gods, galaxies and grains of sand—are connected to each other and interact through myriads and myriads of relationships. In most branches of Buddhism and Hinduism consciousness is thought to be the driving force in these exchanges, while matter is on a lower level; it is sometimes conceived to be a kind of 'frozen' consciousness—approximately as ice is frozen water. The person who through yoga and meditation acquires control of his/her consciousness will therefore—according to the theory—be less enslaved by material restrictions than ordinary people. This is elaborated on in the 196 classic yoga sutras (aphorisms) compiled around 400 CE by the philosopher Patanjali. Here we are instructed in techniques for developing *siddhis*, i.e. paranormal abilities. The treatise explains how one can achieve knowledge of past and future events, knowledge of what is hidden and remote, knowledge of other people's thoughts, how to perform levitation, and other extraordinary skills. We immediately recognize that these are abilities of the psi-type, which in parapsychology would be referred to respectively as post- and precognition, clairvoyance, telepathy and psychokinesis.

Eastern Wisdom and Western Science—Flux and Consciousness as Common Denominators

The Tao of Physics

There have been several attempts to combine Eastern wisdom and Western science; one of the most successful syntheses can be found in the popular science bestseller *The Tao of Physics* (1975) by nuclear physicist Fritjof Capra. He believes that essential insights, which were perceived intuitively in the ancient Eastern wisdom traditions, have in modern times been formulated intellectually in Western quantum physics. One common denominator could then be the notion of nature being essentially a stream, a flux (as in Taoism)—another could be the idea that consciousness is essential, yes perhaps even the basic 'stuff' of the universe (as in Hinduism and Buddhism).

But—as once was said by Jesus: 'A prophet is only without honor in his own country, among his own relations and in his own house.' Many (most) physicists thought (and still think) that quantum physics primarily should be understood and used as a set of mathematical models. These models work very well when performing calculations at the subatomic level (particles smaller than atoms), but they, it is often claimed, are of little or no value in describing our everyday world. So—in addition to his great success, Capra has also taken a brutal beating. This is partly because the special branch of quantum theory he adhered to, the so-called 'bootstrap' theory, quite quickly fell out of fashion, but first and foremost his critics argue that he blends physics and philosophy in an unsustainable manner.

Would it be better, then, if our friend (or fiend?) Capra had kept mum, stayed in his laboratory, and left the philosophy to the philosophers? Well, everyone is entitled to their opinion, but I think it should be noted that some of the greats within quantum physics—Werner Heisenberg, Erwin Schrödinger, Wolfgang Pauli, Niels Bohr, etc.—had distinct philosophical leanings; they weren't afraid to make bold speculations, and were not the least shy in bringing Eastern mysticism into the picture. Bohr even used the symbols of *yin* and *yang* in his personal coat of arms and on his gravestone. And before publishing his book Capra had, in fact, presented his manuscript to Heisenberg, who had apparently approved of the basic tenets.

Anyway, the *Zeitgeist* was obviously hungry for Capra's *cuisine*, and *The Tao of Physics* has for four decades been the most popular quantum course in popular culture with a digestible diet of what, in a slightly derogatory way, is often called *quantum mysticism*—the combination of quantum physics, philosophy, spirituality and consciousness theory. Capra's legacy has in our time, for better or worse, been passed on to many others. One of the books that can be considered both popular and serious is *The Non-Local Universe: The New Physics and Matters of the Mind* by Robert Nadeau and Menas Kafatos (2001).

The World as Flux

Now, one possible meeting point between quantum physics and Eastern mysticism is the notion that basically the world has a 'liquid' nature; if so, the difference between matter and consciousness would not be as insuperable as is held by common sense. David Bohm once stated that matter has a 'mind-like quality.' And even if quantum physics is a patchwork of models and interpretations that sometimes complement, sometimes contradict each other, there is the consistent assumption that at the subatomic level the world is not at all as firm and solid as our everyday experience would suggest. On the contrary, 'down there' the world can rather be described as a cascading mass of elementary particles and wave patterns—'quantum foam,' as it was famously dubbed by the 'physicists' physicist' John Wheeler, who has also coined the well-known concepts 'black hole' and 'wormhole.' Yes, one may even consider the particles to be statistical probabilities rather than existing entities, and they will therefore sometimes be referred to as *possible* particles! So—within modern quantum physics the rock-solid atoms ('atom' means 'indivisible' in Greek) of classical physics have been replaced with 'building blocks' which are highly unstable and fluid—just as unstable and fluid as the ever-changing yin and yang of Taoism!

Maybe this constant state of flux, this 'mind-like quality' of matter, is what conceivably could enable psychokinetic phenomena, e.g. metal bending with the power of thought, for which those such as Uri Geller—rightfully, or perhaps not—became world famous. Physicist John Hasted, former head of research at Birkbeck College, University of London, thought this to be the case. In his book *The Metal Benders*, Hasted has presented many laboratory experiments where mental metal bending allegedly took place under tightly controlled conditions. This uncanny phenomenon is reported to have occurred even when the test subjects were not able to touch the metal at all, e.g. the objects were placed inside sealed glass bottles; this seems to reduce the possibility that the effect was due to cheating. In his own experiments,

Hasted for the most part used ordinary people—often children—as test subjects, and not professional mediums or psychics (who may be wolves in sheep's clothing—cheaters or magicians). Hasted eventually became fully convinced that mental metal bending was for real; nevertheless, he was frustrated with his research since he failed to provide a satisfactory theoretical explanation for the phenomenon.

Consciousness in Charge

Another possible tangential point between quantum physics and Eastern mysticism is, as we have already heard, the preeminent role assigned to consciousness. In some interpretations of quantum physics the observer/consciousness is seen almost as a co-creator of the world. I'll try to explain: It is thought that the world takes shape when the 'potentials are realized' by conscious observation. Etymologically 'realize' stems from Latin: *res* = 'thing, event, deed, fact,' and to 'realize' something basically means to bring it into existence. Many readers will probably know about the mysterious double nature of light. In one experimental setup a beam of light will emerge as waves, while in another setup it will appear as particles! These two different embodiments of the beam—waves, particles—are just *possibilities* until the observer during the experiment *realizes* one of them. There are several interpretations of this highly puzzling phenomenon—one is that the observer by his/her conscious observation virtually *creates* the light beam into becoming either waves or particles. These, I'll have to admit, are not easily accessible matters; I take refuge in the words of physics genius and Nobel laureate Richard Feynman, who has stated that 'anyone who claims to understand quantum theory, is either lying or crazy.'

Some physicists take the extreme view of the role of the observer/consciousness, and claim that if there is no observer to 'collapse the wave function' and 'realize the potential,' then the world simply cannot become manifest, cannot become existent! Based on this idea, the physicist and Nobel laureate Eugene Wigner theorized that there must be some kind of omnipresent Consciousness in the universe—a Consciousness that observes, and thus manifests the world.

Vedanta—Wisdom from Ancient India

Wigner found support for his idea of such an omnipresent Consciousness in the old Indian philosophy called *Vedanta* (*veda* means 'knowledge, understanding' in Sanskrit). Here there is a clear parallel to *panpsychism*, as discussed above, where the whole world is seen as imbued with psyche/consciousness. And from the perspective of the history of ideas it is, in fact, thought that the *fons et origo*, the original source, of panpsychism, via a complex history, can perhaps be found in Vedanta. The possible lineage could be as follows.

There were trade and other exchanges between India and Greece in antiquity, both under Persian rule and increasingly so under Alexander the Great (who during his Indian campaign happened to be joined by Pyrrho, later the founder of skepticism). Via this barter—some historians argue—Vedic philosophy may have infused Greek thought, e.g. the ideas about reincarnation found in Pythagorism and Platonism. Later, Vedic influence may have seeped into the European stock of ideas via Stoic speculations about the *Logos*—the creative Reason, the Divine Word, thought to be omnipresent. This composite baton was in the next leg passed on to Christianity, which can be seen in the famous beginning of the Gospel of John, 'In the beginning was the Word/Logos,' where the *Logos* is identified with Christ. There was also a parallel current in Neo-Platonism and Alchemy, with their ideas of the *anima mundi*, the omnipresent World Soul.

And 'the same old story' seems to continue: Vedanta, with its ubiquitous Consciousness, became a valuable inspiration for Erwin Schrödinger, a preeminent pioneer in quantum physics. To his friends Schrödinger often quoted in Sanskrit from the Upanishads, the sacred texts that Vedanta is based on. And based on Vedanta, Schrödinger conceived consciousness to be a *first fact*—a 'building block' of existence, something having *perseity*, meaning that it exists in and by itself. He therefore did not think that consciousness could be reduced to brain chemistry. And he meant this irreducibility did not only apply to the *existence* of consciousness but also to its qualitative aspects:

> *The sensation of color cannot be accounted for by the physicist's objective picture of light waves. Could the physiologist account for it, if he had fuller knowledge than he has of the processes in the retina and the nervous processes set up by them in the optical nerve bundles and in the brain? I do not think so.*

According to Vedanta there is basically just *one* consciousness. One of the images used to illustrate this is a cut crystal. In its facets it reflects the world in many different ways, yet it is still the same crystal. In keeping with this an individual's consciousness is taken to be an expression of the great Consciousness, much like—to use another image—a vortex in a river is basically an expression of the river, and does not have a separate existence. Schrödinger says: 'Vedanta teaches that consciousness is one, all events are played out within a universal consciousness, and there is no diversity of "selves."' So, this means that both Jack's consciousness and Jill's consciousness, my consciousness and your consciousness, are basically one and the same; we all participate in the one, collective, cosmic Consciousness. And if so, the simple model of consciousness we have proposed in this book—of a Mental Internet in which the separate computers are linked together—seems to fit in perfectly (how very convenient!).

Vedanta also advocates that consciousness reveals itself in many places in nature, not unlike the way (to again use this more modern image) electricity emanates in different types of batteries. Schrödinger has in accord with this argued that even simple organisms, such as earthworms, have consciousness, or, better, *participate* in consciousness, to the degree to which their nervous systems allow. Even if Schrödinger can sound like an ardent New Ager, he seems to have been completely uninterested in whether or not this collective Consciousness enables psi phenomena (and he has argued explicitly against reincarnation). Conversely, a great contemporary physicist, Cambridge professor and Nobel laureate Brian Josephson—also inspired by Vedanta—has long been a warm proponent of the psi hypothesis. Josephson seems to have taken a special interest in telepathy and psychokinesis—phenomena he even claims to have had convincingly demonstrated!

The Perennial Philosophy

An influential proponent for the unification of Eastern and Western thought, who probably is more accessible than the great physicists, is the British author Aldous Huxley (1894–1963). Within fiction he is world-famous for the humorous/dystopian novel *Brave New World*, and in philosophy/religion he contributed with the long-term bestseller *The Perennial Philosophy*. This is a highly influential anthology where Huxley, through a wealth of quotes with accompanying comments, promotes what he conceives to be the essence of both Eastern and Western mystical traditions—an essence which perhaps could be summed up as: the experience of unity with the Divine, the imperative of Love, and openness toward the Miraculous. Huxley had a long-lasting apprenticeship with the Indian guru Swami Prabhavananda; he practiced meditation and wrote well over 40 articles about Vedanta.

Huxley was concerned with understanding how consciousness works, and to a certain extent parapsychology. In his famous essay *The Doors of Perception*, Huxley describes a medically controlled experience with the consciousness-expanding drug *mescaline*. The title of the essay is, as many probably know, taken from *The Marriage of Heaven and Hell*, a series of texts by the great English mystic William Blake, where one of the lines reads: 'If the doors of perception were cleansed, everything would appear to man as it is, infinite.' This line is also the ultimate source for the name of the cult band The Doors. If the mental rust is blown out of the pipes, Huxley suggests, we will have access to the *Mind at Large* where vast amounts of information is stored—yes, when we are in contact with this sphere, we will be virtually omniscient (like one occasionally can feel when browsing the Internet). Huxley sums up his view with a quote from the philosopher C.D. Broad:

Each person is at each moment capable of remembering all that has ever happened to him and of perceiving everything that is happening everywhere in the universe. The function of the brain and nervous system is to protect us from being overwhelmed and confused by this mass of largely useless and irrelevant knowledge, by shutting out most of what we should otherwise perceive or remember

at any moment, and leaving only that very small and
special selection which is likely to be practically useful.

Huxley thus promotes a vision, based on both Eastern and Western sources, which matches splendidly with the view promoted by *Irreducible Mind* (which is not surprising, as Frederick Myers—among others—was a common source for both), namely that our everyday experience of the world is based on a constriction, a limitation, a filtered selection of reality that the brain arranges for us. But—maybe not all of us filter out to the same degree? Perhaps there are some who in a natural way, without the potentially dangerous influence of mescaline and other psychoactive substances (an artificial weakening of the filtration can sometimes cause the mental fuses to blow), slip through larger amounts of information from the *Mind at Large*? And perhaps such people are not only to be found in the secluded monasteries of the Himalayas, or in the mythological mountains of Shambala, but can also be strolling around freely in our own neighborhood? There are, as we soon shall see, good reasons to believe that this is precisely the case!

From the Himalayas to Hallingdal, from Shambala to Snåsa—Space Has No Limits

This chapter opened with a quote by the prominent biologist Thomas Huxley, grandfather of Aldous, where he used the jinni ('jinni' is the correct—singular—form, whereas 'jinn' is plural) in Aladdin's lamp to illustrate the enigma of consciousness. If we now expand this image a little further, we'll remember that one of the properties of this jinni is that it stands outside of the normal spatial limitations. It will in an instant have moved anywhere, there to fetch slaves and camels, silk and khadi, gold and precious stones, perfumes and delectable dishes and everything else that Aladdin's heart should desire. So, even if the jinni (probably for some unknown practical purpose) resides inside the lamp, it is not bound to any specific place, rather it could be described as being *non-local*, as it is often dubbed.

As we will now illustrate, both with examples and with experiments, it can seem as if non-locality is a feature not only of Aladdin's, but also of *our* jinni, i.e. our consciousness. And even if it does not always provide us with the amount of gold and precious stones allotted to Aladdin, it nevertheless allows us to acquire treasures unearthed by the Himalayan sages—jewels of wisdom polished by tradition and given a final luster by writers such as Aldous Huxley. Bringing with us a little of this wealth we now mount our flying carpet and whizz telekinetically back to the shores of home. (The stories about 'flying carpets' are based on out-of-body experiences that happened when Sufis, Islamic mystics, were sitting in deep meditation on their prayer rugs.)

Our first stop is in Hallingdal in Norway—the home of Ivar Flatmo, who was one of the most well-known psychics in Norway until, in 1988, he died under ugly circumstances (stabbed to death in his own home). Flatmo certainly seems to have been a exceptional man: Many have told of how he would describe the interior of their homes where he had never set foot, and also of how, based on his alleged clairvoyance, he succeeded in recovering wedding rings, jewelry and other valuables that had been lost or misplaced. There are also quite a few stories of how Flatmo—sitting in his living room—was able to locate animals lost in the forest. (Flatmo lived in a rural area and local farmers often asked him for help with matters of this kind.)

Flatmo was artistically gifted but socially inept, and periodically he was also given to alcohol, to some extent because his psychic visions imposed a heavy burden on him. When performing daily tasks as, say, going to the store, he would sometimes 'see' the shape of a sideways figure eight (a symbol of infinity) on the back of another customer. In Flatmo's experience this vision of an eight would announce the impending death of the person concerned—obviously not a sight suited to please! Flatmo also had a terrifying vision of the dramatic events on January 28, 1986, when the space shuttle *Challenger* exploded in the air and the entire crew perished. Regardless of how one would explain such an experience—clairvoyance or hallucination—it certainly must have been a most jarring sight for the highly sensitive Flatmo.

Despite his many personal difficulties Flatmo was usually accommodating when people asked for his assistance. Even the Red Cross and the police consulted him from time to time. Once he was asked to help find a person who had drowned. Kjell Askildt at the Hol police station (who later became quite influential in the force, and published a book about his career) relates that when Flatmo appeared at the lake he immediately pointed out where he felt the dead person was lying. Then he went out in a boat together with the search crew and told them where to lower the underwater camera—and the camera bumped right into the corpse! Flatmo subsequently went on to locate the boots and other articles belonging to the deceased. Kjell Askildt summarizes: 'I am convinced of Ivar Flatmo's ability to find missing things and people. His visions were not always correct—there may be many reasons for that. But both I and others in my department have benefited from the information Flatmo was able to obtain.'

Similar abilities are also ascribed to 'celebrity-psychics' such as Anna Elisabeth Westerlund (1907–1995). She had a regular column in a women's magazine and has published several books. In one of them—one that has the almost *too* telling title *I Found the Corpse*—she reprinted letters from both private persons and public officials confirming that she had located their lost relatives and other persons. And like-wise, Joralf Gjerstad, the 'Snåsa Man'—depicted in chapter 5—has been credited with a number of such feats. In 2010 Gjerstad successfully assisted in finding a person who was missing after a snowslide tragedy (two other persons had, by then, already been found dead). The avalanche ex-pert Oddgeir Johansen's report, which was published with the consent of the relatives of the deceased, was reprinted in several newspapers, including the main journals *Aften-posten* and *Dagbladet*. Johansen contacted the Snåsa Man by phone, and was asked to imagine the site of the accident. Johansen relates what then happened:

> He [*the Snåsa Man*] explained that he was now able to see the place and asked me to turn my head to the North. He could then describe the terrain down to the smallest detail, the surrounding mountains and how the slide looked. He then (correctly) indicated the area where the last of the deceased was. I cannot imagine he would have any qualifications to describe the place as precisely as he did, says Johansen. [...] We had already decided to search in that particular area. It was one of the primary sectors. But what was surprising was the description he gave of the terrain and the conditions, because it matched so in-credibly well. He had never been in the area and had lit-tle prerequisite for knowing it [...] I'll just have to bow,

and I think that there are some who see more than others
see [...]. (*Dagbladet,* online version, May 29, 2010.
Link to the article can be found in the bibliography.)

If we are not to believe that the many reliable people who relate such stories—private persons, police officers, avalanche
experts, etc.—for some strange reason should be fibbers
in disguise, it raises the question: Perhaps people such as
Flatmo, Westerlund and the Snåsa Man have fewer filters
in relation to the overwhelming bulk of information which
according to both *Irreducible Mind,* Huxley and Vedanta lies
in the *Mind at Large*? And that they, after having learned
how to relate to this chaotic material, in fact have become
'capable of remembering all that has ever happened [...] and
of perceiving everything that is happening everywhere in
the universe.' Or, as we describe it in step with our more
modern model: Perhaps such people have a somewhat lower
firewall and are kitted out with a somewhat better search
engine on the Mental Internet?

Well, whatever descriptions one should find fitting, both
in the East and in the West, in the wisdom traditions and
in science, from the laboratory and from the field, there are
literally countless reports about phenomena that seem to
demolish 'the standard model,' where consciousness is conceived to be 'brain urine,' a mere byproduct of processes in
the brain. It could therefore be due time to consider more
inclusive and fruitful models that have ample space for the
full grandeur of our consciousness. Because just as Aladdin's
jinni cannot unfold its power if locked within the lamp, also
our jinni will probably be unable to display *its* full beauty
and potential if suffering behind the bars of severely limiting theories!

Immanuel Kant and Emmanuel Swedenborg—Occultism at the Heart of Philosophy

Let us have a closer look at non-locality (spooky action at a distance) by going back to one of the philosophical giants, namely Immanuel Kant (1724–1804). The Norwegian author Jens Bjørneboe humorously referred to him as 'the mastodon' because of his colossal weight in the history of philosophy. In his heyday, Kant and the swarm of interpreters feeding on his work were described by poets Goethe and Schiller in an aphorism:

> Such is it, then, that a rich man will feed droves of beggars,
> Kings build their castles, make carters busy at work!

Let's put our pride aside, and blend in together with the other beggars and gorge ourselves with some of the delicacies served by King Kant!

Space and Time—the Way We See the World

Some of Kant's main philosophical contributions were made regarding consciousness—not so much about how it arises, but rather how it works. Kant's most radical idea in this area, the shift of perspective he himself described as a 'Copernican revolution' (after Nicolas Copernicus, who gave us a radically new understanding of the solar system), was that neither Space nor Time are parts of the physical world, but are rather embedded within our own consciousness! Space and Time are namely used by our consciousness as 'tools' to organize our reality; what we experience will be placed in Space and in Time: 'Let's have a coffee on the pier (Space) tomorrow night (Time),' 'We met in Venice (Space) in the summer four years ago (Time).' Such organizing is all-encompassing, and is done spontaneously, continuously and inevitably. Space and Time are in some sense the 'spectacles' through which we see the world. If you wear glasses with green lenses, everything you look at will seem green. But the beautiful green color you then see when, for example, looking at the sky, certainly does not derive from the sky but from your glasses. In a somewhat similar way, according to Kant, our consciousness is wearing 'Space glasses' and 'Time glasses' and this is the reason why we experience Space and Time as part of the physical world.

The reality lying behind our 'glasses' Kant named *Ding an sich*—the thing for itself. This is a sphere he thinks we cannot really get to know, thus he is extremely reluctant to try to give descriptions—in writing, that is. But from notes made by his students, we can see that in his lectures Kant actually speculates quite a lot about this sphere and our possible experience of it after death. His statements seem to indicate that he thinks that the intellectual part of man may well be immortal and may after death continue to exist in a spiritual state, beyond time and space, where communication is immediate—in fact, quite like by telepathy...

If we speculate further along Kant's 'spectacular' way of thought, we might wonder: Does our consciousness have the opportunity to take off its 'Space glasses' in this life? ('Time glasses' we shall return to in chapter 8). For it could, in fact, seem to be exactly this that occurs when the Snåsa Man, according to the avalanche expert mentioned earlier in the chapter, provides a detailed description of a place where he never has been. It seems that to him—that is, to his consciousness—Space (distance) simply does not exist. And Kant has in fact made statements indicating that it, at least for some people, might be possible to 'throw away the glasses.' The reason for such an occult way of thinking was his preoccupation with Emanuel Swedenborg (1688–1772), a famous Swedish scientist and mystic.

A Swashbuckling Swede

Swedenborg had done research in geometry, chemistry, metallurgy and astronomy, and later he made some highly 'modern' discoveries/suggestions regarding the functions of the nervous system and of the brain. However, after a spiritual crisis around 1740 Swedenborg increasingly turned his focus toward the occult and studied Christian mysticism and the Kabbalah, the Jewish esoteric tradition. Swedenborg had many exalted visions of the afterlife, and felt he could communicate with dead people. And last but not least, he seemed to have developed a strong ability for clairvoyance, of which he gave several astonishing demonstrations. This had given Kant something—in fact, a lot—to think about...

Our knowledge of these matters stems not from Kant's books for here he is usually reticent or even flat-out negative regarding the occult. However, we have a long personal letter in his hand telling a quite different story. Kant had, probably some time during 1762, received a request from Charlotte von Knobloch, a lady who wanted to know what Kant thought about Swedenborg and his alleged clairvoyant abilities. Kant was a thorough man, and spent a lot of time familiarizing himself with the matter. In his reply dated

August 10, 1763 he apologizes to the gracious lady that she had had to wait:

> *I would not have deprived myself so long of the honor and pleasure of obeying the request of a lady who is the ornament of her sex, in communicating the desired information, if I had not deemed it necessary previously to inform myself thoroughly concerning the subject of your request.*

Now, these were times in which one knew how to express oneself! Kant goes on to say that he is not aware that anybody has ever 'perceived in me an inclination to the marvelous or a weakness tending to credulity.' And he relates that he had been, if not completely dismissive, at least very wary of stories about spirits and other occult matters, 'This is the position in which my mind stood for a long time, until the report concerning Swedenborg came to my notice.' (Kant often shortens Swedenborg's name, Hr von Swed, etc. but we'll spell it out in full.) Kant now presents two well-documented cases that he believes show Swedenborg's clairvoyant abilities to be beyond doubt. The story that made the strongest impression on him was related to the great fire in Stockholm in 1756. We'll give the word to Kant:

> *The following occurrence appears to me to have the greatest weight of proof, and to place the assertion respecting Swedenborg's extraordinary gift beyond all conceivable doubt.*
>
> *In the year 1759, towards the end of September, on Saturday at four o'clock p.m., Swedenborg arrived at Gothenburg from England, when Mr. William Castel invited him to his house, together with a party of fifteen persons. About six o'clock Swedenborg went out, and returned to the company quite pale and alarmed. He said*

that a dangerous fire had just broken out in Stockholm, at the Södermalm (Gothenburg is more than fifty miles [one old German mile = c. 7.5 km] from Stockholm) and that it was spreading very fast. He was restless, and went out often. He said that the house of one of his friends, whom he named, was already in ashes, and that his own was in danger. At eight o'clock, after he had been out again, he joyfully exclaimed, 'Thank God! the fire is extinguished; the third door from my house.'

This news occasioned great commotion throughout the whole city, but particularly amongst the company in which he was. It was announced to the Governor the same evening. On Sunday morning Swedenborg was summoned to the Governor who questioned him concerning the disaster. Swedenborg described the fire precisely, how it had begun and in what manner it had ceased, and how long it had continued.

On the same day the news spread through the city, and as the Governor thought it worthy of attention, the consternation was considerably increased; because many were in trouble [upset] on account of their friends and property, which might have been involved in the disaster.

On Monday evening a messenger arrived at Gothenburg, who was dispatched by the Board of Trade during the time of the fire. In the letters brought by him, the fire was described precisely in the manner stated by Swedenborg.

On Tuesday morning the Royal Courier arrived at the Governor's with the melancholy intelligence [news] of the fire, of the loss which it had occasioned, and of the houses it had damaged and ruined, not in the least differing from that which Swedenborg had given at the very time when it happened; for the fire was extinguished at eight o'clock.

What can be brought forward against the authenticity of this event? My friend who wrote this to me has examined all, not only in Stockholm, but also, about two months ago, in Gothenburg, where he is well acquainted with the most respectable houses, and where he could obtain the most authentic and complete information, for as only a very short time has elapsed since 1759, most of the inhabitants are still alive who were eyewitnesses of this occurrence.

So, here we see the Enlightenment's greatest philosopher professing his conviction of the reality of Swedenborg's clairvoyance—a strong testimony, indeed!

It may therefore seem surprising that Kant in 1766 published a tract called *The Dreams of a Spirit-Seer*, where he writes ironically about both Swedenborg's person and his ideas. But nevertheless Kant repeats an abbreviated version of the story of the fire in Stockholm, plus a few other accounts of Swedenborg's clairvoyance. Confusing... so that it's hard to be sure what Kant really intended with this publication. Kant's friend, the Enlightenment philosopher Moses Mendelssohn (grandfather of the composer Felix Mendelssohn of the 'Wedding March' fame), writes that one is left in doubt whether Kant 'wanted to make fun of metaphysics, or whether he wanted to praise clairvoyance.' It seems likely, though, that the tract was a reflection of Kant's disappointment with Swedenborg's *philosophy* (which we know he had studied thoroughly after writing the letter to Miss von Knobloch) due to its vast amount of quirky visions and lofty speculations. As a thinker, Kant was nothing if not rational.

All in all it would be apt to describe Kant's relationship both to the occult and to Swedenborg as *ambivalent*. Outwardly, such as in his legendary *Critique of Pure Reason*, Kant distances himself from 'these things.' While some smaller tracts and letters show that Kant, the rationalist *par excellence*, had a fascination with the guilty pleasures of occultism. Students' notes from his lectures show Kant repeatedly returning to Swedenborg, for the most part with respect, but his descriptions of the mystic/philosopher also portray him as from 'sublime' to 'cheater.' Some think that career considerations could have made Kant speak with forked tongues in relation to this heretical 'enthusiast' (*enthousiasmos* = god possessed). Others think the schism could be due to Kant undergoing internal conflicts, thereby changing his opinion over time. While still others have argued that the ambiguity is founded on Kant's distinction between *philosophy* (which can provide reliable, universally valid knowledge) and *revelation* (which *may* be true, but which could just as easily be wrong). And Kant, in fact, once stated that 'all sight of spirits and ghosts, all dream interpretations, predictions about the future, forebodings and things of that sort are inferior because they cannot be subsumed under any form of law.' *Ordnung muss sein*! (There must be order!) and Truth is too serious a matter to be left to the mercy of visionary whims and flights of fancy.

It has thus been customary to emphasize the disagreements in Kant's relationship to Swedenborg. But in recent times, some commentators have argued that Kant must surely have attributed great importance to Swedenborg since he deliberated over Swedenborg's ideas, engaging in internal, imaginary quarrels with him, for over 30 years! And it is likely that Swedenborg influenced several aspects of Kant's work.

In 1734 Swedenborg launched the now widely accepted *nebular hypothesis*, where the sun and other stars are thought to have been formed out of huge clouds of hydrogen. About 20 years later Kant published a work in which he further builds on this groundbreaking idea, which today is often referred to as the *Kant–Laplace hypothesis*.

Apparently Swedenborg also influenced a central idea in Kant's moral philosophy: that a person should never be considered as a means, but always as an end. Kant expresses this idea by saying that a human being is 'a citizen of the Kingdom of Purpose' (*Reich der Zwecke*). This strange concept is otherwise known only from Swedenborg (in Latin: *Regnum Finium*), where it describes a spiritual realm where souls communicate directly, as by telepathy. There is no physical space, and the 'position' of the individual souls in relation to one another is based on their mutual likes and dislikes, as well as their moral and spiritual levels.

And finally it has been claimed that Kant's radically new ideas about Space and Time, his epochal 'Copernican revolution,' can be seen as a de-theologized version of Swedenborg's philosophy, in which humans are considered to be participating in both a Spiritual World (essentially beyond Space and Time) and a sensual world (subjected to Space and Time). Similar notions are of course also found with other philosophers. But in addition to Swedenborg's *books* there was also, as we know, the impact of the incidents involving his alleged clairvoyance. For example, the episode where Swedenborg was purportedly able to 'see' the fire in Stockholm even when physically in Gothenburg. As we saw in the letter to Charlotte von Knobloch this episode made a strong impression on Kant; yes, he even claims it places Swedenborg's clairvoyance 'beyond all conceivable doubt.' So, this event demonstrated to Kant that Space (distance) poses no insurmountable barrier to consciousness. And perhaps this, then, was precisely what sparked off his idea that Space originates not from outside but from within, from consciousness itself? *If* this really should be the case—and for now we'll have to leave the issue to future archival research, hopefully discovering more letters, more lectures, etc.—then the perhaps most radical idea in Kant's mastodonic influential philosophy would be built on Swedenborg's clairvoyance!

The two men never met face to face, nor did they correspond. Kant sent Swedenborg a letter early in his career, but never received any reply. The collection *Kant on Swedenborg* (listed in the bibliography) contains some interesting texts illustrative of Kant's love–hate relationship with this highly gifted scientist and mystic.

Magic and Modernity

Not only in the case of Kant, but also generally, the emergence of modern philosophy and science was far more influenced by mysticism, magic and occultism than one is usually aware. Goethe, intuitive and precise cultural diagnostician as he was, expresses this connection by making his Doctor Faust—the symbol of modern man—to be a *philosopher, scientist* and *magician.* This modern mentality is certainly not the humility of the medieval monks and nuns, subordinate to God and to the Church. Nay, rather it is the self-reliance of the Renaissance magician, who with his/her will to power and insight into the forces of nature—for better or worse—takes control of the world, hesitant to recognize any heavenly or mundane limitations: Should we go to the Moon—sure, why not? Should we create artificial life—sure, why not? 'Man as Magus' is the classic slogan for this mentality.

This highly exciting theme—the importance of magic and occultism in the emergence of modern science and mentality—has for the past 50 years been charted by historians of ideas, pioneered by the groundbreaking work (although challenged by some) *Giordano Bruno and the Hermetic Tradition* (1964) by the British classicist Frances A. Yates. Unfortunately we do not have the space to delve into this matter here, so we will restrict ourselves to providing some quick examples.

Johannes Kepler, the pioneering astronomer, was also court astrologer and made his living from horoscopes. Giordano Bruno, who was burned at the stake, suffered this fate not only because of his astronomical theories but also just as much—probably even more so—for his occult beliefs. John Dee, England's greatest mathematician in the time of Elizabeth I, was deeply into occultism, mediumship and ritual magic. Robert Boyle, the father of modern chemistry, both researched and defended healing. And the great Sir Isaac Newton wrote in fact more pages on alchemy and biblical prophesies than on conventional science. Occult societies such as the Freemasons and Rosicrucians made significant contributions to the Scientific Revolution of 1500–1700. And to top it all it turns out that Immanuel Kant, the uncrowned king of the Enlightenment, could readily be described as being a closet occultist!

Given this close relationship earlier in history it could perhaps be hoped that science now—quite without shame— would dare to make use of some of the insights that occult traditions might possess regarding consciousness? For instance that it perhaps is able to act non-locally, as Swedenborg seemingly substantiates. Maybe if science could once again start talking more in depth with its black sheep relative, occultism, we could take steps to further develop the model of consciousness called for earlier in this chapter. That is to say, a model that may better encompass the fullness of human experience, including the experiences of telepathy, clairvoyance and precognition that for some strange reason are reported from nearly all cultures, all places and all times.

Those non-ordinary experiences continue to occur even in our modern Western societies, where, as we mentioned in the introduction, more than half of the population according to statistics will have some kind of paranormal experience. If only a single one out of all these millions of experiences should be about *real* telepathy, *real* clairvoyance, *real* precognition—well, this would probably show the need to put the standard model of consciousness up for review. For to repeat William James: 'If you wish to upset the law that all crows are black, you mustn't seek to show that no crows are; it is enough if you prove one single crow to be white.' The award-winning (and controversial) Czech-American psychiatrist Stan Grof has published a fascinating book called *When the Impossible Happens* where herds of snow-white crows are flapping along the pages.

Which is Further Away: York or New York?—Entanglement and Non-Locality

The layman always means, when he says 'reality' that he is speaking of something self-evidently known; whereas to me

*it seems the most important and exceedingly difficult task
of our time is to work on the construction of a new idea of
reality.*

~ Wolfgang Pauli, physicist, Nobel laureate

In 2011 a book with the amusing title *How the Hippies Saved
Physics: Science, Counterculture, and the Quantum Revival* was
released. The author, David Kaiser, a physicist and historian tenured at Harvard, shows how the postwar era saw
a shift in physics, which moved away from a philosophical
orientation toward a more technological approach. What
now became the important thing was physics' *instrumen-
tality*: making better shavers, faster cars, winning the arms
race, getting us to the moon, etc. Reading the writings of
the interwar period grandees, those who gave us the theory
of relativity and quantum theory—Einstein, Bohr, Heisenberg, Schrödinger, etc.—it becomes clear that they were not
only physicists but also philosophers. They intensely debated
the significance of physics in relation to the Big Questions,
and Life itself. The great Danish physicist Niels Bohr said:
'Who is not shaken by quantum theory has not understood
it.' That real physics meant far more than making sophisticated models, and expanding our mastery of the elements
was obvious.

We have already seen examples of both Erwin Schrödinger's and Wolfgang Pauli's mystical philosophical orientation. And as mentioned in chapter 4 in connection with
C.G. Jung, for Pauli this also meant taking the paranormal into account. The quantum-pioneer Pascual Jordan,
who was nominated for the Nobel Prize by Einstein (but
whose Nazi leanings may have cost him the award), wrote
several articles about parapsychology. And even Albert the

Great—Einstein himself—whose interest in general philosophy is well known, was not without an interest in the paranormal. A couple of times he attended séances and recounts having been really impressed with the amount of information the medium was able to provide—yes, he even invited her for supper afterwards, so impressed was he! (We'll take his word that this was the bona fide reason...)

Einstein also took the initiative to write a preface to *Mental Radio* (1930), a book about telepathy by the then famous author Upton Sinclair. Einstein writes: 'I have read the book of Upton Sinclair with great interest and am convinced that the same deserves the most earnest consideration, not only of the laity, but also of the psychologists by profession.' Note that Einstein does *not* claim that the book's many captivating case studies prove telepathy to be a reality, but still he concludes: 'In no case should the psychologically interested circles pass over this book heedlessly.' In 1946, in a letter to the psychoanalyst Jan Eherenwald, Einstein says he is skeptical about telepathy. But he also states: 'I can judge as a layman only, and cannot state that I arrived at an affirmative or negative conclusion (i.e. concerning telepathy). In any case, it appears to me that from the physicist's point of view, we have no right to rule out a priori the possibility of telepathy. For that the foundations of our science are too uncertain and incomplete...'

Even if the great physicists of the interwar period were not actively engaging in spiritual practices, their *longing*, their *urge*—having lost the security of Newtonian physics—may perhaps be aptly summed up in the yearnings of Goethe's Faust as he, having exhausted all normal science and being in deep despair, starts to embrace magic (and modern science has indeed become our form of magic!):

That I may detect the inmost force
Which binds the world, and guides its course.

Postwar Physics—from Philosophy to Engineering

The postwar generation of physicists, however, found that the new mathematical models had legs of their own, and that they worked perfectly without any accompanying philosophical musings. Their ambitions thus became more practical, e.g. delivering new technologies to business, to the military and to space exploration. The Cold War obviously had a marked impact on this shift to the practical as it became of utmost importance to keep apace technologically with the Eastern bloc. But it also seems as if even the *Zeitgeist*, the spirit of the age, was becoming extremely practical. Hence those nightly talks, delving into philosophy that the interwar physicists so fervently had engaged in, gradually fell out of fashion. Of course, there will always be the notable exception of the theoretical physicists but in general physicists in the period from, say, 1945 to 1970 became increasingly seen less as *philosophers* and more as *engineers*. Kaiser says that the *Physical Review*, the most prestigious of the physics journals, systematically refused to print articles having philosophical overtones. And the universities urged physics students to bring their philosophical concerns to heel. And so it came to be, according to Kaiser, that in the early 1970s the educational institutions were collectively chanting the mantra: 'Shut up and calculate!'

The Fundamental Fysiks Group

However, not everyone wanted to join this chorus: A group of gifted and playful young physicists at Berkeley thought they would rather ruffle some feathers and formed the *Fundamental Fysiks Group*—a kind of physics-based philosophical think tank. (They probably used 'f' and 'k,' rather than 'ph' and 'c,' in their name to allude to the great quantum pioneers, mostly writing in German.) This wild bunch of 'hippie-physicists,' like their interwar role models, dared to ask and even answer fundamental questions about the significance of physics for our worldview, not least for our views on humanity and consciousness.

Central names in the Fundamental Fysiks Group were Elizabeth Rauscher (quantum physicist, parapsychologist), Johan Clauser (quantum physicist, experimental physicist), Fritjof Capra (quantum physicist, mystical and environmental philosopher) and Henry Stapp (quantum physicist, awareness theorist; important for the authors of *Irreducible Mind*). Some of the physicists from the Fundamental Fysiks Group were used as consultants for Stargate, where, as we saw in chapter 2, the military and intelligence community tried to use clairvoyance for espionage purposes. More recently, their research has contributed to the development of so-called *quantum cryptography*, applying the principles of quantum physics to ensure that, say, financial transactions and electronic voting become unhackable (but it seems the technology wasn't implemented in the 2016 US elections. Sad.).

The Fundamental Fysiks Group was particularly engaged in *Bell's theorem*, which implies that subatomic particles (the 'building blocks' of atoms) that had once been in close contact may somehow continue their 'relationship' even when moving apart from each other. This strange phenomenon—

strange for particles, not for humans!—is called 'entangle-ment.' The connection between them is said to be *non-local*. Already in the 1930s Einstein understood that bizarre phenomena like entanglement and non-locality lay embedded in quantum theory. But Einstein didn't believe things 'hang together' in this way—quite literally—and critically labeled the idea *spukhafte Fernwirkung*, 'spooky action at a distance.' Nevertheless, despite his impressive intellect, Einstein was wrong about quantum entanglement. And the first to experimentally demonstrate that entanglement and quantum non-locality is indeed real was John Clauser from the Fundamental Fysiks Group.

Einstein was however convinced of the possibility of another type of non-locality, namely the *Einstein-Rosen Bridge*, popularly called 'wormholes.' These are 'shortcuts' through Space and Time, allowing us—just in theory, as for now—to enter the universe in one place and emerge in quite another! This exciting concept has been further developed by the award-winning physicist Kip Thorne.

One classic experiment demonstrating quantum entanglement entails making two electrons collide. In the collision 'sparks' are formed; two particles of light, twin photons, hurtle off in opposite directions. What is really fabulous, then, is that if one measures the movement of one of those photons (e.g. making a turn to the right) then the exact movement, but in an inverted way, can be measured from the other photon (making a turn to the left). The two photons are connected and behave like a unit, even if from all commonly held notions of space they are completely separated. And this applies, at least in principle, even if the photons should travel to either side of the universe!

Non-local connections were first detected between extremely tiny particles, but it has subsequently been demonstrated that they also form between larger molecules. One is unsure as to the extent and importance of the phenomenon. Most physicists apparently believe that non-locality primarily has significance at the micro-level. This is because the entangled particles for the most part will be 'disturbed' and thus decouple within a very short time. And then, falling back to a more stable state (de-coherence), there is no more entanglement but just 'business as usual.' While some argue that since all matter in fact was concatenated when the Big Bang 'banged,' it is in some sense and on some level reasonable to regard the world as forever being a vast network of non-local entanglements.

Regardless: several members of the Fundamental Fysiks Group felt that entanglement exhibits striking parallels to telepathy, in the sense that in both phenomena—the first one physical, the other one psychical—transcend what is usually thought of as Space. Could it be, then, that not only small particles but also our consciousness at a deep level works in an entangled and non-local way? Let's once more use our little model of the Mental Internet: If you, for example, log onto Facebook, the profile of a person in York and a person in New York will in fact be at the same distance from you—if you're online, you're online!

The physicists in the Fundamental Fysiks Group had ideas pointing in this direction, and Elizabeth Rauscher, one of the group's founders, has developed a highly sophisticated mathematical model that she thinks is able to explain the relationship between non-locality and the psi phenomena. This initiative was supported by the aforementioned Nobel laureate Eugene Wigner who, as has been said, was one of the physicists believing consciousness to be ubiquitous.

Another formerly mentioned Nobel laureate is the physicist Brian Josephson, who, although living in England, has fraternized with the Fundamental Fysiks Group. Josephson, who is an outspoken defender of psi, has spent the past decades researching the role of quantum physics and information theory in understanding biological processes. The possibility that telepathy and other psi phenomena are allowed for by quantum theory is frequently evoked by those who are psi positive and almost equally frequently dismissed by skeptics. But Josephson, who thinks that quantum physics is only a step on the road to explaining nature, thinks that entanglement and non-locality could provide useful models to make intelligible how psi phenomena may occur. Josephson has also humorously said that some seem to be so diehard skeptical that they probably would not have believed in psi even if they knew it to exist!

From Twin Photons to Twin Sisters

We are like islands in the sea, separate on the surface but connected in the deep.

~ William James

Both Kant's idea that Space does not belong to the world itself, but rather is embedded in our own 'glasses,' our consciousness, as well as quantum physics' notion of entanglement and non-locality, seem to suggest that spatial distance isn't a barrier as insurmountable as often imagined. For perhaps consciousness in itself is basically a non-local phenomenon? And maybe precisely this is what could explain telepathy and clairvoyance? Now, we may argue and speculate, debate and deliberate, but luckily we need not roam around in complete conjectural darkness, for in fact some 'hard' science has been done that seemingly supports this hypothesis! Let's have a look at an experiment that took place in Denmark in 2010.

Sara and Vicky are identical twins in their late twenties. They have always perceived themselves as being in close telepathic contact with one another—'two souls, one thought' is for them no cliché, but a most real thing. For example: Many times they independently of each other—at least on the physical plane—buy the same object (such as the exact same piece of clothing) at the very same time. Since these things happen regularly, and since they both think there are enough similarities between them as it is, they have made the following agreement: The sister who has the earliest issued cash register receipt gets to keep her object, while the other has to go back to the store and trade hers in! Quirky issues... But—need these coincidences be due to telepathy? Couldn't their shared genes and common upbringing—normal physio-psychological factors—just as well be the reason they act in this coordinated manner? So which is it: paranormal or normal? Both the sisters as well as psychologist Adrian Parker, tenured professor at the University of Gothenburg, were eager to find out. Professor Parker thus designed an experiment that goes as follows.

Sara was placed in an isolated room in a laboratory where she—of course voluntarily—would be subjected to four mild shocks. Meanwhile, her sister Vicky was placed in a remote room where she was connected to advanced apparatus measuring bodily responses such as blood pressure, pulse, respiratory rhythm and electrical skin conductivity. To oversee and control the measurements a British expert on lie detectors had been hired. And to ensure an impartial assessment an inspector from the Danish police was present.

The four shocks Sara would be subjected to were: electric shock (an electric current sent through her finger), cold shock (her legs suddenly exposed to icy water), noise shock (a stack of plates shattered behind her back) and intimidation (a big 'jack-in-the-box' jumping out). But no one—neither the sisters nor the researchers—knew exactly *when* the shocks would be delivered, as this would be decided randomly by a computer. The reason why Parker chose such a procedure was to prevent cheating and/or suggestion from influencing the results. Since the points in time for the shocks were unknown, it was not possible for the sisters (or for the scientists) to coordinate their emotional reactions, either consciously or unconsciously.

The experiment started, and the results were astonishing: When Sara (sitting inside the isolated lab) was given the various shocks, strong bodily reactions were measured from Vicky! This apparently telepathic 'shock-transference' occurred with the first three shocks. But nothing happened in connection with the jack-in-the-box. As this didn't frighten Sara, then, logically enough, no shock could be transferred. Within the boundaries of the standard model, where consciousness is seen to exist only inside the head of the individual, it seems very difficult to explain this result (unless one believes that the whole experiment is just a clever deception). If, however, one instead imagines that consciousness itself is an entangled phenomenon, working non-locally, then it is obviously much easier to understand how one sister spontaneously can have strong reactions when the other sister is subjected to shocks!

There is another interesting peculiarity about this experiment, namely that the sensors measuring Vicky's reactions spiked two to three seconds *before* the various shocks were given. Disregarding, of course, possible cheating and methodological errors, this suggests precognition to have been at work. Many parapsychologists think the different psi phenomena could likely be seen as different expressions of one and the same phenomenon, whose essence is to 'escape' our everyday world of Space, Time and Causality. Consequently, these phenomena are not easily studied isolated from each other, neither in theory nor in practice. In chapter 8, in connection with J.B. Rhine, we will throw a little more light on this tricky side of psi, which is underscored by many parapsychologists and ridiculed by even more skeptics!

I have been communicating with Professor Parker, and he told me the procedures of his experiment are described in the latest edition of *Twin Telepathy* by Guy L. Playfair. Let me add that several other researchers have also performed experiments of a similar type, apparently being able to measure telepathic transference of sounds, lights and other stimuli.

The results from Professor Parker's experiment correspond very well with the many stories circulating about people having strong bodily and/or emotional reactions simultaneously—or even just before—a close relative or friend is exposed to shock, accident or death. And as we know, this is what is often called *crisis telepathy*. An acquaintance of mine related the following little story: a woman, a friend of the family, had—apparently for no reason—risen up in bed in the middle of the night, exclaiming: 'My brother is in pain!' It later turned out that at that very moment her brother had been seriously injured in a car accident. So, was her eerily well-timed exclamation just a coincidence?—well, of course it *could* have been that, but... I'm convinced, based on experience as well as on hard statistics, that quite a few readers will have heard similar stories from *their* friends and/or family, or have themselves experienced such things. Even if nothing is finally proven, I think it is fair to say, though, that Adrian Parker's experiment indicates that such stories need not be based on misunderstandings, lies or coincidences. Rather, it seems to support the possibility that at least some of the accounts of this type could refer to non-local communication between people—or telepathy, as we usually call it.

Summary: Perspectives—'Kantum' Physics and Quantum Physics

Well then, we have now arrived at the end of this little excursion in the highly diverse landscapes of consciousness! God/Fate/Coincidence willing we have avoided drowning in quagmires and swamps, falling prey to the anaconda of angst, the crocodile of confusion and other soul-swallowing monsters. Sure, it has been difficult many a time to overview the hills and the valleys, the jungles and the vast plains. But hopefully we have now and then gained a panoramic glimpse or two, allowing us to see things thought to be well known from a new angle and in a new light. And perhaps that may have opened some exciting new perspectives for us? 'The hard question'—why conscious experience arises at all—we have neither answered nor tried to answer. But perhaps we have succeeded in kneading some stiffened clichés about what consciousness is and how it works? The chapter has in that respect had two main points which are closely related.

First point: There are things that indicate that consciousness in the last resort might be something other and much more than just reflections of flickering brain chemistry.

Tentatively, consciousness may rather be seen as a kind of vast information field with a degree, perhaps even a high degree, of independent existence. Notions of this kind go way back in both Eastern and Western traditions, and lie at the base of many of the classical concepts denoting human consciousness, as for instance soul, spirit, psyche, pneuma, atman, ruach, and neshamah.

Psi phenomena—and several other anomalies, such as savantism, seem easier to welcome and explain with such an understanding than within a standard, 'BrainUrine-based,' model. The alternative models we briefly presented—Irreducible Mind, the Orch-Or, the hologram model, the zero point field—will all quite comfortably allow us to include the strange and exciting psi phenomena, or at least some of them. This is significant, for it has been said: 'An explanatory model is no better than the description it gives of reality.' Hence, if there are too many *anomalies*—experiences and incidents which the established model cannot account for in a convincing way (and concerning psi we are speaking of millions of cases)—it is natural, yes even necessary, that we look for other maps better describing the terrain. Meaning others models of consciousness better suited to accommodate the fullness of human experience.

Second point: Several things seem to indicate that our consciousness—in one way or another, at some level, working in some gear—acts non-locally, that is, without being confined to a specific place. Immanuel Kant's exciting idea that Space does not belong to the physical world, but rather stems from our own 'glasses,' may according to our (perhaps a bit daring!) interpretation be one approach to non-locality. Kant's ideas were likely inspired by the scientist and mystic Emanuel Swedenborg, both his work and the cases involving his alleged clairvoyance—most importantly the incident occurring in connection with the Stockholm fire in 1756.

This extraordinary event, which according to Kant's letter has 'the greatest weight of proof' and places 'Swedenborg's extraordinary gift beyond all conceivable doubt,' if faithfully portrayed by Kant, supports the idea that consciousness may have a non-local dimension.

Quantum entanglement in itself does not say anything about the properties of consciousness. But it does not seem unreasonable to assume that since non-locality is demonstrably real in some connections it could perhaps be in others as well. And as we heard: Einstein, who dismissed the idea of quantum entanglement, suggested the existence of what today is called 'wormholes'—shortcuts through Space and Time. This, in my humble opinion, is non-locality as good as any! That consciousness at its very base could be a non-local phenomenon has been proposed by several eminent physicists, some of them Nobel Prize winners. Moreover, Professor Adrian Parker's experiment with Sara and Vicky (as well as similar experiments done by other researchers) seems to validate the idea that there are non-local connections between people. From our perspective it is precisely these connections—regardless of which model is used to describe them—which eventually could explain telepathy and perhaps also other psi phenomena.

Chapter 7

ABOUT SKEPTICISM— PRIVATE, SCIENTIFIC, DOGMATIC

I am not very skeptical... a good deal of skepticism in a scientific man is advisable to avoid much loss of time, but I have met not a few men, who... have often thus been deterred from experiments or observations which would have proven serviceable.

~ Charles Darwin

It is really quite amazing by what margins competent but conservative scientists and engineers can miss the mark, when they start with the preconceived idea that what they are investigating is impossible. When this happens, the most well-informed men become blinded by their prejudices and are unable to see what lies directly ahead of them.

~ Arthur C. Clarke

Skepticism and Thought Patterns

The word 'skepticism' is derived from the ancient Greek verb *skeptomai* meaning to see, reflect, examine. The skeptical attitude thus initially is to have the mind of an explorer—keen to know and open to the new. The Greek philosopher Phyrro (360–272 BCE) is often seen as the first philosophical skeptic. He believed that since all arguments can be met with counter arguments, there will always be a degree of uncertainty in our perception of reality. For most of us, however, skepticism is probably not primarily a philosophical position, but more a kind of reflex that is triggered when someone utters something that sounds unbelievable. We've no good reason to walk around believing in things we have neither *seen* occur nor have a good explanation as to how they *might* occur. The person who, excited or hesitant, tells us about, say, a healing or a prescient dream may be honest and sane, but maybe he/she still has misunderstood this or that aspect of the experience and therefore has jumped to conclusions? Hence what was just a random event could mistakenly have been interpreted as healing or precognition. We know that such things may easily happen and therefore we are skeptical.

A recurring fallacy is creating patterns from pure randomness, forging something normal into something paranormal. Some hardboiled skeptics therefore believe that *all* experiences of psi could—and should—be treated in this way. Phenomena such as telepathy, clairvoyance, precognition, healing, etc. do not *really* occur, they argue, but are merely misinterpretations: paranormal patterns are being imposed on perhaps unusual but still completely normal events. While the 'believers' retaliate by declaring that the skeptic's opinion could well be symptomatic of his/her own need for imposing clear-cut patterns of understanding on the world, hence the need to deny all 'disturbing' phenomena. C.G. Jung, with his concept of synchronicity (discussed in chapter 4), was of such an opinion, believing that a fear of the irrational is just *so Western*; that we have a well-developed capacity for logical thinking but sparse contact with the immensely complex and paradoxical depths of the soul. However, there is no doubt that the paranormal is an area heavy in speculation and light on confirmed facts, where pitfalls and pratfalls of all kinds are common. So a healthy skepticism toward our own perceptions and conceptions is advisable. Let's become acquainted with a couple of classics in the ignoble art of self-deception, fallacies so well established that they even have their own name!

The Texas Sharpshooter

Our first man out is the impressive marksman from Texas. Imagine a cowboy haphazardly firing a series of shots at a barn wall. Afterwards he goes over to the wall, sees a cluster of bullet holes, grabs a paintbrush and paints a target around the holes, then proudly exclaims: 'Ah, what a sharpshooter I am!' Not so... If he *beforehand* had been able to specify where all these bullets would hit then he would have been a superior sniper, but now he is just a self-deceiver—or a comedian! Now, let's say this cowboy eventually gets tired of shooting and instead ventures into the mysteries of astrology; perhaps he will score just as 'accurately'? Maybe he will immerse himself in the birth chart of, say, Adolf Hitler, and—with the blueprint of history in the back of his mind—find constellations in Hitler's horoscope revealing a character with a penchant for excessive control, brutality, and paranoia? But the question obviously is: Would our man have been able to say these things *beforehand*—if Hitler had been a baby today? I shall refrain from answering the question, but it seems obvious that the temptation to paint targets and zodiac profiles in hindsight is great, not only in shooting and stargazing but in divination of all kinds.

Littlewood's Law of Miracles

Next man out is the Cambridge mathematician John Littlewood with his semi-serious law of miracles. 'Littlewood's Law of Miracles' claims that a person should expect to experience a miracle about once a month. The 'proof'—summed up by one of Littlewood's students, physicist and mathematician Freeman Dyson—goes as follows:

> *During the time that we are awake and actively engaged in living our lives, roughly for eight hours each day, we see and hear things happening at a rate of one per second. So the total number of events that happen to us is about 30,000 per day, or about a million per month. With few exceptions, these events are not miracles because they are insignificant. The chance of a miracle is about one per million events. Therefore we should expect about one miracle to happen, on the average, every month.*

Littlewood's point is that 'the impossible' occurs from time to time. All of us will—because of the immense number of events we experience, the myriads of vortices in the river of life—occasionally experience inexplicable episodes. And it may be tempting to interpret such episodes as something paranormal—as the works of occult powers or spirits.

It is possible to broaden the perspective on Littlewood's law: Suppose we had the opportunity to peek into the dreams of a million different people on a given night. We would then most likely find that some of the dreams were nightmares about plane crashes, as there are many people who regularly travel by plane but are still quite nervous to do so. If one of those having such a nightmare should listen to the news next morning and happen to hear about a plane crash, he/she—if disposed toward the paranormal—might think that the dream had been clairvoyant or precognitive, somehow 'taking in' the plane crash. Whereas in reality there was no real connection between dream and crash, it was all coincidence. Experiences of this kind are common— of course not only related to plane crashes but also to terrorism, illness, and other kinds of drama which stir up strong emotions.

Selective Memory

A more peaceful type of 'paranormal' experience is this: Say you are strolling around town one fine afternoon. Suddenly you meet an acquaintance you haven't seen for quite a while, and at the same moment you remember that some hours earlier you had, in fact, been thinking about just this person! If a little predisposed toward the paranormal you'll perhaps say to yourself: 'Hmm, strange—maybe it was a premonition?' However, during the day you had probably not only been thinking about this specific person but, say, of *twenty* different people—family, friends, colleagues, people in the sports team, club members, etc. But you only remember thinking of the one particular person that you actually met, while the 19 others—all those you did *not* encounter—disappear unnoticed from the saga. So are the workings of our selective memory. It is more fun and interesting to notice, and therefore easier to remember, events that form a pattern than those which don't.

But, having said this, we should not ignore the possibility that paranormal prescience *may* have been involved. For perhaps you had been thinking for much longer and harder about the particular person that you met—yes, perhaps even to the extent that you said to yourself: 'I have a strong feeling that I soon will meet NN!' If *this* was what happened—and you met in a place where encountering NN was not to be readily expected (and you have to be honest with yourself)—then you *might* be a greater oracle than both the Texas sharpshooter and John Littlewood. Because neither of them was able to announce their 'miracles' *beforehand*.

Apophenia and Pareidolia— the Need for Patterns

Let's now have a look at a couple of modern concepts with ancient Greek roots, namely *apophenia* and *pareidolia*. Apophenia (*phenia* = construct, *apo* = of, from) is a concept that was minted by the German psychiatrist Klaus Conrad in 1954, and its essence can be expressed as 'the tendency to perceive meaningful patterns within random data.' Whereas pareidolia (*para* = beside, *eidolon* = image, shape) was coined by the skeptic Steven Goldstein in 1994 and can be described as 'the interpreting of random images and sounds as having meaning or pattern.' Apophenia is often seen as the 'big sister' while pareidolia is the 'little sister.' That is to say, apophenia is when we create a pattern between two or more *separate events*, such as in our example above where a person sees a connection between 1) a dream of a plane crash, and 2) a news report on the same. While pareidolia is seeing a pattern in a single situation, as when a passionate Elvis fan points to an unusual cloud formation in the sky and exclaims: 'Look there—it's Elvis!'

Apophenia and pareidolia will often be combined, however. Suppose you are a good Christian: Sunday morning, when you're making toast for breakfast, you suddenly see that the marks of the grill form a pattern looking somewhat like the face of Jesus (pareidolia). And maybe for a spilt second you have a little feeling of unrest because 'Jesus' appeared at the precise moment as you—perhaps because of yesterday's late night in town...—were planning to skip church (apophenia). Episodes of such and similar kinds happen all the time, and can involve any significant figure and person, as for instance the Virgin Mary, saints, gurus, lovers, parents, children, etc.

A 'meaningful' piece of toast of this type is sometimes called a *Cheesus*, and you can even buy special toasters to make them! Hard-boiled skeptics will argue that all psi phenomena—and also all religions—are no more than an enormous pile of *Cheesuses* where apophenia and pareidolia have caused trivial coincidences to be infused with sacred images and meanings not really there. Such instances are certainly to be found in the history of religion and psychiatry. But, in fact, all normal, healthy understanding—as for instance grasping the content of this book—depends on the ability to see meaning. And as pointed out in connection with Jung in chapter 4, true meaning may also be found in those coincidences which, so it seems, are organized by subconscious forces, the so-called *synchronicities*. The existence of counterfeit money doesn't exclude the existence or the value of real money—it's rather the opposite.

The expression *par excellence* of apophenia and pareidolia is conspiracy theories. I am sure many readers will remember the movie *A Beautiful Mind* where Russell Crowe plays the demon-ridden mathematical genius, John Nash—a true *apophenic*, a notorious pattern finder. Among other things the film shows how Nash finds secret messages, complex codes and intelligence in the pages of an ordinary newspaper. As opposed to common understanding, the apophenic will typically think that the real meaning of things and events is hidden, and that only a privileged few—the Chosen, the Elect (a group to which the apophenic belongs with both its blessings and burdens)—are able to perceive it. The *real* reality to these people, the true nature of things, is different from that grasped by most people; 'Nature is wont to hide herself,' as Heraclitus once said. As conspiracy theories are prone to paranoia they will sometimes be brimming with occult *Cheesuses*—paranormal patterns, symbols, rituals, codes, secret languages and handshakes, sacred geometry, etc. As mentioned in chapter 2, the reason why the *paranormal* so easily bonds with *paranoia* is the emphasis put on connections lying beside the normal ones (*para* = beside).

The paranoiac apophenic (it's getting heavy now…) will—because of his/her desperate need for hidden patterns—easily end up contravening reality. For if the facts don't fit the pattern, then woe to them! Woe, indeed, as the facts will suffer the same fate as the guests of the sinister metal smith Procrustes in Greek mythology. Procrustes tied his guests to a special bed made like a rack. And those who were too short for the bed, he would stretch to fit, while those who were too long got their feet chopped off! Skeptics tend to see a person believing in psi as an apophenic Procrustes stretching and cutting ordinary incidents to fit them into a paranormal pattern. But 'the parapsychotics' immediately strike back and rebuke the skeptics with: 'No, it is actually *you* who violate reality by closing your eyes to the anomalies—the phenomena, the data and the facts that do not fit into *your* system!' (Without having read the statistics I have a hunch that members from these two quarters seldom marry, and if they do they probably live happily never after...)

One could become more than a just a little worried on behalf of the human psyche because of our hardwired desire to find patterns, deceptive and deceiving as they often may be! But our ability to find/see/create/recognize patterns is of utmost importance if we are to establish a world with meaning and coherence; *Ordnung muss sein!*—There must be order!—as the Germans like to say (or at least they do in the movies). And biologically speaking, when wandering through the primeval forest it was precisely our ability to see patterns that helped us interpret the slow, delicate movements in the tall grass...thus avoiding being eaten by the leopard! (And it was obviously better to discern the leopard too often than too seldom...)

Moreover, all reading of signs and language depends in the last resort on our ability to see patterns: semiotics, semantics, words, grammar, and sentences. Also within art and music, indeed in all fields of creative and intellectual life—painting, sculpture, architecture, mathematics, chess, you name it—the ability to find/see/create/recognize patterns is a necessary requirement. Even within the natural sciences the ability to see a possible pattern, a possible natural law, is fundamental. Hence, skepticism about patterns as such is not viable; without patterns our world would dissolve into an amorphous, incomprehensible mass. The advice often given to us in wisdom traditions, Eastern and Western, is therefore not to *avoid* seeing/creating patterns but soberly to *observe* them: do I have a tendency to over-interpret trifles, negative or positive, and imbue them with meanings they don't really have? Am I fully alert, or do I tend to miss out important elements in situations? This type of skepticism, a sober, open questioning, espoused by many wisdom traditions with respect to belief as well as to doubt, is likely the most constructive approach to paranormal as well as normal phenomena.

Between Science and Dogma—CSI, the Committee for Skeptical Inquiry

Previously we have talked a bit about a basic skepticism that most of us probably have—and ought to have. But some do not stop there; rather they see skepticism as a principal virtue in life. The body most strongly associated with this kind of skepticism, and especially skepticism about the paranormal, is arguably CSI, the Committee for Skeptical Inquiry. Since 2015 the CSI has been a subdivision of the Center for Inquiry, a secular humanist organization.

CSI was originally called the Committee for the Scientific Investigation of Claims of the Paranormal, shortened to CSICOP which is pronounced a bit like—the quite descriptive—'Psi-cop'! Please note: For the sake of simplicity I will use only the modern short form, CSI.

CSI: Celebrity Skeptics International— Preconditions and Beginning

Over the years CSI has counted important scientists among their members, and eventually the committee, which originated in the US, has also many international branches and affiliated organizations. Several of the most profiled skeptics in the world today—'the celebrity skeptics'—can be found in the ranks of CSI. Early greats were the astrophysicist Carl Sagan and the biologist Stephen Jay Gould, and today we can, for instance, find the one and only Richard Dawkins, and also the psychologists Richard Wiseman, Susan Blackmore and Ray Hyman (who we became acquainted with in connection with Stargate). The story behind the formation of this powerful skeptic organization, and thereby also behind skepticism as a player within modern mass culture—with festivals, summer-camps, T-shirts, etc.—may roughly be sketched as follows.

The American public had for quite some time been baffled by the unreined, untethered and unbridled behavior of Christian dissenter churches such as the snake handlers, who take the Bible's prophecies literally—'They shall take up serpents; and if they drink any deadly thing, it shall not hurt them,' Mark 16:18—and thus believed themselves to be immune to venom, which they proved by dancing ecstatically with (live) rattlesnakes in their hands! Later, Christianity was augmented by such counterculture congregations as the Children of God, founded in 1968. The leader, David Berg, changed his name to Moses David (no less!), reintroduced polygamy (he 'married' 50 of the members) and prophesied that the comet Kohutek would soon bring death and destruction upon Earth and mankind (in 1974 it passed by Earth smoothly and without incident...).

And eventually the *Age of Aquarius* entered the public sphere, accompanied by tablas and sitars, its acolytes swinging and swaying to the rhythms of the ragas, intoxicated by their golden living dreams of visions, celebrating the dancing Shiva as He trampled Western rationality down in the dust under his lotus feet. In the streets the Hare Krishnas were chanting; on the sidewalks the tarot readers were divining; in the parks Maharishi Mahesh Yogi's followers practiced levitation. Nor could the educational institutions provide a safe shelter from this anti-establishment environment; prophet professors such as Timothy Leary and Richard Alpert, from top universities like Berkeley and Harvard, generously shared their psilocybin and LSD with students, and guided by the *Tibetan Book of the Dead* they all went on psychedelic trips, traveling through spiritual landscapes, inner Heavens and Hells, previously reserved for mystics and schizophrenics.

Richard Alpert followed the trail of the *Zeitgeist*, the spirit of the age, and went to India, the Mother of so many things spiritual, where the guru Neem Karoli Baba overwhelmed him with his demonstrations of telepathy and clairvoyance. And when he at last came home the good Richard was no longer Professor Alpert but had transformed into Baba Ram Dass, and went on to write the bestselling hippie bible *Be Here Now*. The hippies' fascination with the exotic, and everything paranormal, cleared the way not only for well-meaning peace bringers as for instance the Maharishi and Alpert, but also for imported and home-grown gurus and swamis of varying expertise and moral standards—some of them charlatans elevated to pedestals of high esteem who were later convicted of tax evasions, sexual misconduct and economic exploitation, just to mention a few of their trespasses.

Unfamiliar vibes abounded; in the famous hippie song *San Francisco (Be sure to wear flowers in your hair)* Scott McKenzie proclaimed in his sweet voice that a strange vibration was felt all across the nation. This shockwave of strangeness and irrationality made the philosopher Paul Kurtz, a rational man, hit the wall. And as opposed to Major General Stubblebine, who we heard about in connection with Stargate, Kurtz had no intention of trying to walk through it! Neither had he any intention of going to San Francisco with flowers in his hair. Kurtz felt perfectly fine in his New York office, amid his books and with his well-knotted necktie; perfectly fine except, as mentioned, for this ever-increasing irrationality being preached and chanted all around—about mystic crystal revelations, the mind's true liberation and other 'hairy' stuff. This avowed knight of rationality was clearly not at ease with the unfamiliar vibes of this new generation and their new explanation that Scott McKenzie had celebrated.

So, around 1975 Kurtz summoned a band of like-minded people for whom rationality was a hard-earned cultural treasure that was not to be squandered. Thus someone had to be up to the task: to cast a cool and watchful eye on the varieties of witlessness that fluttered, like strings of pennants, over so many religious and 'alternative' camps. The milieu that was soon to become CSI took shape and in 1976 the committee was formally constituted. Important in the early stages were sociologist and magician Marcello Truzzi, astrophysicist Carl Sagan, science writer Martin Gardner, magician James Randi, and science fiction author Isaac Asimov.

The list of things CSI is skeptical of is long and broad and includes everything perceived to be *pseudoscience*, such as astrology, homeopathy, acupuncture, chiropractic, clairvoyance, healing, reincarnation, near-death experiences, etc. CSI operates in a prolonged tradition of the *Enlightenment*—the philosophy that emerged in the 18th century, with people such as Voltaire and Benjamin Franklin, and which touts reason, science, freedom and progress. CSI are intent on *educating*, and one of their main ethical concerns is to short-circuit the irrational power games of diverse paranormal practices: greedy 'clairvoyant' gurus, corrupt 'healing' preachers, fake 'telepathic' mediums, etc. This is obviously a noble and necessary mission considering the many abuses that undoubtedly take place. The problem, of course, is that CSI in their fervor might be in danger of throwing the baby out with the bath water—and might even close their eyes to the possibility that there was a baby in there in the first place...

Is Truth to be Found Only in the Laboratory?

Whoever undertakes to set himself up as a judge of Truth and Knowledge is shipwrecked by the laughter of the gods.

~ Albert Einstein

CSI espouses what is often called *scientific skepticism*. As opposed to *philosophical* skeptics, as for instance Phyrro (mentioned above), a scientific skeptic will often believe that an absolute truth can be found. Among those who describe themselves as scientific skeptics, there is a tendency to consider 'truth' to be more or less identical to what can be demonstrated in a laboratory. If this or that is claimed to be true, it should be possible to count, measure, and weigh, and the phenomenon in question should preferably be replicated in a laboratory by independent researchers. Truly truth is—in the last resort—only what is demonstrated to be an expression of a natural law, lifted high above all arbitrary events and subjective assessments.

However, this *scientism* gives us a narrow concept of truth—so narrow that it easily excludes the truths found in the human sciences and in our *Lebenswelt*—the world of our daily lives. In this connection the truths we arrive at will often, to some extent, rely on anecdotal evidence (testimony, narratives, stories, interpretations) and on such unsteady stuff as interpretation and subjective experience—'How do I puzzle all these facts together to make a meaningful whole?' 'Does he/she love me, do I love him/her?' Skeptics of the CSI ilk have a tradition of being critical of the value of anecdotal evidence and subjective experience. This will of course devalue most accounts of paranormal phenomena as they usually occur under specific conditions—in the complex web of everyday life or in emergency situations—which can never be accurately recreated in a laboratory.

The main social sciences, sociology, psychology and social anthropology, will frequently employ methods based on advanced mathematics. But what a statistical analysis of an opinion poll or a health survey really *means*—what truth may be extracted, what pattern the researcher is able to find in the figures—rests to some extent on subjective interpretation; Jill may very well interpret the results differently than Jack. You simply cannot factor out subjective assessment. The same is evident in history: If a historian is to write about, say, the Battle of Waterloo, he/she will have to make a *reconstruction*, not a *replication*. Footage from the battle doesn't exist (at least I'm not aware of it…), and I predict that you will be deeply disappointed if you are hoping to see Napoleon and the Duke of Wellington march into the laboratory to reenact skirmishes in the presence of independent scientists. But the fact that a battle never can be replicated doesn't mean that it didn't take place…

Even if we may not like the uncertainty of it, anecdotal evidence and subjective interpretation occupy a large place in finding truth in most branches of knowledge other than the 'exact sciences,' the core disciplines of natural science (physics, chemistry, etc.). And, in fact, even here, excelling in objectivity and measurement as these disciplines are, diverging interpretations are widespread. Just think of astronomy: a majority of astronomers are convinced that close to 27 percent of the Universe is made of so-called 'dark matter,' while a (very well-educated) minority think that dark matter doesn't exist at all!

In addition to the examples mentioned above we will often speak about truth in philosophy (valid argumentation), psychology (existential truth, subjective experience), anthropology and sociology (true understanding of people and symbols), in jurisprudence (true assessment of evidence). And perhaps we might also speak about truth in the arts (authenticity, aesthetic laws) and in ethics (natural law, human rights). So, as we can see, only a small part of the truths that we deem important are of a type that can be proved in a laboratory.

According to the opinion brought to the table in this book, paranormal phenomena do not conflict with natural laws and truths, but are rather seen as lesser-known expression of these. Some experiments, such as for instance the one with Vicky and Sara recounted at the end of the previous chapter, seem to indicate that paranormal phenomena may be demonstrated in a lab. But still, perhaps most of them rather ought to be studied as part of human rather than natural sciences, just as is the case with the Battle of Waterloo and most other human phenomena? Thinking of the countless ghost stories, or more specific the poltergeist cases presented at the end of chapter 5, it would obviously be futile—just as with Napoleon and the Duke of Wellington—to expect the specters to troop into the laboratory to replicate their spectacular activities.

Dear reader—please forgive me for having been a bit lengthy! To sum up: the point of delving into all this is simply to show that we probably *can* not and *should* not think of truth as more or less identical to what can be proven in a laboratory, which skeptics of the CSI type have a tendency to do. This narrow concept of truth is what makes their skepticism toward the paranormal so dogged.

A (Gentle)men's Club?

CSI's skepticism often has a markedly different 'vibe' to it than the desire to explore reality. Eviscerating putdowns and scathing repartee are favorite indulgences, with James Randi and Martin Gardner as the classical proponents. Gardner, a pugnacious writer who clearly relished the role of muckraker and whose prowess in virulent rhetoric was undisputed, once justified his method with a quote from the satirist H.L. Mencken: 'One horse-laugh is worth ten thousand syllogisms.' Sure enough, if one's main concern is to denigrate those with different opinions rather than involving them in a dialogue. But how scientific is that, really?—or how fruitful? Hence, moderate skeptics have on occasion been repulsed by such displays of verbal violence and rhetorical machismo.

One of these more moderate skeptics was the psychologist Elizabeth Lloyd Mayer, tenured staff member at the University of California, Berkeley. In her exciting book *Extraordinary Knowing: Science, Skepticism, and the Inexplicable Powers of the Human Mind* she relates a highly interesting episode. She was once robbed of a valuable harp. After some months a friend suggested she contact a dowser, a retired army officer named Harold McCoy. McCoy, who was living in Arkansas, asked to have sent a street map of Oakland, San Francisco, where the harp had been stolen, and he also wanted a photo of the harp. He then proved he was able to locate the harp's whereabouts to a tee, even getting the street address right! Mayer was completely baffled—her worldview simply had no room for such an experience. (Whereas from *our* perspective all the necessary information would of course be available via the Mental Internet...) Mayer later wrote: 'If Harold McCoy did what he appeared to have done, I had to face the fact that my notions of space, time, reality, and the nature of the human mind were stunningly inadequate.' And she also wrote: 'I had the thought: *This changes everything.*'

Filled with a desire to broaden her horizon, Mayer started, among other things, to read CSI's magazine, the *Skeptical Inquirer.* But was she disappointed! It was, she says, 'like reading a fundamentalist religious tract. I found the journal dismayingly snide, regularly punctuated by sarcasm, self-congratulation, and nastiness, all parading as reverence for true science.' Hence, the satirical form in which CSI often present their skepticism does not, it seems, necessarily promote the scientific attitude it professes. Rather, it seems to impart *dogmatism*—a conviction that one from the very outset knows the filthy truth about those darned paranormal phenomena! A 'truth' that implies that accounts of the paranormal are most likely, if not most certainly, gullible nonsense, cynical deception, or, at best, honest madness. This attitude is, to say the least, not very sympathetic, and the high-profiled skeptic Ray Hyman, a central figure in CSI, is alive to the problem and has advised against it. Hyman has also made the following quite candid statement: 'As a whole, parapsychologists are nice, honest people, while the critics are cynical, nasty people.'

Might the 'macho-rhetoric' of the skeptics also be part of a bigger scientific picture? Feminists, e.g. American philosopher Sandra Harding, have sometimes claimed that there is a certain misogyny embedded in traditional natural science as it tends to emphasize conquest, dominance, and control of Nature, a presumed 'patriarchal' way of thinking. This stands in contrast to the more 'matriarchal' ways of, say, the humanities. The alleged difference between a 'masculine' and 'feminine' approach to knowledge has been schematized as follows: conquest/discovery, control/ participation, objective knowledge/subjective knowledge, right-wrong/complex understanding, battle (fight and win)/ synergy (win-win). These may be clichés, but perhaps there could be *some* truth to them, as there are often reasons for a cliché becoming a cliché (which also is a cliché and there-fore perhaps may have some truth to it...). Anyway, the power rhetoric of CSI is obviously leaning, or even tipping, toward the 'masculine' side. The anthropologist David Hess has written: 'Debunking is a very masculine, even macho, art: it represents to skeptics a form of intercourse in which they can roll up their sleeves and have a good fight as hit men, psi cops, boxers, or knights who assault (violate) the castle of pseudoscience.'

According to polls women don't have significantly more telepathic or clairvoyant experiences than men; even so, they tend to make up the majority in most 'alternative' fo-rums. In skeptic forums the majority are usually men al-though latterly this disparity has dwindled. This imbalance is also found in the top layer of CSI; a quick count as of January 2020 tells us that out of the 114 persons listed as 'Fellows and Staff' in CSI only 22 seem to be women; this is no more than one-fifth. That could be a mere coincidence or, if representative of anything, it could be an expression of the traditional male dominance in most organized bod-ies. But still, CSI, of all organizations on this earth, ought perhaps to run its house by reason, and actively dismiss the limiting traditions of gender imbalance?

In *A Skeptic's Handbook of Parapsychology*, edited by Paul Kurtz, the psychologist Leonard Zusne suggests that the typical believer in the occult is 'female, unintelligent, mis-informed, poorly educated, authoritarian, and emotionally

unstable.' A cannonade of invective! Neither women nor occultists—quirky and irrational creatures as they are!—stand
a snowball's chance in hell here. Could this chauvinistic
barrage be just a personal rant from Zusne; an opinion differing from CSI's true profile but allowed in by the editorial
generosity of Kurtz? Or could it rather be an expression of
CSI misogyny—a 'masculine' arrogance toward 'the occult
other'? Well, this is obviously a big theme, so for now let's
just leave it right there, hanging—or perhaps levitating—in
mid-air...

Pseudo-Skepticism

Marcello Truzzi, the sociologist and magician who along
with Kurtz initially chaired the executive council of CSI,
has coined the word 'pseudo-skepticism.' With this expression he refers to a bogus skepticism, usurping the good
name of skepticism—where one *pretends* to have a querying
attitude, while in reality one's mind is hermetically closed
against whatever may threaten one's already established
'truth.' True skepticism, on the other hand, is characterized
by curiosity and openness, and—since all human knowledge
is tentative and fallible—also by a certain humility. Truzzi
writes: 'The true skeptic takes an agnostic position, one that
says the claim is *not proved* rather than *disproved*.'

Moreover, Truzzi states that the burden of proof is not
solely on those who make claims for the paranormal but on
whoever makes a claim; if a critic claims that 'a seeming
psi result was actually due to an artifact,' the critic, according to Truzzi, 'is making a claim and therefore also has to
bear a burden of proof.' Not recognizing this will make you
a pseudo-skeptic, a dogmatist. Truzzi has further stated
that typical of pseudo-skeptics is a tendency to move the

goalposts. They may, for instance, say that if so-and-so is demonstrated, they will admit that the existence of this or that psi phenomenon is likely. But if so-and-so actually *is* demonstrated, the pseudo-skeptic will typically *not* change his/her opinion, but instead resort to such ploys as demanding another trial, another setup, other researchers, etc.

Although Truzzi had been one of the cofounders of CSI in 1976, he left the organization the following year. The reason was that he wanted to admit 'psi-positive' members and thought that the CSI's journal, of which Truzzi was then editor, should print articles from researchers with such perceptions. A true scientific attitude demanded this balanced approach, he thought. However, the majority in CSI was having none of it, and as a consequence Truzzi left the organization—partly by choice and partly after a vote of no confidence. Truzzi has stated that he believes many CSI members are not genuine skeptics but rather pseudo-skeptics—dogmatists in disguise. Truzzi also thought that the concept 'skepticism' itself has been appropriated by hardliners—not unlike how gilded terms like 'Solidarity,' 'Freedom,' 'Brotherhood,' etc. have often been hijacked by extremists within political movements.

The divide between 1) an open scientific skepticism on the one hand and 2) a closed dogmatic skepticism on the other is seemingly at the core of an internal conflict in CSI's ideology. However, admitting to having a closed mind is not easy for a scientific person—yes, it is almost as difficult as admitting one lacks a sense of humor! The American philosopher Daniel Dennett, a prominent CSI member, seems to have his humor intact as he has reportedly said that if paranormal phenomena should turn out to be real he would commit suicide! Although a joke, such a statement nonetheless seems to reflect the dogmatic—pseudo-skeptic—attitude we just discussed. It also seems to reflect the surprisingly strong emotional dedication to skepticism in some that amounts to an almost religious fervor. In light of the model employed in this book, suggesting that paranormal phenomena belong to the natural properties of our consciousness, such vehement dislike is surprising. One gets the same feeling as if watching a person shaking his/her fist angrily against the night sky, cursing in advance those meteorites which might dare to show up, justifying the absurd act by a suspicion that someone, somewhere, might use them as a point of reference for questionable teachings.

And the meteorite metaphor is not only a metaphor: In 1772 members of a committee in the French Academy of Sciences were to assess whether or not meteorites came down from the sky. Their ruling was that no, red-hot stones do *not* come down from the sky! The notion of things coming from above was perceived to be a reactionary superstition—a remnant from those dark, unenlightened times when people believed in divine intervention from Heaven. The observations that these red-hot stones actually *were* dropping down from above was explained either as visions, or that the stones had been ejected from volcanoes, had been spun up in the air by tornadoes or had been 'zapped' upwards by lightning strikes. And—for fear of being reactionary and superstitious, and because of their great respect for the French Academy, many museums—in Denmark, Germany, Austria, Switzerland and Italy—threw their valuable collections of meteorites on the garbage dump! Might the skeptics' fear of superstition lead rational people in our days to dispose of their valuable paranormal experiences for fear of being superstitious?

Important Issues, but How to Handle?

Some CSI members have done important work related to exposing fraudulent healers and mediums. Within charismatic branches of Christianity healing is often (mis)used to underpin the credibility of the preacher. He/she may thereby gain an irrational and potentially dangerous authority over the congregation who—because of the healings, be they real or fake—may come to perceive the preacher as God's extended arm. If the preacher should then require extensive funding, or ask for special favors, spiritual or corporal (!), it would be difficult to say no—after all, you just don't say no to God! The most eager debunker of this form of abuse has been the magician James Randi—probably the most visible CSI member today. Using his extensive insights in 'cold reading' (verbal and mimic techniques for 'reading' people), stage psychology, hypnosis, and technical aids, Randi has on different occasions succeeded in outing and ousting TV preachers faking 'miracles' (psi phenomena as telepathy, clairvoyance and healing), and gripping and grabbing greedily for peoples' hearts and wallets. Among the most famous who has fallen under Randi's axe are W.V. Grant and Peter Popoff. (The latter has recently risen from the ashes, having thus performed yet another miracle...)

Over the past decades there has also emerged a large public market for spiritualist mediums who on stage offer to liaise between the audience and their deceased family members. Without discussing whether this is possible—*if* a component of our consciousness continues to exist after physical death, the possibility of such contact cannot be ruled out—this sphere is obviously densely populated with mediums of less than medium quality! Some of them are undoubtedly cynical rogues, but the larger part would probably better be described as 'honest liars'—people who mean well but who will convey little more than trivia, partly based on 'Barnum statements' (statements so general that they are valid for nearly everybody), and partly on intercepting unconscious cues and clues in people's body language, tone of voice, etc. But, given that our model of the Mental Internet is viable there will also be genuine mediums out there. They will not necessarily be in contact with the dead (this is of course an extensive subject), but they will download relevant and correct information about them from the mental web.

Such mediums can amaze their clients by presenting information—private matters, family secrets—apparently impossible to obtain in any normal fashion. A superlative example is Baba Vanga's initial meeting with Professor Giorgi Lozanov, briefly recounted in the second half of chapter 2. A dogmatic skepticism may in such cases actually seem irrational. This is because in order to establish an explanation of what *really* happened, one has to stack up so many weird 'normal' explanations that the sum of these seems far more paranormal than simply saying: 'Psi seems to be a part of reality not yet well explored.'

Psychologist Susan Blackmore, profiled skeptic and CSI member, is definitely no believer in psi, but she sure is well aware of the dangers of dogmatic skepticism (pseudo-skepticism):

> In skeptical books and magazines we can read again and again authors who prefer to accept even the feeblest and least well-founded skeptical explanation of a claim, rather than consider the possibility that the claim might be true. Yet if we are going to study psychic claims at all, we must always consider the possibility that they are true. Unlikely as it is, ESP and PK might exist. There could be new forces as yet undiscovered. We should accept

the best explanation we can find—not the one that we like the most.

(S)tarbaby—Defending Truth at the Expense of Truth?

CSI has, as has been stated, made important and necessary efforts to debunk various fraudulent and bogus claims within alternative movements, where power hungry individuals, wolves in sheep's vestments, have often gained destructive authority over their devotees by showing off fake (or real) paranormal phenomena—healing, prophecies, revelations, etc. Because of CSI's zeal for sobering people up, their mentality can be compared with that of the Prohibitionists' deep-seated hatred of intoxication, all its works and all its ways. Both groups wield their whips on their respective objects of hate, hoping to have the abominations abolished altogether. But even the most avowed abstainer would hardly attempt to deny that intoxicants *exist*. CSI, however, in their dedication to debunking the paranormal, appear to have attempted just such an unfortunate maneuver in the so-called Starbaby affair of the late 1970s. Here, several of the members of the Executive Council first tried to hide, then to suppress, some unpleasant facts brought to the table by the French psychologist Michel Gauquelin.

Gauquelin, who conducted important parts of his research together with his wife, Marie-Francoise Schneider-Gauquelin, had found statistical correlations indicating that there could be truth to astrology's theories about connections between micro-cosmos and macro-cosmos—that is to say, between Humankind and the Universe, between a person's birthplace, birthdate, characteristics of personality, and the planetary constellations. Gauquelin's statistical material—and Gauquelin was an excellent statistician—bore out that a significant number of top athletes were born when the planet Mars stood either on the horizon or was culminating (at the orbit's high point); this was called 'the Mars effect.' As we know Mars was the Roman god of war, and war certainly followed the Mars effect! Gauquelin's results were ill-matched with CSI's agenda: In 1975 Paul Kurtz had been one of the principal authors of a critical manifest called *Objections to Astrology*. This mission statement was endorsed by a band of scientists and was an important symbol, an intellectual banner, for CSI's endeavors.

'It's Not the Crime, It's the Cover-Up'

A complex chain of events unfolded, the essence of which was that Kurtz and some other central CSI members—among others astronomer George Abell, statistician Marvin Zelen and magician James Randi—attacked Gauquelin's work, dismissing his statistics as faulty and claiming his conclusions to be wrong. But, it seems, they did not act in a truthful manner... The brilliant astronomer Dennis Rawlins, who at the time was one of the nine members of CSI's executive council, in 1981 wrote a critical article called 'Starbaby,' where he describes the questionable steps taken by Kurtz and Co., and admits he himself also 'howled with the wolves' for a while. Rawlins' description is an entertaining and unsparing piece of polemics, where the actions of Kurtz and other central characters in CSI appear in a most unflattering light—the image of a group of vampires writhing in the sunlight comes to mind! Rawlins claims that Kurtz and those in cahoots with him resorted to dubious statistics, intentional forgery, and that they subsequently employed covert actions to hide their initial mistakes and misdeeds. All in an attempt to 'debunk' the unwanted results from Gauquelin's heretical research.

If I understand Rawlins correctly, he states that Starbaby originated as a conflict of interest between good research and good publicity. Early on Kurtz and Co. had made some sloppy calculations, which in itself was not all that serious, but the fear of a *bad press* and an accompanying loss of prestige made it difficult to admit those initial mistakes. Cover-ups were created which caused the affair to escalate over the ensuing years. The name Starbaby alludes of course to stars and astrology, but is also a pun on the 'Tar-Baby'—the old American fairytale about a tar doll which will stick to, and thus trap, the rabbit who starts to fight it. And of course, the more the rabbit fights the stickier it all gets...

If just half of what Rawlins relates is correct it would still have been serious for CSI—an organization touting science, rationality and truth. In 1980, about five years after the Starbaby first saw the light of day, Rawlins left CSI as a consequence of the affair; partly he chose to leave, partly he was squeezed out, much like Truzzi before him. Rawlins for sure maintained his skepticism about the paranormal, but now he had become skeptical of the skeptics as well:

> *I am still skeptical of the occult beliefs CSICOP [the original acronym] was created to debunk. But I have changed my mind about the integrity of some of those who make a career of opposing occultism. I now believe that if a flying saucer landed in the backyard of a leading anti-UFO spokesman, he might hide the incident from the public (for the public's own good, of course). He might swiftly convince himself that the landing was a hoax, a delusion or an 'unfortunate' interpretation of mundane phenomena that could be explained away with 'further research.'*

Rawlins was not known for his diplomatic skills, and later the same year UFO expert Philip Klass (slammed in the quote above), who was also a member of CSI's executive council, wrote an article called 'Crybaby' in which he argued that Rawlins' criticism was motivated by personal 'stuff,' and that by and large it was misleading. Whereas psychologist Richard Kammann, another profiled CSI member, in 1982 wrote an article called 'The True Disbelievers' where he goes through the whole case, and lends support to Rawlins' key points. Kammann also chose to resign from CSI because of this affair. Kurtz and Co. later wrote an article trying to defend their stance but their reputation was still somewhat mired in the aftermath of this case and small, icky-sticky stains from the (S)tarbaby have stuck to CSI's reputation.

This case and how it was handled seem to exemplify—in addition to the personal enmities that have certainly been in the picture—what we above described as an internal schism in CSI's ideology, namely the conflict between an open scientific skepticism on the one hand, and a closed dogmatic skepticism (pseudo-skepticism) on the other.

Why No One Wanted a Million Dollars—James Randi and His Prize

Most people probably know that the magician James Randi over a number of years had a standing offer, that whoever could prove to him that paranormal phenomena are real would receive $1 million. This offer made Randi the most well-known skeptic (or pseudo-skeptic) in the world, and he is also the person with the most widespread success in damaging the reputation of the paranormal. After Randi retired a few years ago the James Randi Educational Foundation decided to discontinue the prize, and since 2015 the offer is no longer valid. But—its impact on public opinion has been, and still is, formidable. So to speak about skepticism and the paranormal without mentioning James Randi and his prize would be to speak about *Star Wars* without mentioning Darth Vader! Within the Star Wars vernacular the prize might perhaps be most aptly described as a manifestation of 'The Dark Side of the Force.' Even if the prize itself belongs to bygone days its ghost continues to haunt discussions about the paranormal, and it is probably still the 'argument' most frequently used to dismiss psi. So let's have a quick look at some important issues concerning both Randi and his prize.

The Lurid Lure

Promising one million dollars obviously has an enormous rhetorical power. For, one almost inevitably thinks, if there is someone somewhere who has paranormal capabilities, why don't they just visit Randi, gave him a convincing demonstration, and collect the prize? Unless one is already a multi-millionaire Randi's should have been an extremely tempting offer. And since the prize was never awarded to anyone it must be because all things paranormal are just bogus, or...? I myself, to some degree, have thought along such lines, and I have sure met others who think likewise. But—things are not always as they seem, especially when dealing with magicians. After all, their profession is to create illusions, to get us to believe in something that is not real—doves appearing out of nowhere, ladies floating on air, etc. A stage magician is by definition a professional cheater. So why should this suddenly change when it comes to competitions and prizes? And obviously, Randi—who has no scientific background—has made a highly successful career as a world-famous skeptic and debunker.

The well-known psychologist and parapsychologist Charles Tart has stated that in serious parapsychological milieux Randi's prize was simply not taken seriously. But why so? Well, among other things Randi's history was never such as to establish confidence in a fair trial. On one occasion, disguised as a journalist and pretending to represent the science supplement of *The Times*, he gained access to a laboratory in London where they were researching metal bending by mental power. Randi brought with him electronic equipment with the intention of botching up the scientists' instruments. However, the attempted sabotage was discovered, and Randi was expelled from the laboratory (but only later did they discover who he really was). One may of course excuse Randi by saying that he did this to underscore the point that cheating may appear even in serious laboratories. But nonetheless: When you more or less constantly over the years have been screaming out loud, accusing other people of cheating, perhaps it is strange as well as unwise for you yourself to engage in cheating?

And there is more—much more: In the early 1980s Randi had two young magicians sign up for psi experiments at the McDonnell Laboratory for Psychical Research. In line with Randi's instructions the two lied to the researchers and said that they possessed paranormal powers. Randi had earlier offered his services to the laboratory—to help expose possible cheaters—but this had been turned down. So Randi chose to change roles and went on to instruct his aides in which tricks to use—bending spoons, making objects move, seeing objects within sealed envelopes, etc. Some members of the staff were, in fact, fooled into believing that Randi's stooges were performing true paranormal feats, and a physicist in charge of the daily operations confessed that he for a while was '80 percent sure' that they were the real deal.

The 'devils in disguise' continued, to and fro, with their scheme over a period of a few years. A couple of senior researchers, however, had become suspicious that a fraud was afoot, partly because the 'paranormal' abilities of Randi's aides for some strange reason seemed to vanish in proportion to the degree that the controls became stricter... And in July 1982 the laboratory terminated working with them (they were still undercover).

Then, in January 1983, Randi went public and made much ado in the media about his stunt, presenting it as if he had succeeded in making the laboratory buy into his assistants' tricks as true psi phenomena. But the truth was, however, that the McDonnell laboratory had never uttered any such statement! On the contrary, on September 1, 1981—more than a year before Randi had weaseled his way to the microphones—the lab declared:

A research brief delivered at the Parapsychological Association Annual Convention in August 1981, at Syracuse University, mentions several events that have occurred, including influence on standard keys, Polaroid photographic film, and electronic fuses. However, ordinary explanations exist for these effects, given the conditions under which they have been observed. Thus, although several events of interest have transpired, we do not claim that evidence conclusive of 'psychic ability' has yet been demonstrated in our research.

As we can see, the lab doesn't jump to any paranormal conclusions! Thus the depiction that the experienced showman
and self-promoter James Randi presented to the public was
just 'fake news' and 'alternative facts.' Sad.

Randi's behavior, the deployment of false subjects and his
misleading press conferences, became controversial; even
some members of his clique in CSI criticized his conduct.
Because of the great commotion the case created, no less
a body than the American Department of Defense filed
a report regarding the incident. At the time the military
were, as we saw in chapter 2 with respect to Stargate, seriously involved with parapsychological research. I strongly
recommend having a look at the DoD report (the link is
found in the bibliography), which is certainly not written
by New Agers! The report says that Randi is guilty of 'gross
distortions' concerning this field of research, and more
specifically:

> *Thus, it is apparent that Mr Randi has presented an ex-
> tremely one-sided view of this hoax attempt. He even
> claims that all parapsychological research is of question-
> able value. Most TV and press coverage thus far also re-
> flect these views. As a result, the general public is given
> highly biased perspectives of this research area in general.
> This could generate negative reactions toward all para-
> psychological research, even for those laboratories where
> controls are tight and where unsolicited subjects are not
> accepted.*

The Department of Defense shows no mercy: 'It is clear Mr.
Randi is solely interested in promoting his image as a clever
magician, and in enhancing his career as a showman, at the
expense of reporting accuracy. The use of tactics involving
"plants" raises significant ethical issues as well.' The report
thus effectively undermines our (or at least my) trust in

Randi's integrity. Having a person this unreliable to organize a test of paranormal abilities… well, one need not be paranoid to suspect the whole thing would have been *very carefully rigged.*

The rules were formulated in such a way that it was Randi himself—not the panel of independent scientists—who in the end would decide if the evidence was strong enough to reward the prize. A little bird tells me that making a decision in favor of the claimant would not have come lightly to Randi, who has spent the better part of his mature (one might wonder…) life in debunking paranormal phenomena. When an illusionist is to act as—to quote Dennis Rawlins, the Starbaby critic mentioned above—'police, jury and judge' in his own case, where one million dollars is at stake as well as his life's work, it would hardly provide the optimal conditions for an impartial ruling…

The edicts, reportedly formulated by a very clever lawyer, entailed that the parties had to 'agree' to the conditions, thus giving Randi the ability to 'disagree' if a serious contender should appear—not just nutcases or people wanting their 15 minutes in the limelight. The candidates also had to waive their right to sue. So if a candidate should feel that he/she had demonstrated the agreed upon phenomenon but Randi refused to approve the result, there would be no possibility to try the case in a court of law. Moreover, Randi appears to have sabotaged applications he found threatening. The Dutch researcher Professor Dick Bierman, a physicist and a psychologist (we'll get back to him in the next chapter), was once in negotiations with Randi to set up a long-term experiment involving multiple participants. A trial of this type would have been regarded as having much more scientific weight than a single phenomenon produced by a single person. But—when things started to become serious Randi suddenly disappeared without leaving a trace (stopped answering Bierman's emails, etc.)—just as magicians have a tradition of doing!

So—one probably need not suffer from *apophenia* (ref. our discussion on thought-patterns above) to feel there is a certain pattern to Randi's dealings...

As to my trust in Randi's offer: the final nail in the coffin was hammered in by Dennis Rawlins. In his *Starbaby* article Rawlings, who at the time was one of Randi's buddies, writes that he had asked Randi if he was not afraid of losing his money, and that Randi had answered: 'I always have an out!' And voilà!—the cat was out of Randi's moneybag, and my confidence in a fair ruling from Randi was reduced to an absolute zero. Randi has later—with varying degrees of success—tried to mitigate this statement. But when the toothpaste is out of the tube it's hard to get it back in again, or as the saying goes: 'You can't unboil an egg!'

So, is Randi just as great a cheater as the fake mediums and healers he has been fond of debunking?—as they say: 'It takes one to know one.' Well, we cannot know for sure, but Randi's words and actions may easily evoke just this suspicion. To me, personally, after I read Rawlings article, Randi has about as much credibility left as a thief caught inside a bank vault. When all due deference has been paid to his efforts as a debunker of charlatans one can hardly get away from the fact that Randi is an illusionist—not a scientist. And wanting to get the better of a professional illusionist is probably as futile as—well, as getting the better of a professional illusionist. The next victim of the illusions is most likely going to be you; that's the name of the game.

There's No Business Like Show Business...

Randi's favorite enemy since the mid-1970s has been Uri Geller, the Israeli who once became famous for his alleged ability to bend spoons with mental power. Their long-lasting feud—sometimes simmering, sometimes boiling—has been fought not only in the public sphere but also in the courtroom as Geller on several occasions has sued Randi for libel—the first time he included CSI. Randi was not convicted but the trial ignited 'fire in the camp of the roses,' as Norwegian poet Henrik Wergeland expressed it, and because of these internal skirmishes Randi left CSI in anger. Apparently he felt thrown under the bus; some say that he was explicitly asked to leave as Kurtz felt Geller's lawsuits to be a threat to the organization's finances. In the first lawsuit, in 1991, Geller demanded no less than $15 million in compensation!—Randi later returned to CSI and has had much skeptical honor bestowed upon him.

What's funny about the whole thing is that Randi is a magician who has chosen to make a career as a man of science, while Geller is a magician who has chosen to make a career as a psychic. Both are basically showmen, and part of their act is to appear as something else. Without here assessing Geller's psychic abilities (we'll get back to him more thoroughly in the next chapter) or Randi's scientific abilities (I'm not so sure if we'll get back to him...oh, well, in a couple of brief comments perhaps) one gets the impression that when it comes to showmanship Randi and Geller are remarkably similar: they both love capturing the headlines and being on TV is good for business.

Geller once had a terrible night on live TV, being seriously debunked on Johnny Carson's *Tonight Show*; Carson had namely conspired with his good friend Randi to sabotage Geller's act. Geller was not able to perform his usual tricks and was visibly insecure and uneasy (the sequence is easily found on YouTube). But paradoxically, Geller's apparent fiasco became a springboard to even greater success. Many viewers thought that if Geller had been just an illusionist employing store-bought and well-rehearsed tricks these would likely have worked smoothly even on 'a rainy day.' But since confusion was writ large in Geller's face he appeared more like a true sensitive than a steely controlled stage magician. So, afterwards Geller, in fact, found that his psychic/'psychic' skills were even more in public demand! Geller has thus had the *chutzpah* to refer to Randi as 'my most influential and important publicist'! Randi for his part sounds a little more reluctant to publicly embrace the importance of the man he 'loves to hate.' Of his death Randi has declared: 'I want to be cremated, and I want my ashes blown in Uri Geller's eyes.' Well, at least they both have a keen sense of humor!

Geller once said, with a cynical little dig, that there's no such thing as bad publicity 'as long as they spell your name correctly.' And multiple headlines with correctly spelled names they have had, Randi and Geller—often helped by each other, propelling them both to stardom in their respective spheres, enabling them both to laugh all the way to their respective banks. I wonder if they share a bottle of champagne now and then when the journalists look the other way...

I think perhaps it might entertain the readers to know what happened when I sent Geller an email with excerpts from the manuscript to get his comments on what I had written about him—if he had been quoted correctly and felt my somewhat cheeky presentation to be fair. Uri's answer consisted of only one line that read: 'You should be worried my legal team is always ready! I have earned millions from settlements.' And I became worried: Had Geller no sense of humor after all? Would he eventually sue me for libel as he had done with Randi? That possibility sent chills down my spine!—$15 million is not pocket money... I immediately mailed him back to sort out matters. No response. I mailed once more, my level of stress increasing. Then came relief: 'Hi Terje it seems that it is you who doesn't have a sense of humor. In my last email to you I was 🥄 joking ☺ what you have written is fine...good luck with your book. Much energy and love ❤ Uri.' And, in fact, I *had* noticed that the mail that had so upset me closed not with an exclamation mark but with an emoji of (what else could it have been!) an endearing little spoon...

Perspectives from Serious Skepticism

With his million-dollar prize stunt and showy look-at-me behavior Randi has succeeded in grabbing the world's (and the present author's) attention partly for the benefit of, but just as much at the expense of, more worthy CSI members. I am thinking of people like the psychologists Ray Hyman, James Alcock, Chris French, and Susan Blackmore. All of them are serious scientists who have worked together with parapsychologists in the form of joint publications and/or laboratory tests—the book *Debating Psychic Experience: Human Potential or Human Illusion?* (2010) is an example of such a collaborative effort between psi positives and skeptics. Here, both parties, in addition to their presentations, were given the opportunity to respond to their critics. That's the way to go! Professor Stanley Krippner, one of the editors, has said in an interview that the skeptics seemed to be pleased with the book, meaning that it conveys their views in a proper manner. In another interview Krippner has said that he, in fact, tends to agree with about 95 percent of the skeptics' objections, but that personal stories/experiences make him believe that psi is real. We'll get back to Krippner and his exciting research on dream telepathy in the next chapter!

Let us briefly mention a few important objections that skeptics often present.

The Treacherous File Drawer...

There are recurring complaints (justified) about weaknesses in the procedures and protocols for eliminating cheating, coincidences and other disturbances. James Alcock mentions the 'file drawer effect,' which is an issue relating to reporting. Say you run a series of experiments; it may then be tempting to eagerly publish your successes (those trials that support your hypothesis) while letting the unsuccessful or ambiguous trials lie unpublished in your file drawer... Over time your hypothesis will thereby appear stronger than it really is. That is not to say that you have deliberately attempted to distort your results—very often it 'just happens.' It is somewhat similar to when a football fan makes a video presentation of his/her team; chances are that you'll get half an hour with goals and thrilling openings rather than long sequences from the (probably more representative) routine games. Fair enough—but it won't give us the whole truth about the team's performance...

I Want It To Be, Therefore It Is—Confirmation Bias

In close relation to this is 'confirmation bias.' Scientists—and this applies all across the field and certainly not only to parapsychologists—have a strange tendency to get results that strengthen rather than weaken their favorite hypotheses. This may often be due to subtle things such as in cases of doubt you will typically have a slight tendency to—spontaneously—interpret your results *just a little bit more positively than what is warranted*. And if you conduct a long series of experiments having a small but consequent bias of this kind you will eventually end up with a distorted picture of what your experiments really show.

Gentlemen Ought to Shave!

Another classic objection is related to the so-called 'Occam's razor.' This is a principle that says that you should simplify your theories and 'shave off' everything unnecessary. The principle is named after the English Franciscan friar and philosopher William of Ockham (1285–1349) who, back in the day, used his 'razor' to trim the firmament of a whole family of angels. In the astrological cosmology of earlier ages it was often thought that the planets were kept in orderly orbit with the help of angels. But Ockham had the distinct feeling that the planets would revolve just as smoothly all by themselves. Hence no steering angels were needed, and swish!—Ockham shaved them off. And in just the same way we, according to many skeptics, should shave off the psi hypothesis. It is, they argue, not needed to explain the (apparent) paranormal phenomena, and parapsychology is an unnecessary science! The suggestion often given is to dismantle parapsychology and rather study experiences of telepathy, clairvoyance, etc. as part of so-called *anomalistic psychology*—a branch of psychology that says 'Yes' to researching all kinds of strange experiences, but (usually) says 'No' to explaining them with the psi hypothesis.

Supporters of the psi hypothesis may also cherish Occam's razor as long as the difference between shaving and cutting off one's chin is kept in mind. Simplification may indeed satisfy our taste for clean lines, they say, but ultimately we are interested not in the *simplest* map but in the map best describing the terrain. As Einstein put it: 'Everything should be as simple as possible, but not simpler.' The psi positives tend to think that many phenomena are impossible to explain without the psi hypothesis—telepathy, clairvoyance, precognition, healing, etc. and perhaps also the extreme skills of the savants. And, by broadening the perspective, which we will do in chapter 9, it could even include the synchronized action of animals (flocks of birds, schools of fish, swarms of insects), and evolution in nature. So instead of attempting to blast away the rocks that are so irritatingly botching up our nice and simple little map, they suggest we'd rather draw a new, bolder and more inclusive map!

No Paradigm

In addition to methodological objections regarding reporting procedures and bias, some skeptics argue against parapsychology that there is no unifying theory for the field. Sure, there is a plethora of strange facts, or alleged facts, but they, it is argued, are only a heap of observations that cannot be gathered into a meaningful whole. Parapsychology has no *paradigm*, as is sometimes said. 'Paradigm' is originally a grammatical term referring to the rules and patterns for the declination of words. The one who first employed the term in a broader scientific context was the historian of science, Thomas Kuhn. He used it to denote the assumptions, theories, and practices that most scientists within a field agree on, and which make up the 'rules' within this science—it's 'the playbook for the game of science,' so to speak.

There are various reasons why parapsychologists have difficulty in finding their paradigm. First, it is the nature of their subject: By definition parapsychology studies phenomena that lie beside (*para* = beside) standard psychology. These phenomena are *anomalies*, they seem to violate the laws already in place (*a* = not, *nomos* = law). A paradigm for parapsychology must therefore be able to include both orthodox psychology as well as the exceptions to it. Creating a unified theory for the whole field of human experience is a daunting task... one has to be almost paranormally brave to attempt it!

In addition there is the practical economic aspect. I once saw a tentative account showing that the field of parapsychology during the past 100 years has had available funds equivalent to two months' research in ordinary psychology! With this limited funding it is perhaps not all that surprising that parapsychology as a science has not quite arrived.

And indeed, even within conventional psychology there is much disagreement about fundamentals in the field. What are psychologists able to tell about our human identity after more than 100 years of research? Competing directions—psychodynamic psychology, behaviorism, biological psychology, Gestalt psychology, cognitive psychology, etc.—differ on basic points. And, as we heard in chapter 6, according to many professionals *consciousness*—the core of the matter, the crux—remains a complete mystery! So even if skeptics have a point in their complaints about a missing paradigm in parapsychology, this also applies—at least to some extent—to its well-established big brother, psychology.

Skepticism and Evidence

Many who are skeptical about psi phenomena are of the opinion that there is no scientific evidence supporting the psi hypothesis. This is not correct, because as we have seen, heaps of evidence has been collected—for example in connection with Stargate, the various individual cases mentioned, and also the research we shall look at in chapter 8. But whether this evidence is strong enough to declare the psi hypothesis proven is, so it seems, still debatable and up to individual judgment. This is partly because evidence in the strictest sense—meaning indisputable proof—is difficult to find in general, and especially in sciences dealing with people, such as sociology, anthropology, medicine, psychology—and parapsychology.

Indeed, it is often said that it is only in mathematics that we may speak about evidence in the strictest sense. As regards other sciences, we must probably be content with more or less well-founded hypotheses. Thus it is often possible to say that a series of trials seem to *strengthen* a hypothesis about, for example, clairvoyance, or that a series of trials seem to *weaken* the same hypothesis. But conclusive evidence—100 percent undisputable proof—is seldom possible to acquire. Most often it will be more like a case in a court of law: all the evidence is assessed with the aim of reaching a conclusion that is 'beyond reasonable doubt' as the phrasing goes. But what cuts it as 'reasonable' will of course vary from person to person.

Some will say that since different experiments in various laboratories have yielded positive results—as for instance those supporting remote viewing, as we saw in connection with Stargate—so much evidence has been accumulated that remote viewing can now be seen as an established reality. This was, as we may remember, the opinion of Professor Jessica Utts, the statistician who was officially appointed to evaluate the results from Stargate. The other appointee, the skeptic Ray Hyman, said that sure, results from this and that laboratory seem to corroborate remote viewing. But what if undetected errors—'dirty test tubes'—were present and that *they* were the true cause of the seemingly convincing results? And serious skeptics will then make suggestions as to where the assumed errors might be hiding. And then the parapsychologists will try to take this into account in their next rounds of trials. That's how science (should) work—'a self-correcting process,' as it is often referred to.

In fact, because of the skeptics' keen criticism parapsychology has become a science with a high level of professionalism, and even many skeptics believe that it is on level with conventional psychology. The leading English skeptic, Chris French, professor of psychology and former chief editor of *Skeptic* magazine, has stated:

> *Many of the most sophisticated experimental designs within parapsychology are easily on a par with the best psychological studies. Furthermore, some parapsychologists appear to produce evidence in support of the existence of paranormal forces even from such apparently well-controlled experiments.*

French therefore believes that even if he himself does not have much faith in psi, only time will tell what conclusions will be drawn. And by the way, French is by no means impressed by his colleagues' understanding of the field: 'Most psychologists could reasonably be described as uninformed skeptics—a minority could reasonably be described as prejudiced bigots—where the paranormal is concerned.'

The Big Picture

Parapsychology is thought to be the science that first started to apply so-called *meta-analysis*—making overall assessments of all trials within a certain field. J.B. Rhine's classic *ESP after 60 Years* from 1940 is often presented as an example; here Rhine evaluated surveys dating back as far as 1882. One of those who has been working with meta-analysis is the versatile scientist Dean Radin—ex-professional musician, psychologist and electrical engineer. Over a period of about 25 years Radin has been trawling through nearly all the parapsychological archives, studying each and every research report (but as he is still alive he must have taken some time off to eat!). And Radin claims that—adjusted for possible sources of error such as those mentioned above as well as various others—there emerges a clear picture suggesting that the most important psi phenomena, the 'Big Five'—telepathy, clairvoyance, precognition, telekinesis and healing—are very real indeed. Whereupon Radin concludes that based on normal scientific criteria the psi hypothesis is proven!

Now, that's something. But more surprising perhaps is that the fervent skeptic Richard Wiseman at first glance appears to agree! Wiseman has namely been quoted as saying:

'I agree that by the standards of any other area of science that remote viewing is proven, but begs the question: do we need higher standards of evidence when we study the paranormal? I think we do.' Wiseman explains this by an amusing example: 'If I said it's a red car outside my house, you would probably believe me. But if I said that a UFO had just landed, you'd probably want a lot more proof.' He reasons further: 'Because remote viewing is such an outlandish claim that will revolutionize the world, we need overwhelming evidence before we draw any conclusions. Right now we don't have that evidence.' As he felt slightly misquoted in the interview, Wiseman has later clarified things and said: '[…] I was using the term in the more general sense of ESP—that is, I was not talking about remote viewing per se, but rather Ganzfeld, etc. as well.' (Wiseman here refers to experiments where ordinary perception is suppressed in order to more easily detect impressions from telepathy and clairvoyance.) 'I think that they [the proofs for psi] do meet the standards for a normal claim, but are not convincing enough for an extraordinary claim.'

It is obviously here that the roads will fork between the proponents of psi hypothesis and Wiseman the skeptic. There is, in fact, little doubt that Wiseman is right in assuming that remote viewing is a revolutionary phenomenon, an extraordinary claim, in light of Newton's physics, where Space, Time and Causality reign the world unrestrictedly. But, as we know, there are those who believe that the worldview—or more correctly, some of the possible worldviews— outlined by quantum physics may comfortably allow for phenomena such as remote viewing. And this opinion is not only held by weirdoes who have gorged on fringe physics from dubious websites, but also by people such as Brian Josephson, who, as mentioned earlier, can boast (but as he is a modest man he doesn't) of having the Nobel Prize in physics. So to some extent the revolution Wiseman spoke about has already silently taken place. And if so, one should not need zillions of replications before allowing the psi evidence to be assessed like other evidence.

In the previous chapter we indicated the direction in which a possible explanation for remote viewing is likely to be found, with non-locality—in one form or another—being the crucial idea. If consciousness in itself is at some level a non-local phenomenon, as our model of the Mental Internet suggests, remote viewing ought not to be compared to something as exceptional as a landed UFO. But—with a little twist to Wiseman's imagery—rather to something as basic as the ever-present asphalt on which cars and any possible UFOs are parked. Perhaps Wiseman's skepticism in the last resort could be due to the fact that he simply hasn't employed the most germane model of consciousness?

Alternative Skeptical Approaches

The Humble Physicist

Skepticism concerning parapsychology is not equivalent to skepticism about the existence of psi. The Anglo-American physicist and mathematician Freeman Dyson (b. 1923) has an impressive reputation; many believe it is sheer robbery on the part of the Nobel committee that he hasn't (yet) received their coveted prize. Dyson believes that the anecdotal evidence—which is overwhelming—suggests paranormal phenomena are real, but he also believes that scientific methods are unsuitable to explore this aspect of reality. Hence he is basically not skeptical about the paranormal, but about parapsychology. Dyson mentions three possible views on evidence with respect to ESP:

> *First, the position of orthodox scientists, who believe that ESP does not exist. Second, the position of true believers, who believe that ESP is real and can be proved to exist by scientific methods. Third, my own position, that ESP is real, as the anecdotal evidence suggests, but cannot be tested with the clumsy tools of science. [...] I put forward, as a working hypothesis, that ESP is real but belongs to a mental universe that is too fluid and evanescent to fit within the rigid protocols of controlled scientific testing. I do not claim that this hypothesis is true. I claim only that it is consistent with the evidence and worthy of consideration.*

It is certainly humble for a great physicist to describe his advanced tools as 'clumsy' with respect to human phenomena. Dyson has said that when he was young he and some friends experimented with precognition in the form of guessing the outcome when drawing cards from a pack. At first they got good results, but as boredom and tiredness came creeping in after hours and even days of guessing and drawing, drawing and guessing, the results declined and eventually leveled off. This is a pattern frequently seen in lab experiments. Perhaps Dyson's thought—that science's practices and procedures are all but optimal for researching something as 'fluid and evanescent' as psi—could be relevant, then? We'll give a few thoughts on this so-called 'decline-effect' in the next chapter, in connection with J.B. Rhine.

The Religious Skeptic

Martin Gardner is sometimes referred to as the 'godfather' of the modern skeptic movement; his was a quite unusual form of skepticism. Gardner, as we heard above, is probably the CSI member who, together with James Randi, has been the most vocal critic of parapsychology. But, strange as it may sound, Gardner would not dismiss the possibility that paranormal phenomena, or even sheer miracles, might occur. As a young man he once wrote that the paranormal effects demonstrated by Stanley Jaks, a well-known *mentalist* (i.e. magician with psi effects as a specialty), were real. However, Gardner thought, based partly on the reasons we have mentioned above, that parapsychology was a murky business, a kind of scientific low-life.

In addition something emerged that I think will surprise most regular skeptics: Although he did not belong to any organized religion Gardner was actually a religious man, who—as he once wrote in a letter to the psi researcher George P. Hansen—believed in 'a personal God, prayer and life after death.' And it was precisely because of his religiosity that Gardner found parapsychology audacious: 'If I were an orthodox Jew or Christian, I would find such attempts to explain biblical miracles to be both preposterous and an insult to God.' He was open to the paranormal: 'It is possible that paranormal forces not yet established may allow prayers to influence the material world, and I certainly am not saying this possibility should be ruled out a priori […].' But parapsychology is definitely not the way to go: 'As for empirical tests of the power of God to answer prayer, I am among those theists who, in the spirit of Jesus' remark that only the faithless look for signs, consider such tests both futile and blasphemous […] Let us not tempt God.'

Gardner thus believes parapsychology to be an abomination, a sacrilege, a desecration, which in a shameful way encroaches on an area of life which ought to be left in peace lest one should trivialize the Mystery—in the famous words of Alexander Pope: 'Fools rush in where angels fear to tread.' Skepticism motivated in this way is rare as most skeptics, especially of the CSI brand, profess a secular humanism where science doesn't need to take heed of such pious taboos. On the surface, then, there is a stark contrast, even contradiction, between Gardner's skepticism and his religiosity. But perhaps a certain puritan streak—the strong passion for truth and the accompanying need to rid oneself of mental trash—can be seen as the common denominator.

Skepticism—a Summary

In this chapter we've had a look at some thought patterns and other possible sources of error that often—and often with good reason—will be used to denounce the paranormal. And we have suggested, sober skepticism coupled with an open and inquiring attitude will be the most fruitful approach to most phenomena—paranormal as well as normal, privately as well as professionally.

Moreover, we have had a look at a couple of cases, the Starbaby and Randi's prize, which, by our understanding, epitomize an inner conflict in the skepticism of CSI; a conflict between science and dogma, between skepticism and pseudo-skepticism. These examples, again by our understanding, also make visible—instructive and cautionary in equal measure—some of the problems arising when science is allowed to function as a prop, letting a *pro forma* openness obscure a *de facto* dogmatism. Let us now close the chapter on skepticism with the wise words of one of the most important CSI members ever, the great astrophysicist Carl Sagan:

> *If you are only skeptical, then no new ideas make it through to you. You never learn anything new. You become a crotchety old person convinced that nonsense is ruling the world. (There is, of course, much data to support you.) But every now and then, maybe once in a hundred cases, a new idea turns out to be on the mark, valid and wonderful. If you are too much in the habit of being skeptical about everything, you are going to miss or resent it, and either way you will be standing in the way of understanding and progress.*

Chapter 8

A VISIT TO THE PARAPSYCHOLOGIST'S LABORATORY

I believe there is no source of deception in the investigation of nature which can compare with a fixed belief that certain kinds of phenomena are impossible.

~ William James

Introduction and Recommendations

In this chapter we'll knock on the door of the parapsychologist's laboratory. As myriads of experiments of multiple types have been conducted over the years, our visit has the modest objective of getting to know a few samples of paradigmatic research—groundbreaking research that has become influential in the history of parapsychology. Since no research occurs in a vacuum, we will also examine important historical preconditions. Furthermore, we'll hand out the *cartes de visite* to some key researchers whose acquaintance it might be worthwhile to make. And—let me now suggest some piquant courses that, if the *hors d'oeuvre* here served should whet your appetite, could preferably be included in a full dinner menu at a somewhat later time.

As a first course I suggest *Entangled Minds: Extrasensory Experiences in a Quantum Reality*. The author is Dean Radin—engineer, psychologist and formerly professional musician—who is head of research at the Institute of Noetic Sciences. Radin is among those who know most about what is going on in parapsychological laboratories. His interesting take on telepathy and clairvoyance is the suggestion that the synaptic fluid between the neurons in our brains might be entangled—as explained at some length in our chapter 6—with the universe at large, thus allowing for transfer of information across distances. His book has a personal approach, and in addition to its presentation of 'hard' science it is brimming with entertaining stories and anecdotes.

As a main course we could then perhaps gorge ourselves with the versatile essay collection *Parapsychology in the Twenty-First Century: Essays On the Future of Psychical Research* by Michael A. Thalbourne and Lance Storm (eds.). I consider this book a 'must,' presenting a broad spectrum of important topics, methods, procedures, problems and results (and lack thereof…) in parapsychology. It also outlines possible ways forward. The contributors are reputable professionals from many disciplines—psychology, psychiatry, philosophy, and the social sciences. This ensures high quality, but—as often is the case with hearty fare—the serving might need to be digested slowly and thoughtfully.

And then, going for the sweet finale, we could enjoy *The End of Materialism: How Evidence of the Paranormal is Bringing Science and Spirit Together* by the very experienced psychologist and parapsychologist Professor Charles Tart. (As usual: Tart will make for a most agreeable dessert…). This is a great presentation, informative and well written, with multiple exciting examples of apparently paranormal manifestations. As Tart has a strong commitment to 'the cause'—the ending of materialism—some readers will probably feel that his book is slightly more 'believing' than what can be considered scientifically healthy. While others probably find that Tart's personal engagement is precisely what gives his book its quality. And after all, who ever said that the only reason for having dessert is for health reasons?

Historical Prerequisites and Obstacles

As mentioned earlier, the great American philosopher and psychologist William James (1842–1910) became the first president of ASPR, the American Society for Psychical Research. James actively campaigned for the recognition of parapsychology, and the US eventually went on to become the first country conducting systematic and statistically rigorous laboratory trials in the field. The biologist J.B. Rhine became the main person in this undertaking and his ESP research at Duke University during the 1930s was truly epochal.

True, that in the 1880s the French Nobel laureate, physician and parapsychologist Charles Richet had experimented with clairvoyance using cards concealed in envelopes; the test subjects would try to 'see' and identify the cards, and afterwards the results were evaluated statistically. However, Richet's research was small scale and did not—at least not there and then—have far-reaching consequences. And although the studies conducted in England by the Society

for Psychical Research were both comprehensive and up-
held high standards (today this is a generally accepted assessment, though many skeptics don't agree), they primarily
examined phenomena that happened spontaneously, and
thus their way of research did not meet the requirements
for *replication.*

The possibility of repeating an experiment—making
replications—is an important criterion in any fully-fledged
branch of natural science. (This does not apply uncondi-
tionally, though. For example, in astronomy and geology
research—the Big Bang, continental shifts, etc.—the replication of experimental conditions is impossible.) In chapter
7 we mentioned that since psi phenomena like all things
human—say, a battle, an election, a marriage—are to some
degree unpredictable and for the most part not replicable—
perhaps it is more relevant to study psi with methods from
the humanities than from the natural sciences. But then,
one method hardly excludes another. Probably a wide array
of approaches—studies both in laboratories and of real-life
phenomena, using both brain scanners and spiritual interpretation, utilizing the expertise of physicians and anthropologists—will give us the best and most relevant understanding of psi.

Bragging Behaviorism

Of the paranormal seeds that William James sowed many
fell upon the stony pavements of the university courtyards,
hibernating in cracks and crevices for a couple of decades
before being able to germinate. This late blossoming was
due to the intellectual movement which from about 1900
became widespread in psychology, namely that of *behaviorism.* This was a climate most unfavorable to occultism's

wild vegetation, as behaviorism tends to disparage all forms of subjective experience: consciousness, thoughts, feelings, introspection. Instead, the focus is—as the term clearly reveals—on behavior. And the objective description (and the possible correction) of behavior is considered psychology's main task; everything else will more or less be relegated to 'fiction,' 'art,' or 'literature.' Thus research on the paranormal—at least as it was conducted under the auspices of SPR—belongs to a completely different universe.

The grand old man of behaviorism—though he did not invent the term—was the Russian physician/physiologist Ivan Pavlov (1849–1936). Perhaps the name rings a bell? I would guess that many readers remember that Pavlov was the one using bells in experiments with 'classical conditioning' in dogs. The dogs were given food simultaneously as Pavlov rang a bell; when the dogs later heard the same bell they would produce the same physiological reaction (salivation) as when given food. 'The dark side' was that Pavlov would also experiment with giving the dogs electrical shocks while ringing another (differently tuned) bell. Later, when hearing this other bell, the dogs would recoil in fear. And when ringing both bells at the same time—one heralding pleasure, the other heralding pain—the dogs would eventually have something close to a nervous breakdown. (Scientific experiment is not an unequivocally nice thing...)

Following on from Pavlov, the American psychologist John B. Watson (1878–1958) invented the term 'behaviorism.' Using Johns Hopkins University as his pulpit Watson fervently preached the gospel of 'classical conditioning.' Newspapers featured serials on the hair-raising experiments he conducted on the nervous system of 'Little Albert,' a young boy used as guinea pig, and so the general public were introduced to the controversial methods and philosophy of behaviorism. Later, the behaviorist's baton was passed on to the psychologist B.F. Skinner (1904–1990).

During the first half of the 20th century behaviorism was the presiding current in American psychology. In Europe it exerted great influence, although there its impact would be cushioned by important figures. For example, European theorists such as Sigmund Freud, C.G. Jung and Karl Jaspers all ascribed the utmost importance to the inner life, whereas a proper behaviorist, *au contraire*, held that the gaze of science should only be bestowed upon that which may be counted, measured and weighed. The philosophy behind this view is called 'positivism' and originated with the French philosopher Auguste Comte (1798–1857). Thus behaviorism and positivism are ideological stablemates: all emphasis is put on the *external* aspects of the person, and existential questions about the meaning of life, love and friendship, contact and communication, personal truth and integrity are perceived not only as a hair but almost as a mammoth in the soup. Hence the 'hairy' paranormal phenomena—which tend to occur in conjunction with a strong inner life—rarely find shelter within the premises of such teachings; structures which often appear almost as mental bunkers designed as a defense against human unpredictability.

The behaviorists' triumph was greeted with rounds of applause from the advertising industry where the newfound tools for manipulating consumers were welcomed 10,000 times, and celebrated with drums, trumpets and jubilant voices as it were, almost resembling an Old Testament coronation. Psychology and advertising courted each other, and some time after having been dismissed from Johns Hopkins University because of an extramarital affair, Watson started working at J. Walter Thompson, then the world's largest advertising agency. Starting out at a low level, he rapidly rose in the ranks. So, at the same time and with the same virtuosity as Jelly Roll Morton played his 'Finger Buster' on the piano, Watson was playing on the psychological keys of customers. He proved to be so successful in creating 'buying behavior,' making that *clinking, clanking sound* ring out loudly and proudly from the cash registers, that the company eventually awarded him the title of 'vice president.'

Boulders in the Stream

However, American psychology had some highly talented people who refused to genuflect to the Baal of behaviorism. One of those unbending men was William McDougall (1871–1938). McDougall had originally been at Oxford University, but in 1920 he accepted an offer from Harvard, more or less taking over William James' old position. However, within a few years—apparently because of skirmishes with colleagues—he left for Duke University to establish an institute of psychology. McDougall wrote influential textbooks in psychology of the mainstream kind, but simultaneously he warmly defended parapsychology. (In England he had for a period been president of the Society for Psychical Research.) McDougall was fully convinced that telepathy was both provable and proven, and to ensure the quality of research within the field he set up a parapsychology lab at Duke—the very first of its kind. Under the leadership of J.B. Rhine this lab was to become a paranormal powerhouse within academia.

Gardner Murphy (1895–1979) was another towering anti-behaviorist—some hold him to be almost as influential as William James. During his career Murphy was associated with various top universities—Yale, Harvard, and Columbia—and for a while he even held the prestigious office as president of APA, the American Psychological Association.

Moreover he was president of the ASPR, the American Society for Psychical Research. Murphy believed that conventional thinking, 'common sense,' thwarted the acceptance of psi, and declared that if another science had provided just one tenth of the evidence presented by parapsychology the case for psi would have been settled, done and dusted. Murphy wrote diverse textbooks in psychology, and was in particular occupied with topics such as personality, motivation and creativity. Within parapsychology his research detected that extroverted and creative people tended to score higher on psi tests than those who were introspective and routine bound. (But he couldn't rule out that this could be because the extroverts felt more comfortable in the laboratory.) Murphy was also a supporter of the idea of a collective field of Consciousness binding us all together.

First We Take the Campus, Then We Take the World—J.B. Rhine

The man who modernized parapsychology and introduced it on the world stage of modern science was J.B. Rhine (1895–1980). Educated as a biologist and definitely not a freak or on the fringe, Rhine was an obstinate man who initially had been skeptical of paranormal claims. But during a lecture given by Sir Arthur Conan Doyle, he was made aware that various prominent scientists were deeply engaged in such phenomena (as mentioned in chapter 5, many early Nobel laureates were members of the Society for Psychical

Research). Rhine made further inquiries, and his wide reading included *Body and Mind* by William McDougall (see above). He was shaken when he gradually came to realize that paranormal phenomena might, in fact, be physically real. This did not mean that he lost his critical sense. On the contrary, in 1926 he exposed the notable Boston medium 'Margery' (Mina Crandon) in such an eviscerating way that Conan Doyle felt the need to counter with running a large ad in a Boston newspaper simply stating: 'J.B. Rhine is a monumental ass'! I have—unsuccessfully—tried to find out which newspaper this was, and the story may, in fact, be apocryphal. Still, it probably is representative of the tension between them.

Rhine, who was neither inclined toward nor had the skills for diplomacy, severed his relations with many of the members of the American Society for Psychical Research. However, William McDougall appreciated Rhine's uncompromising love of truth, and they collaborated professionally.

Rhine's research at Duke University during the 1930s became the model for parapsychology in the ensuing decades. Rhine based his approach on three principles: 1) using ordinary people (not gurus or mediums) as test subjects; 2) having simple, transparent procedures; and 3) making thorough statistical evaluations of the results. The reason why Rhine chose to work with ordinary men and women was that he assumed ESP to be an element of perception just as, say, vision, hearing, etc. Rhine's procedures were sober and methodical, it is tempting to say *tedious*. He was not in it for the spectacular as, say, the conjuring of spirits or sightings of aliens. His attention was rather directed at the small phenomena that (hopefully) could be replicated time and time again in a laboratory; in that respect Rhine was a behaviorist as good as any. This didn't mean, however, that he was without interest in other things. But the task of charting a multitude of spontaneously occurring episodes, collecting and collating paranormal stories reported from all over the United States, was assigned to his colleague and wife, the biologist Louisa Rhine.

Rhine's Experiments with ESP— Basic Methods and Results

Rhine focused primarily on telepathy, clairvoyance and precognition. He also did some, though much less, research on telekinesis, and nearly none on healing. Thus Rhine's research was primarily devoted to ESP (paranormal transference of information) and only to a limited degree to PK (paranormal transference of energy).

Rhine conducted research for several decades, and through the years he employed different methods—the most prevalent was the drawing of cards. Rhine had one of his colleagues, Karl Zener (1903–1964) design a special pack of cards—Zener cards—using only five different symbols. Each card was to have a distinct image so as to make it impossible to confuse them. This is highly important when trying to 'send' and 'receive' the symbols via ESP. The symbols on the Zener cards are: circle, cross, waves, square, and star.

Typically Rhine would use two subjects at a time—let's call them Jack and Jill. To avoid cheating or other leakage of information, Jack and Jill were separated, sometimes even located in different buildings. The different ESP capabilities could be tested as follows:

Telepathy: Jack draws a random card and contemplates the symbol depicted. Now Jill (located in another room/building) will attempt to 'see,' guess, perceive, sense, etc. which

of the five symbols—circle, cross, waves, square, or star—
Jack is contemplating. Hence Jill is trying to read Jack's
mind telepathically. The researchers register Jill's guess, if it
is right or wrong, and act as scorekeepers.

Clairvoyance: Jack draws a random card and—without
turning it—places it face down on the table. Jill (who is still
in another room/building) will then attempt to 'see,' guess,
perceive, sense which of the five symbols is depicted on the
card that Jack has just drawn. Unlike in the previous experiment Jack now doesn't know which symbol is on the card.
Therefore if Jill manages to 'see' the card correctly, it cannot
presumably be due to telepathy but rather to clairvoyance
(or chance).

Precognition: In advance—before Jack has drawn any card
at all—Jill (who is in another room/building) will attempt
to 'see,' guess, perceive, sense which symbol is on the card
that Jack is about to draw. Jill's guess is written down, and
it is only now that Jack will draw a card. As usual, the researchers register Jill's guess and keep score.

Experiments like these were repeated again and again
(and again and again!) for days and weeks on end, eventually
adding up to a series of tens of thousands of draws/guesses.
In this way mere chance and fluke were gradually eliminated from the data, making it possible to obtain results that
were statistically significant.

Rhine's first book was based on an analysis of more than
90,000 draws! From pure chance we should—since there
are five different Zener cards—expect hits in approximately
1/5 of the cases, that is to say a hit rate of 20 percent. But, in
fact, the test subjects had on average a far higher score than
20 percent—one of the subjects even managed to produce a
long series with an average of 39.6 percent hits, close to double the score that would be expected from mere coincidence.

The results therefore appeared to be highly significant, suggesting to Rhine that ESP was very real indeed.

Rhine also thought the results showed that just as there are exceptionally gifted people in most areas of life, there are, in fact, also people with exceptional skills in ESP. Perhaps the most impressive of Rhine's subjects was a theology student who outperformed expectations in a really grand style. When the experimental series were seen as a whole the odds for achieving his score from mere chance was calculated to be less than one in a billion!

So far so good. But, what would happen on various occasions was that the test subjects started out having good results but after some time they would gradually decline. Rhine referred to this as 'the decline effect,' which he thought could be explained by fatigue and boredom—that the exacting toll of hours and days of drawing-and-guessing would impair the subjects' extra sensory perception, much in the same way as it would have impaired nearly any mental functioning, say, the ability to perform mental arithmetic. However, whereas skeptics often argue that the initial good results may have been due to random variations and that over time it was to be expected, with a long series of guessing the results would even out. This is often referred to as a 'regression toward the mean.' If you toss a coin five times you might well get 100 percent heads and 0 percent tails. But if you toss the coin say 500 times you'll get very close to a heads/tails ratio of 50/50.

Laurels, Roses, and Some Thorns...

In 1934 Rhine presented parts of his results to the public in a book simply called *Extra Sensory Perception*. The book received good reviews and became a bestseller, but it also caused a hailstorm of criticism to erupt in this usually quite measured field—ranging from well-meaning objections to pure harassment. In the following years Rhine, a stickler for truth, tried to account for and refute all and every serious objection. In 1937, as part of this process he had the American Institute of Mathematics approve his statistical procedures. He also acquired a machine to shuffle the cards used in the experiments to avoid anyone, intentionally or unintentionally, influencing the order of the cards. The test subjects would now be isolated not only during the experiments but also during the breaks—to prevent blatant cheating as well as more subtle forms of unsanctioned transmission of information—overhearing, side glances, winks, nudges, etc.

At the annual meeting of the American Psychological Association in 1938 Rhine's research was awarded a special debate session, called 'Experimental Methods in ESP Research.' Here Rhine, one of his statisticians, and the aforementioned psychologist Gardner Murphy were to have a face-off against a board of three keen and incisive critics. A lively exchange took place, and the attendees generally felt that the critics' objections were successfully addressed. In fact, the meeting ended with a round of applause for Rhine and his colleagues.

In 1940 Rhine published a new work where he believed he had answered the qualified objections (32 of them, altogether!) that had been raised in the aftermath of his first book. The sequel was called *Extra Sensory Perception After Sixty Years*. The title hints at a book by the French physician and parapsychologist Charles Richet, namely his *Psychic Research After Thirty Years* (as mentioned above, Richet had already initiated the use of statistical methods around 1880). Before the book went to print, Rhine had presented the manuscript to all the critics who were quoted and invited them to give their responses that would then be published in the book. This quite unusual move signifies Rhine's desire for objectivity.

Extra Sensory Perception after Sixty Years—or *ESP 60*, as its pet name goes—was an immediate success, just as its predecessor. It also entered Harvard's list of 'recommended reading' for psychology students. Along with SPR's *Phantasms of the Living*, Rhine's *ESP 60* could easily be the most influential ever book on parapsychology.

Many psychologists found themselves embarrassed by the scientifically rigorous ESP research being conducted at Duke University. On the one hand evidence for the existence of ESP seemed substantial—on the other hand to accept this evidence would break with established perceptions. In 1951, Donald Hebb, the founder of neuropsychology, posed a question to his peers which he answered himself in the next breath:

> *Why do we not accept ESP as a psychological fact? Rhine has offered enough evidence to have convinced us on almost any other issue... Personally, I do not accept ESP for a moment, because it does not make sense. My external criteria, both of physics and of physiology, say that ESP is not a fact despite the behavioral evidence that has been reported. I cannot see what other basis my colleagues have for rejecting it... Rhine may still turn out to be right, improbable as I think that is, and my own rejection of his view is—in the literal sense—prejudice.*

This is certainly a brave admission from Hebb. But just admitting one's own resistance is hardly going to further science... In the autobiographical book *The Invisible Writing* the highly versatile author Arthur Koestler mentions an amusing episode emblematic of the type of shock that could befall a scientist in the slipstream of Rhine's research:

In 1952, I met in Princeton an old friend, the late Hans Reichenbach, a leading mathematical logician and Professor of Philosophy at the University of California. I had not seen him for nearly twenty years. He had aged and become partly deaf; instead of a modern hearing aid, he used an old-fashioned ear trumpet. He asked me what I had been interested in lately, and I told him that I had become interested in Rhine's work on extrasensory perception. He said that it was all hokum, and I said that I did not think so—at least the statistical evaluation of the experiments seemed to show relevant results (meaning that they seemed to confirm the existence of telepathy and kindred phenomena).

Reichenbach smiled and asked: 'Who has checked the statistics?' I said: 'R.A. Fisher in person.' (Fisher is one of the leading contemporary experts in probability calculus.) Reichenbach adjusted his trumpet. 'Who did you say?' I yelled into the trumpet: 'Fisher. The Fisher.' At that moment an extraordinary change took place in Reichenbach's face. He went pale, dropped his trumpet and said: 'If that is true it is terrible, terrible. It would mean that I would have to scrap everything, and start again from the beginning.' In other words, if extrasensory perception exists, the whole edifice of materialist philosophy crumbles. And for a professional philosopher that means the crumbling of his life's work.

Ronald Aylmer Fisher (1890–1962) is regarded as one of the most prominent statisticians in the 20th century; in addition he was considered an important biologist—in fact, Richard Dawkins has described him as no less than 'the greatest biologist after Darwin.' Reichenbach was certainly no insignificant figure either—a leading contemporary philosopher of science, who made contributions in many fields: quantum mechanics, relativity theory, mathematics, probability theory, logic, and more. Reichenbach was an ardent advocate of *logical positivism*—a hardnosed philosophical movement, characterized by an unyielding scientific approach to all aspects of life. The above episode is thus a striking (and witty) example of the vise-like grip that even the toughest skeptics could find themselves in when having to deal with the research conducted at Duke.

Despite huge sales, winning the acclaim of the American Psychological Association, back patting from colleagues and even recognition from multiple opponents, within the course of only a few decades Rhine had fallen out of favor, gradually submerging into *Lethe*, the river of oblivion, to use the ancient Greek description. Part of the reason was the 'vagaries of vogue'—the merciless ever-changing currents of fashion. In addition, when World War II broke out Rhine's lab at Duke lost most of its male staff, who were drafted into military service. And for various reasons— some tragic, some mundane—many did not return after the war. In the post-war period, the pressing issue for society, the universities included, was to repair the damage done. The next step was to counteract the political, technological and military expansion of the Eastern bloc. Parapsychology seemed to have but a faint relevance to the agenda of the day (though this would, to some degree, change later, in the era of Stargate).

Rhine's research was also 'too unique,' 'too one of a kind,' not part of an academic tradition and therefore unable to provide reasonably attractive career opportunities for talented researchers. This problem still haunts the field; the 'pscientists' (parapsychologists) often find themselves impeded by extremely small budgets and even less recognition. The physicist Edwin C. May, who for many years was the leader of Stargate and who thus must be regarded as one of the most successful careerists in parapsychology, has issued strong warnings that trying to eke out a living from parapsychology exacts a heavy toll.

Nonetheless, Rhine at least succeeded in establishing parapsychology as a legitimate branch of scientific research—certainly not with the biggest budgets or with the greatest prestige, but still, how many scientists achieve something similar within their field?

Considerations in Hindsight

And what conclusion should we settle on—did Rhine prove ESP to be real or did he not? It seems (hardly any great surprise) to depend on the eyes of the beholder. If one is open to ESP from the outset, one would likely find Rhine's results to be very convincing. On the other hand, if one starts out as negative toward ESP, one would probably rather attribute the results to potential undetected weaknesses in procedures and methods. Objections that have been expressed are, for instance, the following:

Do we know for certain that information wasn't leaked, either by cheating or by carelessness? Do we know that the judges who assessed the results were completely 'clean' and not biased (by sympathy or bribery), or were otherwise influenced (by gestures, gaze, tone of voice of colleagues or subjects) in ways that could have colored their assessment? Were the test subjects neutral, or were they interested in achieving specific results? How were the results interpreted? Which factors and elements were emphasized, and which were excluded? And further, there are different statistical methods, and it is not a given which should be used to produce the best assessment, etc., etc.

As has been said, Rhine thought that he had taken these as well as the bulk of other objections into account in his *Extra Sensory Perception After Sixty Years*. In more recent times (2007), Elizabeth Lloyd Mayer, professor at Berkeley University (the psychologist with the lost-and-found harp mentioned in chapter 7), vouched for the quality of Rhine's research. She further stated that prejudice seems to be an important reason for not accepting the results.

At the end of chapter 6 we mentioned that it can sometimes be problematic to discriminate between different types of psi. This also holds true when looking at Rhine's research, as it is by no means easy to know which parapsychological ability had been at work. Suppose we wanted to test ESP by guessing which cards are placed in sealed envelopes, and our subjects prove to be right far more often than mere chance would suggest. Given that the results are not due to fraud or other faultiness, should they be interpreted as expressions of a) *Clairvoyance*—meaning that the subjects intuitively have 'seen' the cards within the envelopes? Or should they be interpreted as b) *Precognition*—meaning that the subjects intuitively have 'seen' the future in which the envelopes would be opened and the cards checked? Or, if the cards were placed in the envelopes by an assistant who has seen the cards and not by a machine, maybe the symbols were transferred via c) *Telepathy*—meaning that the receiver 'read' the mind of the assistant? Now, this is not easy to know... not easy at all.

Rhine was aware of these problems but he never fully succeeded in solving them. And what complicates the picture further is, as mentioned in the introduction, that the different psi phenomena can be seen as essentially *one* phenomenon, namely 'the transfer of information/energy beyond the common perception of Space, Time and Causality.'

Even more methodological problems were mentioned in chapter 7. But as also stated: Parapsychology is often, even by skeptics, thought to hold high scientific standards. This level of quality has been achieved because of the large amount of criticism that parapsychologists have had to deal with. However, some parapsychologists—like some psychologists, some medical researchers, etc.—have unfortunately been tempted to garnish their act. In 1974 Rhine, as always doggedly searching for truth, published an article in which he exposed cases of cheating that he had become aware of. And even his own lab didn't escape as a young employee at Duke had recently been caught red-handed 'embellishing' his statistics on animal psi trials. This had of course absolutely nothing to do with Rhine's own research 30 years earlier, but it may serve as a reminder of the skeptic's point: that it is always difficult to be completely sure.

A Norwegian Apropos to Rhine's Experiments

Let me mention that Joralf Gjerstad, the Snåsa Man introduced in chapter 5, was once tested somewhat in the manner of Rhine by the defense lawyer Cato Schiøtz—a well-known culture and media personality in Norway. The short version of the event goes like this.

Together with his friend, the author Ingar Kolloen, Schiøtz visited Gjerstad at home. At the time Kolloen was working on a biography of Gjerstad. After Kolloen had finished his questioning and the two men were about to leave, Gjerstad asked if they had now asked about *everything* they wanted to know—emphasizing the word *everything*. Schiøtz felt his chance had come, as he had secretly hoped to run a little clairvoyance test with Gjerstad. To that effect Schiøtz

374 - *Chapter 8*

had, before leaving home, randomly and face down, drawn a card from a standard pack of 52. He had purposely avoided looking at the card thus making it impossible for Gjerstad to trick him into disclosing its identity using, say, leading questions or cold reading. Schiøtz asked if Gjerstad was willing to demonstrate his abilities and—this turned out to be one of the few occasions where Gjerstad, who mostly refuses to participate in any kind of 'party tricks,' chose to play along.

Schiøtz first placed the card (face down!) on the table in front of Gjerstad, who jotted and scribbled a little, considering a couple of options, and then wrote down his shot. The card was turned and—it was a hit! From pure chance, the probability for this to occur is obviously 1/52. Not completely impossible odds, of course, but it seems weird that Gjerstad proved able to deliver such a hit on demand. I have discussed the incident with Schiøtz, who assured me that he was in full control of the card during the process, and that Gjerstad, in fact, never got to touch it at all. Schiøtz therefore thinks one can rule out palmistry and sleight-of-hand, and believes it must have been either a matter of luck or of ESP. Following an overall assessment, including similar stories reported by others, based on his comprehensive experience and the criteria employed in a courtroom, Schiøtz believes that in a trial Gjerstad would have been found guilty—beyond reasonable doubt—of being psychic!

Dream Telepathy—Our Nocturnal Communications

These disturbing phenomena seem to deny all our scientific ideas. How we should like to discredit them! Unfortunately the statistical evidence, at least for telepathy, is overwhelming

~ Alan Turing, mathematician and logician; pioneer in computer science and artificial intelligence

In the introduction we quoted from a 1922 article by Sigmund Freud, the founder of psychoanalysis, where he claimed it to be 'an undeniable fact that sleep creates favorable conditions for telepathy.' It would take several decades, though, before technological developments, coupled with an increased interest in altered states of consciousness—sown by the Beat Generation, brought to fruition by the hippies—made it feasible to put Freud's claim to the test. The summer of 1964 saw the beginning of what would become a decade of pioneering, systematic research on dream telepathy, conducted at the renowned Maimonides Medical Center in New York. The key researchers were psychiatrist and psychoanalyst Montague Ullman (1916–2008) and psychologist Stanley Krippner (b. 1932). Ullman was, in keeping with his psychoanalytic background, an expert on dreams, and has written diverse books on the subject. For a period Ullman was chairman of ASPR, the American Society for Psychical Research. We have made Krippner's acquaintance already, but in a rather superficial way. Now it seems appropriate to elaborate.

Stanley Krippner is an internationally recognized expert on dreams, hypnosis and altered states of consciousness. He has also been doing in-depth research on shamanism, including what takes place, psychologically, physiologically and chemically, in the brain in the event of trances and trauma. Krippner has been editor for a whole lot of works on psychology, and has, as author and co-author, published about 20 books. Furthermore, he has written almost a thousand articles! Krippner has been head of two divisions of the American Psychological Association, and he has received several prestigious awards for his work. He is often regarded as the 'grand old man' of contemporary parapsychology, and is, so it seems, held in high regard by almost everybody. Even the arch-skeptic, James Randi, has respect for 'Stan' and his integrity, and once stated: 'There are so few things in this field you can depend on, and there are so many people who are prejudiced and biased. But I can depend on Stan. And I don't think he's biased at all.' Truly a strong statement!

Krippner has a liberal lifestyle and hangs out on a regular basis with fringe-dwellers of all kinds, shamans, artists and musicians, and he is also open about his philosophical use of entheogens, psychoactive plants, as, for example, the concoction *ayahuasca*, used by shamans of the Amazon. But in his professional assessments Krippner is extremely sober— almost annoyingly sober, one might think, when knowing just a little about all the exciting things in which he has been involved. For instance, he was a good friend of Jerry Garcia, the leader of the cult band Grateful Dead. Once he hypnotized the band's two drummers to make them more rhythmically coordinated! (They were happy with the result, reportedly having been enabled to interact as one.) Krippner has also conducted exciting group telepathy experiments at their concerts.

From the Dream Lab

The Maimonides experiments covered different aspects of nocturnal ESP, one example was the ability to see the future in dreams. But the primary aim was to investigate whether it would be possible for a person ('sender') to telepathically transmit his/her thoughts to another person lying asleep ('receiver'). A long series of tests seemingly showed there was a remarkably high degree of correlation between the thoughts 'sent' and the thoughts 'received.' Thus the awake person was, so it seemed, able to telepathically affect the dreams of the sleeper! Important results from the trials were published in *Dream Telepathy: Experiments in Nocturnal ESP* (1974)—a work which is considered by many to be epochal, and which has been re-released in several editions.

The experiment protocols varied through the years—one procedure used was this: First, two subjects are assigned the roles as respectively 'Sender' and 'Receiver.' Secondly, these two spend some time together, say, going downtown for dinner to get to know each other and to get 'in tune.' Back in the lab they are ushered to separate rooms. The Receiver's room is soundproof and electromagnetically shielded to prevent 'normal' transfer of information. The Receiver is connected to equipment registering REM sleep (REM = Rapid Eye Movements, referring to the small, very fast eye movements that occur while dreaming). The Receiver then goes to sleep.

Meanwhile, the researchers have prepared a stack of photographs/prints of diverse artwork—often these will be pictures with lively colors and/or depicting intense emotions. Based on dice-throwing the researchers select one of these photographs, which is then placed in an opaque envelope and given to the Sender.

When the equipment shows that the Receiver is in REM sleep, indicative of dreaming, the researchers tell the Sender (who, as said, is placed in a different room) to open the envelope, take out the photo and start 'sending' the content of the photograph to the dreaming Receiver. After some minutes of telepathic transmission, the Receiver is awakened and is immediately asked about the dream. The Receiver's description of his/her dream is both recorded on tape and written down. Let's now have a look at some of the material from *Dream Telepathy*.

In one case the Sender tried to telepathically transmit the *School of Dance* by the French painter Edgar Degas. The painting depicts a group of girls having a ballet lesson. When the Receiver, the dreamer, was awakened she related: 'I was in a class made up of maybe half a dozen people, it felt like a school,' and 'There was one little girl that was trying to dance with me.' It in fact seems like a number of elements in the image that the Sender tried to transmit resurfaced in the dream of the Receiver, e.g. 'group,' 'school,' 'girl,' 'dance.'

In another case (when a somewhat different procedure was used) the Sender tried to make a telepathic transfer of *The Church at Auvers*, a painting by Vincent van Gogh. This painting depicts an old, grey stone church and a woman walking on a cobblestoned street outside. The Receiver, after having been awakened in the middle of the dream, said:

I was dreaming of...Europe. We came to this building. I think it was a dome or something. It was a very old building. It could have been a church. [...] We went into this great hall, and there was the little old lady speaking... I remember walking down a street ...and it was cobblestone...I remember a lot of grey from the buildings.... I think it was a church or something...

Again, it seems that diverse key elements in the image appeared in the dream: 'Europe,' 'old building,' 'church,' 'cobblestone,' 'lady' (albeit placed inside the church), 'much grey.'

After the experiment, the Receiver's taped and written dream report as well as copies of the full stack of photos were passed on to three independent judges—psychologists experienced in the interpretation of perception and imagery, and who also know the relevant statistics (say, of how often different elements occur in people's dreams, etc.). The degree of correspondence between the dream and the 'telepathed' photo was evaluated on a scale from 1 to 6. This assessment was done according to a complex routine involving interviewing the test subjects. In the introduction to the third edition of *Dream Telepathy* Krippner states that approximately two-thirds of the trials yielded significant results, meaning results better than one would expect from mere chance. As the trials were conducted over many years the hypothesis about telepathy in dreams apparently was well corroborated. Or, as skeptics would rather say, the methods apparently were seriously flawed.

As mentioned in chapter 7, it is quite problematic to claim that anything, really, has been completely proven, as there could almost always—someplace, somewhere—be a hitherto undetected source of error. Krippner is therefore circumspect about making extravagant claims. Hence he states his positive assessment indirectly by saying that the hit score was so high 'that coincidence was unlikely.'

In more recent times (2004) Krippner has again spoken in defense of the Maimonides trials, claiming they were conducted with better methods than reference experiments in the field (visual interpretation and pattern recognition). The objection he considers to have the most bearing is that other scientists rarely get similar good results; that is, replication has often been unsuccessful. In the previous chapter we assumed that an optimal functioning of such sensitive capacities as these (if at all real) will depend just as much, or probably even more, on the qualities—enthusiasm, encouragement, etc.—of the 'coach.' The researchers are difficult, or even impossible, to factor out of the experiment, as they—with their attitudes, moods, words, and actions—will unavoidably influence the test subjects, and thereby most likely also their performance, to a certain degree.

So, perhaps the difficulty in getting results similar to those of Ullman and Krippner might be due to such factors—that very few scientists are equally motivating and inspiring to work with as they were. Before Egil 'Drillo' Olsen became coach for the Norwegian soccer team in the 1990s, very few had ever thought it possible for little Norway to reach second place on the FIFA world ranking, even beating the mighty Brazil in two face-offs, in 1997 and 1998.

Assessment by Others

The positive assessment of the Maimonides experiments is shared by other respected professionals. In 1985, in the November issue of *American Psychologist*, Professor Irvin Child, former head of the Department of Psychology at Yale University, published an article called 'Psychology and Anomalous Observations: The Question of ESP in Dreams,' which was mainly based on a thorough analysis of the Ullman and Krippner trials. And Child's conclusion coincided largely with their assessment. In some series of experiments there was, according to Child, less than one-thousandth of a chance that the results could be coincidental!

Child's article was published in *American Psychologist*, often considered to be the most prestigious journal in American psychology, which therefore lent extra gravitas to the work. But of course, not everybody was eager to consider the possibility that the significant deviations might be due to telepathy. In the ensuing debate several critics claimed—some in quite a cocksure way—that the results were expressions of this or that (still undetected) error in the experiments. Child wrote a quite biting counterattack, stating that some of the criticism was irrelevant, while much of the other analysis was based on an incorrect or distorted representation of the trials. Child was certainly not prone to hyperbole and expressed his view in the following understated manner:

> *I believe many psychologists would, like myself, consider the ESP hypothesis to merit serious consideration and continued research if they read the Maimonides reports for themselves and if they familiarized themselves with other recent and older lines of experimentation.*

Well, then, with whom should we join forces?—the skeptics who consider the trials conducted by Ullman and Krippner to be lacking in methodological rigor, and regard dream telepathy as all 'woo-woo'? Or rather with Child, who chose to merit the idea of dream telepathy with serious consideration? The last alternative—which certainly appears to be the most exciting—would also be in keeping with the many esoteric traditions which have described this phenomenon, e.g. the Kabbalah, the Jewish mysticism, where even specific techniques for communicating via dream telepathy are cultivated! Are such ideas just based on mistakes, misunderstandings, misconceptions, misapprehensions, and misinterpretations? Or could their basis rather be the experience of generations with *real* nocturnal communications mediated via the collective field of consciousness, the Mental Internet?

The Ganzfeld—the Lab's Monastic Cell

From the late 1960s on much research has been conducted in parapsychology with experimentation related to the 'ganzfeld effect.' The German word *ganzfeld* means 'total field' and originally referred to the field of vision. The ganzfeld effect will sometimes occur naturally when for an extended period of time we look at, say, a snow-covered, all-white plain, or if we stare into a completely dark room. After a while the brain will start to miss the usual visual signals and 'look inwards' to compensate. Thus the so-called 'neural noise,' the brain's continuous inner 'hum,' will come to the forefront. This may sometimes lead to hallucinations. But amidst this well-known psycho-physiological noise there may also, according to many parapsychologists, pop up some genuinely 'anarchistic' mental content, namely bits of information originating from ESP (telepathy, clairvoyance or precognition). An important pioneer in this special field of research was Charles Honorton (1946–1992). Honorton started out working with Rhine at Duke, and then later collaborated with Krippner and Ullman at the dream lab at Maimonides where he eventually became head of research. Subsequently, in 1979, he established the Psychophysical Research Laboratories (PRL), in Princeton, New Jersey.

A ganzfeld experiment will try to utilize the above-mentioned effect by creating a setup somewhat like the following: the test subject is reclining in a soundproof room wearing headphones playing 'white noise'—diffuse and pleasant sounds, e.g. nature sounds like trickling rain, whispering winds, or breaking waves. The room is dimly lit, perhaps in soothing pink, and the subject's eyes are covered with special goggles (originally ping pong balls cut in half were used). The idea is, as mentioned, to reduce the sensory input from outside as much as possible. Thus ensconced, the test subject becomes more sensitive to subtle inner sensations possibly containing elements coming from extrasensory perception.

This works in the same way as getting all the instruments in an orchestra to play more quietly except for, say, the flutes; in which case the flutes will be more easily heard. Something similar would also happen if you had just the flutes—and none of the other instruments—play louder. This is comparable to the strategy used by Alan Parker in his twin-telepathy experiment (end of chapter 6) where small shocks were used to increase the signals emitting from Vicky ('increasing the volume of the flutes'). But in most cases it will be easier and less painful to dampen 'the orchestra'—reduce distractions from vision, hearing, odors, movements, etc.—as is done in the typical ganzfeld experiments.

A related approach has since days of old been used by mystics in many traditions. 'Mystic' is derived from the Greek word *myein*, meaning 'closing' (of the eyes). Mystics will often spend a great amount of time praying and meditating isolated in hermit huts, subterranean initiation chambers, caves, monastic cells and the like. In this way they significantly reduce sensory input—little or no visual impressions, noise from the marketplace, etc. This partial sense deprivation will often be combined with fasting and vigils. These techniques, especially when combined, may easily cause visions/hallucinations—which really is dreaming while awake, subconscious material entering into consciousness—and experiences of psi, as is well known, have often been reported.

In some sense we are all mystics and parapsychologists, each night entering our own initiation cave to engage profoundly in ganzfeld experiments! During sleep we are deprived of outward sensations to a great extent, thus turning down 'the orchestra' allowing 'the flutes' to more clearly emerge. But of course, our DIY experiments during sleep do not allow for the same degree of observation or active collaboration with researchers. Experimenting in a ganzfeld setup as sketched above is also by far and away the most efficient way to go about researching telepathy, making it possible to send/receive whole series of pictures during a short stint. In contrast, the experiments conducted by Krippner and Ullman were utterly time-consuming: a whole evening was needed trying to send/receive just one single image. The disadvantage of doing experiments where the receiver is awake is of course that most people will not be as relaxed and as receptive as when sleeping. (Some experienced meditators are an exception to this rule.)

Experiments with telepathy in the ganzfeld can be conducted in many ways. However, protocols where the essence is trying to send/receive images are the most widespread. The most vocal proponent of ganzfeld experiments today is likely Dean Radin, head of research at the Institute of Noetic Sciences. Radin's stock-in-trade, in addition to his own research, is the so-called meta-analysis—'doing research on research done.' In that connection Radin has spent a tremendous amount of time reviewing different studies from parapsychological labs around the world. The ganzfeld studies alone number about 2,500 and counting! Having worked his way through piles and piles of material leaves Radin convinced:

We are fully justified in having very high confidence that people sometimes get small amounts of specific information from a distance without the use of the ordinary senses. Psi effects do occur in the ganzfeld.

Prescient Soldiers and Civilians

In his own research Radin has, among other things, worked with precognition. The idea for a novel experiment design was conceived while Radin was a Visiting Fellow at the University of Edinburgh, in 1993, where he helped building a laboratory for testing telepathy. Experiments were conducted somewhat later, in 1993–97, while he ran a psi laboratory at the University of Nevada. Rather than being the preserve of psychics, could precognition be a universal ability? Radin tested this hypothesis by connecting soldiers, used as guinea pigs, to equipment measuring their skin's resistance to electricity—often referred to as 'skin conductivity.' When a person becomes afraid a spontaneous secretion of microscopic drops of sweat takes place, and this moisture immediately decreases the skin's resistance to electricity. Thus changes in a person's level of stress can easily be detected.

Radin had the soldiers watch a screen that would—with pauses of some seconds in between—alternately show pictures with neutral, markedly pleasant, and markedly frightening scenes. And what transpired was, according to Radin, that the soldiers would often get a change in conductivity a few—typically two to five—seconds *before* either a scary or a pleasurable image appeared! Radin thought that the 'gut feeling' that had helped the soldiers survive in the field might actually be based on genuine knowing/perception of the future and that this would strengthen his hypothesis (pre-cognition = fore-knowledge). Scary pictures would create the strongest responses. This makes evolutionary good sense, as it is more urgent to be forewarned of a hungry lion coming your way than of, say, an attractive man/woman. (Chances for mating will most likely appear again—as long as you manage to avoid being eaten by the lion!)

Skeptics would of course think that such results are either caused by faulty devices, or that the pictorial material was not random enough, or that other unidentified methodological faults are lurking somewhere in the protocols. However, serious scientists have been intrigued by Radin's results, thinking something of real interest is going on here. One such scientist is Kary B. Mullis—one of the really trailblazing chemists of our days, who was awarded the Nobel Prize in 1993. Mullis wanted to be tested with the same equipment as the soldiers. He has commented on his experience in hindsight, and has then stated:

> *I sat wired up in front of Radin's machine myself one morning. I was intrigued. My skin conductivity could respond, not every time, but a statistically significant percentage of the time, to what sort of stimulus his absolutely random machine was going to present to me.* [...] *Radin is addressing something to do with human minds on our time scale; whether our minds are really localized in space and time, like we normally think of them.* [...] *He is demonstrating an empirical fact, a strange and unexpected property of things, on a scale of seconds, with which we are personally familiar, and he is doing it in a technically convincing way. I don't know what it means, that's why it's intriguing.*
>
> *I could see about three seconds into the future. It's spooky. You sit there and watch this little trace, and about three seconds, on average, before the picture comes on, you have a little response in your skin conductivity which is in the same direction that a large response occurs after you see the picture. Some pictures make you have a rise in conductivity, some make you have a fall.* [...] *There's something funny about time that we don't understand because you shouldn't be able to do that.*

The physicist and psychologist Professor Dick J. Bierman at the University of Amsterdam has conducted upgraded re-iterations of Radin's experiments. Bierman used advanced brain scans, fMRI, functional magnetic resonance imaging. He further applied extensive and rigorous evaluation methods so as to neutralize sources of errors of all kinds. And Bierman's results came in congruent with Radin's: they indicated that ordinary people—and not only those that are psychics, long-time meditators and/or mystics—really are capable of ESP-based foresight! Links to scientific articles describing the experiments are found in the bibliography.

I once had a conversation with a professional rock blaster, and what he told me fits well with Radin's and Bierman's belief: that precognition is an ability we are subconsciously using all time. He related an incident where he was about 500ft (150m) away from what was intended to be a controlled explosion. Then—simultaneously as the explosives detonated—he suddenly and without thinking found himself swirling around 180 degrees and covering the back of his head with his hands. And in the next moment those hands were struck by chips of stone that could easily have crushed his skull! It was the first time in his career he had done something like this. What, then, was behind his utterly timely swirl—subtle physical signals or paranormal foresight? Who knows? But surely, this episode is easily the epitome of the kind of life-saving ESP prescience that Radin and Bierman have tried to elucidate in their experiments.

Radin believes that the key to explaining precognition could be the 'time-symmetry of quantum events.' This is a complex notion from quantum theory whose essence is that ultra small-scale events—as, say, an electron moving through an electromagnetic field—will look exactly the same whether time is moving forwards or backwards.

Perhaps time-independent processes are also going on in the brain and that precognition simply is our conscious experience of those processes? Radin thinks (something like) this to be the case. Needless to say, skeptics do not agree.

Personally I don't feel competent to make judgments about such complicated matters, but Radin's surely is an interesting idea. Anyway, I think the walk might be more important than the talk, meaning that Radin's enthralling experiments could prove to be more important than his explanatory models. Often strange facts are detected first whereas a proper explanation is found long afterwards. For thousands of years people had observed those tiny flames—burning meteorites—crossing the night sky without understanding their true cause or nature; modern astronomy had to develop before that riddle was solved. Electricity as a phenomenon was discovered by the ancient Greeks and Mesopotamians, but was not explained properly until Maxwell came along with his revolutionary equations around the mid-19th century.

More About Precognition— What Students Can Predict...

Feeling the Future

Quite a number of psychologists probably choked on their coffee when opening the *Journal of Personality and Social Psychology* during March 2011. Because what met the eye in this most orthodox of magazines was a most heretical headline: 'Feeling the Future: Experimental Evidence for Anomalous Retroactive Influences on Cognition and Affect.' This extraordinary article, written by Daryl Bem, an internationally respected psychologist tenured at Cornell University, presents evidence suggesting that humans do, in fact, see/perceive the future! 'Feeling the Future' presents nine experiments that were conducted with volunteer students. Bem believes the results from eight of these experiments to be suggestive of precognition/premonition. 'Precognition' (cognitive; specific knowledge regarding the future) and 'premonition' (affective; general sensations regarding the future) overlap and both are variants of foresight based on ESP. 'Feeling the Future' contains quite a lot of demanding (at least for a lay person) statistics, but there are some accessible parts as well, accompanied by Bem's subtly jocular comments.

'Feeling the Future' created euphoria in psi positive environments and shockwaves among skeptics because Bem is a psychologist of high esteem who has taught at major academic institutions including Harvard. And not least because the magazine that printed the article is among the most respected, peer-reviewed psychology journals in the world. The *Journal of Personality and Social Psychology* is published by APA, the American Psychological Association, and submitted articles must be approved not only by the journal's own editors but also by four external peers. Professor Charles Judd, who oversaw the approval process for 'Feeling the Future,' has stated: 'This paper went through a series of reviews from some of our most trusted reviewers.'

With this article Bem really stomped on the hornet's nest—for which rational person in his/her right mind would believe in such fairytale stuff?—and 'Feeling the Future' has spawned an aftermath of feuding (as well as valuable and thoughtful research). Some critics have even attacked the journal for presenting such eccentric ideas (so much for freedom of research...). Early on, the well-known skeptic James Alcock had a heated debate with Bem in *Skeptical Inquirer*. Shortly thereafter the psychologists/skeptics Chris French and Richard Wiseman issued three replications of one of Bem's nine experiments, the results not being indicative of any precognition whatsoever. The ensuing years have seen much further debate as well as many replications, some successful, some not. Together with three colleagues Bem recently (2014) did a meta-analysis of no fewer than 90 replicated experiments, and—the original conclusions from 'Feeling the Future' were corroborated. Bem's original article, the meta-analysis and other relevant material are easily available (though not as easily readable...) from his website at Cornell University: http://dbem.ws/

Precognitive Detection of Erotic Stimuli

In the first experiment, called 'Precognitive Detection of Erotic Stimuli,' the 'guinea pig students' were presented with a screen displaying two curtains; these could be 'drawn aside' by pressing buttons. The students were told that behind one of the drapes there would be a positively charged image; the computer—that sly dog!—would use highly erotic photographs as bait to awaken the students' precognitive sense. Behind the other curtain, however, there would be nothing exciting. The students' task was, as one would expect, to locate the steamy picture. For this to be a test of *precognition* none of the images—neither the exciting nor the neutral—were present 'behind the curtains' when the experiment started. Instead, the computer chose which images should be displayed *immediately after* the students had made their choice. This meant that the students' detection of erotic stimuli would relate to an event in the immediate future (meaning they had to use precognition) and not something already present (in which case they would have been using clairvoyance).

Bem employed computerized randomization in the experiments—to thwart the possibility of finding answers by, say, shrewd reasoning, detection of subtle clues, cold reading or other tricks in the magicians' repertoire. And by the way, Bem is himself not only a world-renowned psychologist but also an experienced magician and mentalist. Originally he was an ardent skeptic, but eventually he became convinced of the reality of psi following a thorough evaluation of a series of ganzfeld experiments conducted by Charles Honorton (briefly mentioned above).

Bem ran this experiment with 100 different students, 50 of each gender, and performed 36 tests with each student, totaling 3,600 attempts. It turned out that even with randomization in place the students still had the correct hunch about where the eroticism would appear in a majority of the cases! Those students...

The students would on average score 53.1 percent of the time, which may not sound all that impressive. But in a test where the method is specifically designed to eliminate coincidences and a hit rate very close to 50 percent is to be expected—given that no x-factors, as for instance precognition or cheating, are in the picture—a deviation this size is considered to be both certain and important. In a casino the roulette has about this edge versus the players (the casino will win 53 percent and the players 47 percent of the time). And as Bem said in an interview: '[...] casinos are not complaining that that is too small [...] They are making plenty of money with that edge.'

As mentioned above: A full eight out of Bem's nine experiments yielded results, suggesting the students had used ESP to know the future. Therefore, according to Bem, these trials taken together clearly provide the psi hypothesis with more than just a scant evidence base. Bem has analyzed the probability for getting a similar outcome given that precognition does not exist. He found that mere chance would yield a similar result in only one out of 74 billion cases! This sounds quite extraordinary to me, but then I'm only an amateur...

In addition to describing experiments and methods, 'Feeling the Future' also suggests possible perspectives from physics and biology that provide a relevant framework for understanding psi. Bem is also one of those who believe that psi works unconsciously, running as a kind of background program beneath our everyday perceptions—to help us avoid dangers and gain happiness, e.g. find suitable partners. This seems reasonable from an evolutionary perspective; psi would then be an ancient mechanism helping us to be more 'fit for survival.'

Mulling Over the Method

Some of the strength in Bem's trials is that they are based on well-established methods in psychological research, with just some small alterations to make them suitable for testing precognition. For example Bem created a variation on a standard memory experiment. In the classical version the subjects are first shown a list of words on a computer screen. Then they are shown another list that contains half the words from the first list, and are asked to type these words. Finally the screen is blanked, and the subjects are now asked to type as many words as they can possibly remember from the first list. Evidently, the subjects remember more of the words they have typed during the second step. Typing the words makes them easier to remember. No big deal, really.

In Bem's version of the experiment the order between cause and effect was changed. First, a group of students were shown a list of 48 words and asked to remember as many as they could. Second, they were shown a list of 24 words that had been randomly selected from the first list, and were asked to type these words. When evaluating the results it, quite surprisingly, turned out that the students were significantly better at remembering the words (in the first round) that they later chose to type (in the second round)! Thus the well-known memory-reinforcing effect of typing the words apparently worked backward in time. This conclusion is of course utterly confusing and highly counterintuitive! But Bem's methods are generally thought to be sound, which was the main reason the *Journal of Personality and Social Psychology* accepted his article.

To formulate the idea a little differently: Perhaps the explanation could be—if precognition is possible—that the students in the first round would 'see' (by precognition) which 24 words they were going to type in the second round. And that this foresight made it easier for them recognize and remember precisely *those* words when they were displayed during the first round.

Truly, it is interesting—and in my opinion praiseworthy—that a leading journal would 'run the risk of ridicule' by publishing such odd stuff. Charles Judd, the aforementioned editor, said in an interview on the eve of the release (the rumor went that the article would contain explosive material):

What makes these findings so remarkable and certainly controversial is that they turn our traditional understanding of causality on its head [...] *A central as-sumption in lay and scientific conceptions of causality is that a cause precedes its effect, not the other way round.*

Even if Bem reached weird conclusions, Judd and the other peers believed the arguments and the data to be 'well done'—hence he felt the journal had no valid reason to refrain from publishing the article. This, though, is not to say that they shared Bem's opinions: 'This does not mean we agree with his conclusions. We are not endorsing what Daryl Bem says.'

The Confusing Relationship Between Cause and Effect

Retro-causation, even if sounding somewhat sci-fi, is a very old idea. For instance the Arabian collection of fairytales *One Thousand and One Nights* repeatedly weaves retro-causality into the fabric of the stories. In one story the Caliph in Baghdad, Harun al-Rashid, opens a book his library, the *Beit al-Hakim* (*The House of Wisdom*), and reads a tale. Suddenly he falls to the ground, laughing and weeping, and for no apparent reason dismisses his faithful vizier, Ja'far, from sight. Ja'far flees town and gets involved in a series of adventures. After returning to Baghdad, Ja'far reads the book that made the Caliph dismiss him and discovers that it, in fact, describes Ja'far's own adventures! So, the story in the book apparently caused its own fulfilment. But, could it have brought this about if it hadn't been a true precognition? Since Ja'far initially hadn't read the book he obviously wasn't able to turn the story into a self-fulfilling prophecy. So what comes first here, what is cause and what is effect? … a bit confusing. Anyway, I guess many of us would have been curious to have a peek at that book!

Retro-causality is today often invoked in connection with time travel. The sci-fi comedy *Back to the Future* deals with and delves into variants of the so-called 'grandfather paradox.' Imagine you build a time machine, travel back in time, meet your grandfather and kill him before he begets your father/mother. Thus you will not be born, the time machine will not be built, and you will not kill your grandfather. But because of this you are—in fact—going to be born, build the time machine, meet your grandfather and kill him. Thus you will not be born… but, hey…?!

But retro-causality is certainly not only of interest to storytellers, film directors and maverick scientists; even the venerable American Association for the Advancement of Science (AAAS) has given its attention to the subject. In June 2006 a seminar was arranged for physicists and psi researchers where the theme was the physics of time and retro-causation. This symposium was sponsored by the AAAS which afterwards published the proceedings in a book, *Frontiers of Time: Retrocausation—Experiment and Theory* (D.P. Sheenan, ed.). At the conference there appears to have been consensus that fundamental laws of physics are time-symmetric (e.g. as far as quantum processes are concerned, time could just as well go backwards as forwards), and it thus 'seems untenable to assert that time-reverse causation (retrocausation) cannot occur.' This is also, as we have learned, the position of Radin, Bierman and Bem.

Bayesian Brawl

The most thorough critique of 'Feeling the Future' has come from psychologist and statistician Eric-Jan Wagenmakers at the University of Amsterdam. Bem's analysis is misleading, Wagenmakers contends, because his statistical methods are not 'fit for the job.' Wagenmakers worked his way through Bem's numbers applying so-called Bayesian statistics—a method for weighing and interpreting data with uncertainties attached to them. Some think of the Bayesian method as almost a revelation, while its critics see it as little more than truisms poshed-up with complex equations. An excellent and funny intro to 'the Bayesian thing' can be found at: https://blogs.scientificamerican.com/cross-check/bayes-s-theorem-what-s-the-big-deal

Well, then, using the Bayesian system, Wagenmakers did not find Bem's data to be suggestive of precognition. He says: 'Evidence is a relative concept, and although some data may be unlikely under one hypothesis, this does not mean that therefore we should accept the other.' Simply put, even if Bem may have demonstrated that chance does not readily account for his findings, this does not mean we should immediately accept the psi-hypothesis.

Wagenmakers' attack would have been a serious blow to many a strong hypothesis. But precognition bobbed and weaved and struck back forcefully. Bem invited two experts on Bayesian statistics to his corner; together they did a second Bayesian analysis, and before long precognition was again ruling the ring! If I understand Bem correctly, he thinks Wagenmakers had set an unrealistically high bar for how strong a psi effect must be before it can be counted as significant. It is often said that 'extraordinary claims require extraordinary evidence.' But exactly *how* extraordinary the evidence should be is of course difficult to decide.

The White Queen, Alice and Us

Bem rounds out 'Feeling the Future' with a *coda* containing some amusing references to *Through the Looking Glass, and What Alice Found There* by Lewis Carroll. Apart from being a writer, the versatile Carroll was a theologian, mathematician, logician, inventor and a photographer, and in his highly personal way he delved deeply into questions of both time and the paranormal (and as mentioned in chapter 5, he was a member of the Society for Psychical Research). Bem quotes from a scene where Alice has an encounter with the White Queen, who is 'living backwards,' meaning she is experiencing time as running in the opposite direction, from the future to the past. The Queen tells Alice that living this way 'always makes one a little giddy at first,' but that the advantage is that you will have a memory that works both backwards and forwards. Alice, however, has—at least as far as she knows—no such memory: 'I'm sure mine only works one way,' Alice remarked. 'I can't remember things before they happen.' The Queen then declares: 'It's a poor sort of memory that only works backwards.' I think the Queen's point here is that time does not necessarily limit the scope of our consciousness. And precognition is clearly integrated in the sort of 're-collection' that the Queen has (and that we perhaps have too?), as her mind is able to collect information from both past and future.

Bem closes his article with a dialogue where Alice confides to the Queen that she has an inability to believe impossible things. The Queen, however, is having none of that, and gives Alice an almost scathing reply: 'I daresay you haven't had much practice,' said the Queen. 'When I was your age, I always did it for half-an-hour a day. Why, sometimes I've believed as many as six impossible things before breakfast.' In contrast to the White Queen Bem is not asking his colleagues (or us) to believe impossible things. But teasingly he assumes that perhaps reading 'Feeling the Future' will prompt those psychologists who haven't excluded psi from the outset to raise their 'posterior probabilities'—a joke on statistical terms, which refers to how in hindsight one reassesses the probability of something—of believing at least one anomalous thing (precognition, that is) before breakfast!

Bem has constructed the experiments so as to be easily replicable, and if you wish to try them out yourself you may contact Bem directly via his website and get 'replication-packages' for both Mac and Windows—for free. If you should be a teacher in high school, at college or university I would think this could make for an exciting and sobriety twisting scientific project to carry out in cooperation with your students.

Some Time-Out Thoughts on Time

For what is time? Who can readily and briefly explain this? Who can even in thought comprehend it, so as to utter a word about it? But what in discourse do we mention more familiarly and knowingly, than time? And, we understand, when we speak of it; we understand also, when we hear it spoken of by another. What then is time? If no one asks me, I know: if I wish to explain it to one that asketh, I know not [...]

~ Saint Augustine, *Confessions* Book XI

Time is truly one of the great mysteries of existence from physical, psychological and philosophical perspectives, giving the philosophers and scientists manes of grey hair. Henri Bergson, French philosopher and Nobel laureate, said that grasping time is possible only by intuition and not by reason. Our maps won't fit the territory and inevitably we confuse the menu with the meal, as Zen master Alan Watts said. The word is never the thing; it is just 'a finger pointing to the moon.' And according to Jean-Jacques Rousseau, our concepts tend to cover the world like a film, often hiding reality rather than revealing it. So perhaps I had better stop right here before confusing things even more... But as to be human is to share, I shall convey some very simple 'time-out thoughts' on time and it wouldn't surprise me to find that they mirror some of the reader's own thoughts (in which case we both will feel a little less alone).

Time—Real or Not?

When dreaming, many of us probably have had the experience of understanding something profound, but then, when waking up and trying to grasp our newly won insight and place it in the constraints of language, it slips through our fingers, becomes vague, evaporates. And suddenly, the insight, and maybe even the memory of what the dream was about, has slid back into the murky depths of the subconscious from where it first arose, leaving us with nothing more than a feeling of having been touched by 'meaning.' It could easily have been an experience of just this sort that impelled Salvador Dalí to create his famous painting *The Persistence of Memory*. This painting, with which many readers will be familiar, displays a dreamlike landscape with an enigmatic, sleeping figure (which is probably a representation of the artist himself) in the middle ground, and a few mysterious objects scattered about, including three watches, melted and deformed. Dali seemingly managed to capture the insight he had glimpsed: using his artistic intuition he appears to have perceived that behind the structuring of consciousness there is no time.

However, common sense, and also most philosophy throughout history, considers time to be objectively and harshly real, an integrated part of our physical reality. But exceptions exist. As mentioned in chapter 5, Parmenides had completely other ideas; his *grand thesis* being 'It is'! The totality of Being—past, present, future—IS, while change, becoming and time are but illusions caused by the flimsiness of the senses. And in chapter 6 we saw that Immanuel Kant, the Enlightenment's greatest philosopher, was convinced that time does not belong to the physical world at all, it isn't 'out there' but is a creation of consciousness—a 'matrix,' an arrangement made by the mind to give structure to our world. Because of Kant's enormous impact much philosophy and physics, especially in Germany, would hereafter have a Kantian slant to it, suggesting that the reality we usually take to be real is a projection. Scientists and philosophers such as Ernst Mach (who did not accept atoms as real but thought of them as mental constructs) and Hans Vaihinger (who regarded all ideas to be 'as ifs,' just practical fictions) belong to this tradition. Furthermore, Einstein's idea about the relativity of time and quantum physics' notion about time symmetry (claiming that quantum processes are indifferent to time) can clearly be seen as part of the Kantian cargo.

Eternalism—All Things Always Already There

I must confess that I am even a little worse off than Saint Augustine as quoted above, as I don't dare say that I know what time is even when no one asks me. But I have, in fact, had experiences that with some credibility could be interpreted as seeing the future while awake and—mostly— while asleep. I am by no means special in this respect; Louisa Rhine, the colleague and spouse of J.B. Rhine, who for many years systematically collected and collated stories about anomalous experience, has stated that seeing the future in dreams is one of the paranormal phenomena most frequently reported. I could of course be fooling myself by taking my experiences to be instances of true precognition; but on the other hand I could probably also be fooling myself by denying that possibility. But, if seeing the future at all should be possible then the future must in some sense— at one level, on some plane, in some dimension—already be present.

Let me again quote Oliver Lodge: 'The events may be in some sense in existence always, both past and future, and it may be we who are arriving at them, not they which are happening.' Time, then, would not be a process of *becoming* but a process of *revealing*. In chapter 5 we mentioned that such a view is sometimes called 'block time' or 'the B-theory of time' with reference to John McTaggart's 1908 book *The Unreality of Time*. And, as said, also used is 'eternalism.' A modern proponent of a variant of eternalism is the English physicist Julian Barbour; in his book *The End of Time: The Next Revolution in Our Understanding of the Universe* (1999) he strongly defends the position that time is non-existent. Time is a measure of movement: the Earth rotates around the Sun in 365 days; Usain Bolt has run the 100m in 9.58

seconds, etc. But time isn't 'out there'—its apparent reality is merely a habit of the mind. Such a position is, I would think, primarily theoretical, presumably having little practical bearing. One might wonder what would happen if Barbour visited a friend, even a most philosophical one, at 4 o'clock in the morning, trying to convince him that—since time is non-existent—it is not late at all ...

Barbour's position has of course been contested, perhaps most vocally by Lee Smolin, a theoretical physicist who in his book *Time Reborn* (2013) argues that physicists who, to a greater or lesser degree, deny the reality of time mix up their mathematical models with reality (precisely what Alan Watts warned about, confusing the menu with the dinner, taking the map to be the territory). Smolin, on the contrary, regards time as absolutely fundamental in the sense that even the eternal laws of nature may not be eternal after all, but may have developed—and may still be developing—over time.

If the eternalist perspective is valid—in one or other of its variants—perhaps we could be likened to train passengers traveling through ever-changing landscapes and passing the many stations. Looking out the window, we only see what presents itself before our eyes. But this does not mean that the landscapes and stations we will pass a little later do not yet exist!—they are already there but it will take *time* for them to be revealed to us as we are not able to process the totality of being all at once. In the interwar period Albert Einstein wrote to a friend: 'People like us, who believe in physics, know that the distinction between past, present, and future is only a stubbornly persistent illusion,' and on another occasion Uncle Albert stated with the usual twinkle in his eye: 'The only reason for time is so that everything doesn't happen at once.'

The considerations we are making here with regard to time are to some degree parallel to those made regarding space in chapter 6. There we suggested that non-locality might be a property integral to consciousness and could be compared with the internet. If you are logged into say, Facebook, a friend in York will be no further away or closer than a friend in New York—if you're online, you're online! We also suggested a few possible explanatory models (there are definitely many more) with perspectives from quantum physics and from Immanuel Kant ('Kantum physics'). And further we supported the idea of non-locality in a concrete way by presenting Adrian Parker's exciting telepathy experiment with Vicky and Sara.

In the present chapter we have seen that there are also experiments that can be interpreted as consciousness having a non-temporal, a timeless property. And if this should be the case, maybe there is nothing strange at all about precognition—perhaps it is precisely what we should expect! But—if it really is possible to 'see' the future, how does this go together with the notion of free will, which most of us probably are not ready to dispense with? Are precognition and free will mutually exclusive? Or could it perhaps be rather the opposite: that getting to know the future will give us a unique opportunity to change it? If you get to know that your train is heading for Siberia, perhaps this knowledge will provide you with opportunities that you hadn't been aware of until then? For it is only after getting to know this that you will be able to make an informed decision about whether you should change trains or not. Dick Bierman, who is both a physicist and a psychologist, is definitely no stranger to these complex themes, but his take on them is quite simple:

*This phenomena [precognition] allows you to make a
decision on the basis of what will happen in the future.
Does that restrain our free will? That's up to the philosophers. I'm far too shallow a person to worry about that.*

The Solution of No Solution

The solution to the problem of freedom vs. destiny—which
of course is no solution in the normal sense, but merely a
recognition of the problem and its likely insolubility—is
probably to acknowledge, as highlighted earlier, that our
words and concepts—time, freedom, choice, causality,
etc.—do not truly represent the reality they purport to describe. So when we try to use them to solve our problems we
are bound to roam around in labyrinths of paradoxes and
contradictions, perhaps even being devoured by the Mino-
taur of despair! The word is not the thing, the menu is not
the dinner, the map is not the territory—the words of adventure novelist (*King Solomon's Mines*) and spiritualist H.
Rider Haggard could perhaps be apposite: 'Thinking can
only serve to measure out the helplessness of thought.'

This, then, could be seen as a quite depressing state of
affairs. But it could also be seen as an important first step
in attaining freedom from our limiting interpretations of
the world. Such an attitude of conscious non-knowing or
un-knowing is considered wisdom e.g. by Socrates, and in
traditions like Zen, Sufism and Christian mysticism. And
in the first of his *Elegies of Duna*, the often extraordinarily
profound poet Rainer Maria Rilke says: 'And the diligent
animals know it already: we are not truly at home in the
deciphered world.'

Let us now run the train metaphor to its terminus: Our consciousness might possibly be pictured as sitting inside a small mental compartment, enjoying the cozy comfort but also suffering the limitations that go with it—a perception limited to seeing things as they roll up along the railway line, bound to linear time. But maybe we are able to step out of the compartment, climb up on the roof of the train compartment, and—in classical action style—be lifted up into the sky by a helicopter? Our vision would then expand tremendously! All the great religious traditions—Hinduism, Buddhism, Taoism, Islam, Christianity, Judaism—are replete with accounts of people getting such bird's-eye views, being lifted out of time. Are such reports just nonsense and superstition? Or could they be referring to experiences of real precognition? Or perhaps a mixture of both?

Well, whatever religious beliefs the reader might or might not have, maybe he/she would be willing, for a moment, to imagine being (as great as) God? Imagine that you are throwing Kant's glasses to the floor, crushing them under your heel. Then imagine that you are climbing out of the compartment, flying up in the air, expanding infinitely. Let your Being spread out in the Universe, filling the entire space-time with all its events both Past and Future. From this supreme position Space and Time don't exist anymore; rather, the world appears as an eternal Here and Now. At this moment you are non-local and non-temporal, ubiquitous and ever-present; you see everything and know everything. And now I ask you to consider for a moment: What if this should be more than a mere thought experiment? What if the consciousness that you—perhaps a little too much as a matter of course—refer to as your own is, on one level, *already* outside the compartment and is participating and present throughout the totality of space-time?

Mind Over Matter—
Some Experiments
With Psychokinesis

If we are to believe the statistics, many readers will have had experiences that can (but don't have to) be seen as ESP—telepathy, clairvoyance or precognition. Whereas PK, psychokinesis, 'mind over matter'—moving/influencing the physical world directly with the power of thought—is reported far less often. This phenomenon is also referred to as telekinesis (Greek: *tele* = remote, *kinesis* = movement). The terms overlap, and are often used interchangeably but it is not uncommon to use psychokinesis as an umbrella term covering absolutely all instances of this kind: the ability to influence objects, electricity, computers, the weather, living beings, etc. Whereas telekinesis has a more limited use, referring mostly to the moving and influencing of physical objects: tables, keys, spoons, etc.

Few claim to have experienced this phenomenon—apart from being able to move their body by acts of will, which, when thinking about it, actually is a form of psychokinesis. And even fewer claim to be able to control it. The real-life stories largely disclose uncontrolled and even chaotic events, often connected to poltergeists ('noisy ghosts'). Still, some researchers claim to have documented various forms of psychokinesis in the laboratory. Their experiments have involved a variety of things: bending of metal, influencing bingo and Lottery balls (a most useful feat, indeed...), influencing the growth of plants and bacteria, controlling the behavior of insects, evaporating clouds, etc.

A distinction is often made between macro PK and micro PK, the line being drawn some place between those effects that can be seen with the naked eye and those that will need to be measured by instruments. Media reports have often revolved around macro PK and in particular showpieces such as metal bending. Scientists, however, are usually more interested in micro PK, which they consider more fit for research—easier to succeed with and easier to control. In practice this will often mean experiments in influencing electronics, as, for example, in so-called random event generators (see below) and computer programs.

Many suggestions have been made to provide an explanation as to how PK may be possible. As we've heard earlier, both C.G. Jung and Wolfgang Pauli claimed to have experienced diverse incidents involving psychokinesis. One of their suggested explanations for the phenomena was that the archetypes (the collective fields of 'psychic energy,' as we discussed in chapter 4) would facilitate exchanges between our consciousness and the outside world—which deep down are not separate entities at all but different manifestations of the underlying oneness. Such ideas may perhaps sound a little 'airy-fairy,' but Pauli was, as we know, awarded the Nobel Prize in physics, so it is probably worthwhile to pay attention to his speculations.

Matter and Mind—Different Sides of the Same Reality

The basic thought in a number of the suggested explanations is that behind the various objects and entities in the world—behind galaxies and quarks, behind consciousness and matter—there is a basic unity, an *arché*, a *unus mundus*, an all-unifying principle that is seen as the source of everything. Some will name this principle 'energy,' others 'information,' yet others again 'akasha,' etc. But anyway, the idea related to psychokinesis is that any event happening within our consciousness is simultaneously also an event happening within this underlying reality; a movement within a drop is simultaneously a movement within the ocean. Given this entangled state of affairs it doesn't seem a far stretch to imagine that if certain activities take place within our consciousness, corresponding activities might take place in the surrounding world. For more specific ideas one might perhaps want to check out the brilliant collection of essays I recommended at the beginning of this chapter, namely *Parapsychology in the Twenty-First Century: Essays on the Future of Psychical Research* by Michael A. Thalbourne and Lance Storm (eds.). Also the various books of the Bohmian quantum physicist F. David Peat may prove helpful.

However, several parapsychologists will confess that they don't have a satisfactory theory of how PK may eventually work. An interesting discussion of important problems arising out of psychology, biology and physics when trying to explain PK is provided by Adrian Parker in the chapter 'The Mind-Body Problem and the Issue of Psychokinesis' in *Mysterious Minds: The Neurobiology of Psychics, Mediums, and Other Extraordinary People* (Krippner and Friedman, eds.). It includes a useful bibliography for those who wish to delve deeper into the matter—or maybe even better, into the mind's potential power over physical matter.

Macro PK

In addition to his celebrated ESP studies J.B. Rhine also conducted some lesser-known research on PK. For quite some time he hesitated to publish the results in this field, apparently because he felt he was controversial enough as it was. In his PK trials Rhine would often use dice throwing. The subjects were given the task to 'will' the dice to land showing a specific face—say, the one with six spots. At first the subjects themselves threw the dice. Obviously, this was highly unfortunate as it provided opportunities for cheating by sleight of hand. Hence Rhine changed the routines and employed a machine to throw the dice to ensure proper randomization. In 1941 Rhine evaluated the results from 651,216 trials, and the statistics showed a high degree of success. According to Rhine, the chance for the hit rate to be coincidental was 1 to 10,115, meaning the odds were less than 1 in 10,000!

Some critics will argue that if your method is skewed, the results may become more and more swayed the more trials you run, and that Rhine's results therefore need not be utterly impressive but could instead be utterly misleading. However, Rhine's statistics had, as we heard, been evaluated by none less than '*The* Fisher' himself (Sir Ronald Aylmer Fisher) and the dice throwing was eventually completely automated. So, where a fault with such far-reaching consequences could be hidden is not easily explained. And there are few, even among the hardline skeptics, who suspect Rhine as having engaged in deceit.

In general, PK trials have been fraught with obstacles, not least of which has been rampant fraud; this has proved surprisingly difficult to avoid even in cases that have been witnessed by both magicians and scientists (who may be professionals in lab work but amateurs in conjuring). For example, the Austrian medium Rudi Schneider (1908–1957), who managed to manifest 'spirit hands' in the air, move objects and affect electrical apparatus while sitting almost motionless in a chair under meticulous surveillance, including cameras shooting from three different angles. Several scientists declared him to be a real paragnost. Schneider even managed to baffle the eminent illusionist Will Goldston, who had authored books on magic (and who also was a life-long friend of Houdini). Goldston stated that he didn't see how Schneider's effects could be brought about by mere tricks. Whereas other magicians were convinced that Schneider was no more than a clever fraud. Without drawing any clear-cut conclusions from this, let me just mention that Schneider eventually gave up acting as a medium and went back to his original trade as a car mechanic.

Nina Kulagina, the Russian alleged paragnost who was introduced at the beginning of chapter 2, underwent thorough testing, and at least some of the results seemed very convincing. Many skeptics will argue that Kulagina and her act may have been no more than a carefully orchestrated Soviet propaganda piece—rigged instruments, actors playing their paid-for parts, etc.—and perhaps they might be right; the Soviet state was notorious for producing 'alternative facts' supporting their claim to superiority. But still, let me mention that Montague Ullman, Stanley Krippner's colleague during the dream telepathy experiments, once met Kulagina in a private setting and was impressed by the demonstration she gave him. And, what about the significant experiences reported by Benson Herbert (chapter 2)? He claims he nearly collapsed from a strange kind of heat/electricity coming from her hand. Could such an effect have been caused by an unknown concealed technical device? Or was it an extreme and unpleasant demonstration of the 'warm hands' that healers are so often reported to possess?

Another exciting (alleged) telekinetic is the Frenchman Jean-Pierre Girard. He claims his special abilities were activated after he was struck by lightning as a child. Girard excels in mental metal bending, and has also bent objects placed inside sealed glass bottles. In some cases the metal was placed in the bottle while it was being cast. Girard's demonstrations have impressed many *professeurs*, including the Nobel laureate in physics, Alfred Kastler, and the esteemed metallurgist Charles Crussard. What impressed the metallurgist most was not the bending itself, but the alterations in the metal's molecular structure that had taken place. Crussard has also stated that some of Girard's demonstrations 'were even followed by no less than seven reputed illusionists who saw the deformations of the metal but were unable to find any sign of faking [...].'

On May 27, 1994 Géraldy, Stavisky and Ranky, three members of Comité Illusionniste d'Expertise des Phénomènes Paranormaux (CIEPP), an organization of French magicians specializing in paranormal phenomena, conducted a trial with Girard; this also included a subsequent laboratory test on the structure of the metal he had bent. After the trial, Ranky, who was the president of CIEPP, signed a declaration supporting Girard's claim to be the real deal (though I would guess a number of his colleagues would still look for other explanations...). Girard can be seen doing his thing in videos available on YouTube.

Uri Geller and the Spoonbenders

Suspicions of fraud have always loomed big time over Israeli TV star and paragnost (or 'paragnost') Uri Geller. Cheating has even been caught on film (Geller is once clearly seen bending a spoon with his hands and not with his mind). And Geller has actually admitted to using tricks early in his career when he worked as an entertainer for military personnel in Israel. And from time to time he has, as it seems, hinted about also doing so afterwards. So perhaps it is all fake?

Anyway, Geller's position as a completely unique paranormal pop-cultural icon justifies a mention, and perhaps—as we'll see—it cannot be entirely ruled out that he could have a little more than just tricks up his sleeve (perhaps…).

As many are probably aware Geller became known through his television appearances in the 1970s, where he dazzled by bending spoons, keys and other metal objects, apparently by using solely the powers of his mind. Uri became a celebrity, and hung out with VIPs of all kinds. Wernher von Braun, the rocket scientist who first worked for the Third Reich and later headed NASA (from Nazi to NASA), claimed that Geller made his wedding ring change shape—without even touching it! And in an interview the one and only Clint Eastwood told Reuters:

> *The only thing I have ever had that is sort of offbeat, that is I have watched Uri Geller spin the keys and things like that… I have seen that so I am a believer. It was my house key and the only way I would be able to use it is get a hammer and beat it out back flat again. So there are certain energy things that are outside of the norm…*

Whereas the physics genius and Nobel laureate Richard Feynman, who was an amateur magician, has said that Geller did *not* manage to bend a key while he was watching.

The common perception among magicians is that Geller belongs to their own flock. But some of the pros, like David Ben and David Blaine—known among other things for having been frozen in a block of ice!—think that Geller perhaps could have 'something more.' (If we can take Ben's and Blaine's word for it—magicians will often have an agenda or two more than the rest of us.) Blaine has stated:

> *Uri bent a spoon for me, the first time he did it, I thought there must be a trick. The second time I was stunned,*

*completely, completely stunned and amazed. It just bent
in my hand. I've never seen anything like it. It takes a
lot to impress me. Uri Geller is for real and anyone who
doesn't recognise that is either deluding himself, or is a
very sad person.*

And Blaine is not alone: the Danish magician Leo Leslie,
who once tested Geller, became completely perplexed. As
co-founder of a magician's guild and editor of a Danish journal for magicians, Leslie apparently was a respected crafts-
man—which was probably the reason Danmarks Radio, the
national broadcaster in Denmark, chose Leslie to conduct
the test. In his 1974 book *Uri Geller: FUP eller Fakta* (*Uri
Geller: Fraud or Facts*) Leslie relates that he had wondered
if Geller made use of chemicals on his fingers. He therefore
had keys prepared that were plated and lacquered. One of
these keys was held in front of Geller by a journalist. Leslie
tells what happened next.

*Uri stroked the key a few times with his index finger.
'No, I can't' he said. 'You have done something to it. I
cannot get in contact with the metal!' I licked my lips.
Now he was trapped. Then it was chemicals after all, I
thought. I took the key from the journalist and studied it
closer. While I sat looking at the key, the varnish began to
crackle and the next moment flakes of the plating curled
up like tiny banana peels while the key started to bend
between my fingers!*

Also various eminent physicists were fascinated by Geller
and some of them also ran experiments with him. (Might
there here be new natural laws to discover? And perhaps
some Nobel Prizes to win?) One of those was John Hasted,
head of experimental physics at Birkbeck College, University of London, who we briefly encountered in the middle

of chapter 6. After some experiments during the summer of 1974 Hasted wrote the following in a report:

> *We possess four numbered and weighed brass Yale keys which were bent through angles of between 10 and 40 degrees under light stroking action by Mr Geller. If, under symmetrical four-point loading, force pulses of the order of 500N (say 50kg of weight) had been applied to the keys, similar bends would have been produced. [...] Geller applied a light, stroking action between forefinger and thumb, or by forefinger, with key placed on the table. In all cases, several witnesses watched the entire operation intently from within 1 meter. In one case, the key was not stroked but was simply, held under a cold-water tap. In all cases the bending took a time of the order of minutes to complete, and it usually appeared to continue for a short while after the stroking had been terminated. No physical or chemical explanation of these phenomena is readily apparent. The mean grain size at the bent surface has been compared with that in unbent and mechanically bent specimens by x-ray reflection and electron micrograph. No significant change in grain orientation or size was noted.*

Hasted clearly sounds intrigued, but he still does not conclude that telekinesis has taken place. The report ends as follows: 'Continued experiments are planned.' But, as far as I know, such follow-up sessions never happened. However, what—according to Professor Hasted—*did* happen was a series of mysterious episodes in his own home. It supposedly started one beautiful day in the kitchen when a small ivory figurine descended from the ceiling, followed by an old clock key suddenly appearing seemingly right out of thin air (these items were usually kept in the living room). Over the next weeks such spontaneous movements—

'apportations'—happened to many other items as well, while the ivory statuette and the clock key continued to regularly take a trip from the living room to the kitchen! The key belonged to an antique clock that had not been functioning for 30 years. But one evening this clock allegedly started to chime, something that made Hasted's wife greatly perturbed. Things hardly improved when the clock gave no sign of wanting to stop its rampant behavior that night...

Others have also reported strange events happening in connection with Geller. Several articles in Norwegian newspapers from the 1970s report that ordinary people tell of suddenly having bent metal objects (apparently) with the power of thought after having seen Geller exercise his crafts on television. Mere delusions? Eager imagination in overwrought people who want to believe in such things and/or want to have their 15 minutes in the limelight? Probably in most cases, but who knows? Geller has explained that he thinks such episodes may occur because there are many people with latent PK capabilities, and when they see his demonstrations their own dormant skills are triggered and come alive.

Okay, this sounds kind of plausible, but skeptics of course regard it as just part of the typical Gellerish hogwash concerning non-existent powers. And sometimes, even Geller himself cast doubts on his abilities. In 2008 he received the prestigious David Berglas International Magic Award. When the question 'Are you a magician [i.e. and not a psychic]?' was raised from the audience, Geller—who nowadays calls himself a 'mystifier'—then really mystified. If he was not a real paragnost, he said, he would perhaps be the greatest of all illusionists:

I thrive on controversy, looking back on my career, I called myself a psychic, I constantly need to re-invent

myself, you will not get a straight answer. I have to pro-
tect the performers in my show, I owe it to them, I don't
want to know how they do it, I just want to see the most
mind blowing show there is. Let's say I wasn't real, let's
say for the last years I've fooled the journalists, the sci-
entists, my family, my friends. You. If I managed to fool
them, I must be the greatest?

Well, should we then once and for all conclude that Geller is nothing more than a trickster? Most of us would probably be inclined to draw this conclusion. But, interestingly enough, David Copperfield—the mega-magician who once 'conjured away' the Statue of Liberty and who readers will be familiar with from the TV screen—surprisingly said this about Geller on German television in 2009 (the program is easily found on YouTube): 'I think some of the things he shows are illusion. But I cannot claim for sure, that this applies to everything.' Copperfield says that he has not experienced telekinesis himself, but that he—who I would think knows all the tricks in the book, and who also has added diverse new ones—would not rule out that this phenomenon may be real. However, he believes that it would be very difficult to demonstrate this on a stage.

Let me *en passant* mention that in general magicians are much more open to psi than perhaps could be expected. Several surveys have been conducted with very different methodologies and very different results, but just to present a few 'fun facts.' In 1980, a German survey found that 72 percent of magicians in the German Magic Circle thought ESP probably was real. In 1993, Marcello Truzzi, the American skeptic and sociologist we mentioned in chapter 7, polled the Psychic Entertainers Association and found that 47 percent believed that ESP 'truly exists.' And in 2008 the skeptic Richard Wiseman, also mentioned earlier, made a Web Survey among magicians, one of his questions being: 'Do you believe that you have had a paranormal experience?' to which a surprising 26.25 percent answered, 'Yes.' So, as opposed to what many think, it's not at all like 'we magicians know all the tricks so we don't believe in this stuff!'

In the wake of Geller's performances 'PK parties' were organized around the world. This trend was initiated in 1981 by the late Jack Houck, an engineer at Boeing aircraft factory. Houck has theorized quite a bit about PK and he has also created an informative website: http://www.jackhouck. com. At PK parties people get together attempting to use mental power to bend cutlery and other metal objects. The late American author and scriptwriter Michael Crichton (who graduated as a medical doctor from Harvard and as a visiting lecturer taught anthropology at Cambridge) is perhaps best known for having written the book behind Spielberg's blockbuster *Jurassic Park*. In his book *Travels* Crichton tells of his experiences at a PK party:

> *I looked down. My spoon had begun to bend. I hadn't even realized. The metal was completely pliable, like soft plastic. It wasn't particularly hot, either, just slightly warm. I easily bend the bowl of the spoon in half, using only my fingertips. This didn't require any pressure at all, just guiding with my fingertips.—I put the bent spoon aside and tried a fork. After a few moments of rubbing, the fork twisted like a pretzel. It was easy. I bent several more spoons and forks. [...]*
>
> *Uri Geller, an Israeli magician, who claims psychic powers, often bends spoons, but other magicians, such as James Randi, claim that spoon bending isn't a psychic phenomenon at all, just a trick.—But I had bent a spoon, and I knew it wasn't a trick. I looked around the room and saw little children, eight or nine years old, bending*

large metal bars. They weren't trying to trick anybody.
They were just little kids having a good time. [...]

Astonishing, indeed! But still, the cutlery *might* conceivably have been fatigued (e.g. by repeated bending) in advance. Or it *might* have been made of *nitinol* (nickel titanium) or some other shape-memory alloy. These are alloys with a particular molecular structure that are able to 'remember' their original mold. Say you cast a fork, giving it a sharp bend in the middle. When it has cooled down you straighten it out and it then both looks and feels like any other fork. But, inside the molecular structure the fork's original shape is 'remembered,' and if heated slightly (which may happen when being stroked repeatedly) it will gradually regain its original shape (the bend starts to return). So, if you want to appear as paranormally gifted to your circle of friends I recommend that you buy a set of nitinol cutlery!

Dean Radin relates a funny episode in *Entangled Minds*. He had long been highly skeptical of stories about the mental bending of metal. But once at a PK party he suddenly managed to do it himself! He had beforehand decided he would only be persuaded if *the bowl* of the spoon bent (as the shaft is more easily bent one may—at least in theory—bend it by unconscious muscle use). After having held a spoon in his hand for a while without anything special happening his attention had settled on the activities of a neighboring lady. Then, suddenly, he experienced the bowl of his spoon becoming like putty between his fingers and folding without out the use of any force. In his blog Radin has written that he later dipped the spoon into boiling water but nothing happened. This indicates that it probably *was* an ordinary spoon and not just some heat-sensitive magic device. (When he tried to bend a similar spoon in the normal way he had to use a couple of pinchers.) However, I still wish Radin had taken his PK bent spoon to a metallurgical laboratory!

Well, anyway, *if* Radin's spoon should have been no more than an elite specimen of trick equipment, this could hardly have been the case with Clint Eastwood's key that Geller bent. Eastwood said it was his own house key, thus it seems fair to assume that Geller couldn't just have replaced it with some copy. And moreover, the anti-chemical keys that the Danish magician Leo Leslie had prepared specially for testing Geller were clearly not trick keys. (*Unless*, of course, Geller, before arriving in Denmark, had made an unholy arrangement with Leslie: 'Hello Leo—it's Uri here; listen, I have a really interesting suggestion for you!' etc.)

So, could Geller perhaps be a true paragnost after all? Or maybe he is simply the best in the world at creating the illusion of spoon bending? Many magicians say Geller isn't *that* good, really. But as the great David Berglas thought him worthy of his prestigious award maybe the naysayers are just envious of Geller's almost magical/paranormal success? Regardless, what we can agree on is that the most famous among the world's spoon benders is—without comparison—Uri Geller!

Let's now briefly return to the lab: In his 1985 book *Bak Tid og Rom* (*Behind Time and Space*) the Norwegian philosopher and environmentalist Erik Dammann has, among other researchers open to unusual perspectives, interviewed the abovementioned Professor John Hasted and had him describe the control procedures used when conducting research on metal bending. Crucial for Hasted was that the subjects—the would-be metal benders—never got to touch the objects. (As we read in Hasted's report, Geller had, in fact, been allowed to touch the keys, but that was many years earlier). And still, Hasted claimed that many of his subjects, including children, managed to perform metal bending using only the power of thought. In retrospect Dammann felt the need to pose a direct question to Hasted, and wrote him a letter: 'Do you—after about ten years of serious research in this area—consider some people's ability to bend metal by mental influence to be proved beyond all reasonable doubt?' The answer he got was: 'Yes. Sincerely J.B. Hasted.'

Micro PK—the Devil is in the Details

Serious study of micro PK is often regarded as having begun in the 1960s and early trials were conducted by the renowned French biologist Remy Chauvin (1913–2009). Chauvin has written close to 40 books and was eventually created honorary professor at the Sorbonne, the most prestigious university in France. Chauvin happened to be the mentor of my father, the biologist Tore Albert Simonsen, and I met him when I was a boy and we were living in France, but I was too young to ask him about his science. When testing for psychokinesis Chauvin had his subjects attempt to increase and decrease the frequency of 'clicks' in a Geiger counter—which, as most readers probably will know, is an apparatus used for measuring radioactivity. The results were reportedly astounding but were lacking in consistency. Chauvin conducted, however, other experiments, and in combination with the research of others this eventually convinced him of the reality of psychokinesis. Moreover, Chauvin studied psi in animals, so-called AnPsi, and his writings cover diverse aspects of the paranormal, including UFO and ET-ish stuff. One of Chauvin's books, which for fear of the 'emperor's wrath' (see chapter 3) was published pseudonymously, is called *Nos pouvoirs inconnus*. This literally translates as *Our Unknown Powers*! I swear that I was not aware of the title of Chauvin's book when I subtitled mine. But of course, it is a somewhat obvious title for a book on the paranormal.

A few years later the German-American physicist Helmut Schmidt (1928–2011) entered the paranormal scene. Schmidt had originally worked as a senior researcher at Boeing's aircraft factory, but from the early 1970s on he devoted himself to other—in a certain sense—even loftier matters as he became head of the laboratory at Duke University that had previously been led by Rhine. One of Schmidt's projects was to find out whether psychokinesis could influence Random Event Generators (REG). These machines generate series of random events (I guess that's why they are called random event generators...) e.g. colored flashes or numbers appearing on a screen. The original REGs utilized the activities of unstable atomic nuclei, radioactivity that is, or so-called electrical noise; the order of the flashes or numbers they produced thus became completely unpredictable. (These REGs have been largely superseded by computer programs that are much cheaper but not necessarily as reliable.) Schmidt's subjects would attempt to exert micro PK by influencing the distribution of flashes and numbers, typically by steering the generator to come up with specific colors or numbers more often than others.

Schmidt claimed to have demonstrated that when using a generator with one green and one red light—where an equal blink distribution between the two colors was expected—the subjects got their chosen lamp to blink approximately 1–2 percent more often than the other. When running a series with a great amount of blinks the distribution should eventually become almost equal; there should *not* be a consistent deviation of 1–2 percent in the 'forced' direction.

And if this happens it has to do with an effect that requires an explanation. Schmidt believed that the explanation was psychokinesis—that the subjects' intentions, to a small but very real degree, intervened directly in the nuclear processes and electrical circuits of the REGs. Needless to say, skeptics do not agree. They prefer to attribute Schmidt's results to possible errors—either in the apparatus, or in the statistics, or eventually in the reporting procedures. For, what if Schmidt consciously/unconsciously was eager to report successes but a little more sloppy with reporting the experiments that yielded either zero or negative results? Then, over time, we could get a very wrong impression of what had happened in his laboratory...

The well-known skeptic James Alcock has often highlighted this problem, which is typically referred to as 'publication bias' or the 'file drawer effect' (results not to one's liking are left unpublished in the drawer). Without commenting on Schmidt's case specifically, let me mention that in one of his meta-analyses Dean Radin went through older trials with random generators (more than 800 studies as of 1987!). And the meta-analysis seemed to confirm that psychokinetic effects really were taking place. Because, for the positive results to be explained by publication bias/the file-drawer effect—as Alcock et al. tend to do—then, according to Radin, there had to be more than 50,000 'unwanted' studies concealed in the file drawers of the parapsychologists—a completely unrealistic number.

Also in recent times many REG experiments have been conducted and Radin believes that taken together the newer trials confirm that our intentions can have a small but measurable effect on micro-processes. The French physicist Costa de Beauregard (1911–2007) thought that such effects did not pose any problem with respect to either the laws of physics or to rationality. His interpretation of quantum physics—in which consciousness is seen to have an important role—implies rather the opposite: 'phenomena such as psychokinesis or telepathy, far from being irrational, should, on the contrary, be expected as very rational.' And the physicist and Nobel laureate Eugene Wigner has stated that since matter has an impact on consciousness we should expect consciousness to have an impact on matter. If not, it would be the only known relationship in the universe where influence goes only one way.

For those readers who don't feel convinced by the research of others, I have good news to herald: Computer programs for testing micro PK are publicly available. Diverse websites will also offer such tests for free, but buyer beware: my humble opinion is that there is quite a lot of unreliable stuff out there. The Institute of Noetic Sciences (IONS) had a free testing platform running for some time, but as of writing it seems to have been dismantled. But I would guess they could still help you to buy the right program.

The Global Consciousness Project

'A micro PK experiment in macro format' seems to be the *mot juste* for describing the Global Consciousness Project, which was started in 1998 at Princeton Engineering Anomalies Research Laboratory at Princeton University. The lab closed in 2007 but the project is still running, led by psychologist Dr Roger Nelson and supported by the Institute of Noetic Sciences. About 70 random event generators, generating 0s and 1s, are deployed in different parts of the world and the data are sent back to computers in Princeton for analysis. The Global Consciousness Project seeks to detect if movements in our hypothesized collective Consciousness are reflected in the output of the generators. For example, if events affecting many people emotionally—natural disasters, war, terrorist attacks, strikes, etc.—make the generators depart from their usual distribution pattern of 0s and 1s. And many of the physicists and engineers engaged in the project really think this is the case! On the project's website it is stated that 'when a great event synchronizes the feelings of millions of people, our network of RNGs becomes subtly structured.' Hence, in the locution of *Star Wars* they claim to be able to detect 'a great disturbance in the Force.'

The Global Consciousness Project has a great amount of different events on file, including the September 11 terror attack, where 'a great disturbance in Force' was allegedly measured. Critics claim, however, that the project's methodology is dubious, e.g. that the results could be due to an arbitrary choice of 'time window.' Meaning that if the collection of data had started/ended a little earlier/later—for when, exactly, does an earthquake or a battle begin/end?—the results may not have been significant.

The project has, in fact, been criticized on many grounds; I shall not enter the debate but just mention that I find the project to be quite interesting. Let me also mention that one can find the degree of 'force disturbance' pertaining to recent events measured on their website. Some of the latest measurements give you the numbers for Obama's farewell address, Trump's inauguration, the Women's March on Washington, and the Muslim ban protests.

Thoughts on Healing

Healing at a Distance—Remotely Plausible or Plain Placebo?

Obviously it is a daunting task to correctly identify how healing works—or if and when it works—if the eventual effects are due to chance, conveyance of energy, transference of information, intervention of spirits, or you name it. Among skeptics the trend is to attribute all possible effects to the so-called placebo effect (*placebo* = I please), meaning that an expectation of recovery will help to mobilize the organism's inherent resources and may bring about healing. Imagination is clearly a powerful force; in some surveys, placebo medicines ('sugar pills') have actually worked better than real medicine! But could this effect, powerful as it is, explain everything there is to healing? The well-known British healer Matthew Manning is a great fan of activating the placebo effect by the means of 'creative visualization'—i.e. creating mental images that vividly symbolize that healing takes place—but he also believes there's much more to healing. Based in part on laboratory experiments, he argues that healing can have a distinct impact on living systems even where placebo effects are highly unlikely, for instance when it comes to the growth of plants, which seemingly can be accelerated by healing. Manning gives interesting examples of this in a small book with the charming title *No Faith Required* (1995).

Another star on the healing firmament is Eric Pearl, who was originally a chiropractor. In his book *The Reconnection* (1998) he claims to have discovered his healing abilities when patients he treated for spinal and muscular problems surprisingly and spontaneously—without the use of suggestion, hypnosis, etc.—recovered from other and often more serious diseases. If his descriptions are correct it seems unlikely that a placebo could account for such healings. Pearl explains that other strange psi phenomena of diverse kinds began to occur in this period of his life. This resembles a pattern reported by various other outstanding healers, e.g. the Snåsa Man, Matthew Manning and Harry Edwards. Of course, all such stories could be merely lies or delusions, but they could also be an indication of what we hinted at earlier: that the different psi phenomena may be expressions of one phenomenon, which in turn—as shamanic drumming and meditative practices seem to suggest—may be connected to the presence of certain brainwave patterns.

The well-known TV hypnotist Paul McKenna, who some years back moved on from being a mere entertainer to using his hypnotic skills to help people stop smoking, control their weight and eradicate phobias, has said that his father, a skeptic, was cured of severe arthritis by the healer Seka Nikolic (the father more or less had to be tricked into the hands of the healer). This experience made McKenna—who being a hypnotist has an unusually profound understanding of the placebo effect—think that healing might be something more than this. McKenna and Nikolic have subsequently worked together with clients, based on the idea that a combination of placebo (induced through hypnosis) and healing may give the best possible result. For a discussion of studies on healing, there is a most helpful article by L. Dossey and S.A. Schwartz, called 'Nonlocality, Intention, and Observer Effects in Healing Studies: Laying a Foundation for the Future' (the link can be found in the bibliography).

I myself have been quite intrigued by the placebo effect, and I actually registered 'Placebo' as a trademark in Denmark (VR 2006 01402). The idea was to use it as the name of a lozenge, with the slogan: 'Placebo, the lozenge that will cure everything—as long as you believe it!' There would also be a strong version with large, red tablets called 'Placebo Forte.'

Some people believe that healing is a kind of psychokinesis, namely *direct mental interactions with living systems* (DMILS). If this should be correct, we may need to modify the statement made earlier in the chapter claiming that psychokinesis is rare, for healing is, in fact, a phenomenon which is reported quite often. But others believe that healing should rather be understood as a form of telepathically triggered 'System Recovery.' This is based on the idea that by its genetics the body is able to 'remember' its earlier optimal function. Thus healing tries to 'remind' the body to reset its system to 'factory specifications.' Or eventually to do just a little 'system restore'—partially reverting the system back to a condition when it was working more properly.

Regardless, if one understands healing as caused by psi in one form or another one will not just, and not even primarily, emphasize psychological factors—placebo, acceptance, security, etc.—which obviously can be important in eliciting healing. Nor will one consider the therapeutic touch, such as the laying on of hands, to be crucial. If healing really is a psi phenomenon it is actually possible to imagine that it might take place without any normal contact—touch, sight, conversation, etc.—between the healer and the patient. This is what is often called 'remote healing.'

Remote healing is reported from days of old and from various corners of the earth: in the New Testament, in ancient China, in shamanic traditions, etc. But we certainly don't have to visit remote times or remote places to find remote healing! According to Norway's most respected newspaper, *Aftenposten*, the famous cross-country skier Petter Northug (13 world champion titles, two Olympic gold medals, etc.) received remote healing from Joralf Gjerstad, the Snåsa Man, during the 'Tour de Ski' in 2009. The sixth leg was held in Italy on January 3. The day before, Northug was feeling terrible, 'his sinuses were completely stuffed and he had a headache.' Northug called the Snåsa Man—and what happened? 'The day after he crushed Axel Teichmann in the Monster hill in Val di Fiemme, having made an almost full recovery.' (Teichmann won this race, though, but Northug finished before him on the final list.) (*Aftenposten*, October 15, 2011. Link to the article can be found in the bibliography.)

In an interview 10 days later with Northug in *Her og Naa* (*Here and Now*) the Norwegian ski ace said: 'When I got the Snåsa Man on the line my sinuses suddenly opened. It may sound unbelievable but the Snåsa Man actually helped me. We talked for a while, but what he said I vowed should be between him and me.'

As there was a conversation between the Snåsa Man and Northug (*Nor-thug*—Norwegian thug, what a name for an athlete!) his sudden improvement was not necessarily only (or at all) due to remote healing but perhaps also (or only?) to an efficient pep talk.

Let me also mention that about two years later Northug again consulted the Snåsa Man, this time with a personal visit. Severe fatigue was now completely thwarting his preparations for the upcoming world championship in Holmenkollen three months later. According to his biography, *Northug: A Family History*, he became better almost immediately after talking to the Snåsa Man, and was able to resume training later the same day. (Northug went on to win three gold and two silver medals in Holmenkollen.) Perhaps the Snåsa Man's placebo eliciting abilities are nothing short of miraculous? Or perhaps it was all coincidental? Or perhaps the old man really has some serious psi abilities?

For neither placebo nor coincidences seem likely to account for the following case involving the former Norwegian Minister of Health, Bjarne Haakon Hanssen. In 2009 Hanssen told both national TV and the press that because of colic his baby boy had cried almost continuously, day and night, for two months (ugh!). At last Hanssen was so exhausted and wretched that out of sheer desperation he called the Snåsa Man. We let Hanssen tell the story himself:

I was then a basically skeptical but desperate person who called for help, says Hanssen [...]—Gjerstad said just: 'That's okay, I'll see what I can do.' Then we hung up, and I thought that this is unlikely to help, says Hanssen. But just ten minutes later there started some dramatic processes in that tiny body.—Haakon [the baby boy], was reclining in a tilting chair, and then he began farting, or releasing air, as it is called here. In ten to fifteen minutes there came such amounts that both I and Rigmor [his wife] thought it totally implausible that this really was possible, says Hanssen. This was about 6 pm, and after a quarter of an hour expelling gas the baby fell asleep. He slept all evening, all night and well into the next day. This was the first good night he'd had [in two months], says Hanssen.

The next days the baby was well, but after three or four days he gradually began to deteriorate. After a week I called Gjerstad once more and explained what had happened. He said again 'Okay, I'll see what I can do again.' After ten to fifteen minutes the process in the baby's body started again: Exactly the same thing happened once more. He let out huge amounts of air, fell asleep and had thereafter no more problems with his stomach, says Hanssen. (Verdens Gang, February 26, 2009. Link to the article can be found in the bibliography.)

The Health Minister has made a partial reassessment of his own skepticism after his experience with the Snåsa Man:

> *I don't have much faith in healing and other alternative things like fortune telling. But neither do I think it is right to deny my own experience with the Snåsa Man. I just convey what I experienced, says Hanssen.*

It seems difficult here—with an absent patient who doesn't have the faintest idea of what healing is, and a father who was skeptical even after his first conversation with Gjerstad—to see where such a potent and acute placebo effect could come from. And, honestly, is it really likely to be coincidental that—after two months of colic around the clock—the baby is healed in an instantaneous (and humorous!) way when the Snåsa Man was contacted? And moreover: that this weird scenario not only manifested itself once but twice? Strange... strange indeed. Well, thus spoke Health Minister Hanssen!

A Trip to Hawaii

There has, in fact, been quite a lot of research conducted on healing; a comprehensive overview from 2005 suggests that even back then there were more than 2,000 studies on file. Unfortunately, many of them suffered from methodological weaknesses and limitations. Some of the best are found in the peer reviewed *Journal of Alternative and Complementary Medicine*. In December 2005, the magazine published one that I think deserves to be called 'a classic' and which is often referred to as 'The Hawaii Study.' This is because (you're right!) it was conducted in Hawaii, more specifically at the Department of Radiology, North Hawaii Community Hospital at Waimea. Even if essentially healing-related, the Hawaii study did not assess the possible benefits of remote healing but rather—somewhat more modestly—if intent from a distance would have a measurable effect at all. This is a *sine qua non*, an absolutely necessary condition, if remote healing should be possible.

The chief scientist was Jeanne Achterberg, PhD, professor of psychology at Southwestern Medical School, and together with her colleagues she presented the study in an article named 'Evidence for Correlations Between Distant Intentionality and Brain Function in Receivers: A Functional Magnetic Resonance Imaging Analysis.' It can be downloaded from the journal's website, and a link to a partial reprint can be found in the bibliography.

A short description: Eleven healers of different traditions—shamanism, qi gong, kahuna, etc.—had each chosen a receiver. Based on the assumption that emotional rapport helps facilitate the process, the healers had been told to choose a receiver to whom they felt a close connection. The receivers would be placed in a magnetic brain scanner, while the healers—located in an electromagnetically shielded control room, physically and optically isolated from the receiver—would attempt to influence the receivers by 'doing their thing.' Such an arrangement was put in place to prevent the exchange of audio-visual clues and possible radio transmission (e.g. by concealed spy apparatus) between the healers and the receivers.

The different healer/receiver pairs were then tested—one pair at a time. The healer would send 'good intentions' to the receiver in a series of 12 turns, each turn lasting two minutes. The order was randomized so only the researchers would know when the good intentions were to be 'switched on' and 'switched off' respectively. This protocol was partly employed to avoid cheating but just as much to neutralize the placebo effect. Since the 'sending' schedule was unknown, the receivers could not coordinate their expectations with the healers 'sending.'

And as for the results? The scans showed a marked difference between experiment and control—that is, between when the healers were sending 'good intentions' and when they were pausing. Clearly measurable changes in brain functions took place with no fewer than nine out of the 11 receivers. Dr Achterberg said that on the monitors one could see that the receivers' brains 'lit up like Christmas trees'!

Much like the telepathy experiment with Sara and Vicky (end of chapter 6) and the dream-telepathy experiments of Ullman and Krippner (mid chapter 8), the Hawaii study seems to support the hypothesis that there is, in fact, a non-local connection between people. The researchers discuss possible sources of error, but conclude quite confidently: 'In summary, these findings support previous research on distant healing suggesting that human intentions may directly affect others in ways that are not entirely understood.' Skeptics will of course think that the findings—if not due to error or fraud (e.g. that nurses divulged the time schedule of the healers' sending)—must be due to chance, a statistical fluke. The researchers in turn claim that the odds for such effects to appear based on pure chance are less than 1 in 5,000! And I think it is fair to say that this is where the case stands as of now.

The Hawaii study was by no means the first time that brain scanning was used in psi research. It is well known that in 1924 the German psychiatrist Hans Berger was the first to measure human brainwaves electronically (animal brainwaves had been measured some years earlier). What is less well known, though, is that Berger had invented his device to detect telepathy! The history behind this was as follows: In the early 1890s Berger was enrolled in the military. There he became the victim of a dramatic and near-fatal accident; in the very same moment his sister, living in another town, got a stark sense that Hans was in peril. She therefore insisted that her father send a telegram to check if he was all right (it was the first telegram the father had ever sent him). Berger writes: 'It was a case of spontaneous telepathy in which at a time of mortal danger, and as I contemplated certain death, I transmitted my thoughts, while my sister, who was particularly close to me, acted as the receiver.' So—having survived and having become obsessively curious as to what happens in the brain in connection with telepathic activity, Berger started to study psychology, and many years later he developed his revolutionary electroencephalography (EEG).

Problematic Prayers

Apropos distant healing, let me mention that the 2006 April issue of the *American Heart Journal* presented the results from the so-called STEP—the Study of the Therapeutic Effects of Intercessory Prayer. This was a long-lasting collaborative project between researchers from several prestigious institutions, including Harvard, which evaluated cases pertaining to about 1,800 patients who had gone through coronary artery bypass graft (CABG) surgery (I'm surely no medical doctor, but I think I got it right!). The point was to map the eventual effects of intercessory prayer—in this case prayers from strangers—whose purpose was to reduce complications and mortality following surgery.

The patients were divided into three groups: 1) those who received prayer after being informed that they may or may not receive prayer; 2) those who did not receive prayer after being informed that they may or may not receive prayer; and 3) those who received prayer after being informed they would receive prayer. The intercessors, those praying, were from different religious backgrounds—Protestant, Catholic and Jewish. They were assigned one patient each, and got to know their patient's first name and the initial of the last name: 'Wendy, will you for the next 14 days please pray for the successful recovery of Peter P!'

And the results? Well, STEP did not show any healing effects of this kind of prayer; in fact, the patients in group 3)—those who were prayed for and who knew that they had been prayed for—had on average slightly more complications than the two other groups! It is not obvious how this should be interpreted (if it was more than just a fluke). It has been suggested that some people get a quite stressful performance anxiety by being prayed for (by strangers): 'I must not disappoint the kind people who spend time and effort praying for me!' And also it could be perceived as a make-or-break situation related to God: 'If I don't get well, maybe it's because God doesn't like me!'

STEP has been criticized from diverse quarters; for being mere folly (skeptics) and for methodological flaws (psi-positives) and a number of doctors have claimed it is impossible to conclude anything on the basis of STEP. Without going too deeply into the discussion, let me just mention that it is obviously problematic—regrettably, one might think—to assume that the prayers of different people will have equal or even comparable effects. Remote healing will from a parapsychological perspective—mostly—not be thought of as an intervention by non-human powers (it lies outside our book's framework to discuss such aspects) but rather as a function of the human mind—the workings of our secret powers. There is research supporting that such an ability may exist, e.g. the abovementioned article by Schwartz and Dossey. And if this is the case, it seems likely that—as with any human ability—based on talent and training some people will possess remote healing skills outshining the average. Just as one cannot assume that most people have the same capacity for understanding physics as did Einstein, one cannot assume that average persons have the same capacity for healing prayers/remote healing as, say, an experienced healer or shaman.

Furthermore: In STEP the intercessors had no personal contact with the patients, and from what we know—or what we think we know—personal connection cannot be disregarded when it comes to psi; rather it seems to be crucial. People report telepathic contact with family and friends and (mostly) not with strangers; people report precognitive dreams concerning family and friends and (mostly) not concerning strangers. Quite obviously, it seems. Therefore, research on prayer 'by strangers for strangers'—as in STEP—is unsuitable to tell us anything about a) whether individually performed prayers/remote healing have effects and b) who eventually may exercise such effects. With respect to these questions it seems much more relevant to study individual, targeted intentions—just as was done in the Hawaii study. The way to go, then, is probably to conduct a large-scale study partly patterned after the Hawaii study—and, as 'aloha' means good wishes and love, what would be more fitting than to conduct it in Hawaii, the Aloha state?—where not only the impact on brainwaves but also the eventual health benefits of the healers' good intentions are assessed.

Leaving the Lab—a Summary

Well, we have now served and consumed some tidbits and morsels of what psi research may involve! What conclusions, then, might we reach based on the experiments presented? Some would argue that ESP is substantiated by solid evidence, whereas PK is a somewhat different story. Others would view this the other way round. And yet others will—for different reasons—reject the psi hypothesis altogether and contend that the observed effects should be explained within established theories. Anyway, what *can* be concluded with absolute certainty is that one doesn't need to be naive, dishonest nor dimwitted to regard psi as a very valid option to account for a string of otherwise seemingly incomprehensible results.

Controversial perhaps, but 'naive, dishonest or dim-witted' is far from an apt description of the psychologist Hans Eysenck (1916–1997), a professor at King's College, University of London. Eysenck is considered one of the most important thinkers in modern personality psychology; he authored/co-authored about 80 books and over 1,600 scientific articles (unbelievable!), and at the time of his death he was the world's most cited psychologist in articles and books. Eysenck was notorious in his positivistic approach: 'If it cannot be measured, it doesn't exist!' He does not seem to have been convinced that *every* person possesses paranormal abilities, but he was completely certain that some did. At the height of his career he 'perpetrated'—a psychology professor rarely writes in favor of psi without being indicted by his colleagues—a small book called *Are you Psychic?* that contains diverse puzzles for testing the sixth sense. This peculiar book came not as a complete bombshell, as Eysenck had already confessed his belief in our secret powers in *Sense and Nonsense in Psychology* (1958). And with some plainspoken remarks from this book we let Eysenck close the chapter:

Unless there is a gigantic conspiracy involving some thirty University departments all over the world, and several hundred highly respected scientists in various fields, many of them originally hostile to the claims of the psychical researchers, the only conclusion the unbiased observer can come to must be that there does exist a small number of people who obtain knowledge existing either in other people's minds, or in the outer world, by means as yet unknown to science.*

***N.B.** *We could be right in the middle of a turning of the tides, because the last few years no less than three mainstream scientific journals – The American Psychologist, The Psychology of Consciousness, and The International Journal of Dream Research – have featured lengthy articles with positive assessments of the evidence of telepathy, remote viewing and precognition. Most groundbreaking is likely American Psychologist's release of 'The experimental evidence for parapsychological phenomena: A review'. Assessing an enormous amount of research the article's author, professor Etzel Cardeña of Lund University, Sweden, concludes that, taken as a whole, the studies support that our dear phenomena are real, indeed! American Psychologist is the flagship-journal of the American Psychological Association and is often considered to be the world's most prestigious psychological journal. So that the editors dare risk its excellent name to print a 'psi-positive' article speaks volumes.*

Chapter 9

OUR PARANORMAL DAILY LIFE

There are only two ways to live your life: One is as though nothing is a miracle. The other is as if everything is.—I believe in the latter.

~ Albert Einstein

Introduction: Pearls or Plastic

On July 7, 1998 the *South China Morning Post* (the largest English language newspaper in Hong Kong) printed a piece that could hardly be to the taste of the arch-skeptic James Randi: Masanobu Sakaguchi, the spokesperson for electronics giant Sony, announced that after conducting a multi-year-long research program Sony had reached the conclusion that ESP is a reality! However, Sakaguchi also reported that Sony—for what perhaps could be seen as somewhat trivial reasons—would not proceed with this particular strand of research: 'We found experimentally that, yes, ESP exists but that any practical application of this knowledge is not likely in the foreseeable future.'

Most of us are probably far less concerned about the technological and financial implications of ESP than Sony, but even so, perhaps our situation is not entirely different? For even if the scientists who vouch for psi should be right—then what? Aren't such phenomena, regardless of whether they are objectively real or not, just curiosities—perhaps entertaining, but in the last resort devoid of meaning? Or could these phenomena perhaps have the possibility of conveying a meaning—and a meaning that could not have come from elsewhere?

Special Experiences and Special People

The psychotic drowns in the same waters in which the mystic swims with delight

~ Joseph Campbell

Let's go back to the work mentioned in the introduction to this book, namely *Varieties of Anomalous Experience*, which was published by the APA, the American Psychological Association. As we stated, the editors think that anomalous experiences in themselves are not necessarily an ominous sign. And, as also mentioned a couple of times, statistics tell us that more than half of us will experience something outside the 'normal.' Hence one is definitely not whacky or otherwise at variance with reality just because one experiences such phenomena! Typically many have related some sort of special *meaning* connected with their atypical experiences—a feeling they will often describe as 'spiritual but not religious.' The editors argue that many psychologists are not sufficiently familiar with such anomalous spiritual experiences as to be able to welcome and embrace them rather than meet them with derision and ridicule. If the field of psychology aspires to encompass our human experience in its fullness, it ought to come up with something better than name-calling—'dissociation!,' 'delusion!,' 'psychosis!,' 'madness!'—to portray the broad array of unusual occurrences that a human being might experience.

It seems as though people with extraordinary creative abilities—in the arts, music, science, philosophy, politics—tend to have unusual experiences more often than other people. One likely reason for this is that these creative people to a larger degree dare to open the door to our combined treasure trove and cabinet of horrors, the subconscious mind, from which all sorts of mental content may bubble forth, including experiences of the paranormal. It is no coincidence that the word 'visionary'—literally, a person who has visions—will often be used to describe creative people of many varieties. Abraham Lincoln was precisely such a visionary, and the poet Walt Whitman, thought him to be a 'mystical' man. And as stated in the introduction to this book, Lincoln occasionally felt information about the Civil War was given to him in dreams. The 'Captain'—as Whitman famously titled Lincoln—seemingly also participated in some of the spiritualistic séances his wife arranged in the White House. Some say Lincoln did this just to please her, while others have argued that Lincoln was genuinely interested in what the medium, while in a trance, could tell about the political agenda of the day.

If we now throw a glance even further back, to ancient Greece, we will find that Socrates, often considered to be the founding father of Western rationalism, believed he had received a special gift from the gods: an inner voice, a *daimon* (which in Greek would mean 'divine force' rather than 'demon'), which would instruct him, 'often warning, rarely impelling.' The *daimon* gave him ethical directives and also, at least as Plato portrays it, the strength to drink the cup of hemlock with the greatest serenity after having been sentenced to death.

Some depictions also suggest that Socrates experienced what we would call psi phenomena related to his *daimon*. The historian Xenophon, a younger contemporary of Socrates, writes that people said Socrates thought the *daimon* 'let him know things, or gave him signs that would let him know them.' And further that he 'often would advise those in his company to do certain things and to avoid others, in keeping with the directions given by the *daimon*.' Here, Socrates seems to act much more like a psychic adviser than a philosopher! When Xenophon asked Socrates whether or not he ought to join a military campaign, Socrates—completely without irony—referred Xenophon to the Delphic oracle for an answer. Apparently Socrates believed the oracle to be divinely inspired by Apollo, the same god who had provided him with his *daimon*. So—the incomparable philosophical saint seemingly had a high degree of openness toward anomalous experiences and what we would call psi!

We could then mention important religious founders such as Buddha, the Jewish prophets, Jesus and Muhammad, who all, according to tradition, had revelations and experienced phenomena of the psi type. Without raising the question as to what degree religious texts can be regarded as historical documents it seems reasonable to assume that the said persons had intense and unusual experiences setting them apart from other people. Within the mentioned traditions it is also taken for granted that not only the founders but also (some of) the followers are going to have similar experiences, whether bestowed as divine gifts or as fruits of prolonged meditative work. Among Christian mystics, Sufis and Kabbalists (i.e. Islamic and Jewish mystics) there are innumerable stories of revelations and paranormal phenomena. And in Buddhism it is thought that all people, at least in principle, may realize their inherent 'Buddhanature.' This may also—even if often regarded as a stumbling block rather than an impetus to growth—involve developing special abilities such as clairvoyance, contact with spirits, etc. And as we heard in chapter 3, similar stories abound within the shamanic traditions.

The point of mentioning these people and traditions is to highlight that paranormal phenomena, regardless of whether they are taken to be subjective experiences or objective manifestations, tend to occur around people in contact with 'the depth dimension' in life—someone seized by the quest for meaning, by an 'ultimate concern,' to use an expression from the philosopher and theologian Paul Tillich. Such a state of mind may be extraordinarily challenging, creating a plethora of emotions, sometimes with such an intensity that makes it nearly impossible to bear. But it may also prove extraordinarily rewarding; as stated by Friedrich Nietzsche: 'One must still have chaos in oneself to be able to give birth to a dancing star.'

In the light of the ideas found in *Irreducible Mind* (see chapter 6), perhaps it is precisely this chaos, these existential tremors, that sometimes may suspend our otherwise quite rigid filtering, allowing our slumbering abilities to awaken and come to life? Maybe psi can thus sometimes be seen as a herald to new life?—like the shoots, sprouts and buds springing forth when the sap starts to flow after winter, heralding the arrival of the all-rejuvenating spring.

Of course, there are disturbing and distressing paranormal phenomena—poltergeists, haunted houses, people being possessed, etc. These scary kinds of phenomena are, regrettably, often the ones writers and filmmakers enjoy delving into, fattening their coffers most effectively... But there are, as we have heard, a lot of people who report deeply satisfying paranormal experiences—healing, meaningful telepathic contact with family and friends, helpful warnings through dreams, etc.

Whether the experience of the paranormal is to become a blessing or a curse will often depend on 'set and setting.' That is to say, having a constructive mindset and supportive surroundings could make all the difference. This seems to be the prevailing sentiment within esoteric schools. Thus the 'awakening person'—the seeker, the initiate, the neophyte—will often seek the supervision of a guru, a sheikh, a rebbe, giving them the advantages as well as the traps (dependency, power-abuse) that typically go with such relationships. Within Western culture, however, it would probably be best to seek out an experienced therapist open to transpersonal perspectives.

Intuition—the Synthesis of Normal and Paranormal Abilities?

Perhaps the majority of us are a tad more occult than we are usually aware of? Many of us have probably had the experience of thinking of a particular person, one who has been out of both sight and mind for quite some time—weeks, months, perhaps even years—and then, just a few hours later, to receive a call from this very person. Many have also experienced suddenly having an inexplicable worry about a friend or a family member, later to learn that at this particular time the person concerned went through something very unpleasant. Such intuitions might sometimes be caused by the interplay of randomness and the perception of subtle signals, physically or verbally. Perhaps one unconsciously had spotted that Jack was a little paler than normal at the party last weekend. Or perhaps one *en passant* had—subconsciously—picked up a casual remark that 'Jack has not looked well lately' or the like.

But what if these experiences occur more or less regularly; that again and again one's hunches prove to be correct? Well, it *could* of course mean that one is an extremely keen observer. Or, if just a little prone to self-deception, it could mean that one has a touch of *apophenia*—the tendency to see patterns where there are none, as we discussed in chapter 7. Or perhaps it could—as this author through the years has become more than ready to consider—be due to our 'consciousnesses' being interlinked? That our antennae are much longer than we realize, and that subconsciously sweeping through the 'mental Facebook' they might pick up things of interest—as, say, that our old friend Jack has planned to give us a call, or that our dear cousin Jill has just been painfully dumped by her boyfriend? Perhaps this—and infinitely much more—information is virtually 'in the air.' If so, our intuition must obviously be much more than just the sum of accumulated experiences. To get a better overview of this somewhat complex theme let's first have a look at 'normal' intuition.

Intuition from Logical and Artistic Perspectives

In 2006 the leading journal *Science* published an article called 'On Making the Right Choice: The Deliberation-Without-Attention Effect,' by the prize-winning Dutch psychologist A.J. Dijksterhuis (the links to this and the other articles used below are found in the bibliography). The results indicated that in uncomplicated situations—such as, say, when choosing home appliances—*reason* will be our best counselor; meaning that based on reason we are likely to make choices with which we are happy in hindsight. While in more complex situations, where there are a whole lot of pluses and minuses to be weighed against each other—for example when choosing a roommate, purchasing an expensive car, or even a house—Dijksterhuis believes it will often be favorable for us to resort to 'unconscious thought.' By this he means using a slow-working kind of intuition (and *not* the fast-working intuition described by Daniel Kahneman, as we will see below).

The reason Dijksterhuis makes such a recommendation is that we are able to process far greater amounts of information unconsciously than consciously. Perceiving and relating to *the essence* in a situation of choice—which out of these six cars should I buy? Ought I to move in with this particular person?—is when 'unconscious thought' may prove more helpful than mere logical thinking. This applies only if you first take the time and effort to garner the necessary facts and data so that your unconscious mind has sufficient and relevant material available to work with. But after having familiarized yourself thoroughly with the situation, you should not engage in endless brooding and analyzing—what we usually call 'overthinking'—as this, according to

Dijksterhuis, may cause you to lose perspective, leaving you wrapped and trapped in outsized concerns for trifles.

In an interview with the *Harvard Business Review* in 2007 Dijksterhuis said:

> *Use your conscious mind to acquire all the information you need for making a decision—but don't try to analyze the information. Instead, go on holiday while your unconscious mind digests it for a day or two. Whatever your intuition then tells you is almost certainly going to be the best choice.*

Dijksterhuis holds that this kind of intuitive processing is often derided by those who feel compelled to verbalize the reasons for their choices. In the article 'A Theory of Unconscious Thought' Dijksterhuis writes:

> *A major reason that people distrust intuition is the belief, which is often implicitly held, that intuitions are snap judgments that arrive in the consciousness with little or no prior information processing. However, such a belief may not be justified. In many cases, intuitions may well be the result of extensive unconscious thought. Intuitions are the summary judgments the unconscious gives us when it is ready to decide.*

Intuitive decision-making should not be carried out lightly, though. There are prerequisites that should be in place to ensure the quality of your decisions. To that effect Dijksterhuis suggests we ask ourselves two questions. The first is: 'Did I give myself enough time to engage in unconscious thought?' If you conclude that yes, you probably have given your unconscious mind sufficient time for processing, then ask yourself the second question: 'Did I have all the important information, or are there additional things I really need to know first?' If you think you have all the information you need, Dijksterhuis says: 'Go with your intuition. It likely is the best advice you will get.'

Similar advice is often given to us in fairytales: To be able to win the princess, the Ash Lad—the poor but skillful young man who is the hero in many Norwegian folktales— once needed to build a vessel able to 'fare on water, on land, and in the air as well'—obviously a very demanding task. The Ash Lad wanders out in the woods and close to a giant oak tree he meets an old man (a symbol for his own higher self?) with whom he shares his food. In return the old man gives him the following guidance:

> 'Now, chop out a chip of wood [from the oak tree], and then put it back just where it sat, and when you've done that, you can go to sleep.' Yes, the Ash Lad did as the man said, then he lay down to sleep. And in his sleep he thought he could hear the noise from hewing and hammering and sawing and crafting, but he couldn't wake up until the man woke him up. Then the ship stood fully finished along with the oak.

There is always a risk in overanalyzing the poetry of a story, finding things that are not really there, but I'll take the chance. I think the 'hewing and hammering and sawing and crafting' that the Ash Lad heard in the background were the mighty, unconscious processes. In fact, Dijksterhuis has stated that we unconsciously are able to process about 200,000 times as much information as we are able to do consciously! The superlative example of this outrageous capacity is the savants' unbelievable but proven feats in calculation and memory (chapter 6). When the normal, rigid ego filtering is partly suspended—either by autism or in various other ways (the Ash Lad had to go to sleep to get the vessel built)—the untethered and unreined unconscious mind is able to perform some really mind-blowing amazing stunts.

However, the Nobel laureate psychologist Daniel Kahneman does not think relying on intuition is always a boon. In his erudite and widely recognized book, *Thinking, Fast and Slow*, Kahneman maintains that when making decisions we think in two different ways. Either we think 'fast' (intuitive, feeling-based) or we think 'slow' (analytical, logical). When we think 'fast' our judgments are to a great extent based on our previous experiences. Hence we use our ready-made clichés with the advantages (speed) and drawbacks (lack of nuances) that go with them. Many who act on intuition, says Kahneman, are therefore simply not in touch with *the present situation* and its specifics. Rather, they are 'living on memories'—and are proud of it! In addition, Kahneman believes he has demonstrated that intuitive assessments often suffer from 'optimism bias,' meaning that decisions based on intuition tend to be overly optimistic. Trite but true: misplaced optimism may easily lead to ugly results—in traffic, in politics, in the stock market, etc.

Dijksterhuis and Kahneman thus seem to be in profound disagreement as Dijksterhuis explicitly recommends that complex decisions be taken based on intuition, while Kahneman spots trouble in the offing whenever intuition is given primacy over analytical deliberation. To sort out the matter I contacted Dijksterhuis, who told me that he and Kahneman, in fact, are speaking about different things: Kahneman distinguishes, as mentioned above, between two kinds of thinking, fast and slow. While Dijksterhuis distinguishes between *three* types of thinking: fast and slow (much like Kahneman), but moreover an even slower form, working unconsciously, as we discussed above in connection with the Ash Lad. And, according to Dijksterhuis, Kahneman does not take this type of slow, unconscious thinking into consideration at all.

So, to Kahneman, 'intuition' means instant thinking based on memory—a pattern recognition happening in the blink of an eye, typically without the need for acquiring new information. For example, decisions of the kind that experienced pilots make when sitting at the controls; they know the situation in and out, thus they will intuitively—in Kahneman's sense of the word—know how to deal with almost any possible issue. Whereas to Dijksterhuis 'intuition' refers to those prolonged unconscious processes so often prized by creative persons such as artists, inventors and entrepreneurs—for example the Apple founder Steve Jobs, who spoke warmly about intuition and who, as many probably will know, had a related interest in mysticism and altered states of consciousness. (Jobs said that Bill Gates would have become more creative if he'd tried LSD...) I would guess Jobs was not so much interested in Kahneman's intuition (recognizing established patterns) as he was in Dijksterhuis' intuition (creating new patterns).

Dijksterhuis explained that people involved in such unconscious processes will typically use even more time than Kahneman does when he is 'thinking slowly.' But unlike Kahneman's slow thinking, these processes are—as stated above—not about protracted logical analysis but about allowing for fermentation and maturation in the unconscious mind. And only when this brewing process is reaching completion will it be time to 'go with your gut.'

Such maturation may result in 'reframing' and an 'escape to a higher level' as it is sometimes called within systems theory, meaning that one will intuitively (in Dijksterhuis' sense) see the issue in question in a new and liberating way. Understanding the connection between A and B (analysis) is important when you want to go from A to B. But sometimes it will be even more important to see both A and B in a new light (reframing). Doing so, you may find that you are not so interested in going to B after all but would rather like to go to C! For example, rather than deciding to buy this or that fancy car, you might suddenly surprise yourself by thinking, No, I'd rather buy a bike as I will feel freer if I don't increase my mortgage. And that freedom—and getting in shape—is more important for me than keeping up with the Joneses.

Perhaps the reason why Kahneman and Dijksterhuis differ in their approach to intuition could be traced back to their different personalities? Kahneman seems, in writing and in interviews, to be an utterly analytical and logical person; he so loves to expose the fallacies of intuition (as he understands the concept), and his book contains some funny (and important) examples. Whereas Dijksterhuis appears to be more of an artistic and even bohemian type. In practical play the difference is probably not decisive, though, as both recommend that we, in addition to being well informed, take our time when making complex decisions.

This is hardly a shocking new insight for most of us, but maybe it is good to have it put on a solid foundation. Links can be found in the bibliography to some pertinent articles. To get the most out of them you should probably first—as Kahneman prescribes—think slowly through their content, and then—in keeping with Dijksterhuis' recommendations—do something else and let the material get a good and long unconscious maturation!

Intuition from an Occult Perspective

In this book 'intuition' is used in a broad sense that smoothly encompasses both Kahneman's and Dijksterhuis' ideas, and where the essence would be 'the feeling of knowing but without quite knowing why you know.' A couple of examples: 'Well, I met my sister's new boyfriend yesterday, and immediately I just knew he was a psychopath—I don't know why!' (Perhaps it was the sadistic glint in his eye similar to that of another, formerly met, psychopath?) 'When I woke up this morning I just knew I needed to change jobs—I don't know why!' (Perhaps a long repressed need for a quieter lifestyle had surfaced in a dream?). The question is of course whether such intuitions, such gut feelings, only stem from the conscious and unconscious learning from past experiences. Or if in addition telepathy, clairvoyance and precognition might enter the picture and 'fortify' one's intuition, have it working 'on steroids,' such as occultists think is possible. Our intuition would then become a sixth sense.

As we have heard, many parapsychologists—Ryzl, Lozanov, Parker, Radin, Bierman, Bem and others—think this is the case. They think psi is doing its job silently in the background, unconsciously, sometimes allowing paranormal information to seep (mostly undetected) into and blend with our usual mental processes. Only a few of us have visions à la the prophets and mystics, but most of us will from time to time have intuitions, gut feelings, and hunches which, based on the understanding mentioned above, will sometimes contain paranormal information. Maybe this is why 'unconscious thinking' and gut feelings can help us make decisions that are remarkably clairvoyant (perhaps even literally). The experiments of Radin, Bierman and Bem are suggestive of just that.

Imagine that you have been looking at an attractive house and consider buying it. Then, suddenly you get a weird sensation that something is wrong. Such a feeling may of course be nothing more than a whim. But applying the occult perspective on intuition, one would want to take such a vibe a little seriously, and perhaps ask oneself some questions, such as: 'Could it be clairvoyance/clairsentience that is giving me this rotten feeling, signaling that the apparent dream house is a nightmare of undetected rot?' Or, 'Maybe it is telepathy that is giving me this feeling that the broker is not telling me all that I ought to know?' Or, 'Perhaps precognition is occasioning this weird *déjà vu* (French = already seen), warning me that trouble could be about to happen?'

In addition to the lab experiments conducted by Radin, Bierman, Bem et al., a paranormal perspective on intuition is also suggested in the diverse field cases we have discussed, as for instance Elizabeth Lloyd Mayer's experience with the lost harp (chapter 7). Kahneman thinks that the 'seeming magic' of intuition is merely due to its capitalization on large amounts of accumulated experiences. But the kind of intuition that was demonstrated to Mayer—the dowser was located in another city where he specified the whereabouts of the harp using a pendulum over a map—can obviously not be explained by former experience, fast or slow thinking. Here we are talking real clairvoyance or real deception! Mayer was a recognized and respected psychologist, and the introduction to her book was written by the maverick physicist and mathematician Freeman Dyson. In other words, there are hardly good reasons to believe she is deceiving us.

And it has become clear during our extensive hike in the borderland of consciousness, Mayer is by no means alone; there are many presumably credible and resourceful persons who have recounted experiences of related kinds. Thus, perhaps it is the occultists' perspective—viewing intuition as a seamless synthesis of our normal and paranormal abilities—that may provide us with the most satisfactory understanding.

Well, whether we choose to listen mostly to Dijksterhuis, Kahneman or to the occultists, they all seem to agree that our intuition should not be dominated by Hopes or Fears, the two largest sources of error when assessing information, normal or paranormal. This is probably one of the reasons that from time to time we should put all thoughts of decision-making aside and simply 'sleep on it.' Just as was taught us by no less than the Ash Lad himself!

YES.

DIY

Given that the occultists' perspective on intuition is relevant—is there anything we could do to make our intuition more open to ESP? Can we learn to know gold from garbage, diamonds from dust, distinguishing fanciful neurosis from truthful intuition? Can we, in other words, go from five-sensory to six-sensory functioning? If we choose to say, somewhat like the military did when setting up Stargate: 'Well, maybe this could be possible,' then the esoteric schools—Kabbalists, Sufis, Rosicrucians, Hermeticists, etc.—have exciting schemes to offer us, as over the centuries they have developed methods of training precisely for this purpose.

The easiest technique of all is doing deliberate guesswork. Empty your mind of thoughts as much as possible and guess: What's in the letter that the mail carrier just delivered? Who's calling right now? What is it that he/she wants? Who is going to win the game tonight? What will the scenery be like at our holiday destination? In short, guess at all and everything, but preferably at that which you cannot know in the usual way! Afterwards, write down and evaluate your scores. If there is to be any point in such an exercise, one must of course be uncompromisingly honest;

this is the only way that—if at all possible—one may learn to tell the difference between true 'downloads' and fanciful imagination.

Errors will be abundant, but have no worries: shedding the fear of mistakes is part of the training. If the esoteric masters are right, slowly but surely one will develop a 'taste' for quality and truth, and thus one's score will supposedly get better. When learning to play the guitar or the piano you will make many mistakes at first. But eventually your fingers will find the right positions with greater ease, and your ear will also become more precise and nuanced. After some time, chances are that you will get the chords right much of the time. And you will also hear whether your instrument is out of tune, or if the strings resound with that magical, silvery sound, that Orpheus got from his lute.

However, talent is unevenly distributed in the world, and there is no reason to think that an eventual sixth sense should be an exception to this rule. Given that psi is real, it seems reasonable to think that most of us—figuratively speaking—could learn to play for pleasure, but far fewer will be talented enough to be musicians, and only rarely will a person or group be able to develop the necessary qualities for creating a new craze. Perhaps one could say that from an occult perspective people function basically in one of three ways: Some work 'offline,' filtering out practically all information from the Mental Internet. Others, probably most of us, download information to a greater or lesser extent, usually without thinking about it, as has been suggested by Radin, Bierman, Bern, Parker, et al. While the third group both utilize this special kind of information and are also very much aware that they are doing it. It is of course such people who will often be referred to as 'psychics' or 'paragnosts.'

Becoming a Real Psychic?

Perhaps some readers have a more ambitious goal than just to spice up their intuition, and want to dedicate a serious amount of time, effort and even money trying to develop their paranormal abilities to their full potential so as to be able to excel in telepathy, clairvoyance, healing, telekinesis, astral projection, etc. To what extent this will be possible I can't say—traditionally it is often held that the true psychic or magician is born, not created—but it is certainly possible to go from dreaming about it to start experimenting!

Given that it should be possible to attain some degree of success with a project of this type, one should probably consider whether such an expansion of consciousness is something one is truly ready for. As we have heard, experienced psychics tell of the strain that goes with constantly 'taking in' human pain, grief, anxiety, and also forebodings about unpleasant future events. During WWI, Rudolf Steiner, the Austrian esoteric teacher, was contacted by a flight commander who, before the missions started, would 'see' among the pilots those who would be killed. And he was often right. This was a great burden to him, hence he asked Steiner to help him 'shut down' his precognitions. (Steiner prescribed some specific mental exercises that reportedly accomplished the task.)

And if, for example, you should succeed in developing healing skills, you are likely to get unsolicited calls 24/7, and I promise your social life will never be the same. Hereafter you will be continually confronted with the 'doctor's dilemma': 'Oh, this back of mine! I've heard you're into healing; could I ask if you would just very quickly, etc.' On the other hand, maybe you think your psi abilities already are somewhat active and it feels right to initiate a closer cooperation with them? Or maybe you feel the need for something new, a plunge into the unknown, thus expanding your horizons in this direction seems promising?

There are lots of 'psychic gyms' of different brands and qualities; let me briefly mention a couple which I think are serious.

Many who work with cultivating ESP claim to have benefited from the Silva courses. Here you will learn techniques for relaxation and 'going to alpha,' i.e. learning to regulate (to some degree) your brainwaves, thus changing your mental gears. You will also learn to sort your inner stream of images, words and sensations where the ESP information might possibly show up. Silva courses have been tried and tested for quite some time; however, they are fairly expensive, and results cannot be guaranteed.

An esoteric school sharing their occult skills on quite idealistic grounds is Servants of the Light (SOL)—an offshoot of the Hermetic Order of the Golden Dawn (mentioned in chapter 5). However, their courses progress slowly as they want you to mature personally in parallel with developing psychic abilities. Hence you will have to digest far more esoteric philosophy than most of us are motivated for.

Anyway, it is probably best to take the first steps peacefully in the safety of your own home, becoming familiar with some of the extensive how-to literature on psychic skills. As mentioned, a simple instruction in remote viewing is found in the links to chapter 2. It will also be useful to learn to relax at will—meditation, yoga and autogenic training are proven aids. Many people also tell of the benefits from using soundtracks with 'binaural tones' that utilize so-called 'brain entrainment.' As with shamanic drumming, these sounds are intended to alter your brainwave pattern so as to trigger relaxation and/or induce altered states of consciousness. The two most well-tested systems are probably

Holosync and Hemisync. (Personally, I have used the former, and with some quite good effects.)

If I should dare to recommend a specific book to help in becoming psychic I think, in fact, it would have to be *Becoming Psychic: Spiritual Lessons for Focusing Your Hidden Abilities,* by Stephen Kierulff with contributions from Stanley Krippner. Kierulff is an experienced psychologist who has published articles in peer-reviewed journals; Krippner needs no further introduction. In a laid-back way Kierulff gives us snapshots from physical and psychical journeys during which he—much to his own surprise—managed to develop (some) abilities for extrasensory perception (as he sees it). He recounts many personal psychic experiences of different kinds, and suggests targeted exercises for the reader: how to open up for telepathy, how to develop foresight, etc. Each chapter is equipped with enlightening and entertaining comments from the expert Krippner.

Seeing is believing—and often believing is seeing. At the end of his book Kierulff provides contact information for a number of psychics he assumes (though cannot fully guarantee) are the real deal. If you doubt whether psychic functioning really exists at all, Kierulff suggests that you test out some of these folks. And when/if you then meet a person who proves able to provide you with information that he/she could not possibly have acquired in any customary way this, according to Kierulff, will make it easier for you to activate your own extrasensory perception. (If you constantly repeat to yourself that 'extrasensory perception is bogus!' this will of course make you prone to overlook possible impressions of this kind.)

If you are starting out on the road to paragnosis, it is probably wise to remind yourself that these are not 'divine' qualities that—if real—will make you able to 'see' every number in the Australian phone directory or pinpoint the correct Lottery combinations. Surprisingly many people think that since such feats cannot readily be achieved, extrasensory perception must surely be synonymous to extrasensory deception. Our proposal, however, which is based on the model of the Mental Internet, makes it possible to find a middle ground between the extremes of believe-all or believe-nothing. We suggest that such abilities might very well be real and—if sufficient talent and training is in place—occasionally can bring about astonishing results. But at the same time we mustn't forget that they, like any other human skills, are not infallible; *errare humanum est* (to err is human) as the ancient Romans used to say. Even the best batter can't be expected to hit the ball every time. Accordingly it is unreasonable to expect that a psychic will have hits on all occasions. What *is* reasonable, however, is to expect that those who present themselves as professionals— be they batters or be they psychics—should have far more hits than the rest of us. This leads us quite naturally to the next section.

Costly Truths?— Professional Psychics

Via telephone, internet, letters and personal consultations, professional psychics are running multi-multi-million-dollar schemes worldwide. Without going too deeply into the matter I would like to share some brief reflections. Among the obvious dangers within the psychic business are the professional cheaters. Some readers may recall the Maria Duval scam, apparently managed by an international network of con-psychics. Clients all over the world—often vulnerable people with health problems, in existential crises, etc.—were swindled, paying exorbitantly for 'psychic' services. In the US and Canada alone the amount of money involved in this mail fraud scheme is estimated to have been a whopping $200 million. Another scam is Rinalda—'she' is a computer—who impresses many visiting 'her' website by imparting such things as 'You will soon approach London'—a feat which 'she' performs by logging into your computer's IP address. (I once used a proxy server to move my IP address to Kuala Lumpur, a move that for some reason left the poor girl completely confused...)

Fortunately, such cases are rare. More common are 'honest liars'—people who believe themselves to be psychic but who do not deliver. This does not necessarily mean that they are completely devoid of talent; from the perspective we employ in this book almost all humans have psychic abilities to some degree. But the 'honest liars' typically overestimate their skills, either because of naivety or because of ego, conveying much muck with their grains of gold. The ads for telephone psychic services are often found right next to the ads for sex services. If we should interpret this as some kind of a meaningful coincidence, it could probably be explicated as follows.

There are certain natural phenomena that people may want more of in their lives. It cannot be excluded that the person on the other end of the line has some relevant skills, but one also ought to know that in such contexts the supplied goods will often be of very poor quality.

If one accepts this, it will perhaps—if one should feel a need for any of these stimuli—be possible to enjoy both types of service. The one type of line may—if you are lucky—perhaps provide you with an experience of extrasensory perception. While the other type of line will usually be limited to experiences of pure (or impure) sensory perception.

Many of the professional psychics are people who have been around for a while, and some of them are quite competent as coaches. Thus they will often provide their clients with a much-needed pat on the back when going through hard times. The danger is of course a possible addiction that can be unhealthy both for soul and for wallet (but, as we know, this will apply to several of our more routine pleasures as well…). Many will also attribute much too much weight to the words of psychics. If, say, a bureaucrat should happen to drop a stupid comment in passing it will usually be an easy matter to shake it off. But if the idiotic remark is made by a professional psychic, a person who reputedly has strong intuitive abilities, then it might not perhaps be that easy to ignore. A scene from the French comic album *Asterix and the Soothsayer* now comes to mind: An augur, a Roman priest and soothsayer, is performing his rituals before a pleased-looking Caesar and his adopted son, Brutus, who is fiddling with a dagger… The augur solemnly declares: 'As long as Brutus is near you, O Caesar, you will have nothing to fear!'

At last it should be mentioned: When a person feels utterly alone and deeply distressed, perhaps even on the verge of suicide, and desperately needs another human being to talk to, it may—especially during the night—be difficult to pick up the phone and call friends or family, or a mental health service. In such situations many have chosen to call a 24/7 psychic line—and many have also received help. Perhaps one's primary need was to break the loneliness, something that could have been accomplished by chatting with just about anybody? Or maybe the person who came on the line was a real intuitive, being able to 'tune in,' to find the right words and provide consoling perspectives not readily available from an average person? An elderly man, who for a couple of decades has been working on a psychic line, once told me that 'when the weekend comes the suicide candidates will call, and I don't let them off the line before I hear their pills being flushed down the drain!' Those of you who treat your clients in this way, regardless of whether or not you are psychic, be thanked, for you have saved lives.

One Heretic, Two Books, Four Legs and Six Senses—Rupert Sheldrake and His Ideas

Many people have related stories of having a close, yes, almost a telepathic contact with animals. Is this just a result of projection, or could such contact really be possible? According to, for example, the Indian Vedanta philosophy, as outlined in chapter 6, consciousness is not something peculiar to humans; rather it belongs to Nature itself, and is part of all life to varying degrees (and perhaps it could even be latent in 'dead' matter). And if we accept the ideas of Daryl Bem found in 'Feeling the Future'—where he suggested that ESP is part of an evolutionary survival kit—there is no reason why animals shouldn't have the capacity for extrasensory perception. And maybe they might even be more proficient at these feats than us while leading a life more in tune with nature.

Telepathy—a Shared Language Between All Living Beings

One who advocates such a position is the British biologist Dr Rupert Sheldrake. Having a very solid academic background, Sheldrake is by no means a typical fringe theorist; for six years he was Director of Studies in biochemistry and cell biology at Clare College, Cambridge University. But as the years have gone by Sheldrake has become more and more controversial, primarily because of his ideas on evolution, which he ascribes to 'morphic resonance'—a natural circuit of non-local information, closely resembling telepathy.

Sheldrake first put forth his heretical thoughts with the article 'A New Science of Life' in the *New Scientist,* June 1981. The science writer Colin Tudge then wrote an editorial that presented Sheldrake's thoughts under the incendiary heading: 'Scientific proof that science has got it all wrong.' About a week later, Sheldrake released his book *A New Science of Life: The Hypothesis of Formative Causation.* The sequel, *The Presence of the Past: Morphic Resonance and the Habits of Nature*, was released in 1988. I remember finding and buying this latter book at the University of Oslo bookstore when I was a student in the early 1990s, the back page sporting a panegyric blurb reading something like: 'If reading this book, in 50 years you'll be able to say, I was there!' More than 25 years have passed since then and the book has gained very solid traction within 'alternative' milieux. Perhaps before the next 25 years are up it will have gained recognition within regular academia also?

In the aforementioned two books Sheldrake discusses much complex biochemistry and genetics—spheres where I fear to tread. Thus the following is just a simple summary of the main features of his thinking.

Heretical Core Ideas

Sheldrake maintains that evolution does not happen out of the blue; on the contrary, there is a feedback circle at work—meaning that Nature somehow learns from its experiences with itself. The original scientific version of this strain of thought is called 'Lamarckism,' named after the French biologist Jean-Baptiste Lamarck (1744–1829). The problem that has always haunted Lamarckism is to explain *how* such learning takes place—what is the mechanism causing this alleged natural self-schooling? Sheldrake believes he has answers to offer, namely his theory of 'formative causation.'

He postulates that Nature is governed by 'habits' that give all organisms their structures, shapes and functions. Evolution, says Sheldrake, is the build-up and development of these habits via 'morphic fields.' These are fields of information generated by the experiences had by generations and generations of organisms. For example crocodiles: When millions of crocodiles make 'deposits' of information (their experiences of hunting, mating, sensations, pleasure, fear, etc.) in the collective memory bank, their descendants will become the beneficiaries of the heritage. This means that today's crocodiles are 'in-formed' (shaped, directed, governed, modified, etc.) by these fields. And their experiences will in turn make new 'deposits' in the collective memory bank. Ad infinitum. This feedback circle of information does of course not only apply to crocodiles, but to all species in nature ranging from single-celled organisms to mammals. And that's the way of the world!

The exchange that takes place between the 'morphic crocodile field' and the crocodiles is, as mentioned, called 'morphic resonance.' This resonance is very tempting to describe as 'Nature's telepathic education of itself.' Sheldrake explains that:

organisms are subject to an influence from previous sim-
ilar organisms by a process called morphic resonance.
Through morphic resonance, each member of a species
draws upon, and in turn contributes to, a pooled or col-
lective memory. Thus, for example, if animals learn a
new skill in one place, similar animals raised under sim-
ilar conditions should subsequently tend to learn the same
thing more readily all over the world.

Sheldrake does not use the t-word in this connection; in 'normal' telepathy the exchanges of information take place between individual senders and receivers. But he has stated that he thinks telepathy, which he warmly espouses, can be seen as an expression of the same type of non-local communication as is morphic resonance. And the good Sheldrake goes further: He thinks that inanimate, 'dead' matter—for example the structure of crystals—also develops as part of nature's ever-evolving habits. And in the last resort, Sheldrake holds, even the natural laws themselves are habits—formed over enormous time spans. In keeping with this Sheldrake thinks that several of the so-called 'constants' in nature—for instance the 'big G,' a formula which describes the gravitational force between two bodies—are not that constant after all.

Sheldrake's scientific research is informed by the works of older scientists such as Hans Spemann (Nobel laureate in Medicine/Physiology, 1935), Alexander Gurwitsch (biologist/physiologist, likely the originator of the concept 'morphic field') and Paul Albert Weiss (biologist, recipient of the American Medal of Science). Moreover, Sheldrake has cited C.G. Jung, with his ideas about 'the collective unconscious' that we discussed in chapter 4, as an influence. Sheldrake developed his seminal thoughts during a period when he headed the International Crops Research Institute for the

Semi-Arid Tropics, a plant research center in Hyderabad, India. Later he spent some time in an *ashram*, a spiritual workshop. And some of Sheldrake's ideas definitely have a whiff of Vedanta. For example, he regards consciousness to be inherent in Nature (and so it also has to be, I guess, since we—conscious human beings—are a part of Nature). Sheldrake has said his thinking has also been inspired by an eccentric, philosophical lady—a kind of elderly female Mowgli—who lived in an old house teeming with birds and other animals, and where wasps were allowed to build their nests unhindered!

Morphic resonance may help to explain why Life has not been standing still but in fact has evolved dramatically. After all, it is an extremely long way (in most cases, that is…) from amoebae aswim in the primordial ocean to space-traveling humans! This evolution cannot, according to Sheldrake, be accounted for just by chanting the Darwinian mantra 'survival of the fittest.' Surely, the un-fits will die out. But—thinking about it, innumerable simple life forms are obviously better fitted for their kind of life than we humans are for ours. Thus they have had no real reason to evolve, so it seems. So what, then, is the impetus for evolution to happen at all? Could it be, as Sheldrake imagines, that the morphic fields gradually grow over time, and as they in-fluence and in-form organisms, generation after generation, pushing and pulling them ever so slowly, ever so slightly—thus molding their genetics over millions of years—, Life on Earth will be led in the direction of more complex forms and higher levels of consciousness?

To validate his ideas Sheldrake has cited among other experiments a classic designed by William McDougall (featured early in chapter 8). This experiment, which was conducted at Harvard, allegedly showed that when a breed of laboratory rats managed to solve a problem (finding their way through a particular maze) their counterparts in laboratories in Scotland and Australia would be able to solve the same problem a little more quickly. If this really should be the case, 'morphic resonance' might be a possible explanation. When the first rats solve the puzzle their insight becomes a part of the 'morphic field' and the other rats can, to some extent, 'download' and utilize the first rats' experiences.

But this doesn't end with the rats, mind you! It turns out that ever since standardized IQ tests were introduced, new generations score higher than their predecessors. This effect, which isn't overly big but still is recognized as a fact, is called the 'Flynn effect.' According to Sheldrake, the Flynn effect cannot be accounted for just by the—acknowledged—increased stimulation through the media, electronic gadgets, schooling or the like. While in light of morphic resonance this scenario is exactly what we should expect! Our collective memory bank has received lots of 'deposits' by all the IQ tests that have been carried out over the years, thus our morphic field has been more 'educated.' Hence today's humans—through morphic resonance, nature's internal telepathic education—will benefit when taking *their* IQ tests.

As an extension of his basic ideas Sheldrake suggests that collectives, swarms and shoals also make daily use of this kind of direct 'telepathic'—as it were—information; for instance, when the ants in an anthill coordinate their immensely complex activities. There are experiments that, according Sheldrake, suggest that genetic programs and chemical signals alone cannot fully explain the complex communication and exchange of information that are obviously taking place between the ants. Some early entomologists (insect researchers) thought likewise and suggested that an anthill, a beehive, a termite mound, etc. may be seen as a *super-organism*, where the individual insects can be regarded as the cells constituting the organism, and where a kind of group telepathy helps to organize the whole thing.

The same goes for fish and birds. In the 1980s the American researcher Wayne Potts filmed flocks of dunlins and afterwards examined their movements, frame by frame. According to Sheldrake, Potts found that

> the rate of propagation of what he [Potts] calls the 'maneuver wave' is extremely fast: about 20 milliseconds from bird to bird. This is much faster than the birds' minimum reaction time to stimuli. He measured their startle reaction time using dunlins in the laboratory in dark or dim light. He set off photographic flashbulbs and measured how long it took the birds to react. He found that it took the individual birds about 80–100 milliseconds; that is, they reacted as individuals four to five times more slowly than the rate at which the maneuver wave moved from bird to bird.

So, according to Sheldrake, the coordinated movements of the birds are simply going much too fast to be ascribed to the normal visual reading of the flight patterns of their 'wing men.'

A Book for Burning?

On the eve of the launch of *A New Science of Life* in 1981 the *New Scientist*'s editorial said that Sheldrake's ideas were off the beaten track, but that 'the science in his ideas is good […] This does not mean that it is right but that it is testable.' Colin Tudge introduced him as a polymath, 'Sheldrake is an excellent scientist; the proper, imaginative kind that in an earlier age discovered continents and mirrored the world in sonnets.' However, a little later *Nature* responded quite differently. Sheldrake's ideas obviously stuck in the craw of the editor, Sir John Maddox. His review, which is close to a writ of summons, had the ominous headline: 'A Book for Burning?' Maddox wrote that, 'This infuriating tract [...] is the best candidate for burning there has been for many years.' And further, that it was 'ridiculous' to claim that such a hypothesis could be tested, and that the experiments Sheldrake suggested would be inconclusive.

Maddox did not conclude that the book ought to be burned, though—he in fact says 'Books rightly command respect [...] even bad books should not be burned; [...] [Dr Sheldrake's] book should not be burned.' But still, the mighty Maddox employing this inquisitorial and bigoted rhetoric stamped Sheldrake as a heretic fielding a 'science from Hell.' This sulfuric attack greatly contributed to the ruin of Shedrake's, until then, untainted reputation.

One may wonder if Maddox here really was in his sound scientific mind, and some of *Nature*'s readers also reacted to what they perceived to be an irrational rant. Maddox did not relent, though, and followed up later by explicitly naming Sheldrake's thoughts 'heresy.' This is certainly strange vocabulary for a science editor, because in contrast to religious dogma the essence of science is applying (as far as possible) neutral methods, formulating hypotheses, designing experiments and running tests. As long as one makes one's theory testable—which Sheldrake had done by proposing specific experiments—any theory may be brought to the table. In a later review Maddox, still being sulfurous, accused Sheldrake of lack of controls during the experiments. As a response Sheldrake invited Maddox to attend the trials to see for himself. But not only did Maddox not accept—he did not even reply.

One thing is *scientific* disagreement, but what is surprising is how irrationally vexed some people become by

Sheldrake. By many he is seemingly perceived as a traitor to the 'true teaching'—the prevailing theories in biology. Irrationality may well fester in the crannies of rationality and if one is perceived as having committed high treason one runs the risk of being hanged, drawn and quartered by the self-avowed guardians of science. In 2008 Sheldrake, after giving a lecture in New Mexico, was stabbed by a Japanese attendee. The attacker claimed that Sheldrake had tried to control him by telepathy so clearly mental health issues were in the picture. But still, mainstream academics very seldom encounter accusations of this type.

Regardless of the controversy that surrounded Sheldrake, some highly competent scientists have been fascinated by his ideas and have bravely defied the taboo of not touching the unclean. Steven Rose, the English biologist and neuroscientist, conducted experiments with Sheldrake during the 1990s, but an agreement on how the results should be interpreted was not reached. Sheldrake also received support from the great physicist David Bohm (briefly presented in chapter 6). Bohm believed that Sheldrake's ideas meshed well with his own theory of Nature as an explicate manifestation of an implicate order (the morphic fields).

Revenged by the People

First and foremost Sheldrake has exacted his revenge through the large fan base he has acquired among lay people. He is an accomplished educator, and his later books are aimed at a general readership. He has suggested many entertaining low-budget experiments for testing telepathy and other oddities. People obviously also appreciate that Sheldrake is paying heed to the intrinsic value of animals. He tells of having reacted strongly to the 'objectifying' attitude prevalent in parts of his own profession, and which is poignantly expressed in René Descartes' obnoxious statement that when an animal screams (in pain) it is equal to the squeaking from an ungreased wagon wheel. According to Descartes animals don't think and therefore they are not able to have a conscious experience of pain. Cartesian ideas, which have been—and to some extent still are—widespread in academic circles, may obviously pave the way for unnecessary brutal experiments on live animals.

Sheldrake paints a completely different picture and defends animals as sentient beings, and in the book *Dogs That Know When Their Owners Are Coming Home* he also defends them as telepathic beings! Few are those in the academic community who will publicly admit to a belief in telepathy—be it in relation to humans or to animals. But as Sheldrake has experienced several times: after two or three glasses of good wine tales of telepathy are told even among biologists! Sheldrake has built up a large database of reported cases, amounting to thousands, which appear to support the case for telepathic exchange between humans and animals. He doesn't claim it is possible to discuss the presidency of Donald Trump, Brexit, the situation in the Middle East or the environmental policy of the Green Party, but Sheldrake is convinced of the possibility of telepathic exchanges of essentials as say, care and fear, and also of other things that are important to the four-legged: food, going for a walk, homecomings, etc. What I find especially moving are the stories where animals, apparently based on telepathy, have intervened to stop their owners from committing suicide.

Jay-T—the Telepathic Terrier

Sheldrake has not been content just to collect other people's stories but has also conducted his own experiments. The most noteworthy was with Jaytee, a 'telepathic terrier' living close to Manchester, England who mysteriously seemed to know when Pam Smart, his owner, was heading for home. Pam and her parents had noticed that Jaytee strikingly often would be in the front porch when Pam got home—as if the dog knew she was on her way and was waiting for her. But— maybe Pam arrived home at quite regular times and the dog somehow was able to adjust to this? Or perhaps Jaytee, in fact, would stand quite close to the porch much of the time when Pam was away? Or maybe he was able to hear familiar engine sounds from afar and based on this recognition stood at the porch just as Pam's vehicle was approaching?

Sheldrake wanted to find out and started digging into the matter. He writes:

> *Preliminary observations revealed that Jaytee usually started waiting for Pam just before she set off homewards, apparently when she formed the intention to do so. He did this whatever the time of day on 85 out of 100 return journeys.*

Sheldrake installed cameras in the houses where Jaytee stayed (trials were run both from Pam's place and from that of her sister) to document the dog's behavior: 'In formal, randomized tests, Pam went at least five miles away from home. While she was out, the place where Jaytee waited was filmed continuously on time-coded videotape.' Sheldrake tested out Jaytee's alleged skills again and again, and had Pam arrive at varying times so there were no routines to indicate when she would be approaching. He also had her use different vehicles to avoid the sounds of familiar engines that could give her away. And, according to Sheldrake, the film footage showed that Jaytee was near the porch around 4 percent of the time in general, while when Pam was on her way home Jaytee was by the porch about 55 percent of the time—a massive difference!

If Sheldrake has interpreted the dog's movements correctly such a difference in percentage would be a stark indicator that Jaytee actually had true perceptions—true extrasensory perceptions—of when Pam would be coming home. Admittedly, Pam's parents and sister were in the house together with Jaytee in some of the trials. But as they didn't know the time schedule they were not able to divulge Pam's homecoming to the dog via subtle signals such as excitement, restlessness, etc. Unless, of course, *they themselves* telepathically perceived Pam's arrival!

However, the well-known skeptic Richard Wiseman has also conducted some experiments with the selfsame Jaytee, even borrowing and using Sheldrake's equipment. And Wiseman's results did—I almost said 'of course'—*not* come in similar to Sheldrake's. Hence Wiseman has cast aspersions on Sheldrake's conclusions and suggested that he may have interpreted the dog's behavior selectively—in favor of his hypothesis, that is (how close to the porch counts as 'close,' etc.). Sheldrake on his part has claimed that Wiseman's factual basis is too weak (as far as I have ascertained Wiseman ran just four filmed trials with Jaytee whereas Sheldrake ran a hundred). And in addition, Sheldrake claims that Wiseman, both in writing and on TV, has presented 'alternative facts,' in the Conwayan sense (willful misrepresentations of the truth). In some of Wiseman's trials Jaytee, so it would seem, did not do all that bad. But, according to Sheldrake, Wiseman has not been willing to admit this.

Sheldrake, who exudes tweedy old-style etiquette and high-table bonhomie, has said that he perceives Wiseman's behavior to be 'completely outrageous.' The lack of consensus between these two profiled researchers is glaring and the trust is tenuous, to put it mildly. As of today I don't know if they speak *with* or only *about* each other. On Sheldrake's website one can find a presentation of the controversy with links to the essential facts—also the alternative ones!

Telephone Telepathy

Another area where Sheldrake has been involved is 'telephone telepathy.' The experience of thinking about a friend whom you have not heard from in a long time and then, shortly after, to have a call from this same friend is, as we know, quite widespread. But perhaps such occurrences could be purely coincidental? Perhaps one has been thinking of many friends during the day but in hindsight one tends to remember only the one that (accidentally) called that afternoon? Or could it, in fact, rather be due to telepathy? This will obviously be difficult to determine under ordinary circumstances. Sheldrake was curious to figure this out, and designed a simple experiment going roughly as follows.

The conductor of the experiment has a volunteer subject make an agreement with four of his/her friends or relatives (emotional connections must be a factor). These four people are located in separate houses with access to telephones but without individual answering tones! At random times the conductor contacts one of the four friends and tells him/her to call the subject. The subject will now—before answering the call—try to guess who is calling. A research assistant who is with the subject writes down the guess, and the subject is then asked to pick up the phone to check who is actually calling. As there are four friends who may call we should—based on a normal distribution of results—expect that the subject will guess correctly one out of four times, meaning 25 percent of the cases. But what turns out, according to Sheldrake, is that the subject on average will guess correctly much more often, typically in about 40 percent of the cases!

Sheldrake has eventually had over a thousand persons participate in this experiment, which in addition has been replicated at the universities of Amsterdam and Freiburg with quite similar results. The experiment was carried out with variations giving slightly different scores, yet the results differed significantly from mere chance.

If Sheldrake's depiction really is true and faithful we'll have to consider factors other than mere coincidence. If we for the sake of argument disregard possible flawed reporting—either consciously (cheating) or unconsciously—telepathy could be a relevant explanation. Viewed from an evolutionary perspective it seems obvious that in antediluvian times—meaning before God created the mobile phone!—having such contact with kinsmen could favor survival.

The aforementioned experiment with telephone telepathy is quite easy to organize, something that is important to Sheldrake who wants lay people to actively engage in science—to become 'citizen scientists.' He has even developed an app to facilitate experiments of this kind. I haven't conducted the experiment myself (yet) but it could obviously be fun to try it out with friends and—for those who are teachers—with pupils/students.

Other Ideas

Sheldrake has also experimented with other things, including the so-called 'stare effect'—that people (might) have an ability to know when they are being stared at. And as usual he has designed experiments for people to test things out themselves. One of Sheldrake's later books is called *The Science Delusion* in the UK, in the US, *Science Set Free*. His main concern here is that much of science, as he sees it, operates with a series of tacit dogmas—e.g. that (an outdated variant of) materialism is seen as the 'obligatory' philosophy—which is obstructive to new insights. Sure enough, most natural scientists have ignored the book, but it has fared quite well with some philosophers and also in the media. It could be refreshing and expand your horizons to spend some time in the company of this persistent heretic, even if you don't swallow his every word hook, line and sinker. And Sheldrake should, in fact, be completely happy with that. In a debate with the well-known skeptical psychologist David Marks he stated:

> *Like Marks, I am a sceptic but of a different kind. His scepticism is directed towards anything he regards as 'paranormal,' taking as normal that which lies within the limits of current scientific understanding. My scepticism is directed towards the assumption that we know enough to proclaim what is possible and what is not.*

Continue Blogging With a New Computer When the Old One Breaks?

It is not more surprising to be born twice than once; every-thing in nature is resurrection.

~ Voltaire

Historical Perspectives and Early Research on Reincarnation

As many readers will probably know the idea of some form of reincarnation—'transmigration of souls'—is prevalent in various parts of the world; both in Hindu and Buddhist traditions, and also with several peoples native to Africa, America and Australia. It is less well known that such ideas were by no means introduced to the West by the 1960s counterculture, but that they, in fact, have a long tradition in European history. Just to give an indication: notions of rein-carnation are found in the teachings of Greek philosophers such as Pythagoras, Plato (in some works) and Plotinus; in some of the early Christian churches; in Jewish esotericism (Kabbalah); in Sufism, the Islamic mysticism; with Gallic druids (Getafix in Asterix); in the occult philosophy of the Italian Renaissance; in the teachings of the Freemasons; with some of the French Enlightenment philosophers, the German Romantics and the American Transcendentalists.

The official religious European expectation regard-ing life after death as we know has been that Heaven or, alternatively, a less pleasant place (or even total annihilation) is the next station. Whereas diverse materialist secularist philosophies espouse the idea that the end of the body is the end of everything. If the computer is broken then it is 'Game over—no replay.' There will be no more gaming or blogging after the processor has said good night! But, as mentioned above, the notion of reincarnation flows as an ever-present undercurrent in the Western history of ideas and diverse New Age movements have ensured that this idea has become common property. Surveys indicate that we are not far from the truth if we estimate that approximately 20–25 percent of Westerners believe in reincarnation in one form or another. And they do so unashamedly and with broad smiles, right in the face of both skeptics and priests, who for their part are pulling their hair out over such naivety and/ or heresy.

Reincarnation has thus become established as an important modern symbol—perhaps *the most* important modern symbol—of *transcendence*; that our being exceeds the seemingly unfair and sad limitations of having only one life at our disposal. And perhaps reincarnation to some degree might provide a plausible answer to the world's injustices? For some (but by no means all) variants of this idea include the belief that one's life is part of a larger accounting governed by an ethical natural law—the law of *karma*, as it is often referred to in the East. Personally, I first heard about reincarnation when reading that the double murderer Gary Gilmore, executed in 1977, had said that reincarnation is the only way there could be some justice in the world.

But—longing for transcendence or justice does not mean that it will be provided; being hungry does not mean that there is food in the fridge. So—could there be other reasons to believe in reincarnation beyond the comfort this might give with respect to our desire to continue living and our yearning for justice? Or—in some cases—our desire to be Alexander the Great, heading victorious Macedonian armies on spectacular campaigns in the Near East? Or to be Cleopatra sailing lazily down the Nile, surrounded by servants waving their fans of palms, all the while the eye of Ra the sun god is glowing dazzlingly in the sky above the Pyramids of Giza?

The literature on reincarnation is enormous, as are the variations in quality. Beyond stories passed on by traditions and gurus some anthropologists, psychiatrists and psychologists have related astonishing and apparently well-documented stories that seemingly are indicative of people having lived past lives. A famous case is published in the book *The Cathars and Reincarnation: The Record of a Past Life in Thirteenth-Century France* (1970) by the—up to that point—well-respected English psychiatrist Arthur Guirdham. He describes the case of 'Mrs Smith,' a woman who presumably was fully sane, but who for years had suffered from powerful nightmares involving burnings, murders and massacres. In addition, her dreams would provide accompanying historical depictions, including information about medieval costumes, rituals, strange vernaculars and songs.

Guirdham, who was unable to find a plausible psychiatric explanation for all this weirdness, but who was interested in spiritual perspectives on life, eventually consulted a historian, a certain Professor Nellie at the University of Toulouse. Nellie informed Guirdham that Mrs Smith's accounts were astoundingly descriptive of the life and times of the Cathars. The Cathars—'the pure ones'—were members of a medieval Gnostic-Christian sect in France who in the 13th century were massacred several times by armies of crusaders initiated by Pope Innocent III (!) and the Inquisition. Some of the information imparted by Mrs Smith was apparently not publicly known at the time. This, if true, is of course highly interesting with respect to our theory of a Mental Internet... The life of the Cathars has been admirably described in the book *Montaillou* (1975) by the French historian Emmanuel Le Roy Ladurie.

Guirdham was a prolific and versatile writer who published novels as well as books on spirituality and psychology; he has also contributed to a textbook on psychiatry. Over the years he may possibly have taken the Cathar thing a bit too far—but then, who am I to say?—as he eventually came to believe that not only Mrs Smith but a large group of Cathars had reincarnated in the region around Bath, England where he lived.

The quite famous stories collected by the Jewish rabbi Yonassan Gershom, can be found in *Beyond the Ashes: Cases of Reincarnation from the Holocaust* (1992), and *From Ashes to Healing: Mystical Encounters with the Holocaust* (1996). During the 1990s Gershom experienced, to his surprise, various people presenting him with powerful stories of what appeared to be their former lives in Europe during the Holocaust. Like Mrs Smith some of Gershom's subjects would reveal specifics—say, about the appearance of objects in a concentration camp—that they, so it seemed, could hardly have learned of in a regular way. Interestingly enough, some of these reincarnation/'reincarnation' stories were disclosed to Gershom by people with no known Jewish ancestry.

Ian Stevenson: Reincarnation, Again, and Again and Again...

The one who above all others is associated with research on 'the transmigration of souls' is the Canadian psychiatrist Professor Ian Stevenson (1918–2007). He devoted over 40 years of work probing the mysteries of reincarnation! Interestingly enough, he was no sectarian but an utmost sober and 'boring' researcher. Stevenson published in peer-reviewed journals both before and after he chose to sail into the dangerous waters of reincarnation research, thus challenging the 'emperor's wrath'—risking the lack of academic respect, support and position, as we saw in chapters 3 and 4.

One of the reasons that Stevenson went down this particular lane was that some patients exhibited neuroses that, as he saw it, couldn't reasonably be ascribed either to trauma or to genetics. Working from his base at the University of Virginia, where he was director of the Division of Personality Studies, Stevenson collected and examined about 3,000 (three thousand!) cases where children seemingly had remembered past lives. These kids described and named specific things such as past-life domiciles, past-life spouses, past-life children, past-life occupations, etc. It was possible to check many stories against public records, registers, etc., and several of them proved, according to Stevenson, astoundingly correct.

It is important to be aware of two things: Many of the people Stevenson examined were children between the ages of three and seven. And substantial parts of his research took place before the creation of the internet (the *physical* internet, mind you!). Although the parents could have given the children this or that piece of information there seemed to be little chance that regular channels (TV, movies, books, etc.) could have provided such detailed information as the children were sometimes able to deliver. For example, the case of Suzanne Ghanem.

She was a Lebanese girl from Beirut who, when just 16 months old, time and again had picked up the phone trying to contact a certain Leila. Around the age of two Suzanne had started claiming she used to live in another and bigger house, and that she was Hanan Mansour, a recently deceased woman. A person who happened to be acquainted both with the Ghanem family and the Mansour family recognized the names Suzanne had mentioned, and arranged for the two families—who did not know of each other—to meet. What turned out was, among other things, that the recently deceased Hanan Mansour had tried to call her daughter Leila from the hospital where she had died. There are of course lots of Leilas and Hanans in Lebanon, both dead and alive. But, at first glance Suzanne was, so it seemed, able to identify multiple persons depicted in the Mansour family's photos; she could name no fewer than 13 of its members! Furthermore, Suzanne would relate events only known to the close family. For example, she seemingly recounted parts of a speech that had been made at the funeral of Hanan's brother! And there were lots of other oddities as well.

Reception of Stevenson's Work

Stevenson's first book, *Twenty Cases Suggestive of Reincarnation*, was released in 1966, and it has become a bestseller as well as a point of reference within the field. Stevenson went on to publish 13 more books with the same theme, the last being *European Cases of the Reincarnation Type* (2003). In addition Stevenson wrote around 300 related articles.

For sure, the academic communities had for the most part no problems in curbing their enthusiasm, but in 1975 one of Stevenson's books actually got an appreciative review in the *Journal of the American Medical Association*. The journal's book review editor, Dr Lester Snow King, a pathologist and prolific author on medical history, wrote that

> *in regard to reincarnation he [Stevenson] has pains-takingly and unemotionally collected a detailed series of cases from India, cases in which the evidence is difficult to explain on any other grounds. He presents his corpus of evidence in an interesting way, providing careful detail, and discussing the procedures that he used in attempting to verify the assertions. He provides a critical analysis of the strong and the weak points.*

In 1977, the peer-reviewed *Journal of Nervous and Mental Disease* devoted nearly their entire September issue to presenting Stevenson's work. The editor, psychiatrist Eugene Brody, justified publishing this type of research—which normally would have been regarded as unscientific—with reference to the 'scientific and personal credibility of the authors, the legitimacy of their research methods, and the conformity of their reasoning to the usual canons of rational thought.'

One of the contributors was the well-known psychiatrist, psychoanalyst, sex therapist and educator Dr Harold Lief. He was both a colleague and friend of Stevenson's but of a more skeptical disposition. Lief says: 'In writing this commentary, I find myself in an awkward position. I am far from being a convert to a belief in parapsychological phenomena during this incarnation, let alone a believer in the survival of the soul or spirit [...].'

Still, he had the greatest respect for Stevenson's work and confesses: 'I am a "true believer" in his methods of investigation.' Some years earlier Lief had conducted 'normal' psychological fieldwork with Stevenson, and about this cooperative effort he recalls, 'I was able to observe, first-hand, his thoroughness in assembling the data on which we based our report, and to recognize the clarity of his thinking as we explored the various hypotheses we were testing in a real life situation.' Lief also made an often-cited remark about Stevenson: 'Either he is making a colossal mistake, or he will be known [...] as "the Galileo of the twentieth century."'

One person who wanted to find out which of these two options was most likely—Dr S. making a colossal mistake, or being a new Galileo—was Tom Shroder, a prize-winning journalist who, among other things, has worked as an editor at the *Washington Post*. In 2010 Shroder was awarded the coveted Pulitzer Prize. In the late 1990s Stevenson, after having been 'courted' for a long time, allowed Shroder to accompany him on his travels and to check on how he collected all his stunning data. Schroder soon found that Stevenson was very thorough; he would often make multiple return visits to his subjects and sometimes question more than 20 witnesses for just a single case. Shroder began the journey as an interested skeptic but after some months he had become convinced that Stevenson's work was to be trusted—that he was not a victim either of lying children or attention-seeking parents, and that his interviews were neutral and did not implant 'false memories,' etc. Shroder, the award-winning journalist, would certainly know a thing or two about interviewing...

In 1999 Shroder published the book *Old Souls: The Scientific Search for Proof of Past Lives,* in which he relates his experiences and reflections from the journey. Many interesting cases are presented; Shroder has dedicated a full chapter to the story of Suzanne Ghanem, which I briefly mentioned above. *Old Souls* was well received and got favorable reviews, e.g. in the journal of New York University School of Medicine, Professor Jack Coulehan wrote:

> *As a participant observer, Shroder tells a sympathetic, yet questioning, story of Stevenson's investigation (or follow up) of a few recent cases. In the process, he presents a compelling portrait of the maverick 80-year-old psychiatrist. [...] The data is very impressive. Stevenson's work has nothing to do with (and long antedates) the deluge of remembered lives that constitutes one of the least endearing aspects of New Age culture.*

Shroder admits that for his own part the accumulation of cases, across cultures and circumstances—all with diverse, independent witnesses who in a down-to-earth way confirmed 'unimaginable' things—eventually wore away his 'skeptical prejudices.' Perhaps it is a bit sacrilegious to say but if one is interested in Stevenson's work it will probably be more rewarding to read, at least to start with, Shroder's fluently written text rather than Stevenson's own, more academic, writings.

Reincarnation and Birthmarks

Okay—maybe some of these kids actually presented information not available to them in a normal way. But does this mean that reincarnation has to be the answer? Based on our model all the necessary information about these other lives could have been telepathically downloaded from the Mental Cloud. This would be parallel to a person visiting YouTube and watching a documentary about Elvis Presley. Afterwards the person would be able to present us with a lot of details about Elvis' life. But knowledge of these facts would certainly not turn this person into a reincarnation of Elvis!

Stevenson was familiar with this train of thought, and he, in fact, thought it to be a *likely* explanation. But what made him think that reincarnation was *the most likely* explanation was that quite a few of the children had very unusual birthmarks and deformities that matched well with the violent deaths the children told of having experienced in their former lives. There was a Mexican boy who was born with a scar-like mark in the midriff area and who told a story of having been killed about 30 years earlier by a gunshot to the diaphragm. And there was a Thai child who was born with a marked and rare skin lesion at the back of the head and who claimed to remember having been killed with a blow on the head from a heavy knife. And there was a Turkish boy who was born with a starkly deformed ear claiming to have been shot in the head at pointblank from the side. And... and...and...

But maybe the children (fanciful creatures as they are) or their parents (honor-defending creatures as they may be) had constructed these stories to embellish the—unwanted and perhaps even shameful—marks? This seems very reasonable. However, in a dozen cases Stevenson, in addition to the stories and birthmarks, also found specific evidence— autopsy reports and forensic photographs—that supported the children's stories. The typical case would be something like this: A child between three- and six-years-old would tell about being another person with such-and-such a name who had lived in such-and-such a town and had died in such-and-such a way. When Stevenson then visited the hospital in the town concerned he would on a number of occasions find that they had in fact a person, a corpse, 'on file' matching the child's descriptions of both the biography and cause of death.

Stevenson has submitted much of the documentation concerning these somewhat eerie cases in a work of over 2,000 (!) pages called *Reincarnation and Biology: A Contribution to the Etiology of Birthmarks and Birth Defects*. Parts of the material can be found in an abridged version called *Where Reincarnation and Biology Intersect*.

I must admit that the forensic photos have made a lasting impression on me; with my own eyes I could see the dead bodies with serious injuries fitting surprisingly well with the children's stories about the death of the people they had allegedly been. How on earth could this be possible? Could it be a plot with cleverly fabricated stories, reports and photographs? Had perhaps publicity-obsessed parents—or even Stevenson himself—manipulated or bribed staff members at diverse hospitals into faking the records? Or could it instead be possible that...?

According to Stevenson's intellectual heir, the psychiatrist Dr Jim Tucker, birthmarks or deformations resembling the injuries of the person whose life the child recalls are present in roughly 20 percent of the reincarnation cases. These are, as could be expected, often cases where the deceased person has suffered a markedly violent death—murder, car crash, etc.

Objections

Most of Stevenson's colleagues, even those who had no faith in his project, regarded him to be utterly serious and honest. But some believed, of course, that he was probably a tad too eager to believe in the stories he was told. What critics often hold against Stevenson is that he hasn't provided a proper explanation for *how* reincarnation may be possible; are we to believe that our minds can be popped in and out of bodies like batteries in a flashlight? That our consciousness is a kind of spiritual 'lump' which can jump into another body, sporting its memories and defects? Or how should we imagine this? Providing an exhaustive explanation for a mystery of this magnitude would probably have been awarded multiple Nobel Prizes, and is probably much too much to demand from a pioneer researcher. As mentioned earlier: Peculiar observations and phenomena will often precede—sometimes by centuries or even by millennia—the theories that explain them (e.g. comets, solar eclipses, bird migrations, hereditary traits, etc.).

Another objection to Stevenson's research is that to a large extent it relies on field interviews and not on 'hard' facts. This, of course, makes the information more susceptible to error than is the case with information collected in a lab. But, as we saw in chapter 7, such an objection is equally valid (or invalid) for other research as well; anthropologists, ethnographers and folklorists, for instance, will often rely heavily on field interviews. And as we heard, the award-winning journalist Tom Shroder espoused Stevenson's approach and thought his data difficult to explain within the 'sanctioned' Western horizon of understanding (i.e. explaining the children's stories as fantasy and/or fraud). Stevenson himself defended his scientific approach as follows:

> *Modern psychologists imitated physicists by only being interested in what happened in a lab, not in things like love and death, and parapsychologists imitated psychologists. That is, you have tight control of conditions. But it seems to me that it's far better to be 90 percent certain of something important than 100 percent certain of something that is trivial.*

And 'trivial' is certainly not what comes to mind when taking a look at Stevenson's research! The high-profiled atheist and skeptic Sam Harris, author of *The End of Faith*, is one of those who has been intrigued, and on one occasion he stated that 'either he [Stevenson] is a victim of truly elaborate fraud, or something interesting is going on.' Harris has later mitigated his statement somewhat, but still...

Stevenson reputedly never said that he 'believed' in reincarnation; rather he said that if a person has a wish to believe in reincarnation there would, from a scientific point of view, be nothing against it. There are obviously many who will disagree with him but Stevenson was, however, fine with that, and said that his own opinions were not what mattered but that one was willing to evaluate the evidence. He also stated: 'There are, as I tried to show, various alternative explanations of the data, some of which are also "likely." I do believe, however, that survival is the "most likely" interpretation.'

Taking Over the Baton

One person who became fascinated by Stevenson's research and who today manages his archives is Dr Jim Tucker, psychiatrist and director of the Child and Family Psychiatry Outpatient Clinic at the University of Virginia. Tucker has written extensively on reincarnation stories; films have been made based on his work, and he has also become a household name with the media and with the stars; he has appeared on *Larry King Live*, and in 2019 he was interviewed by John Cleese of Monty Python. Tucker has focused his work on American children. I would guess this is mainly for practical reasons, but likely it is also because a frequent criticism of research of this kind is that much of it has been conducted in countries where a belief in reincarnation is widespread, for example India. One could therefore suspect that the children's stories merely reflected the culture's common belief. Tucker's research effectively counters this assessment, as it makes clear that such stories are also plentiful in the US (and other Western countries). Tucker presents some newer cases in the book *Return to Life: Extraordinary Cases of Children Who Remember Past Lives*.

Stevenson was, of course, aware of this objection—that the children's stories might just reflect common belief. But as he had also found such stories in cultures neutral or even negative to reincarnation he thought that 'common belief' didn't quite cut it as an explanation. Just as a culture open to reincarnation may sometimes elicit false stories (thus causing 'over-reporting'), it is equally true that an environment negative to reincarnation—as e.g. most materialist and Christian milieux—will often suppress such tales (thus causing 'under-reporting'). Stevenson thought this could be the reason that relatively fewer cases are reported from Western countries.

The iconic astrophysicist and skeptic Carl Sagan has stated in his book *The Demon-Haunted World* that one of parapsychology's claims that merits study is the assertion that 'young children sometimes report the details of a previous life, which upon checking turn out to be accurate and which they could not have known about in any other way than reincarnation.' Since the one and only Carl Sagan, a man who hardly could be called naive, thought this particular subject worthy of study, perhaps we ought not put it to rest so easily. And who knows: Maybe we will be able to continue the blog with a new computer when the old one eventually breaks?

The Grand Narrative: Worlds are Fading, the Field is Upgrading—a Basis for Cosmic Optimism?

Don't urge me, friend, to solve these dark equations;
I'd rather ask; my job's not explanations.

~ Henrik Ibsen, from 'A Rhyme-Letter' (1875)

The full meaning of life, the collective meaning of all hu-
man desires, is fundamentally a mystery beyond our grasp.
As a young man, I chafed at this state of affairs. But by
now I have made peace with it. I even feel a certain honor
to be associated with such a mystery.

~ Eugene Wigner

The Myths We Live By

The atheist philosopher Bertrand Russell (1872–1970) was a tireless advocate for truth, human dignity and world peace. In this commitment, he seems to have found a deep fulfillment, albeit his views on the big picture rather sound like the pinnacle of pessimism. In the small masterpiece *A Free Man's Worship* he says we have to face that:

> *all the labors of the ages, all the devotion, all the inspi-*
> *ration, all the noonday brightness of human genius, are*

destined to extinction in the vast death of the solar sys-
tem, and that the whole temple of Man's achievement
must inevitably be buried beneath the debris of a uni-
verse in ruins—all these things, if not quite beyond dis-
pute, are yet so nearly certain, that no philosophy which
rejects them can hope to stand.

In devotion to Truth, Goodness and Beauty—'the Platonic trinity'—many experience a deep meaning even within the, let's say, gloomy scenario that Russell sketches. Others feel, however, that without a God (theism), and/or spiritual beings such as spirits and angels (spiritualism) and the associated parallel dimensions, it is difficult to find a 'grand narrative,' a larger, encompassing story that may provide us with a credible meaning in life. While still others feel that such entities and dimensions, regardless of whether they exist or not, are in any case secondary to the Cosmos itself—divine, eternal and elevated, ever-becoming conscious of itself through its creations and creatures, continuously unfolding its own inherent meaning (pantheism).

Seemingly, most people have, consciously or unconsciously, adapted a myth, a 'grand narrative'—some story that circumscribes their life and gives meaning to their existence. Such stories may neither be verified nor verifiable, but they still provide the frame for Life as a whole. For example, the different religions and philosophical *credos*—as the belief in Mankind, the belief in Progress and the belief in Reason—as well as the various nationalisms, can all be seen as examples of such 'grand narratives,' stories to live by.

Thinking Big with Ervin Laszlo

The highly versatile Hungarian systems and environmental philosopher Ervin Laszlo (b. 1932), whose model of consciousness we discussed briefly in chapter 6, has launched what we could call a 'meta narrative,' a great-grand story, that seemingly has ample space for the 'grand narratives' of both atheists, theists, spiritualists, pantheists and agnostics. We are often recommended to 'think big,' and Laszlo's story is nothing if not big: you almost inevitably become giddy as he does not confine his storyline to just one universe. Rather, Laszlo draws an infinitely large circle around the whole Cosmos and postulates a *Metaverse*—an unending chain of universes, one after another, separated by occasional 'Big Bangs' in between.

Laszlo has described his vision as 'imaginative but not imaginary.' Here we are dealing with a cosmological story, not empirical research. Thus it should not be evaluated by the same criteria for verification and falsification as, say, Ian Stevenson's research on reincarnation discussed earlier in the chapter. It is not necessary that such stories are *provable*; it is sufficient if they are *probable*. This apparent limitation needs not be at all disqualifying. In his 1931 book *Cosmic Religion and Other Opinions and Aphorisms*, Einstein says: 'Imagination is more important than knowledge. For knowledge is limited, whereas imagination embraces the entire world, stimulating progress, giving birth to evolution.'

The reader may perhaps remember from chapter 6 that an important concept for Laszlo is *akasha*; which refers to *ether* in Sanskrit. It may further denote space, sky and essence, whereas the original meaning is 'radiation' or 'brilliance'—indeed a rich and complex concept! And, as mentioned, Laszlo's onus is on akasha as an eternal hotline between all and everything, an all-encompassing field of information and memory. Hence in our terminology akasha is some sort of cosmic Mental Internet. In his book *Science and the Akashic Field: An Integral Theory of Everything* Laszlo elaborates on some of his thoughts about, well, about everything, including akasha:

> *The informed universe is a universe where the A-field [the akashic field] is a real and significant element. Thanks to this field, this universe is of mind-boggling coherence. All that happens in one place happens also in other places; all that happened at one time happens also at all times after that. Nothing is 'local', limited to where and when it is happening. All things are global, indeed cosmic, for the memory of all things extends to all places and all times.*

But what does this have to do with our own, apparently small, lives? Or with psi? Well, if all our experiences—everything that we have felt and thought, the values we have fought for, our love, our hopes and our dreams, our discoveries, our art and our science, the increased consciousness we have contributed to—if all this information and also much more (the experiences of animals, all nature's genetic codes, the crystalline structures, etc.) is 'uploaded' and integrated in the world's own inherent memory, that could be really good news. Because when an old universe dies and a new one arises, this new universe will—because the akasha endures—have available all the lessons learned from previous universes. Nothing is lost, all files are transferred; the contributions we have made to progress, a better world and increased consciousness, no matter how small they may be, will be there for the benefit of all future universes!

And as for the role of psi? In *Science and the Akashic Field* Laszlo also discusses and endorses various types of paranormal phenomena. For example he describes many, apparently highly successful, experiments with telepathy or—under another name—'transpersonal communication.' Laszlo thinks transpersonal communication presents an opportunity to both scientifically detect and to personally experience 'the interconnectedness of all things.' And that the latter— the possibility to personally experience this interconnectedness—is not just available for a few elect, for specially gifted, for prophets or psychics, but for nearly everybody.

> *Identical twins are only the top of the tree of bonded pairs. Some form of telepathy has been observed among all people who share a deep bond, such as mothers and children, lovers, long-term couples, close friends. In these cases all but the most conservative psychologists are forced to recognize the existence of some transpersonal contact. But only exceptionally broad-minded psychologists admit that transpersonal contact includes the ability to transmit thoughts and images, and that it is given to many and perhaps all people. [...] It appears that almost all people possess 'paranormal' abilities.*

Hence such phenomena may function as a guarantee for the eternal and intimate liaison between fellow human beings and between Humankind and the Mystery. Laszlo has even suggested that, given that there are conscious beings in other places in the universe—which its size definitely allows for and perhaps even makes an odds-on possibility—the akashic field would likely make it possible for us to telepathically contact and exchange information with them!

Laszlo is clearly a thinker off the Western beaten track, but he cannot be dismissed as a lightweight. A short CV: He has been employed at Princeton and Yale, and is a honorary doctor at several universities; he has been a member of the prestigious Club of Rome, and has himself started the Club of Budapest, another think tank boasting a number of political and cultural celebrities. Laszlo has conducted studies for the UN, and published more than 70 books and hundreds of articles. In his youth, he was a classical pianist, touring the world and making a number of recordings. Furthermore, Laszlo has engaged in peace work with the Indian guru-philosopher Sri Sri Ravi Shankar. Like several of the thinkers we have met earlier in the book, Laszlo has also been digging deep into the treasure trove of Indian philosophy. Perhaps there is some truth to the words of the German-Swiss novelist and sage Hermann Hesse when he paradoxically says, 'the oldest texts are always the most contemporary.'

So—maybe Laszlo's perspectives could enhance the ambiance, standing as a rebuke to pessimism, giving us a brighter outlook on the big picture. Both his highlighting of the interconnectedness of all things manifested via psi, and his exciting thought that even our smallest contributions to increased consciousness and human evolution will never be lost and therefore will never be in vain—both these closely related perspectives might perhaps impart a zest to our sometimes joyful, sometimes painful, and sometimes drab grey existence. In short: perhaps Laszlo's notion of *akasha* could form the basis for a cosmic optimism?

Farewell and Blessings

I want to thank the readers so much for being willing to sign up with the suggested thought experiment: that our 'consciousnesses' can be seen as some sort of Mental Internet. And also for being my travel companions on this journey in the borderland of consciousness! Perhaps our simple model has enabled us to shed some light on phenomena that otherwise would seem incomprehensible? And, if nothing else, hopefully our playing around with this thought has brought attention to the fact that no one—neither lay nor learned—knows what consciousness is. And moreover, that the prevailing notion of consciousness—that it is just 'brain urine,' the product of chemical processes in our heads—is not satisfactory, insofar as many phenomena seem difficult, even impossible, to explain within this horizon. So maybe it is due time to seriously consider different models? In the course of the chapters we have looked at some options that could represent steps toward a model with greater explanatory power.

As mentioned above, Einstein considered imagination to be more important than knowledge. He once elaborated on this to his good friend, the Danish mathematician and humorist Piet Hein, and said: 'Knowledge often assumes too narrow a form, and imagination is often right in thinking that there is something more, and that everything could be completely different.' It is stimulating for the imagination to meet with people who do not march in step and who dare to think thoughts other than just the correct ones (yawn!) sanctioned by consensus and various edicts. When people like the double Nobel laureate Marie Curie out of serious interest repeatedly participated in spiritualist séances, and the physics genius Wolfgang Pauli found it rewarding to exchange ideas with the 'occult mud-wrestler' C.G. Jung for over 20 years, I believe *we* should neither fear being 'tainted by association'—mingling with the scientific *Einzelgänger,* the lone wolves, that we have become acquainted with: archaeologists, secret agents, anthropologists, occultists, philosophers, physicists, consciousness researchers, neuroscientists, psychiatrists and psychologists.

This colorful assembly comprises, as has been made clear, highly skilled professionals. Perhaps encountering these mavericks, their research and their stories, might cause us to revise a couple of our cherished but outworn opinions? This, in fact, could be a most healthy thing to do: using the trope of clothing the Norwegian novelist Alexander Kielland once, with an air of noble virtue, remarked: 'It is rather unhygienic not to change opinion once in a while.'

Our journey into the borderland of consciousness has also brought us face to face with numerous sobriety-twisting episodes; some will perhaps take these to be miracles whereas others will certainly see them as chimeras or bluff. We, however, have suggested that they might be expressions of secret powers, unconsciously and discreetly used every day, without thought and without drama, but which sometimes—especially in emergency situations—may manifest in astonishing ways. And now, toward the close of the book, we have also seen examples that such phenomena might be more than just curiosities, and that they could conceivably serve us in many ways—in making decisions, in our relations to animals and relatives (sometimes they are not identical...), in our quest for personal growth, and in relating to *the* big questions.

Although these phenomena at first glance may seem puzzling, when looking closer they are probably not any stranger than anything else in this, our mystical, mystical world—such as the paranormal phenomenon that my body consists of the same chemical substances found in the flowerbed outside my window, yet having completely different properties, so that by a psychokinetic miracle I can conduct its physical movements with my non-physical will. Perhaps the psi phenomena, then, might be seen as a symbol of an essential feature of our world: that everything is intimately interrelated but in ways that we do not fully grasp?

And even stranger than how the world *works*, is the incomprehensible fact that it *is*. As once said by a girl in primary school (she later became my mother): 'Why does *something* exist—why not *nothing, nothing, nothing*?' There is hardly a more profound question, and often an old philosopher or a young child is needed to truly pose it. Nor is the answer obvious; to some degree we'll probably have to content ourselves by being aware *that* the world is, but without forgetting to wonder. The great sociologist Max Weber believed that our time is characterized by an *Entzauberung der Welt*, a de-enchantment of the world. 'Instrumental rationality' has for many reduced the world to an object for exploitation—they think trees are valuable just for making paper, and animals just for making food. For people of this thinking, the world has become trivial.

And if Magic disappears then *Meaning* will also easily disappear. We are usually not able to give full value to ourselves and our fellow humans, to our four-legged, winged and otherwise equipped friends, to nature, yes, to the entire wide world, unless the grey veil of triviality is drawn aside. And perhaps the psi phenomena, regardless of how they are explained, can help us achieve this?

And perhaps we might surmise, as the transpersonal thinkers often suggest, that the psi phenomena can form part of an evolution toward an extended and expanded consciousness—a Consciousness that perhaps in one way or another, either individually or collectively, either in new lives or in new worlds—may transcend physical death? An exciting proposal, that is…

With these words, I thank you once more for being my fellow travelers! For me our journey has been a great pleasure, and I really hope you have enjoyed it too. So until next time: Goodbye, Jedi knights—and may the Force be with us all!

BIBLIOGRAPHY

Literature and Links

As this book is intended as a popular work and not a research project, the bibliography doesn't cover all sources. Let me mention that some quotes, and also some etymologies, can be found in different versions. So, if my rendition should differ from what the reader knows from other places, neither source need to be incorrect. Several of the main works listed are available for free download on sites such as Project Gutenberg, the Internet Archive and Google Books. I have also provided web links—listed by theme, not alphabet—to a string of relevant articles, reports and websites (let's hope they stay active!).

Introduction

Literature

Cardeña, E., Lynn S.J. & Krippner, S. (eds.). (2000) *Varieties of Anomalous Experience*. American Psychological Association Publications, Washington, DC.
Lamon, W.H. (1999) *Recollections of Abraham Lincoln 1847–1865*. University of Nebraska Press (pp. 116–117).

Links

Harris, S. http://www.samharris.org/site/full_text/response-to-controversy

Chapter I

Literature

Bond, F.B. (1989) *The Gate of Remembrance.* Time Life Education, Fairfax, VA.
McMullen, G. (1995) *One White Crow.* Hampton Roads Publishing Company, Newburyport, MA.
Schwartz, S.A. (2001) *The Secret Vaults of Time.* Hampton Roads Publishing Company, Newburyport, MA.
Schwartz, S.A. (1983) *The Alexandria Project.* Delacorte Press, NY.

Links

Bligh Bond, F. 'The Gate of Remembrance': http://www.gutenberg.org/files/48568/48568-h/48568-h.htm
Emerson, J.N. 'Intuitive Archaeology: A pragmatic Study': http://www.sacaaa.org/Phoenix3-1979-fall.pdf
Schwartz, S.A. 'The Alexandria Project' (video): https://www.youtube.com/watch?v=Q0QZTwpCAFo
Weiant, C.W. 'Parapsychology and Anthropology': http://bit.ly/125gC8A

Chapter 2

Literature

Atwater, F.H. (2001) *Captain of My Ship, Master of My Soul.* Hampton Roads Publishing Company, Newburyport, MA.
Krippner, S. (1980) *Human Possibilities: Mind Exploration in the USSR and Eastern Europe.* Anchor Press/Doubleday, NY.

Ostrander S. & Schroeder L. (1974) *Psychic Discoveries Behind the Iron Curtain.* Prentice-Hall, Englewood Cliffs, NJ.

Ryzl, M. & Kysucan, L. (2007) *Ancient Oracles.* Trafford Publishing, Bloomington, IN.

Schnabel, J. (1997) *Remote Viewers: The Secret History of America's Psychic Spies.* Dell Publishing, NY.

Smith, P. (2005) *Reading the Enemy's Mind: Inside Star Gate, America's Psychic Espionage Program.* Tor/Forge, NY.

Targ, R., & Puthof, H. (1977) *Mind-Reach.* Dell Publishing, NY.

Targ, R., Tart, C. & Puthof, H. (2002) *Mind at Large.* Hampton Roads Publishing Company, Newburyport, MA.

Targ, R. (2012) *The Reality of ESP: A Physicist's Proof of Psychic Abilities.* Quest Books, Wheaton, IL.

Links

Stargate's report on the Taurus experiment, part 1: http://www.remoteviewed.com/blogdocs/taurus1.pdf

Stargate's report on the Taurus experiment, part 2: http://www.remoteviewed.com/blogdocs/taurus2.pdf

Stargate leader Edwin C. May, interviewed by Terje Toftenes, October 2017: https://vimeo.com/239626460 (Use password Stargate)

Utts, J. (report on Stargate): http://www.ics.uci.edu/~jutts/air

Hyman, R. (report on Stargate): https://www.ics.uci.edu/~jutts/hyman.html

Smith, P. (DIY remote viewing): https://www.shift.is/2019/02/how-to-do-a-simple-remote-viewing-session/

Smith, P. *Coordinate Remote Viewing Training Manual* (used by Stargate): http://www.remoteviewed.com/files/CRV%20manual%20full.pdf

Schwartz, S.A. (1977): 'Two Application-Oriented Experiments Employing a Submarine Involving a Novel Remote Viewing Protocol, One Testing the Elf Hypothesis': https://bit.ly/3bJxj4s

Chapter 3

Literature

Bäckman, L. (1982) 'The Noaid and his Ecstasy—a Contribution to the Discussion,' in Holm, N.G. (ed.). *Religious Ecstasy*. Almquist & Wiksell International, Stockholm, Sweden.

Connor, N. & Keeney, B. (2008) *Shamans of the World: Extraordinary First-Person Accounts of Healings, Mysteries, and Miracles*. Sounds True, Louisville, CO.

Dodds, E.R. (2004) *The Greeks and the Irrational*. University of California Press.

Elkin, A.P. (1994). *Aboriginal Men of High Degree: Initiation and Sorcery in the World's Oldest Tradition*, University of Queensland Press.

Flower, M. (2009) *The Seer in Ancient Greece*. University of California Press.

Fyhn, H. (2001) *Shaman in the World of Experience*. Norwegian University of Science and Technology, Trondheim.

Harner, M. (1980) *The Way of the Shaman*. Harper & Row, NY.

Keeney, B. (2004) *Bushman Shaman: Awakening the Spirit through Ecstatic Dance*. Destiny Books, Rochester, VT.

Long, J.K. (1977) *Extrasensory Ecology: Parapsychology and Anthropology*. The Scarecrow Press, Metuchen, NJ. 1977.

Markides, K. (1989) *The Magus of Strovolos: The Extraordinary World of a Spiritual Healer*. Penguin Books, NY.

Storm, L. (ed.) (2008) *Synchronicity: Multiple Perspectives on Meaningful Coincidence.* Pari Publishing, Italy.

Swanton, J.R. (1953) *Superstition—but Whose?* Swanton, Newton, MA.

Young, D.E. & Goulet, J.-G. (1994) *Being Changed by Cross-cultural Encounters: The Anthropology of Extraordinary Experience.* Broadview Press, Peterborough, ON, Canada.

Links

Procopius. *The Secret History of the Court of Justinian*: http://www.gutenberg.org/cache/epub/12916/pg12916-images.html

Darwin, C. (Diary from the Voyage of the Beagle): http://bit.ly/16tTSVW

Freuchen, P. *Book of the Eskimos*: http://bit.ly/ZUfx22

Ballo, O.G. Interview, VG 29.1.2009: http://bit.ly/12tEcfS

Weiant, C.W. 'Parapsychology and anthropology': http://goo.gl/ntH2N

Schwartz, S.A. 'Boulders in the Stream: The Lineage and Founding of the Society for the Anthropology of Consciousness': http://www.stephanaschwartz.com/wp-content/uploads/2010/02/Boulders-in-the-stream-SA.pdf?x23564

Laughlin, C. 'Transpersonal Anthropology Then and Now': https://drakenberg.weebly.com/irdc-blog/transpersonal-anthropology-then-now

The Cyprus Weekly, September 1–7, 1995 (obituary for Daskalos): http://www.researchersoftruth.org/daskalos_researchers_of_truth_system-htm/obituary

Combs, A., & Krippner, S. 'Collective Consciousness and The Social Brain': http://noosphere.global-mind.org/papers/docs/others/Collective.Consciousness.Brain_08.doc

Turner, E. 'The Reality of Spirits': http://www.shamanism. org/articles/article02.html
Hunter, Jack. http://psi-encyclopedia.spr.ac.uk/articles/an-thropology-and-psi-research
Paranthropology: Journal of Anthropological Approaches to the Paranormal: http://paranthropologyjournal.weebly.com
The Society for the Anthropology of Consciousness (SAC): http://www.sacaaa.org/

Chapter 4

Literature

Enz, C.P. (2002) *No Time to be Brief: A Scientific Biography of Wolfgang Pauli*. Oxford University Press.
Jung, C.G. (1989) *Memories, Dreams, Reflections*. Vintage, NY.
Jung, C.G. & Pauli, W.E. (2012) *The Interpretation of Nature and the Psyche*. Ishi Press International, San Jose. CA.
Manning, M. (1987) *The Link: The Extraordinary Gifts of a Teenage Psychic*. Colin Smythe Ltd., Gerrards Cross, UK.
Peat, F.D. (2014) *Synchronicity: The Marriage of Matter and Psyche*. Pari Publishing, Italy.

Chapter 5

Literature

Bomann-Larsen, T. (2011) *Roald Amundsen—En Biografi*. Cappelen Damm, Oslo, Norway.
Dimitriadis, Dicta. (2006) *Marie-Anne Lenormand: Portrait einer berühmten Seherin*. Cascada Verlag, Munich, Germany.
Dumas, A. (2012) *The Whites and the Blues*. Ulan Press, San Bernadino, CA.

Gronow, R.H. (2010) *Celebrities of London and Paris.* Kessinger Publishing, LLC, Whitefish, MT.

Kolloen, I. (2008) *Snåsamannen—Kraften som Helbreder.* Gyldendal, Copenhagen, Denmark.

Lerum, M.-G. & Grimstvedt, G. (1988) *Synsk.* Grøndahl & Søn, Oslo, Norway.

Mayer, E.L. (2007) *Extraordinary Knowing; Science, Skepticism, and the Inexplicable Powers of the Human Mind.* Bantam Books, NY.

Puhle, A. (2005) *Mit Goethe durch die Welt der Geister.* Reichl Verlag, St Goar, Germany.

Westerlund, A.E. (1968) *Synsk—Av en Clairvoyant Kvinnes Erfaringer.* Gyldendal Norsk Forlag, Oslo, Norway.

Links

Magazin für die Literatur des Auslandes, No. 49, 23. April 1838, 'Mamsell Lenormand und der Minister von Malchus': https://goo.gl/e2kYTR

Greer, Mary K. (blog post about Mlle Lenormand): https://marykgreer.com/2008/02/12/madame-le-normand-the-most-famous-card-reader-of-all-time/

Schjelderup, H.K. 'Det Skjulte Menneske': https://goo.gl/QwXLhX

Hygen, G. 'Vardøger—Vårt Paranormale Nasjonal-fenomen': https://goo.gl/9v79RC

Hygen, G. 'Telepati—Vår Medfødte Mobiltelefon': https://goo.gl/oJM8oZ

Aall, Thomas L. 'Fra en Ukjent Verden': https://goo.gl/a1eX1U

Flekkøy, K. 'Lalm barnehage: Oversikt og vurdering av uvanlege hendingar frå 26. april til 15. juni 2010': https://bit.ly/37B9XuC

http://www.namdalsavisa.no/artikkel/2017/01/17/Sn%C3%A5samannen-tror-Trump-blir-skutt-14074784. ece

Chapter 6

Literature

Bohm, D. (2002) *Wholeness and Implicate Order.* Routledge, London, UK.

Capra, F. (2010) *The Tao of Physics: An Exploration of the Parallels Between Modern Physics and Eastern Mysticism.* Shambhala Publications, Boulder, CO.

Frackowiak, R.S.J. *et al.* (2004) *Human Brain Function.* Academic Press, Cambridge, MA.

Grof, S. (2005) *When the Impossible Happens.* Sounds True, Louisville, CO.

Johnson, G.R. (ed.) (2003) *Kant on Swedenborg.* Swedenborg Foundation Publishers, West Chester, PA.

Hasted, J. (1981) *The Metal Benders.* Routledge & Kegan Paul, London, UK.

Huxley, A. (2009) *The Doors of Perception: Heaven and Hell.* Harper Perennial Modern Classics, Harper, NY.

Huxley, A. (2009) *The Perennial Philosophy: An Interpretation of the Great Mystics, East and West.* Harper, NY.

Kaiser, D. (2011) *How the Hippies saved Physics.* W.W. Norton & Company, NY.

Kelly E.F. & Kelly E.W. (eds.) (2010) *Irreducible Mind: Toward a Psychology for the 21st Century.* Rowman & Littlefield, Lanham, MD.

Laszlo, E. (2007) *Science and The Akashic Field: An Integral Theory of Everything.* Inner Traditions, Rochester, VT.

LeShan, L. (1980) *Clairvoyant Reality.* Turnstone Press, Winnipeg, MB, Canada.

Nadeau, R. & Kafatos, M. (2001) *The Non-Local Universe: The New Physics and Matters of the Mind.* Oxford University Press.

Penrose, R., Hameroff, S., Stapp, H. & Chopra, D. (2011) *Consciousness and the Universe: Quantum Physics, Evolution,*

Brain & Mind. Cosmology Science Publishers, Cambridge, MA.

Playfair, G.L. (2014) *Twin Telepathy.* White Crow Books, Guildford, UK.

Talbot, M. (2011) *The Holographic Universe: The Revolutionary Theory of Reality.* Harper Perennial, NY.

Treffert, D.A. (2011) *Islands of Genius: The Bountiful Mind of the Autistic, Acquired, and Sudden Savant.* Jessica Kingsley Publishers, London, UK.

Yates, F.A. (2001) *The Rosicrucian Enlightenment.* Routledge, London, UK.

Yates, F.A. (1991) *Giordano Brand the Hermetic Tradition.* University of Chicago Press.

Links

Ananthaswamy, A. 'Quantum weirdness may hide an orderly reality after all.' (Test of David Bohm's theory, conducted by Steinberg *et al.*) *New Scientist*, February 6, 2016: https://www.newscientist.com/article/2078251-quantum-weirdness-may-hide-an-orderly-reality-after-all/

Bohm, D. 'Soma-Significance: A New Notion of the Relationship Between the Physical and the Mental': https://pdfs.semanticscholar.org/9e6d/2cd741429ebfccbb8d-031c808732af8109c0.pdf

Hameroff, S. & Mishlove, J. Conversations 1–6 on the Orch-Or model of consciousness: https://goo.gl/aJJFuS

Dagbladet, article about the Snåsa Man (healer, psychic): http://goo.gl/LY8zp

Chapter 7

Literature

Hansen, George. P. (2001) *The Trickster and the Paranormal*. Xlibris, Bloomington, IN.

Krippner, S. & Friedman, H.L. (eds.) (2010) *Debating Psychic Experience; Human Potential or Human Illusion?* Praeger, Santa Barbara, CA.

Mayer, E.L. (2007) *Extraordinary Knowing: Science, Skepticism, and The Inexplicable Powers of the Human Mind*. Bantam Books, NY.

Phillips, P.R. (2016) *Companion to the Project Alpha Papers*. (Kindle) Pari Publishing, Italy.

Radin, D. (2009) *The Noetic Universe: The Scientific Evidence for Psychic Phenomena*. Corgi, London, UK.

Links

Eskenazi, J. 'The Psychic World of Stanley Krippner.' *San Francisco Weekly News*, April 25, 2012: http://bit.ly/19i8l3W

Rawlins, D. 'Starbaby.' *FATE Magazine*, No. 34, October 1981, pp. 67–98: http://cura.free.fr/xv/14starbb.html

Kamman, R. 'The True Disbelievers: Mars Effect Drives Skeptics to Irrationality': http://bit.ly/bNGEB9

Klass, P. 'Crybaby' (refuted by *FATE Magazine*, privately distributed): https://goo.gl/JHPNHJ

Department of Defence, report on James Randi: http://www.remoteviewed.com/blogdocs/James%20Randi.pdf

Thalbourne, M. 'Science Versus Showmanship: A History of the Randi Hoax': http://www.aiprinc.org/para-c05_Thalbourne_1995.pdf

Chapter 8

Literature

Bierman D.J. & Radin D.I. (1997) 'Anomalous anticipatory response on randomized future conditions.' *Perceptual and Motor Skills*, No. 82, pp. 689–690.

Bierman D.J., & Radin D.I. (1998) 'Conscious and Anomalous Non-conscious Emotional Processes: A reversal of the arrow of time?' *Toward a Science of Consciousness*, Tucson III, MIT Press, pp. 367–386.

Braud, W. (2003) *Distant Mental Influence: Its Contributions to Science, Healing, and Human Interactions.* Hampton Roads Publishing Company, Newburyport, MA.

Dossey, L. & Schwartz, S. (2012) 'Nonlocality, Intention, and Observer Effects in Healing Studies,' in L.J. Miller (ed.) *The Oxford Handbook of Psychology and Spirituality*, Oxford University Press, USA.

Leslie, L. (1974) *Uri Geller: Fup eller fakta.* Samlerens Forlag, Copenhagen, Denmark.

Manning, M. (1995) *No Faith Required.* Colin Smythe Ltd., Gerrards Cross, UK.

Margolis, J. (1999) *Uri Geller: Magician or Mystic?* Welcome Rain Publishers, NY.

Radin, D. (2006) *Entangled Minds: Extrasensory Experiences in a Quantum Reality.* Paraview Pocket Books, NY.

Tart, C.T. (2009) *The End of Materialism: How Evidence of the Paranormal is Bringing Science and Spirit Together.* New Harbinger Publications, Oakland, CA.

Thalbourne, M.A. & Storm, L. (eds.) (2004) *Parapsychology in the Twenty-First Century: Essays On the Future of Psychical Research.* McFarland & Company Inc., Jefferson, NC.

Ullman M. & Krippner S. (2002) *Dream Telepathy: Experiments in Nocturnal Extrasensory Perception*. Hampton Roads Publishing Company, Newburyport, MA.

Links

Bem, D.J. 'Feeling the Future: Experimental Evidence for Anomalous Retroactive Influences on Cognition and Affect.' Online version: http://dbem.ws/FeelingFuture.pdf

Bierman, D.J. & Steven Scholte, H. 'Anomalous anticipatory Brain Activation preceding Exposure of Emotional and Neutral Pictures,' Tucson Conference Presentation 2002: https://www.quantumconsciousness.org/sites/default/files/presentiment_0.pdf

Cardeña, E.: The experimental evidence for parapsychological phenomena: A review. https://psycnet.apa.org/record/2018-24699-001

Ranky (on the paragnost J-P. Girard): http://paranormal.blogspirit.com/tag/jean-pierre+girard

Hasted, J. (report on Geller): http://www.urigeller.com/brief-psychokinetic-investigation-mr-uri-geller/

Jack Houck's homepage (on psychokinesis): http://www.jackhouck.com

Dean Radin's blog: http://www.deanradin.com

Achterberg, J. *et al.* 'Evidence for Correlations between Distant Intentionality and Brain Function in Recipients': https://pdfs.semanticscholar.org/197e/9eb52c-802920532b9ea80db281873d1abed7.pdf

Aftenposten (on the Snåsa Man): http://www.aftenposten.no/norge/Northug-reddet-av-Snasamannen-268794b.html

Verdens Gang (on the Snåsa Man): http://www.vg.no/forbruker/helse/helse-og-medisin/snaasamannen-kurerte-min-soenn/a/546595/

Chapter 9

Literature

Freeman, A. (ed.) (2005) 'Sheldrake and his Critics: The Sense of being Glared At.' *Journal of Consciousness Studies* (Book 12), Imprint Academic, Exeter, UK.

Gershom, Y. (1992) *Beyond the Ashes: Cases of Reincarnation from the Holocaust.* A.R.E. Press, Virginia Beach, VA.

Gershom, Y. (1996) *From Ashes to Healing: Mystical Encounters with the Holocaust.* A.R.E. Press, Virginia Beach, VA.

Guirdham, A. (1990) *The Cathars and Reincarnation: The Record of a Past Life in Thirteenth-Century France.* C.W. Daniel Company Ltd, London, UK.

Kierulff, S. & Krippner, S. (2004) *Becoming Psychic: Spiritual Lessons for Focusing your Hidden Abilities.* New Page Books, Wayne, NJ.

Laszlo, E. (2007) *Science and the Akashic Field: An Integral Theory of Everything.* Inner Traditions, Rochester, VT.

Maddox, J. (1981) 'A Book for Burning?' *Nature,* No. 293, pp. 245–246.

Parker, A. (2004) 'Psi and Altered States of Consciousness,' in Thalbourne, N. & Storm, L. (eds.) *Parapsychology in the Twenty-First Century,* McFarland & Co., Jefferson, NC, pp. 65–89.

Sheldrake, R. (1995) *A New Science of Life.* Park Street Press, South Paris, ME.

Sheldrake, R. (1995) *The Presence of the Past.* Park Street Press, South Paris, ME.

Shroder, T. (1995) *Old Souls.* Simon & Schuster, NY.

Stevenson, I. (1980) *Twenty Cases Suggestive of Reincarnation.* University of Virginia Press.

Stevenson, I. (1997) *Where Reincarnation and Biology Intersect.* Praeger, Santa Barbara, CA.

Links

Grof, S. (speech at VISION-97): http://www.vize.cz/
wp-content/uploads/2016/05/laureat-stanislav-grof-en-
speech.pdf

Havel, V. (speech at VISION-97): http://www.stan-
islavgrof.com/wp-content/uploads/pdf/Havelspeech-Vi-
sion97.pdf

Dijksterhuis, A. & Nordgren, L.F. 'A Theory of Unconscious Thought': http://www.newcode.ru/media/UTT.pdf

Dijksterhuis, A. & Nordgren, L.F. 'On Making the Right
Choice: The Deliberation-Without-Attention Effect':
http://bit.ly/1008xUX

APA, presentation of Dijksterhuis' thoughts: http://www.
apa.org/science/about/psa/2009/10/sci-brief.aspx

Freeman, A. 'The Sense of being Glared At,' on the Sheldrake Controversy: https://www.sheldrake.org/files/pdfs/
FreemanSenseOfBeingGlaredAt.pdf

Holt, J. 'Two Brains Running', on Kahneman's Thinking,
Fast and Slow, *New York Times*, November 25, 2001: http://
nyti.ms/ZUhP19

Kahneman, D. 'Debunking the Myth of Intuition' (interview): http://bit.ly/JJdTax

Tsakiris, A. (podcast/script on Sheldrake/Wiseman):
http://www.skeptiko.com/134-rupert-sheldrake-on-rich-
ard-wiseman-deception/

Stevenson, I. 'Birthmarks and Birth Defects Corresponding to Wounds on Deceased Persons': https://med.
virginia.edu/perceptual-studies/wp-content/uploads/
sites/360/2016/12/STE39stevenson-1.pdf

ACKNOWLEDGEMENTS

The author gratefully acknowledges the following for permission to quote from material in copyright:
~ Pages 115–116 reprinted by courtesy of Stephan A. Schwartz
~ Pages 135–136 reprinted by courtesy of Kyriacos C. Markides
~ Page 365 reprinted by courtesy of the Koestler estate by Peters Fraser & Dunlop

Warm thanks to:
family, friends, acquaintances and others, who by their help and support, and by sharing their paranormal experiences, have made this book possible. Among them there are some that I want to thank in particular:
~ Roald Storaker for giving me the encouragement and motivation to take on the daunting task of writing this book
~ My Norwegian editor Elisabeth Bjelland at Pax Publishing, for accepting my proposal for an unusual project, and for giving me an unusual amount of freedom, support and cheers during the writing process. I bow to thee!
~ Maureen Doolan and Eleanor Peat at Pari Publishing for accepting my manuscript for its first English release. Thanks to Maureen also for improving on my translation, removing errors and adding valuable information
~ Fiona Robertson for ushering the book through the gates into Watkins' courtyard and for an always splendid communication! Thanks also to Etan for graciously accommodating the book, and to Daniel and the others at Watkins for skillfully sprucing it up and helping it to enter the world stage

~ Cecilie Mohr, Andrea Barbieri and Francesca Corsini for designing covers for releases at Pax Publishing, Pari Publishing and Watkins Publishing, respectively

~ Svein Olaf Evjen Olsen for his endurance and invaluable support and encouragement, following the book from idea to manifestation, and for diligently reading through the translated chapters time and again, helping me getting things right

~ Kirsten Marianne Bessesen, my competent translator-cousin, for contributions to both the Norwegian and the English edition, and for being my semantic sparring partner, always and in all ways

~ Lars Fjell Hansson for, as always, insightful and constructive criticism, and for valuable advice on social science and philosophy

~ Svein Erik Syvertsen, for graciously supporting the project by helping the cow to avoid dying whilst the grass is growing!

~ Anna Kari Evjen Olsen for commenting, suggesting and advising based on her multicultural (and multispecial) wisdom

~ Terje Toftenbes and Ragnhild Løken, for being supportive and encouraging in serveral ways, helping me spread the word

~ My aunt Kirsti MacDonald for indispensable material and spiritual support during difficult times, without which this book might not have been written

~ Undis Mjelva, the Norwegian Sibylle, for readings out of another world, and for radically expanding my understanding of psi. RIP

~ Bjørg Tofte, my mentor, for guidance and encouragement through many years. RIP

Furthermore, for contributions of different sorts I want to thank (in alphabetical order) Aase Bessesen, Atle Lund Christensen, Jan-Erik Ebbestad Hansen, Oda Helene Evjen, Olaug Fostås, Jan Arild Fredriksen, Jan Guttulsrud, Anne Kalvig, Jarl Christian Kind, Aase Camilla Løkling, Lise Klemsdal Løkling, Jon Mansåker, Ole Mauseth, Eivind Reierson and Gunnar Tungland.

Thanks also to Bjørg, Liss Mette, Elias, Sara, Øystein, Turid, Karina Neema, Olaf Amani, Solveig Jalia, and (of course!) Mama Kari, and all the other members of the 'Olsen-clan' who in various ways—with ideas, conversations, good food and/or just by being their beautiful selves—have helped the author as well as the book.

And finally: thanks to the competent and charming staff in Mandal's cafés and restaurants for always being accommodating to the author's whims and wishes!

INDEX

Index of subjects

Index of names

WATKINS
Sharing Wisdom Since 1893

The story of Watkins began in 1893, when scholar of esotericism John Watkins founded our bookshop, inspired by the lament of his friend and teacher Madame Blavatsky that there was nowhere in London to buy books on mysticism, occultism or metaphysics. That moment marked the birth of Watkins, soon to become the publisher of many of the leading lights of spiritual literature, including Carl Jung, Rudolf Steiner, Alice Bailey and Chögyam Trungpa.

Today, the passion at Watkins Publishing for vigorous questioning is still resolute. Our stimulating and groundbreaking list ranges from ancient traditions and complementary medicine to the latest ideas about personal development, holistic wellbeing and consciousness exploration. We remain at the cutting edge, committed to publishing books that change lives.

DISCOVER MORE AT:
www.watkinspublishing.com

Read our blog

Watch and listen to
our authors in action

Sign up to
our mailing list

We celebrate conscious, passionate, wise and happy living.
Be part of that community by visiting

 /watkinspublishing   @watkinswisdom

 /watkinsbooks   @watkinswisdom